PROPERTY, SUBSTANCE AND EFFECT

CW01497021

Hau
Books

Director
Anne-Christine Taylor

Editorial Collective
Deborah Durham
Catherine V. Howard
Nora Scott
Hylton White

Managing Editor
Jane Sabherwal

Hau Books are published by the
Society for Ethnographic Theory (SET)

www.haubooks.org

PROPERTY, SUBSTANCE AND EFFECT

ANTHROPOLOGICAL ESSAYS ON PERSONS AND THINGS

Marilyn Strathern

Reprint

WITH A NEW INTRODUCTION BY ERIC HIRSCH

Hau Books
Chicago

Cover image: Pen drawing by Georgina Beier, property of Marilyn Strathern
Cover design: Daniele Meucci and Ania Zayco
Layout design: Deepak Sharma, Prepress Plus
Typesetting: Prepress Plus (www.prepressplus.in)

ISBN: 978-0-999-1570-7-7 [paperback]
ISBN: 987-0-999-1570-9-1 [PDF]
LCCN: 2022932273

Hau Books
Chicago Distribution Center
11030 S. Langley Ave.
Chicago, Il 60628
www.haubooks.org

Hau Books publications are printed, marketed, and distributed by The University
of Chicago Press.
www.press.uchicago.edu

Printed in the United States of America on acid-free paper.

For R., E., and A.

Contents

Introduction: Working Through Other People's Descriptions

Eric Hirsch

Concepts and Themes

The reissue of Marilyn Strathern's *Property, Substance and Effect* provides an opportunity to look afresh at a collection of essays that were originally published eleven years after her seminal volume *The Gender of the Gift* (1988). In the intervening period, Strathern's thinking had taken important new directions. What anthropological as well as wider political influences were at work in the chapters she assembled? In this introduction I highlight the themes and concepts that are the focus of *Property, Substance and Effect*. I contextualize the issues examined in its chapters and consider how Strathern's analyses here connect with her previous and subsequent work. I also briefly consider how other anthropologists have elaborated the insights provided by Strathern in work that takes us into the twenty-first century. Published twenty-three years ago, how, in short, is *Property, Substance and Effect* relevant to readers today?

The subtitle of the book—*Anthropological Essays on Persons and Things*—is revealing and allows us to begin mapping out the themes and concepts of concern in the book. The first matter to note is that the distinction between persons and things is of concern to Euro-Americans.[1]

---

1. By Euro-American Strathern refers to a specific "worldview" and intellectual canon that stresses European and North American ideas and voices, but which is not restricted to these geographical areas.

Why does this distinction matter? Ideas of property and property ownership organize much of Euro-American social life and maintaining the difference between persons and things is intrinsic to specifying property and ownership. By contrast, and until recently, such a division was of no relevance to Melanesians. This difference between Euro-American ways of thinking and Melanesian ones is associated with the way Melanesian persons perceive relations. All entities associated with persons in Melanesia are composed of relations and all relations derive from persons. What Euro-Americans perceive as "things" in the Melanesian context are perceived by Melanesians as versions of persons.

The distinction between persons and things that *Property, Substance and Effect* draws attention to is connected to another theme of central concern to the analytical framework deployed by Strathern. The chapters in this volume, as with Strathern's earlier work and all her subsequent publications, deal with a binary contrast between Euro-America and Melanesia. And with respect to these contexts, she is interested in the perspectives and descriptions that inform their particular worlds. When people act in Euro-America or in Melanesia (or elsewhere) they act with respect to specific descriptions, such as a spoken or written account of a person, event or object. If particular descriptions are not available then it is not possible to act in the way those descriptions prescribe. This is a matter of logic, if nothing else. Descriptions and actions are intrinsically connected. Euro-American descriptions include ideas of property and property ownership and this influences the actions and perspectives of Euro-Americans. From a Euro-American perspective persons are distinct from things and this matters in determining which person or persons owns which thing or things. Melanesian descriptions and actions, as documented by anthropologists, are not informed by this distinction and ideas of property ownership do not figure in Melanesian perspectives. That is, until recently, and it is one aim of *Property, Substance and Effect* to examine the implications of this shift (see especially chapter 6).

Having said this, it is of course the case that what is attributed to Melanesian and to Euro-American perspectives and descriptions are already the perspectives and descriptions of Euro-American discourse. A principal theme in Strathern's writing is a persistent struggle with the language of description.[2] She observes that social anthropologists conduct their work through the descriptions of the people they engage

---

2. As Strathern notes in her preface to this volume.

with, either directly, in the course of fieldwork, or via descriptions in the ethnographic writings of other anthropologists: getting the descriptions right matters.

Nonetheless, and as noted, the descriptive language anthropologists use to describe Melanesian accounts and actions derives from the Euro-American world. This is an unavoidable fact of anthropology (see Geertz 1988). What Strathern does is place this reality front and center. This had been a concern of Strathern's earlier research and it informs the pages of *Property, Substance and Effect*. So, for example, pointing to a dominant feature of Euro-American societies and economies, she states in *The Gender of the Gift*, "a culture dominated by ideas about property ownership can only imagine the absence of such ideas in specific ways" (Strathern 1988: 18). That specific way, she suggests, following Gregory (1982), can be a contrast between commodity exchange and gift exchange, each associated, for the purpose of description and analysis, with different societies and economies. The contrast between gifts and commodities is a Euro-American one, not a Melanesian one. Nevertheless, the contrast allows ethnographic material to be organized in different ways: "To talk about the gift constantly evokes the possibility that the description would look very different if one were talking instead about commodities" (Strathern 1988: 19). The point to emphasize again is that the contrast between Melanesia and Euro-America as much as that between gift exchange and commodity exchange is for descriptive purposes. That is, it is to generate a space, so to speak, where the accounts, actions and perspectives created by Melanesian peoples can be disclosed, while simultaneously making apparent that that disclosure must be through Euro-American modes of description.

The chapters in this book stem from this understanding of description and perspective as well as the model of Melanesian personhood illustrated by Strathern in *The Gender of the Gift*. Relations between Melanesian persons, in all their variety, are established through forms of transaction (gift exchange). Building on the ethnography of other Melanesianists, Strathern has demonstrated in significant detail that Melanesians, contrary to how it might appear from the established ethnography, actually hold their conventions in common.

These common conventions are based on the idea that persons are composed of relations and it is through relations that persons reveal their capacities: "persons must in themselves be what they can become" (Strathern 1988: 220). According to this perspective, then, persons must be able to accomplish the abilities they are imagined to have. So, for

example, a girl can already be imagined as a woman as she can be seen
to have within her the ability to give birth to children. But the capacity must be made visible in an appropriate form. In English this sounds
like "stating the obvious." The point, though, is that in "'Melanesian' (as
it were)" people work so as to make this apparent. They endeavor to reveal these capacities as "objects of knowledge for themselves" (Strathern
1988: 220).

Of course, the concept of relation used by Strathern, and anthropologists more generally, is a Euro-American notion. Melanesians do not
speak explicitly about "relations," as such. In its dominant Anglophone
outlines the relation has two properties.[3] The first of the concept's properties is that it "can be applied to any order of connection" (Strathern
1995: 17). This is a property of scale. The relation has a second property
to do with complexity. Complexity is a property because the relation
"requires other elements to complete it"—a relation must be between
this and that (Strathern 1995: 18). The complexity stems from the fact
that "the relation always summons entities other that itself" (Strathern
1995: 18).

When the relation is applied by anthropologists to the elucidation
of Melanesian materials such as the Melanesian person, the person can
be revealed to act as the measure of all things; the person can appear
in all forms of life—exist at any scale—from yams to humans to clan
ancestors and so forth (see Wagner 1991). Strathern's interpretation of
relations stems from her analysis of Melanesian materials but she also
seeks to make the idea of relations obvious with respect to the English/
Euro-Americans. She makes this specific analytical move because of a
distinctive feature of English and Euro-American perspectives regarding relations.

In writing about the English Strathern indicates that she is also writing about Euro-Americans more generally but from the perspective of
her English context. She uses the contrast described with Melanesia in
order to draw attention to the difficulty Euro-Americans have in con-
ceptualizing relations.

On the one hand, and based on an understanding deriving broadly
from the writings of Roy Wagner, Strathern suggests that Melanesians
take relations as given. Relations are the "vital supports" for any living

---

3. Already in 1981 Strathern was using the notion of "relatedness" to describe
    how notions of class fed into ideas of kin by blood and kin by marriage as
    found in a Cambridgeshire village (Strathern 1981).

person (Leenhardt [1947] 1979). What Melanesians do is continually exert effort so as to differentiate persons from each other—from a certain set of relations—in order to have the capacity to act. On the other hand, Euro-Americans take "individuality" for granted, as a kind of natural condition. As a result of the taken-for-granted nature of individuality, the manner in which persons relate to one another becomes like a "cultural enterprise." She suggests that representations of individualism are deep-seated in areas of Euro-American discourse and, like the notion of "nature," individualism is a kind of "cultural artefact" (cf. Strathern 2020: 167–90).

A further aspect of the relational and transactional universe is examined in the present collection and that is the idea of substance. In Melanesian perspectives, substance is understood as the outcome of people's actions, contained in a physical form (such as a pig or other kind of wealth) that they have created. The substance can be then be revealed as an object obtainable through exchange relations. Substance is thus implicated in the exchanges that people enact in order to produce and sustain relations: to make relations out of relations (see chapter 3). By contrast, something different is considered in the Euro-American context which speaks to the prominence of its property thinking. Here, human substance (such as components of the anatomy) is perceived to have the potential to be transacted as a commercial entity through transformations effected by biotechnology (see chapter 8).

As with property and substance found in the book's title, the third and last concept of the title is that of effect. As it is deployed in the pages that follow, effect has a distinctly Melanesian resonance. Consider one of the first examples examined in chapter 2: adornments worn by Mt. Hagen dancers. Strathern describes a feather plaque displayed on the head as part of the dancer's ornaments. The plaque as well as the other adornments (feathers, shells, and face paint) can be understood as bits of other persons attached to the dancer, summoning their presence. The description captures how the relations with other persons are foreshadowed in these decorations. The decorated assemblage will have an effect on others, exemplifying the dancer's efficacy. Adornments make visible the support the dancer has had through relations with other persons. This is why Strathern suggests that the decorations are bits of other persons—the decorations display the support that enabled the dancer to perform. Yet, simultaneously, the decorations reveal how the dancer had to separate from these same relations in order to have the capacity to perform.

These exchanges are what Strathern refers to as the "exchange of perspectives." There is reciprocity at work here whereby each person perceives themself from the point of view of the other. This might suggest a comparison with the Euro-American "reflexivity of selfhood": "I know who I am because you can see who I am." This is not, however, an exchange of gazes between persons as if the above dancer views the spectators and the view of his performance is returned to him. It is not, in Melanesia, a Euro-American perspective where each gaze is from an individual position onto the world. Euro-Americans, according to Strathern, do not have exchanges of perspectives. What they do have are collections of individually diverse perspectives on themselves and the world around them. By contrast, the idea of "effects" is essential to the exchange of perspectives that concerns Strathern: there is an exchange of effects between persons. The person views him or herself transformed through the effects he or she has on other persons. And the presence of other persons is the cause of one's own actions. Thus, a pregnant mother and her unborn child have reciprocal effects upon one another—each grows and elicits the other—just as later the child and its clan will have mutual, reciprocal effects in growing one another (numerically increasing the clan size and the food on clan land which is growing the child). These effects are the product of reciprocal interactions; the concern of persons, as argued by Strathern, is not on being reflexive or on being focused on the self.

Persons and things; property, substance and effect; the ubiquity of relations; perspective and description: These are the key concepts addressed in this volume and they are applied to a range of issues arising in Melanesia, as well as Euro-America.

The Ethnographic Moment

The Melanesia (and specifically Papua New Guinea) that Strathern writes about in this book is the Melanesia she experienced when undertaking fieldwork at various times from the 1960s through the 1990s. The ethnographic material that forms the core of many of the book's chapters is the outcome of her immersion in the social lives of the people whose descriptions and actions she attempted to capture in her fieldwork notebooks (as reported most recently, for this volume, in chapters 5, 7, and 9). Her second immersion is the one in which the anthropologist (Strathern) seeks both to grasp and re-create the sense of the accounts and practices of the people she was involved with in fieldwork. It is the movement between these fields—the "field" of fieldwork and the "field" of the study—that Strathern refers to as the ethnographic moment.

This moment is comparable to the relation (discussed above). What are related are the "understood" (at the time of observation in fieldwork) and the "need to understand" (what is examined at the time of analysis). However, this movement between fields occurs over different time scales. To illustrate this point I consider an example of description deployed by Strathern from her earlier research and a different descriptive lexicon from more recent writings.

Producers and transactors are the terms she used to mark the differences between women and men in the Mount Hagen area of Papua New Guinea (PNG) following her fieldwork there in the 1960s. Production was the mode in which women's work was valued by Mt. Hagen people, while men were judged locally as transactors. Men were also producers, but this was not valued by Mt. Hagen people in the same way the ability to engage in exchange relations were. As Strathern (1972: 135) notes:

> For a man, his own involvement in production (e.g. clearing gardens) carries relatively little prestige. Industry alone does not lead directly to big-man status. Anyone can make gardens if he applies himself; it is simply a matter of hard work. Renown comes from being able to influence people, demonstrating power over exchange partners and one's clansmen alike.

However, by the end of the 1970s this form of description was perceived by Strathern as inadequate. She changed her view due to transformations in anthropology, especially the influence of feminism and interest in gender identity which meant that new descriptive terms were required. Drawing on the extensive range of comparative Melanesia ethnography Strathern introduced the distinction between same-sex and cross-sex gender relations. She argued that a male or female person's gender assumes a given or inactive androgynous state, known as cross-sex. In dealings with other persons, that is in engaging in action, a person's gender identity is made uniform in a single-sex form. Previously it was sufficient to understand how the fame acquired by men derived from the influence they had over people and the ability to exhibit power over exchange partners as well as clansmen. Now, the ethnographic moment had changed, and a more fine-grained analysis of gender was required to understand these processes of influence and power. It was necessary, for example, to understand the transformed same-sex relations men assume in their exchange relations with other men, where their cross-sex relations with women are obviated at those moments. Men and women, depending on their particular actions, oscillate between being perceived in a cross-sex condition or a same-sex one.

To illustrate further the changes in forms of description consider the following examples from chapters 1 and 5 of the present volume. Strathern recounts being "dazzled" by the first Mt. Hagen ceremonial exchange event she witnessed in the mid-1960s where mounted pearl shells, heavy in weight, were being carried hurriedly by men as some form of gift exchange. At that time, competitive exchanges between clans were common. The increase in competitive exchanges was stimulated by the colonial suppression of interclan warfare and the influx of large quantities of pearl shells into the local economy, brought by Australians needing goods to trade with Mt. Hagen men. By the mid-1990s social life was, of course, different, but Strathern does not describe those differences directly. The ethnographic moment Strathern creates asks the following question: What does 1995 seem like from the perspective of descriptions that were valid thirty years before? While many anthropologists argue that historical change is crucial to understanding (e.g., Thomas 1991), Strathern adopts a different point of view and argues in turn that the categories of analysis used to understand other people's descriptions and actions cannot themselves remain timeless. It is in this regard that she applies the categories of same-sex and cross-sex relations to describe the differences between now (mid-1990s) and then (mid-1960s), especially where the acquisition and circulation of money came to eclipse the dominance of pearl shell exchange in Mt. Hagen. The inflation of cross-sex relations she describes, with maternal kin in particular, provides an original take on the emergence of individually minded consumers some twenty years after PNG independence in 1975.

Of course, what is Euro-America, as much as what is Melanesia, is not fixed in time but transforms under specific conditions. Strathern (1975) early on considered an example of these transformations in PNG among Mt. Hagen migrants in Port Moresby. Such changes—the urbanization of Port Moresby, labor migration, and changes to courts and legal institutions, among countless other changes—were the outcome of Euro-American interventions. Strathern (1985) subsequently uses research among urban Mt. Hagen migrants to interrogate ideas of personhood and transactions informing Euro-American and Melanesian conventions and expectations of conduct. In doing so she examines the relations between a white *masta*[4] and his *hausboi*[5] and their differing perceptions of what "wages" (commodity exchange) and "gifts" mean given the two men's different social backgrounds. Her discussion is informed by a reading of John Locke's writings on property, domestic labor, and the master-servant relationship (see Tully 1980). This comparative exercise not only anticipates the core of the analysis elaborated in *The Gender of the Gift* but also that of *The Relation* first presented as an inaugural lecture in 1994 (Strathern 1995) and then expounded most recently in *Relations: An Anthropological Account* (Strathern 2020).

For Strathern, the ethnographic method as fashioned by social anthropology, with its demands of fieldwork immersion, is what enables such descriptions to be accomplished. As she emphasizes at the end of her first chapter—a chapter she entitles "the ethnographic effect"—ethnography allows the study of the immediate here and now from which anthropologists create their knowledge of the world. It is a mode of inquiry that has unpredictable outcomes in relation to realms of knowledge and social activity. And importantly, it permits the recovery of material that investigators did not know at the time they were collecting. Strathern's take on ethnography and its effectiveness is in contrast with those accounts that are concerned with ethnography largely as a "genre of writing" (cf. Clifford and Marcus 1986).

Global Property Regime

As the above examples illustrate, changes in Euro-American descriptions and actions came to hold an ever-increasing place in the style of anthropology practiced by Strathern. By the 1990s, for instance, new international policy instruments such as the Convention on Biological Diversity (CBD) and especially an agreement on Trade-Related Aspects of Intellectual Property Rights (TRIPS) meant that countries like PNG needed to reconsider claims to the ownership of all kinds of resources. This was not a voluntary move. It was a pressurized change intended to protect outside investment by introducing intellectual property provision. Powerful, "developed" countries via the World Trade Organization wanted intellectual property law to be standardized on a global scale.

4.　White man or European in Tok Pisin; Tok Pisin is an English-based creole language spoken throughout Papua New Guinea.

5.　Male domestic servant in Tok Pisin.

In contrast to developed countries, so-called developing countries were imagined to be prevented from "catching up" by their entrenched "traditions." Aligned to this view was one that characterized such countries as having collective or communal forms of ownership, forms of ownership that were contrary to individualized ideas of property rights.[6] These were highly charged political developments that captured Strathern's attention.

At this time intellectual property had shifted from its primary existence in legal discourse to having greater public prominence in the media. And this shift, in turn, was connected to the expansion of new things—electronic and biogenetic—that could be owned. As a result, the sphere of patenting was expanded. PNG was thus compelled to standardize intellectual property law through legislation although concerns were raised by interested parties about the legitimacy of the legal categories. The legislation concerned with copyright and patent made no attempt to query whether such a conceptual framework was the best way to regulate often conflicting international, national, and local objectives. This enlargement was not without controversy and people from PNG were at the forefront of disputes. In 1996 a patent was granted to

---

6. Many decades ago Malinowski (1926) confronted a similar set of perceptions then current among a certain generation of anthropologists. Rivers (1924), for example, argued that canoes in Melanesian culture were the subject of common ownership. He also referred to a "communistic sentiment" that governs Melanesian ideas about property. More generally, Rivers (1923) speaks of the "communistic behavior" in Melanesian societies (Malinowski 1926: 19). Malinowski argued by contrast that any notion of "ownership" among the Trobriand Islanders he lived with was defined by how the object—such as a fishing canoe—is manufactured, used, and perceived by the group of men who created it and delight in what they possess. There are different relations each man has with the canoe as well as with each other. One man initiated production of the canoe and through relations of kinship and marriage other men assisted with the construction process. These men are all connected through reciprocal exchange obligations that are enacted during the canoe's construction and subsequently when it is used on fishing expeditions. In the latter case, the catch is distributed in accordance with each person's contribution to the canoe production (Malinowski 1926). What Malinowski demonstrated is that any idea of ownership among Melanesian peoples is intrinsically connected with notions of transaction and how such exchanges enable creations—like that of the Trobriand canoe.

scientists associated with the US National Institutes of Health for a cell line that had been obtained from a blood sample of a Hagahai man from the Schrader Mountain area, PNG. There was widespread international condemnation of the patent as it was perceived to be commodifying human body parts and the patent was subsequently withdrawn. An earlier controversy in the United States concerned the patenting of a cell line from a surgically removed spleen that was upheld in court (see Rabinow 1996; and below).

It is in the context of this international expansion of property regimes that Strathern fixes her analytical attention on notions of property. Is the intellectual property model appropriate for the protection of rights and claims over intangible resources such as performances and sources of ancestral knowledge that originate in "Indigenous cultures" and are part of long-standing "traditions"? Can culture become a form of property (see also Brown 2003)? These issues were at the forefront of her concerns. On the horizon was a UNESCO initiative to create a standard-setting device concerned with the realm of intangible cultural heritage. How might these international changes be understood in light of the descriptions and actions coming from PNG ethnography?

Intellectual property rights as applied internationally require that persons and things, as discussed above, exist as separate entities. This is a necessary requirement for putting such rights into practice. This precondition appears uncontroversial from a Euro-American perspective but Papua New Guineans do not have the ideological necessity to separate things and persons. Again, what ethnography repeatedly discloses instead is that "people divide people": difference is recurrently created in how Papua New Guineans conduct their social relations. And they conduct their social relations by dividing themselves from others through transactions (see the example above from chapter 2 for an illustration). Although Papua New Guineans appear to be preoccupied with "things" in how they exchange items of the same kind—pork for pork or money for money—what is disclosed by such transactions is not their "thingness" but their social origin and social endpoint. The transactions of "things" reveal people's capacity to act, to transact: the "things" from a Euro-American perspective are just things, but from a Melanesian viewpoint are an index of a person's capacity.

At this time, Strathern was concerned with how intellectual property rights would deal with Indigenous culture and intellectual property often referred to as "traditional knowledge" and what legal difficulties and local problems this might cause. Papua New Guineans are mainly concerned with regulating access to and use of this Indigenous knowledge so that laws can be implemented to protect such cultural and intellectual property. Related to this is the issue of economic profit arising from the use of traditional knowledge materials for which people want to be properly compensated. However, there is a problem with such a solution and that is the idea that this kind of intellectual property exists as a "thing" owned in a conventional Euro-American sense. The problem emerges because the "property" does not really have an intellectual aspect. Rather, traditional knowledge dwells in a social collective. No one person has the right to alienate this version of property; it inheres in the social formation (Kalinoe 2004: 43).

An important take on these matters that Strathern highlights is the contrast between dispersal or dissemination connected with cultural property and that connected with intellectual property. In order to claim that certain cultural knowledge belongs to a particular social formation or collective people in it may need to demonstrate that their cultural knowledge has been passed on from one generation to the next. The authenticity of cultural property, then, hinges on the fact that it has been passed on. Intellectual property is just the opposite. One can only claim intellectual property by showing that it has not been dispersed.

Property, Substance and Effect: Wider Influence

Fred Myers (2004) has drawn on Strathern's analysis of intellectual property for his own study of the Aboriginal artist and activist Wandjuk Marika, who in the early 1970s requested the Australian government to investigate the use of Yolngu clan designs on a range of commodities which had not been authorized. Following Strathern, Myers discusses the inability of legal discourses of cultural property to apprehend the perspectives and concerns of Indigenous Australians with regard to their ideas of creativity and cultural expression. In contrast to Indigenous Australians' perspectives concerning their cultural creations, Euro-American ideas of ownership are radically different—they are about individual ownership, whether that individual is a corporation, culture, or individual author. Myers (2004: 10) quotes Strathern's succinct formulation (chapter 8) in this respect: "Ownership gathers things momentarily to a point by locating them in the owner, halting endless dissemination, effecting an identity" (p. 170, this volume). This idea of ownership is in conflict with indigenous Australian ideas of cultural creations.

As the above example suggests, the ideas and analysis in this volume have inspired scholars in their own studies. A simple Google Scholar search of *Property, Substance and Effect* will show that the book has been influential, cited by a wide range of scholars both inside and outside of anthropology. It is beyond the scope of this introduction to map that influence in its entirety. What I want to do instead is to briefly consider how some of the insights provided by the chapters in the book have been carried forward by a number of anthropologists (including Strathern herself) pursuing diverse areas of research. How might the reader new to *Property, Substance and Effect* perceive its relevance for contemporary times?

One interesting answer to this question is provided by Stefan Helmreich (2008). Since the publication of *Property, Substance and Effect* there has been a proliferation of developments in biotechnology in areas such as genomics, stem cell research, and reproductive technology as well as that of bioprospecting. The entangling of biotechnology with its commercialization has been examined by a number of researchers who are the focus of Helmreich's publication. What is of interest to me is the genealogy of scholarship provided in his article. In the forking figure he presents, inspired by the diagram at the end of Darwin's *On the Origins of Species*, one fork connects Strathern with a group researchers influenced by her thinking, including Sarah Franklin (2007), Cori Hayden (2003), and Charis Thompson (2005), among others.

Hayden, in particular, investigates an aspect of the new global property regime that was foreshadowed by Strathern. As I mentioned earlier, the UN-sponsored Convention on Biological Diversity (CBD) and specifically the agreement on Trade-Related Aspects of Intellectual Property Rights (TRIPS) required countries like PNG to introduce legislation concerned with the ownership of diverse kinds of resources. Hayden considers a similar issue in the context of Mexico, the site of her research. She frames the CBD and TRIPS as neoliberal innovations designed to facilitate or enforce the escalation and enlargement of capitalist markets and trade. Bioprospecting is the focus of her study and bioprospecting is meant to be a utilization of resources that is, in principle, in tune with the CBD. The goals of the CBD are realized through bioprospecting by conserving nature while converting plant material into information and thus into potentially valuable patents and drug therapies. The ideology behind bioprospecting weds ideas of sustainability with fair and equitable sharing of the profits arising from the use of genetic resources. The benefits stemming from nature are meant to be shared amongst the interested parties, for the most part being pharmaceutical companies, universities from the Global North, and Indigenous peoples from the Global South.

However, TRIPS runs counter to the principles and ideas contained in the CBD and requires intellectual property protection that is significantly different from that promoted by the CBD. As Hayden (2003: 95) argues:

TRIPS requires that member states recognise patents on microorganisms and the biological processes used to produce them; at the same time, it holds no requirement for benefit-sharing or even obtaining consent when companies patent compounds based on natural products from nations such as Mexico. And unlike the CBD, if member nations do not sign TRIPS, they are subject to trade sanctions.

Nations of the Global South are forced to abide by the intellectual property regime of TRIPS rather than the redistributive mechanisms of the CBD. However, and regardless of this potential conflict, an additional problem arises and the source of this problem reminds us of Strathern's interpretation of the Euro-American distinction between persons and things that runs throughout *Property, Substance and Effect*. Bioprospecting can only operate if scientists are able to identify the benefit-recipients (persons) that are linked with their plants (things). But a problem arises when plant material is collected from places with no discernible local people, such as the sides of roads. Hayden (2003: 175) notes that plant ecologists find roads to be especially important for the spread of "exotic" species as they act as effective corridors along which plants move with great efficiency. When it comes to roadside flora it is virtually impossible to identify the local "owners" of plant life. The same holds true for flora obtained in markets which comprise a large proportion of bioprospecting collections. In this case, money changes hands and virtually all obligations end as a result (Hayden 2003: 144). In short, Hayden documents that bioprospecting plant collections have always been multiply authored and generally do not correspond to the Euro-American ideas of "persons" (as local benefactors) connected to identifiable "things," so that proceeds from intellectual property can be shared.

Hayden's study thus expands an important theme in *Property, Substance and Effect* concerning Euro-American ideas of property, whether it is intellectual, cultural, or more conventional things such as land. Property requires a boundary so that a network of relations is cut, the claims of other persons are severed, and a singular identity created. Property presupposes the existence of distinct persons and distinct things. At the same time, what Hayden reveals is that relations of various kinds pervade all aspects of the bioprospecting endeavor, and taking her lead from Strathern she states that "ownership brings relations ... to a stopping point, even if only temporarily" (Hayden 2003: 224).

DNA sampling raises comparable issues to that of bioprospecting regarding benefit-sharing and patents involving donors and scientists. The complexity of these issues is examined in Michael Montoya's study of DNA sampling among Mexican-Americans and its use for diabetes research. As for Hayden, Strathern also stimulates his understanding of these transactions. He is critical of the perspective which suggests that patent policy proposals should focus on the "equitable material transfer agreements between donors and scientists" (Montoya 2011: 155). Montoya perceives this as accepting the "logic of possessive individualism" that informs patent case law—the idea that cells or tissue were owned and could then be exchanged depending on the party's relation to the biological substance.

It is certainly the case that biological samples have become like crops, land, and minerals where scientists use the metaphors of harvesting, extraction, and procurement to refer to the scientific techniques they deploy. The famous (or more likely infamous) case of Henrietta Lacks and the HeLa cell line that scientists immortalized from her cancerous cells in the 1960s and 1970s is a case in point (see Skloot 2010). Unquestionably, such language indicates certain suppositions about the human body, in particular, that the body can be divided into parts and the parts can be abstracted from the living humans and the social context in which they are situated.

Montoya argues that the above critical perspectives on DNA sampling, although important, fail to recognize the social relations "that make possible the production and circulation of DNA samples" (Montoya 2011: 155–56). Attention needs to be given, he suggests, to the actual social context of sampling and the "social life" of the sample. What is too often obscured is how the transactions at the core of sampling generate "regimes of value." Instead, Montoya follows the insights of Strathern in this volume, where he argues that

[O]ne modality of making property out of bits of biological organism (animal or plant) requires the delinking of the product from its origins ... This enables the reassignment of ownership at each stage in the development of knowledge. This is not magic. It is the emergent form of property relations manifest in intellectual property rights discourses. (Montoya 2011: 156)

Bioprospecting and DNA sampling are two areas of research where ideas presented in *Property, Substance and Effect* have had considerable influence (see, for example, Fullwiley 2011; TallBear 2013). These two areas are ones that fall at the intersections of anthropology and science studies. Although Strathern does not see herself as a Science Studies scholar, many of her interventions in this volume speak directly to the concerns of this research area. One in particular is her analysis of Euro-American kinship systems and the connection between these forms of relations and that of science (see chapter 4).

Strathern observes that Euro-American kinship systems contain an array of fundamental suppositions concerning knowledge which makes what we call "science" very easy to contemplate. In particular, she argues, Euro-American kinship involves knowledge that can be externally verified by information relating to the natural world. Information about biological processes, in particular, is one source that provides persons with knowledge of how they are related to each other. These significant and in many ways ground-breaking ideas are further developed by her in a later publication (Strathern 2005). There she writes about "embedded science." Her starting point is the claim made by scientists and policy makers alike that society is implicated in science. If science is "in" society, Strathern (2005: 33) asks, "where is it?" To answer that, one must first recognize that science did not emerge like an island from the sea: "ways to conceptualise its descriptions and claims emerged through borrowings from other domains of life" (Strathern 2005: 46).

The idea of relation is, again, central here. The Human Genetics Commission, for example, was a body that advised the UK government on the social and ethical aspects of genetics, including genetic testing, cloning, and other procedures connected with molecular medicine. Strathern notes that the commission advised that people "should recognise the extent to which they are related" (Strathern 2005: 46, emphasis removed). With this in mind, she asks why Euro-Americans need to acknowledge and inform themselves of the degree to which they, as people, are related. "And why, then, are they surprised when they discover that they are *already* related?" (Strathern 2005: 46, original emphasis). In the present volume she suggests that Euro-Americans live out a "scientific" system of knowledge, where kinship is one amongst other objects of knowledge (cf. McKinnon and Cannell 2013). Given the centrality of the concept of relations to both scientific knowledge and knowledge associated with kinship, Strathern (2005: 46) proposes that Euro-Americans have a "scientific kinship system."

To this point I have touched briefly on how ideas in *Property, Substance and Effect* have informed anthropological research in the Euro-American context. What about in Melanesia? Here, concepts articulated in this volume have been applied in different ways. One of the implications of the concept of effect is that it requires the person to appear—to become visible—in a particular form. In the concluding chapter of the book (which concludes chapter 1) Strathern reflects on the way she previously described (in Strathern 1988) how persons in Melanesia make visible the relations of which they are composed. She writes: "I had no account (description) of the apparent need I imputed to these Melanesians to make relations visible" (this volume, 247–48, emphasis removed). It was a "blind spot." Effect is how she now understands the motive. A person sees what there is to be seen because the witness is in the correct social condition to "register the effect." Another person, in turn, is the cause of the effect.

Based on her research in the Madang Hospital, located in Madang Province, PNG, Alice Street found that the patients as well as the medical staff were concerned with making themselves visible in distinctive ways. Her research expands the range of contexts in which the insights presented in *Property, Substance and Effect* are applied, especially that connected with "effect." Street examines two technologies of visibility that are familiar in Euro-American medical contexts: government health cards and audit practices. In the PNG hospital setting she studied these technologies do not operate as they would conventionally in Euro-American institutions. That is, they do not act as "tools of governance that fashion self-reflexive subjects who turn a normalising gaze inward on themselves" (Street 2012: 2). In this context the state is largely absent, although also desired, both for the poorly resourced hospital medical staff, and its patients.

Hospital audit practices—such as a public open day—and government health cards are interpreted by Street as "relational technologies." The power they are perceived to possess lies in their ability to coerce responses from others. It is through assuming a specific form of visibility that the medical personnel and patients alike are able to forge a relation with the generally nonexistent state.

Audit in this case is not used as a system of governmentality that functions by persuading organizations or persons to reflect on and control themselves. Rather, the use of transparency, Street suggests, has more "relational effects," by potentially causing government personnel to recognize the hospital and force a monetary response.

The government health cards are used in an analogous manner by patients. They perceive the state, which is largely absent, as having obligations towards them which they seek to have the state recognize. The government health cards are not how the state governs patients. Instead, patients perceive and use the cards as relational technologies. That is, they seek to entice the state (in the form of medical professionals) to see them as patients and cause the medical personnel to give medical care. Unlike in the Euro-American context, Street argues, the use of the government health cards does not transform patients into "biomedical subjects." The cards act as transactional devices and not as a technology of the self. As she notes:

> I very rarely encountered patients who described their condition in biological terms, most referring instead to the fact that only doctors and white people understood the causes behind sickness pertaining to white people's medicine (*sik bilong marasin* [Tok Pisin]). In contrast to the claims of biological citizenship, patients in Madang Hospital are uncertain about what kind of person they need to appear as to elicit care from the doctor or the state. They cannot comprehend what is written in their clinic books and complain that the workings of "white men's medicine" and the state remain hidden to them. Patients only know that they have appeared in the correct form as patients when the desired response is elicited. (Street 2012: 15)

In other words, the patient perceives that s/he can only achieve an effective relation with the doctor by becoming visible in an appropriate way. The relation can only be formed through what Strathern has referred to as the correct aesthetic.

Relations as Ubiquitous

Whether it is Melanesia or Euro-America Strathern's anthropological focus has been on relations. Relations are as central to Euro-American social life as they are to Melanesian social life. But relations assume different forms in these contexts. In the English context of Euro-America, a person has relations with a mother and father, for example, each of those relations being a particular kind of parent. Motherhood or fatherhood in turn can be related to numerous contexts outside of parenting such as education, medicine, law, and so on. So the domain of fatherhood/parenting contains elements that can also be seen as part of these other domains. This kind of relation between domains is what Strathern (1992: 73) refers to as merographic.[7] The ability to shift perspectives and redescribe something from another point of view is, Strathern argues, distinctively English/Euro-American. The existence of merographic relations is bound up with the pluralistic societies and cosmos that Euro-Americans inhabit.

With reference to the discussion about science I raised in the previous section, Strathern also posits an association between the advent of the scientific revolution and that of merographic relations. Under the remit of science, the natural world and cosmos became an object of knowledge, but the ontological status of science was uncertain. In a parallel manner this raised questions about the ontological status of society. Given the undetermined makeup of the natural world and cosmos, comprehension was rendered through relating separate particles of matter to one another. The establishment of such relations enabled evidence of new kinds of relations that could be further added. The conceptual world that was thus created had a vast ability to expand internally. The reason for this is because "every domain contain[ed] elements that [could] also be seen as parts of other domains" (Strathern 2014: 56).

And certainly, in the English context, relations as deployed in the scientific revolution were simultaneously a way of thinking and speaking about relations between persons. Relations were also a way of describing kinspersons. Knowledge about how persons were related was confirmed from information deriving from the natural world, which was itself grounded on a range of basic assumptions concerning knowledge. It is this particular configuration of knowledge that makes science as

---

7. Merographic calls to mind the concept of mereology which is the study of part-whole relations. Strathern's intention is not to suggest part-whole relations but something connected to this. Namely, she means "that anything may be a part of something else, minimally part of a description in the act of describing it. In this view, nothing is in fact ever simply part of a whole because another view, another perspective or domain, may redescribe it as 'part of something else'" (Strathern 1992: 73).

an object easy to envision. It is for this reason that Strathern suggests, as noted above, that Euro-Americans have a "scientific" kinship system.

With the idea of the merographic in mind and as a final, brief example of how ideas associated with *Property, Substance and Effect* and Strathern's larger corpus of writings have been applied I turn to research on the "new genetics."

The "new genetics," as it is called (see Pálsson 2007), is increasingly implicated in Euro-American kinship, an example being the genetic diagnosis of embryos undertaken in IVF laboratories. This is an area that has been studied by Sarah Franklin. She draws on the notion of the merographic to productively interpret her ethnography. Strathern deploys the idea of merographic connections to make sense of English kinship thinking which is comprised of both biological and social facts. Franklin quotes Strathern who describes the biological and social facts of English kinship in terms of parts and wholes.

> The popular supposition that kinship is only "part" of society rests on the fact that it is also "part" of biological process. Such parts are not equal to one another. The perspective that gives each of them its distinctive nature appears always as a different order of phenomena. Each order that encompasses the parts may be thought of as a whole, as the individual parts may also be thought of as wholes. But parts in this view do not make wholes ... Thus the logic of the totality is not necessarily to be found in the logic of the parts, but in principles, forces, relations that exist between the parts (Strathern 1992: 76). (Franklin 2003: 66; emphases removed)

Strathern's formulation points to the way "parts" overlap in the creation of ideas of relatedness, such that biological fact of relatedness, for example, is a kind of totality or "whole." Franklin uses these ideas to interpret how the new genetics and kinship thinking are connected. So, for example, in English (and Euro-American) kinship thinking biological relationships are treated as social facts and named accordingly as mother, father, sister, brother, and so on. In a comparable manner, Franklin (2003: 66–67) observes

> [T]he names that are given to the protein sequences that comprise "genes," or "genetic markers" belong to the realm of science, which describes its objects in terms of technological processes of identification and intervention. Both kinship and the new genetics connect

these distinct domains "merographically" because in the idea of a kinship relation, or a genetic marker, is the idea of a co-mingling of parts that belong to different wholes.

What is knowable about genetic screening for breast cancer, or paternity testing, for instance, is already "built into the conception of kinship as a hybrid of individual and society, of natural and cultural facts" (Franklin 2003: 74). At the same time, though, there is a dilemma about genes and the supposition that it is genes that makes us who we are. This is what is referred to as "geneticization," where genes take on an overdetermining part in the biological blueprint of living forms. Franklin suggests that the new genetics proceeds merographically, that is, it draws together parts that belong to diverse orders of phenomena corresponding to the "logic of the totality [that] is not necessarily to be found in the logic of the parts, but in principles, forces, relations that exist between the parts" (Strathern 1992: 76).

Thus, efforts to relate genetic treatments with forms of social obligations will always be partial. This is what the merographic perspective highlights. DNA is both a social object and a natural object and there is a lack of common measure between the totalities to which DNA belongs. Based on her deployment of the merographic perspective, Franklin is able to demonstrate that DNA will continuously supplant its social context just as the social context will continually supersede DNA. "This is the same as saying, too, that the assumption that genes make us who we are is both too true to ignore, and too partial to be enough truth by itself" (Franklin (2003: 83).

By contrast, the idea of merographic connections is not applicable to the Melanesian context—a statement that could only be made by someone from where merographic relations do apply. Melanesian societies and cosmos are not divided into domains with overlapping orders of phenomena and knowledge that persons work to bring into relationship, providing them with different perspectives on the world. Knowledge does not take this form in Melanesia. If anything, forms of knowledge are continually taken apart to disclose their composition. Knowledge of garden magic, for instance, is assessed by the yams that are grown and displayed. The capacity to grow yams must be revealed and that capacity becomes an object of knowledge. This is analogous to how the person is understood from the standpoint of the relations that compose her or him. The person (she or he) is "objectified" in those relations and simultaneously revealed in them. However, "for the relations to exist, they must already be there"; and, as already quoted above, "persons must in themselves be what they can become" (Strathern 1988: 220).

Conclusion

The binary divide between Melanesia and Euro-America which runs through the chapters of the present volume and much of Strathern's writings over several decades places relations at the center of her descriptions and analysis. This is as true for Melanesia as it is for Euro-America, although in different ways, as has been shown above and as further elaborated in the pages that follow. The Melanesian exchange of perspectives and the Euro-American gaze are very different sorts of things. Both are made possible by relations, and in the final words of this volume Strathern expresses her central point most succinctly: "one could say that relations are what make people 'see' anything at all."

Twenty-one years after writing those words Strathern reiterated the importance of the anthropological focus on, and vocabulary of, relations. This is because the language of relations joins a range of languages from the life sciences among others, "for bringing home the lamentable blindness that has led to the present ecological [crisis]" (Strathern 2020: 12). Relentless property ownership that Strathern analyzed in *Property, Substance and Effect* and the exploitation of resources associated with such individual proprietorship is one aspect contributing to our present climate catastrophe. Property relations are relations of a particular kind and ones that often obscure a pressing requirement of the present: to grasp the "interdependence of beings and entities of all kinds" (Strathern 2020: 167–68). It is the previous blindness and continuing reluctance to properly acknowledge the pervasiveness of the relations between humans and nonhumans that has resulted in our current ecological predicament.

At the time of its original publication *Property, Substance and Effect* furthered the understanding of the complex relations between persons and things that was initiated in *The Gender of the Gift*. The book before you captures a moment in the ongoing analysis and understanding of the relations that constitute the diverse worlds we inhabit with diverse others. The book simultaneously shows the enduring relevance of anthropology for examining these worlds and the power of ethnographic insight for illuminating the intricate relations of persons and things of all kinds.

Acknowledgments

I thank my Brunel colleagues Will Rollason and James Staples for reading early drafts of this Introduction and offering very useful and helpful comments. The anonymous reviewer for the publisher read two drafts of the Introduction and on each occasion made comments that were both critical but helpful in pointing me in the correct direction. Finally, I thank Deborah Durham for inviting me to write the Introduction and who wisely and gently guided me along the way. For any errors of style, fact or form that remain I only have myself to thank.

References

Brown, Michael F. 2003. *Who Owns Native Culture*. Cambridge, MA: Harvard University Press.

Clifford, James, and George Marcus. 1986. *Writing Culture: The Poetics and Politics of Ethnography*. Berkeley: University of California Press.

Franklin, Sarah. 2003. "Rethinking Nature-Culture: Anthropology of the New Genetics." *Anthropological Theory* 3 (1): 65–85.

———. 2007. *Dolly Mixtures: The Remaking of Genealogy*. Durham, NC: Duke University Press.

Fullwiley, Duana. 2011. *The Enculturated Gene: Sickle Cell Health Politics and Biological Difference in West Africa*. Princeton: Princeton University Press.

Geertz, Clifford. 1988. *Works and Lives: The Anthropologist as Author*. Cambridge: Polity Press

Gregory, C. A. 1982. *Gift and Commodities*. London: Academic Press.

Hayden, Cori. 2003. *When Nature Goes Public: The Making and Unmaking of Bioprospecting in Mexico*. Princeton: Princeton University Press.

Helmreich, Stefan. 2008. "Species of Biocapital." *Science as Culture* 17 (4): 463–78.

Kalinoe, Lawrence. 2004. "Legal Options for the Regulation of Intellectual and Cultural Property in Papua New Guinea." In *Transactions and Creations: Property Debates and the Stimulus of Melanesia*, edited by Eric Hirsch and Marilyn Strathern, 40–59. Oxford: Berghahn Books.

Leenhardt, Maurice. (1947) 1979. Do Kamo*: Person and Myth in the Melanesian World*. Translated by Basia Miller Gulati. Chicago: University of Chicago Press.

Malinowski, Bronislaw. 1926. *Crime and Custom in Savage Society*. London: Routledge and Kegan Paul.

McKinnon, Susan, and Fenella Cannell, eds. 2013. *Vital Relations: Modernity and the Persistent Life of Kinship*. Sante Fe: SAR Press.

Montoya, Michael. 2011. *Making the Mexican Diabetic: Race, Science and the Genetics of Inequality*. Berkeley: University of California Press.

Myers, Fred. 2004. "Ontologies of the Image and Economies of Exchange." *American Ethnologist* 31 (1): 5–20.

Pálsson, Gísli. 2007. *Anthropology and the New Genetics*. Cambridge: Cambridge University Press.

Rabinow, Paul. 1996. "Severing the Ties: Fragmentation and Redemption in Late Modernity." In *Essays on the Anthropology of Reason*, 129–52. Princeton: Princeton University Press.

Rivers, W. H. R. 1923. *Psychology and Politics*. London: Kegan Paul, Trench, Trubner.

———. 1924. *Social Organisation*. London: Routledge, Trench, Trubner.

Skloot, Rebecca. 2010. *The Immortal Life of Henrietta Lacks*. London: Macmillan.

Strathern, Marilyn. 1972. *Women in Between: Female Roles in a Male World: Mount Hagen, New Guinea*. London: Academic Press.

———. 1975. *No Money on Our Skins: Hagen Migrants in Port Moresby*. Canberra: New Guinea Research Unit, Australian National University.

———. 1981. *Kinship at the Core: An Anthropology of Elmdon, a Village in North-West Essex in the Nineteen-Sixties*. Cambridge: Cambridge University Press.

———. 1985. "John Locke's Servant and the *Hausboi* from Hagen: Some Thoughts on Domestic Labour." *Critical Philosophy* 2 (2): 21–48.

———. 1988. *The Gender of the Gift: Problems with Women and Problems with Society in Melanesia*. Berkeley: University of California Press.

———. 1992. *After Nature: English Kinship in the Late Twentieth Century*. Cambridge: Cambridge University Press.

———. 1995. *The Relation*. Cambridge: Prickly Pear Press.

———. 2005. *Kinship, Law and the Unexpected: Relatives are Always a Surprise*. Cambridge: Cambridge University Press.

———. 2014. "Kinship as a Relation." *L'Homme* 210: 43–61.

———. 2020. *Relations: An Anthropological Account*. Durham, NC: Duke University Press.

Street, Alice. 2012. "Seen by the State: Bureaucracy, Visibility, and Governmentality in a Papua New Guinea Hospital." *The Australian Journal of Anthropology* 23: 1–21.

TallBear, Kim. 2013. *Native American DNA: Tribal Belonging and the False Promise of Genetic Science*. Minneapolis: University of Minnesota Press.

Thompson, Charis. 2005. *Making Parents: The Ontological Choreography of Reproductive Technologies*. Cambridge, MA: MIT Press.

Thomas, Nicholas. 1991. *Entangled Objects: Exchange, Material Culture, and Colonialism in the Pacific*. Cambridge, MA: Harvard University Press.

Tully, James. 1980. *A Discourse on Property: John Locke and his Adversaries*. Cambridge: Cambridge University Press.

Wagner, Roy. 1991. "The Fractal Person." In *Big Men and Great Men: Personifications of Power in Melanesia*, edited by Maurice Godelier and Marilyn Strathern, 159–74. Cambridge: Cambridge University Press.

Preface

The National Research Institute (NRI) in Port Moresby facilitated two months research in Papua New Guinea in 1995. I am most grateful to the people who took care of me so generously, and to the Department of Western Highlands, Western Highlands Province. My hosts will know what I owe them. Special appreciation must go to Reya, Henry, Mberem and Pale, as well as to Mande and her daughter Lucy, and to Snow. John Kenny (Puklum El) provided much wise guidance. On this occasion, as many times previously, Ru Kundil has contributed far more than acknowledgement of an ongoing intellectual debt can indicate. Fieldwork was funded by the British Academy and Cambridge University, while a brief visit to Port Moresby in 1997 was at the invitation of the NRI and Conservation Melanesia. Cyndi Banks and James Baker, and Claudia Gross and Mark Busse, were unstinting in their hospitality on both occasions, as were Mr and Mrs Oiee. My particular thanks to Kupi Kundil (Mrs Oiee) for the photograph of her as a girl.

A Papua New Guinea kina was approximately 50p in 1995.

Recent Melanesian anthropology has engaged in much more sophisticated commentary than I do justice to here. Over the last decade, along with James Weiner at Manchester University and then with Gilbert Lewis at Cambridge, I have had the privilege of quite exceptional company from several social theorists and ethnographers who have also at some stage been apprentice Melanesianists. They have included, in Papua New Guinea, Tony Crook, Melissa Demian, Claudia Gross,

Andrew Holding, James Leach, Patricia Peach, Adam Reed and Hélena Regius, as well as Lissant Bolton (Vanuatu), Annelise Riles (Fiji), Jude Philp (Torres Strait) and Gerhard Schneider (Solomons).

The essay format is derived from the original impetus for several of these pieces being contributions to conference topics: *Portraiture and the Problematics of Representation,* University of Manchester, 1993, convened by Marcia Pointon and Joanna Woodall (Chapter 2); *Cultural Poetics,* University of Southampton, 1996, convened by Peter Middleton and Julian Thomas (Chapter 3); *The Culture of Biomedicine,* Cambridge, 1996, convened by Alberto Cambrosio, Margaret Lock and Allan Young for the Social Science Research Council, New York (Chapter 4); the European Society for Oceanists biennial conference, Basel, 1994 (Chapter 6); *Actor Network Theory and After,* Keele University, 1997, convened by John Law (Chapter 9). Chapter 10 was originally given in 1997, under the title of 'Scale, culture and the imagination: an anthropological puzzle from Papua New Guinea', as a lecture to the British Psycho-Analytical Society, at the Institute of Psycho-Analysis, London.

The following chapters are also published elsewhere. Many thanks are due to volume editors for their willingness in the matter, while permission to draw directly on the material is gratefully acknowledged to the publishers in each case. For the purposes of this edition, some minor changes have been made.

Chapter 2 (1997) in *The Australian Journal of Anthropology,* special issue ed. by Diane Losche, 8: 89-103. Abridged version published in J. Woodall (ed.) (1997) *Portraiture: Facing the Subject,* Manchester: Manchester University Press. These include the photographs in the chapter.

Chapter 5 (1998) in *Mana, Estudos de Antropologia Social,* 4: 109-39). (Translated as 'Novas formas econômicas: um relato das Terras Altas de Papua Nova-Guiné'.)

Chapter 6 (1998) in V. Keck (ed.) *Common Worlds and Single Lives: Constituting Knowledge in Pacific Societies,* Oxford: Berg Publishers.

Chapter 7 (1998) in Chris Hann (ed.) *Property Relations: Sharing, Exclusion, Legitimacy,* Cambridge: Cambridge University Press.

Chapter 8 (1996) in *Social Anthropology,* 4: 17-32.

Chapter 1 includes a paper, 'Writing societies, writing persons' (1992), published in *History of Human Sciences,* 5: 5-16.

Conserving these, and other pieces written on separate occasions, as discrete essays means that the reader will find some overlap in the materials which they treat. Certain of the essays were also written in tandem with further papers with which they share material. To avoid the tedium of repeated reference, I note them here. 'The New Modernities' (Chapter 6) is a companion paper to 'Cutting the network' (1996), *Journal of the Royal Anthropological Institute*, (NS) 2: 517-35. Chapter 3 ('The Aesthetics of Substance') and Chapter 5 ('New Economic Forms') form a trio along with 'Same-sex and cross-sex relations: some internal comparisons', presented at the 1996 Wenner-Gren symposium on *Amazonia and Melanesia: Gender and Comparison,* convened by Don Tuzin and Tom Gregor. Finally, the last two chapters (9, 'What is Intellectual Property After?' and 10, 'Puzzles of Scale', with its photographs that appear as the endpiece) go together with a lecture, 'Environments within: an ethnographic commentary on scale', given in the 1996-7 Linacre Lecture series, Oxford (to be published in *Culture, Landscape and Environment,* Oxford: Oxford University Press).

The principal reason for bringing these essays together is at once very personal and very typical for an anthropologist. I have been affected more than I can express by my time with people in Mt Hagen in Papua New Guinea, starting in 1964-5, and including the much longer periods I have spent not there and on other things. I wanted to record that in a direct way and in a way which would make evident their influence. So these essays are in that sense retrospective. That personalises a professional conviction that social anthropology does not always do enough with its past. It has contributed uniquely to human knowledge by its studies of human knowledge. In doing so, it draws attention to one consistent characteristic of social life, namely the complex kinds of reflections upon themselves that people afford one another through their relations with one another. The material which results, rich with the distillation of many minds, becomes in the past even as it is written down, but continuing to write about it also continues to make it present.

Of course there are many ways of demonstrating this. And it is just as well that we have different projects! In this connection, I wish to note where I stand in the division of labour between myself and colleagues. These essays document, among other things, a continuing struggle with the language of description. Description presupposes analysis, and analysis presupposes theory, and they all presuppose imagination. The issue is how we may best describe knowing the effect which descriptions have on one another, that one description is always interpreted in the company of others and nothing is in that sense by itself. Social anthropologists make the question explicit: they work openly through other people's descriptions. Those descriptions invariably include people referring to fellow people as thinking and feeling beings, and attribute what they say and do to how they think and feel, but that is not the same as studying how people think and feel and this is not intended to be such a study. As on other occasions, the present work remains agnostic as to the emotions, states of mind or mental processes of the people mentioned here.

Getting the description right (a matter at once of accuracy, faithfulness and aesthetic alignment) applies anywhere. So that goes for the 'Euro-American' features I summon quite as much as the 'Melanesian' ones. These essays are certainly concerned with getting the Euro-American right, but, with one or two exceptions, they do so in an indirect sense. Euro-American is there, so to speak, in the analytical and theoretical turns. One way or another, what gets into the writer's vocabulary matters.

Cambridge, March 1998   Marilyn Strathern

CHAPTER I

The Ethnographic Effect I

If at the end of the twentieth century one were inventing a method of enquiry by which to grasp the complexity of social life, one might wish to invent something like the social anthropologist's ethnographic practice.

The practice has always had a double location, both in what for a century now it has been the tradition to call 'the field' and in the study, at the desk or on the lap. In the 1990s, it hardly need be added that it does not matter where the fieldworker's 'field' is geographically located nor how many sites it is spread across, nor even if sites are accessible through the laptop. Indeed, time rather than space has become the crucial axis of isolation or separation. I shall argue that it does matter that the ethnographic moment is moment of immersement. But it is a moment of immersement that is simultaneously total and partial, a totalising activity which is not the only activity in which the person is engaged.

Insofar as the ethnographer's locations can be seen as alternating, then each offers a perspective on the other. One of the elements which makes fieldwork challenging is that it is carried out with a quite different activity (writing) in mind. And what makes the study which follows in its own way equally challenging is that it turns out in fact to be much more than a matter of writing-up – for the writing only works, as the student discovers, as an imaginative re-creation of some of the effects of fieldwork itself. While any would-be author may find his or her account thronging with the words of other authors, for the returned fieldworker these companions sit side by side with a whole other society of people.

At the same time, the ideas and narratives which made sense of everyday field experience have to be rearranged to make sense in the context of arguments and analyses addressed to another audience. Far from being a derivative or residual activity, as one might think of a report or of reportage, ethnographic writing creates a second field. The relationship between the two fields can thus be described as 'complex' in that each is an order of engagement which partly inhabits or touches upon but does not encompass the other. Indeed, either may seem to spin off on its own trajectory. Each point of engagement is thus a replacement or a reordering of elements located in a separate field of activity and observation altogether. And the sense of loss or incompleteness which accompanies this, the realisation that neither can ever match up to the other, is common anthropological experience. So it becomes a kind of premonition perhaps to take loss with one. The members of the 1898 Cambridge Anthropological Expedition to the Torres Strait took a great sense of loss with them, although as they saw it it was the Melanesians who were suffering loss, loss of population and loss of culture. They were certainly anxious to record, as fully as possible, activities they thought were bound to diminish even further. It was the organiser, Alfred Haddon, who is credited with borrowing from natural history the term 'fieldwork' itself.

One kind of complexity lies, then, in the relationship between ethnography's double fields: each creates the other, but each also has its own dynamic or trajectory. The field ethnographer often learns the trajectory effect the hard way. What back at home had made sense as a field proposal can lose its motivating force; the preoccupations of the people on the spot take over. Yet for all sorts of reasons, they cannot take over completely. The fieldworker has to manage and thus inhabit both fields at the same time: to recall the theoretical conditions under which the work was proposed, and thus the reason for being there, while yielding to the flow of events and ideas which present themselves. To 'return from the field' means throwing those orientations into reverse.

All this is very familiar to social anthropologists; equally familiar is critical scrutiny of such practice. Some of the implications of moving between fields have been the subject of contentious debate over the last decade, if not longer, a debate addressed to the politics of writing anthropology and specifically to literary renderings of fieldwork experience. Social anthropologists have become sensitive to the image of movement, both because it mimics the kind of travelling that fieldwork and return often but not invariably imply, and because of its politically troubling connotations of intrusion and of freedoms taken at other people's expense. In turn, the fact that the intellectual journey traditionally required total immersement has become either a platitude or an embarrassment. Yet it is by contrast with the traveller's expectations of novelty that immersement yields what is often unlooked-for: it yields precisely the *facility and thus a method* for 'finding' the unlooked-for. This should be of considerable interest to students of complex phenomena.

UNPREDICTABILITY

The juxtaposition of different orders of phenomena, the linking of trajectories, as between observation and analysis, makes for complexity of the kind Lévi-Strauss adumbrates in the idea of complex structures in kinship (by contrast with other kinds of comprehensive arrangements which mesh kinship and marriage together, complex structures define who is related but leave open to completely different criteria who should marry whom). Such structures contain different orders or dimensions of existence, and any set of human dealings can be seen to be complex in this sense. Juxtaposing orders of data as part of its overt mode of collecting and analysing information simply renders the ethnographic method a highly visible case. When one thinks of different parts of a social system as having their own trajectories, one can see that the system is going to change through time in uneven and unpredictable ways. Here is another connotation of complexity. Over the same period as social anthropology has confronted the 'complex' effects of writing in the knowledge of new perceptions of the relationship between writing and fieldwork, outside anthropology ideas about complex systems – derived in the first place from mathematics, as well as biology and other natural sciences – have been applied to the study of human organisations. One consequence of this is of interest in the present context: it renews a long-standing challenge to the very idea of data collection.

The ethnographic moment

Now, from several points of view, the idea of data collection has come to seem suspect in recent years – both the collecting (because of its political connotations) and the data (because of its epistemological ones). The former, it seems, appropriates other people's possessions, while the latter mystifies social effect as fact. Indeed the pair of terms carries colonising resonances one would not necessarily wish to shrug off; the critiques do an important job in their utilisation of Euro-American views of what is appropriate to relations between persons in respect of things (in short, property relations). However, these challenges are not what I have in mind. The challenge is rather to the kind of breadth of information one might eventually wish to have. In a world which thinks of itself as information-driven, there is always too much and too little data. For where there seems to be more and more data in circulation, and in multiple formats, old questions about provenance need to be asked, repeatedly, again. These may turn into questions about authorship or proprietorship, or about forms of ownership or attachment that do not necessarily entail property, such as dispositional control. There are certainly issues over distribution and access. There are also, and quite separately, questions of responsibility. Taking responsibility for circulating data turns it already into information (about its provenance) for the users of it. This leads to the question of content. One also has to take responsibility for the object of study, and in the case of anthropologists this consists in elucidating and describing the contours of social life. More than that, social anthropology is committed to a certain view of social life as complex: it is a relational phenomenon and by its nature cannot be reduced to elementary principles or axioms. This has always been a problematic in the act of description. The challenge is indeed to the breadth of information one wishes for. It is renewed in challenges posed by new perceptions of complexity.

Any social organisation can be thought of as a complex evolving system insofar as it generates behaviour that is unpredictable, non-linear and capable of producing multiple outcomes. Because of the overlapping and dove-tailing nature of multiple factors working upon one another, systems generally show a sensitivity to their initial conditions. Events do not unfold with regularity, and small changes can produce major outcomes in quite unpredictable ways. Translated into the need to generate information (about outcomes), this means that conditions may be overlooked because they are too small to be or are simply not recognised as initial conditions in the first place. The challenge is apparent: how does one argue back from an unforeseen event, an unpredictable outcome, to the circumstances of its development?

While models of complex systems may well appeal to management practices which have to be able to predict outcomes, or to ways of seeking to be innovative within an institutional framework, they also hold an obvious interest for the study of social change or of evolution in human behaviour. However, looking to innovation or development gives a secondary, superfluous dynamic to the primary activity of describing social processes; there is a dynamism already built into the activity of description itself. When it comes to building up *knowledge* about any complex organisational system, with its diverse outcomes, it is the initial conditions themselves that emerge as unpredictable – they are unpredictable from the point of view of the observer or whoever is striving to describe the social processes at issue. After all, what must be taken into account is what has been overlooked. The investigator does not know at the outset the full range of factors which are going to be relevant to the end-analysis, nor indeed the full range of analyses which are going to be relevant to comprehending material already filling notes and papers.

One social science strategy is deliberate selection through coupling specific methods with the expectation of specific types of data. But since there will have been factors at the beginning whose influences and effects were unpredictable, or which only came into operation when other conditions subsequently arose, how does one deliberately factor those in? One answer is that we can always try working backwards with our archaeologies. Closer to hand, however, is the conundrum posed by fieldwork undertaken over an isolated stretch of time. Has it not always been a problem to encompass enough to include material which cannot be seen at the time, let alone be specified in advance, but which could well be useful later? If it did not exist, we might have to be inventing the anthropologist's ethnographic method and its strategies of immersement. Immersement itself is a complex phenomenon, as we shall see.

It is significant that field immersement is repeated in the subsequent study away from the field. Ethnographers set themselves the task not just of comprehending the effect that certain practices and artefacts have in people's lives, but of re-creating some of those effects in the context of writing about them. Of course analysis ('writing') begins 'in the field' as much as the ethnographer's hosts continue to exert a pull on the direction of his or her energies long after. Now the division between the two fields creates two kinds of (interrelated) relationships. There is the acute awareness of the pull of divergent paths of knowledge, and the anthropologist may well regard one of these trajectories as pertaining to observation and the other to analysis. But there is also the effect of engaging the fields together, and this we might call the *ethnographic moment*. The ethnographic moment is a relation in the same way as a linguistic sign can be thought of as a relation (joining signifier and signified). We could say that the ethnographic moment works as an example of a relation which joins the understood (what is analysed at the moment of observation) to the need to understand (what is observed at the moment of analysis). The relationship between what is already apprehended and what seems to demand apprehension is of course infinitely regressive, that is, slips across any manner of scale (minimally, observation and analysis each contains within itself the relation between them both). Any ethnographic moment, which is a moment of knowledge or insight, denotes a relation between immersement and movement.[1]

I cannot avoid a personal note about my particular understanding of my first fieldwork field, Hagen in the Highlands of Papua New Guinea. I am not referring to the products of discourse, to dialogic interchange or mutual authorship, important as these can become both to relationships with persons and to the writing of anthropology. Nor to the reader over my shoulder: to the fact that while I might think I am organising my account of Hageners' doings, they are also organising my writing of the account. I want rather to find a way of acknowledging the fact that my attention has been transfixed at certain (ethnographic) moments I have never been able – wanted – to shake off.

On being dazzled

Movement between fields is only part of the flexibility of the ethnographic method – the paradox is that flexibility of a kind lies also in the very state of immersement, in the totalising as well as the partial nature of commitment. In yielding to the preoccupations of others, the fieldworker enters into relationships with people for which no amount of imagining or speculating can serve as advance preparation. It is not just that fieldwork, or writing for that matter, is full of surprises, but that there is a point of method here crucial to the fieldwork side of the double field(s). To comment on an obvious aspect of this: people are more than respondents answering questions; they are informants in the fullest sense, in control of the information they offer. I mean this in the sense that the ethnographer is often led to receive it as information, that is, as data which has become meaningful, by putting it into the context of general knowledge about these people's lives and situations and thus the context of its production. This in turn encourages, even forces, the ethnographer into the position of collecting data that is not yet information and thus whose relevance to anything may not be immediately obvious at all.

One of the rubrics under which Haddon and his colleagues worked in the Torres Strait was to gather as much material as possible. The accompanying sense of urgency was in part an outcome of Haddon's solo visit as a marine biologist ten years previously; he had not been prepared for the impact which the islanders had upon him, and he had returned with all kinds of observations about what he saw as the effects of colonial rule on them.

But how could such an imperative about gathering material be sustained beyond the initial rescue reaction in the face of what appeared then, a hundred years ago, to be vanishing cultures and disintegrating societies (we know now that they refused to disappear)?[2] Collecting data before it became information had to be made interesting to do for its own sake. Here reflective practice ('writing') had its role to play. One of the motivations that galvanised a good part of twentieth-century social anthropology in Britain was known by the analytical shorthand 'holism'. This had a multiple reference – drawing anything and everything interesting within the focus of enquiry, regardless of scale; rooting this in the supposition that societies and cultures have an internal coherence, so that all would in the end connect up; developing this in a theory of the functional interrelations of social phenomena, at the very least in order that different parts of the data could serve as a context for understanding other parts; and evincing this coherence and interconnection in a battery of constructs such as 'organisation', 'order', 'structure', 'pattern'. No matter that latterday commentators have argued that the coherence was largely an artefact of anthropological writing itself, that all the mid-century metaphors of social order gave way to processual ones, and that structure, coherence and interconnection came to be regarded as suspicious rhetorical tools. The project of holism was the project of imagining an encompassing social field to which any aspect of social life, however apparently 'small', would contribute; it was also the project of imagining that any information might be relevant to a larger account. As a methodological axiom for the fieldworker, it meant therefore that a larger accounting was necessarily and always waiting future elucidation. It became a trivial point whether or not such an encompassment proved attainable.

For it was of course pointless to imagine that one could gather everything: items of knowledge multiply and divide under one's eyes. Rather, the enterprise of field anthropology, at once modestly and scandalously, endorsed the possibility that one could gather *anything*. Perhaps this reconciled the fieldworker to the directions in which his or her hosts might be pulling – it certainly gave licence to curiosity and to following up paths that at the outset simply could not have got on the map.

On my part, I shall never forget my first sight of mounted pearlshells in Mt Hagen, in 1964, heavy in their resin boards, slung like pigs from a pole being carried between two men, who were hurrying with them because of the weight, a gift of some kind. It was only a glimpse; the men were half-running and their path was almost out of my field of vision. But it belongs to a set of images which have mesmerised me ever since. In those early days, time was divided between walking around gardens, getting some idea of the settlement pattern, doing rudimentary genealogical work and acquiring a sense of relations between political groups (clans and, as they were called in the emergent Highlands literature of the time, tribes). The original proposal that I investigate the effect of sibling order on cash cropping success, stimulated by recent reports of Highlands entrepreneurial activity, was put on hold. My supervisor, Esther Goody, might now be amused to think that although the question of sibling order did not prove to be a particularly interesting one, the effect of cash cropping and the property relations it had introduced most certainly did – although it has taken thirty years to loop that back through the visual display that diverted me off the path. A report of sorts can be found in Chapter 5. Some of the other chapters also attempt to work out by what kind of ethnographic account one might render the role that the pervasive market relations of capitalism play in people's lives when there are new objects and desires (cash crops were an early example) at their disposal. As we shall also see, Papua New Guineans, let alone Hageners, are by no means the only people to whom that question applies.

It was impossible to anticipate the role that prestations were to play in my understanding of Papua New Guinea Highlands social life, as it was impossible to anticipate the significance I was to put on the gendered nature of the event (one would never see women carrying shells like that). Not to know what one is going to discover is self-evidently true of discovery. But, in addition, one also does not know what is going to prove in retrospect to be significant by the very fact that significance is acquired through the subsequent writing, through composing the ethnography as an account after the event.

The fieldwork exercise is an anticipatory one, then, being open to what is to come later. In the meanwhile the would-be ethnographer gathers material whose use cannot be foreseen, facts and issues collected with little knowledge as to their connections. The result is a 'field' of information to which it is possible to return, intellectually speaking, in order to ask questions about subsequent developments whose trajectory was not evident at the outset. These might be developments in the anthropologist's understanding generated by the writing process or they might be social and historical changes in the social life under study. One way of ensuring that at least there will be some resources to hand lies in an old axiom which once accompanied the rubric of holism, namely that data has to be collected 'for its own sake'. And one way of doing that is for the fieldworker to commit him or herself to the social relationships people wish to establish with him or her – for if they so wish it, the fieldworker then becomes part of their relationships with one another. It is back to front to imagine that this either can or should be undertaken in order to collect better data. The relationships must be valued for their own sake. Any resulting information is a residual – often initially unknown – product. This is what immersement means.

Much information is amassed, hopefully, by the field ethnographer with specific intentions in mind. But, at the same time, knowing that one cannot completely know what is going to be germane to any subsequent re-organisation of material demanded by the process of writing can have its own effect. It may create an expectation of surprise, for instance; one looks for the untoward, for small revelations. The expectation of surprise reappears in the ethnographic text as a revelation of a different kind. The diverse ways in which social anthropologists 'make sense' of bizarre materials, or put events into a wider context, or uncover ideology or demonstrate – an analytical preoccupation for a while – that there is a relationship to be explored between the real and the ideal: these are all analytical moves which pass on the effect of surprise. As it has often been pointed out, material is managed so as to divide the less evident from the more evident and thus show up the work of elucidation. Sometimes it is assumed that the anthropologist is making claims to know 'more' than those he or she works with, although I do not know any practising fieldworker who would ever put it that way. Yet to pass this off by saying that really the anthropologist knows differently, to my mind misses an important point. Rather, the anthropologist is equally trying to know in the *same* way – that is, recover some of the anticipation of fieldwork, some of the revelations that came from the personal relationships established there, and even perhaps some of the surprises which people keep in store for one another.

Indeed there is a form of revelatory knowledge bound up in the antinomies by which much anthropology has proceeded in the second half of this century: norm and deviance, ideology and practice; structure and process; system and agent; representation and evocation: each creates the possibility of escaping from the other, and thus relies on its trajectory being tied at some point into the other in order to emphasise its own path of flight. Its counterpart remains (half) hidden. The expectation of surprise becomes further routinised in the adage that one is never content with what is on the surface and looks behind or looks underneath or otherwise questions what seems taken for granted.

Perhaps it is to conserve some of the original effect of surprise, then, that ethnographers have been drawn to those arenas of social life where people appear to be reflecting on their practices and often seem to be 'revealing' to themselves facts about themselves not always immediately apparent. This can lead to an emphasis on the interpretation of ceremonial or myth, or other esoteric material, which brings in turn the problems of special knowledge to which Maurice Bloch has consistently, and importantly, pointed. It is worth remarking, however, that special knowledge which inheres, say, in theological or scientific expertise has never held quite the place in anthropological accounts as materials which appear esoteric *because* they require revealing (beg immediate interpretation). An initial surprise becomes a suspension, a dazzle, and some kinds of 'special knowledge' are more likely to dazzle than others. One is held, as it were, on the threshold of understanding. I referred to having been mesmerised; it is the dazzle effect of certain revelatory practices which occupies me here.

REIFICATIONS

Why should the Highlands of Papua New Guinea have dominated analytical forms influential now in the social anthropology of Melanesia for more than three decades? While their saliency is periodically contested, displacing one regional view with another seems no solution. We might instead address that influence through some of the forms which knowledge takes in this region. I would suggest that there has been a powerful fusion between the 'expository' practices of anthropologists and the 'display' practices of certain Highlanders. Their effects are both revelatory.

A comment on revelatory practices

The impact of Highlands display on anthropological expositions of group dynamics is widely known. Men in general and big men in particular seem to organise the people around them in the same way as the anthropologist would like to organise his or her account. Yet there is more to this impact than the question of those dominant social forms and the public visibility of men's (by contrast with women's) affairs which have been the subject of thorough-going theoretical attention. Part of the fascination lies I think with the way in which the unfolding of these practices themselves mimics the kind of discoveries ethnographers make through analysis; they invite one to consider what is hidden and concealed behind the acts of revelation. (Is it partly because of this very invitation that such acts may be dubbed 'ceremonial' or 'ritual', as in 'ceremonial exchange' or 'initiation rituals'?) Highlands men and women alike have their own answers to what can or cannot be seen in these ceremonial and ritual events. In being shown what is concealed, however, the ethnographer may well conclude that, among other things, he or she is dealing with knowledge practices, and the different kinds of knowledge that become appropriate on different occasions. It may thus seem that people themselves are managing what is to be known, and to whom when.

For the anthropologist that knowledge will be distributed between the work of observation (what is already understood) and the work of analysis (what needs understanding). I believe I am here speaking for more than myself, though indubitably I am speaking for myself. I have come to realise[3] the extent to which certain Hagen practices have had enduring effect on my anthropology. These include the gestures and practices of ceremonial exchange by which men, as donors and recipients, alternate their perspectives on one another. What is revealed to the audience on the occasion are the signs of capacity – the properties of persons and things, the substance of body and mind – to which people lay claim; what is simultaneously revealed (to whomever might be paying attention) is the already known fact of the origin of these capacities in other people.

It was dazzling at the time. Exchange involved a whole nexus of activities including the creation of a public life, negotiations over the giving and receiving of items of wealth, as well as visible interaction and performances, and accompanied life-crisis events such as bridewealth and mortuary occasions, being epitomised in what exactly came in the literature to be known as ceremonial exchange *(moka)*, and on which Andrew Strathern has written extensively. The dazzle effect (for me) endured in the analytical work that was done afterwards. The ethnographic moment, then, was necessarily also an artefact of analysis and of writing. Partly it was a result of realising the revelations behind the revelations; partly it was a result of these events creating the further effect of there being quite different dimensions of life to be uncovered. Thus what was to be further uncovered were the processes of production behind these transactions, the life of women which the public life of men seemed to conceal, and the cross-sex relations that lay athwart these same-sex ones.

Each ethnographic moment will belong to a field of such moments, and is in turn composed of others. In describing Hagen in relation to other societies and other materials, I have found myself repeatedly coming back to this particular 'moment', to the way in which donors and recipients alternate their perspectives on one another, for explanatory purchase on the character not only of Hagen but of Melanesian sociality. (What took off from men's performances did not of course remain there.) Those mounted shells which I first glimpsed half-disappearing over the brow of a hill as the path took the men out of view were still in general circulation when anthropological investigation in the Highlands of Papua New Guinea began. Neither their historical absence since (shells have gone out of circulation) nor subsequent theoretical arguing and counter-arguing seem to have lessened their presence in my work. On the contrary, I have been taken aback by the extent to which they have reappeared in these essays. It is as though they have been summoned by the character of changes and developments – and not only in Papua New Guinea – which the essays also touch upon.

Relational knowledge

The argument can be put another way. It should be evident that this particular ethnographic moment has become for me a paradigm, a theoretical passage point which mobilises several issues: in short, it has become a category of knowledge. The moment objectifies a certain observation (the gift of wealth) and its accompanying analysis (the exchange of perspectives). To borrow back terms given a particular analytical emphasis in the context of Melanesian material,[4] the object (of knowledge) is here reified. By reification I simply intend to point to the manner in which entities are made into objects when they are seen to assume a particular form ('gift', 'exchange'). This form in turn indicates the properties by which they are known and, in being rendered knowable or graspable through such properties, entities appear (in Euro-American idiom) as 'things'. A parallel process of objectification lies in what in the Melanesian context I have needed to call personification. The Euro-American notion of humanising non-human entities is a special case and I mean more broadly the way in which entities are made into objects through the relations which people have with another.

These terms derive from an earlier elucidation of materials which there is no necessity to rehearse here (see note 4). A few more words about reification are, however, in order.

The focus on form comes from what has seemed to be a useful contrast between Euro-American assumptions about the naturalness or givenness of the properties of things, and the way in which Melanesians sometimes think of themselves having to work to make things appear in their appropriate guise. A clan of men and women only appears as a 'clan', or a human child as 'human' rather than spirit, if the contours, the shapes, are right. In the past, making the right form appear included having to ensure proper growth – of persons, plants, pigs – hence the anxious application of magic as part of people's endeavours. Now Euro-Americans take the form of many things in their world for granted. It is when obvious intellectual effort is applied to them, as for instance in the theoretical decision as to what is to count as a clan, or these days how human a human embryo is, that the role which people's (intellectual) work plays in the construction of such 'things' becomes evident to them (Euro-Americans). Among scholars a special place is given to intellectual work, and again to the work it takes to understand that and thus to epistemological self-consciousness about ways of knowing. We should not lose sight of the fact, then, that the effort of 'knowing' which goes into making an analysis or model of the world 'appear' in a written account is a process which involves reification. It is a cultural curiosity that reification is of course frequently attacked for its very properties – for being an edifice of knowledge, and thus obviously artifice.

There are many already established and thus conventional reifications in social anthropology, in the recent past the most powerful being the concepts of 'culture' and 'society'. These things, consistently shown up not to be things at all while all along continuing to behave just like that in people's writings, condense into concrete images whole spectra of relations. They thus present themselves as (analytical) categories of knowledge; a universe of data is at once bound up in these terms and is organised by them so as to appear as certain kinds of information. One can as a consequence interrogate such categories, and use them to interrogate other categories. At what moments is it appropriate, for example, to label events as social or cultural? However, that question is not restricted to these particular categories alone. Anthropological models in general organise knowledge about human affairs in terms of social relations and the complexities of social life and thought. They determine the contours of what is recognisably relational in people's dealings with one another.

Those contours may be 'seen' in certain recurring images. When I write about exchange of perspectives, for instance, I have in mind the image of a Hagen man handing over an item (shells, pigs, money) with the expectation of a return gift and, thus, with the counterflow contained in that same gesture.[5] There is much more to my understanding of such an event, but the form which that gesture takes is durable: it reminds me that regardless of previous analysis there remains a moment to be understood. What I reify here is of course an understanding about sociality, and specifically about a rather particular, and particularly gendered, set of social relations. What I see in the gesture I then see over again in the wealth items themselves. These gifts had a further compelling effect on this ethnographer for the reason that they seemed to compel responses from people who saw them. They were generally handed over in a public context to critical and judgemental recipients before a critical and judgemental audience. The scrutiny of form drove home the fact that, *ipso facto*, a form can only appear with its appropriate properties – or else it has not appeared. A return gift is not a return gift if the items are too few or poor; prestige does not emerge from a display if the display fails. In that sense these entities have an aesthetic effect. In that sense, too, they hold something of the status of 'art objects' in Euro-American culture, minimally because whether or not an artefact is deemed art at all is a debate precisely about the appropriateness of form.

Now I am self-conscious about this particular act of reification as an artefact of observation/analysis because that is how I also wish to describe the gesture from a Hagen perspective. It would be a mistake, however, to jump to the conclusion that, for Hagen people, shells and pigs and such are reifications (things) because they are objects. Rather, they become objects, in the sense of becoming an object of attention or of people's regard, by being grasped or apprehended as things. That I put it round this way must be understood in relation to the second mode of making objects, which also gives us the generic Hagen entity which is (so to speak) the object of objectification: social relations. Objects may also be grasped or apprehended as persons.

Wealth items (among other things in Hagen) objectify relations by giving them the form of things; they may also objectify relations by making persons, that is, positions from which people perceive one another. For these items separate persons from persons. It is through the separation of persons from one another that specific relations are created, and through relations that persons are defined in respect of one another. The relationship between donor and recipient is my paradigm here, for it is in each distinguishing himself from his partner – in order to undertake the transaction – that the relationship between them becomes visible. Each acts with the other in mind. But note that relations are thus personified in the separation of persons to the extent that persons (continue to) (thereby) have an effect on one another. Those effects also have to be conveyed, and wealth items can convey them. We can now return to reification, and to the place which it holds in several of the chapters which follow.

Relations wither or flourish according to the properties seen to flow alongside them. The *effectiveness* of relationships thus depends on the form in which certain objects appear. What is reified, we may say, are capabilities and powers, that is, relations are reified, endowed with effect, in anticipation of – or in commemoration of – being activated. If Hagen people were to think of it this way, they might put it as follows. Wealth items, gifts, do not reify society or culture, which is an object of the anthropological analysis of social relations; they reify capacities contained in persons/relations. They are thus predicated on activity, and the direction of flow indicates the immediate source of agency.[6] In short, social relations are made manifest through action.

If the ethnographer has been more elaborate than is necessary with these definitions, it is because the dazzle of the ethnographic moment forces on her, or out of her/me, certain conceptualisations which I try to hold steady with these terms. The terms themselves belong to a much wider field of discourse – there are other, overlapping anthropological usages.

Alfred Gell has provided a wonderful example. The phrase 'social relations are made manifest through action' comes from his book *Art and Agency* (1998).[7] When Gell set out to delineate an anthropological theory of art, it was to be a theory which resembled others in social anthropology. That is, it (the theory) was to take as its subject the working of social relations. This was not to be an account of art as representation or a disquisition on cultural meaning or the exercise of putting art productions into a 'social context'. It was to theorise art as operating within a nexus of agency. Agents cause events to happen. Art, he argues, may be actor or acted upon, agent or patient, in a field of agents and patients which take diverse forms and have diverse effects on one another. As far as efficacy on others is concerned, one may thus see an art object in the same way as one may see a person. It embodies capacities. Euro-Americans often think agency inappropriately personified when it is applied to inanimate entities, but that is because they link agency to will or intention. Magnificently, Gell sweeps all that aside. In terms of the effects of entities upon one another, and it is the analysis of relational effect which in his view makes analysis anthropological, 'things' and 'persons' may be co-presences in a field of effectual actors.

From his perspective on art, Gell has his own battery of terms; apart from 'agent' which signals the effective source of an act, he uses the term 'index' in a rather similar way to my usage of reification (a thing), and his 'patient' overlaps with my person as a (personified) object of people's regard. It is of course the concepts, not the terms as such, that matter. Although I do not pursue it very far here, the advantage of his vocabulary is that it frees our two otherwise troublesome constructs, thing and person, for their phenomenal apprehension in an ordinary language sense.

Social agency manifests and realises itself in the effects of actions. An agent thus requires a relational counterpart, that which shows the effect of another's agency, hence Gell's use of the term 'patient'. He argues that primary agents and patients proliferate in secondary, artefactual, form. Artefacts may, in his words, be persons, things, animals. There is interest here for the sociologists' actor network theory, briefly introduced in Chapter 9, which comes from the quite different theoretical stable of science and technology studies. Actor network theory pays attention to the way in which social relations, and their self-empowering manifestation in human skills, summon the properties of, and thus enroll the effectiveness of, artefacts and techniques regardless of whether these are (in the Euro-American ordinary language sense) persons, things, animals or, for that matter, events.

There is also interest here for the analysis of property relations. Property as a relation has long been central to anthropological theorising, with or without reference to theories of political economy, and the long-standing indigenous Euro-American critique of property forms as containing or concealing social relations. In fact property relations could have provided Gell with a secondary model for his analysis of art. Like 'art', property is a specific cultural form whose counterparts elsewhere social anthropologists may demonstrate or deny. (They may either regard property as responding to an innate human disposition towards possession or else regard it as having emerged under certain, localised social conditions.) When they are being Euro-American, anthropologists may regard art and property as attached to persons in somewhat comparable (not necessarily similar) ways. Art already appears to be (has the phenomenal form of) the work of persons, so that the products of this work thus appear as a reification of their capacities. To Euro-Americans, art thus has visual or acoustic properties whereas there is nothing necessarily visual or acoustic about property. In comparison, where things already appear to exist in the world then establishing 'property' is a question of creating personal claims in them. Behind the thing, analysis may in turn uncover social relations, for instance – in fact especially – the social nature of production, either as a manufactured item or as a piece of the natural world made known by intellectual effort, routinised in the understanding of property as a bundle of rights. Property rights appear as at once the possession of persons and, by that act, as dividing persons off from one another.

These are of course only moments in the unfolding of comprehension. For Euro-Americans, the application of knowledge (analysis, the writing of an explanatory account) brings a further, recursive, comprehension of these entities. When the 'thing' which becomes property through the claims people make on it is then perceived as the product of social relations in the first place, that fresh perception may itself be perceived as a product of social effort, for it requires and constitutes knowledge. Knowledge may in turn be the subject of property rights, provided, that is, it assumes an appropriate form.

The Reification of Social Relations

Language can work against the user of it. One of the problems with the Euro-American-derived language on which anthropologists draw for making phenomena appear in their accounts is that it makes other, unwanted, things appear as well. There are intrusive evaluative overtones to many of the key terms in the analytical vocabulary. Sociality is frequently understood as implying sociability, reciprocity as altruism and relationship as solidarity, not to speak of economic actions as economistic motivations. Here terms can even carry insulting connotations, as 'object' and 'objectification' often do.[8] Thus reification can be regarded as making things abstract, artificial and depersonalised, personification as absurdly fetishist or mystical. As for my ethnographic moment, the recapitulated and recursive gesture of exchange, that can sound either too materialist or too sentimental for words. Dazzle, on the other hand, is likely to connote the fascination of enchantment.

In order to divest the dazzle effect of some of its positive overtones, I have included in these essays reference to the troubled nature of episodes quite difficult to think about. Head-hunting seems no more nor less barbaric than much human activity; but the image of the witch-child has a different effect (on me), more akin to some of the morally problematic issues raised by Euro-American interventions in human reproduction, and in particular the technical availability of choices which hold out the idea that one might select a child for particular characteristics. Although in the Papua New Guinean case to which I refer (see Chapter 3) men as well as women may hunt down witches, it is the actions of the female parent, the mother, that made me pause. The case bears directly on what people wish to make visible about themselves.

When Hagen men display shells and pigs (not heads), they present a version of themselves as they would like to be seen. Hagen women do not present themselves in the same way. If I think of a counterpart to the two men with their shells, I think of the women I would visit in the evenings, returned from the gardens, having washed their cull of sweet potatoes in a stream on their way. Or another meeting, in 1995, with a now elderly companion. What sticks in my mind is her retreating back, humped with a netbag full of tubers, digging stick clasped over the head, a steep path in front of her, hurrying home. This was not a display, any more than men have any particular desire to be seen when they are work-ing in their gardens. It is an ethnographic moment, but one that disap-pears in what (misleadingly as it turned out) seems to have been already understood.

If one were to ask what is going on here, the chances are that one would focus on the evident effects of work, of daily rhythm, of obliga-tion. No surprise that on the other side of ceremonial exchange lies the work of women and men in their gardens and the daily grind of feed-ing people and pigs. And why is it no surprise? Perhaps because that image is likely to have been preempted by the counter-effect of certain Euro-American knowledge practices. These have many components, but they also share one crucial point of substance or content. Perhaps one could refer to it as auto-dazzle.[9] Knowledge involves creativity, effort, production; it loves to uncover creativity, effort, production! Specifically it uncovers effort applied to a given world (whether that world is social or natural), so that it (the effort) can be made visible apart from its ori-gin and outcome. Like the hilly path, the arduousness of producing the necessities of life seems all too evident evidence. And the fact that in this case it involves gardening, and thus work akin to productive activ-ity in Euro-American eyes, is likely to summon further Euro-American notions about the underlying reality of human intervention in natural or biological process. Moreover this reality is open to constant discov-ery and re-discovery; I am almost inclined to see the uncovering of the 'reality' of human intervention in such processes as having a counterpart dazzle to the revelatory practices of ceremonial exchange where what is revealed is the origin of one person's gift in another person.

The Euro-American reification of effort or productivity takes various forms. 'Property' once held the place of the self-evident/mystifying demonstration of human effort which had gone into the appropriation of nature; in the late twentieth century, it seems, 'technology' has become a new exemplar of human enterprise. Technology adds the further crucial element of 'knowledge', for technology embodies not just the modification of natural realities, and the recognition of the human handiwork that has gone into them, but evidence of the knowledge of how to do it.

It is the cultural place which technology has come to play in Euro-American perceptions of their place in the world which has in turn given an impetus to the concept of intellectual property – intellectual property rights (IPR) hold up a mirror to the dazzle of creativity. For 'intellectual property' points simultaneously to an item or technique made available to knowledge, authorising its use and circulation, and to the knowledge, on which claims are made, which has made it into an item or technique. Knowledge embedded in technology has already been productive in the manner that labour is productive, while knowledge rendered as a subject of property rights can be put into productive circulation as commodities are. 'Intellectual property rights' takes its place as part of the current international language of commerce and human rights alike.

In its wake come all kinds of indigenous (Euro-American) critiques, including outright criticism of the saliency of property as the overwhelming legal response to claims which could be conceptualised in other ways (as in use rights, disposal, licence). This critique addresses the fact that the last twenty or thirty years has seen an unprecedented development not just of new things to own but of things which suggest that Euro-Americans need to devise new ways of laying claim. New reproductive technologies (NRT) are one area of interest. Questions about relations based on substance and relations based on intention or mental conception, questions that could not have been foreseen twenty years ago, come to influence the kinds of claims kin make on one another. Thus Euro-American ideas about the interrelation between different components of the procreative process, the place of biology and the nature of (re)productive 'substances', have become problematised by claims (made possible through technologies of assisted conception) arising from intellectual or conceptual work and invention. These add new complexities to relations. Indeed we could identify a double trajectory, each spinning off in its own orbit while making repeated contact with the other. For in debates over NRT, and the ideas of personhood caught up in them, Euro-Americans witness on the one hand an increasing emphasis on corporalisation (biology), and on the other hand an increasing value given to conceptual or mental effort. Thus what are constantly (re)created as the underlying realities of genetic makeup are counterbalanced by the accord given to human invention.

The essays which follow touch both on the claims people make through relations with others imagined as relations of body substance, and on the increasing visibility of intellectual work as a factor in property relations. They exploit one of the facilities of the ethnographic method: being able to re-describe something from another viewpoint not just as a view on it but from a new point of entirety or holism. I have of course written my own invitation when I say it invites one to return to earlier formulations with fresh intent.

The chapters in Part I are ethnographically heterogeneous. Chapter 2 draws attention to an explicit aesthetic effect as the aim of Hagen body decoration. The effectiveness of a man's exchange relations with others are given form, reified, in the items he attaches to the body and of which it thus appears composed, and specific ceremonial exchange occasions entail the display of this form. A parallel with Euro-American notions of genetic composition is briefly explored through questions about the representation of individuality raised by a conference on portraiture. But reification can carry a penalty. The subject of Chapter 3 is the production of images in a world of excess. Excess of consumption (the body image of a greedy witch) finds a parallel in Euro-American perceptions of excess of meaning (analytical work run riot), and raises the question of how to hide or dispose of image/meaning. One 'solution' lies in alternating states of depletion and plenty. In Chapter 4, the penalty of reification is raised again by a different kind of excess: for some, no amount of theoretical arguing and counter-arguing can seemingly subdue the effect of biological knowledge. The role of knowledge in debates over procreative rights (here, the right of the child to know its biological parentage) is examined from two perspectives raised by a Canadian case. The approval with which information is gathered in order to make public opinion about the new reproductive technologies visible and explicit is contrasted with the ambiguous consequences on Euro-American ideas of kinship of data about ties of substance where parents may wish to hide the information it brings.

Part II turns to the vocabulary of analysis stimulated by changing configurations of property. It asserts the need of – and one which could be taken much further – a new conceptual repertoire for understanding traditional anthropological materials. Chapter 5 opens with the ways in which social relations appear to have expanded in Hagen over the last three decades; this is put down to an excess of sorts (inflation, new patterns of consumption). Not being able to detach relations from one another is in the 1990s, and under the impact of economic change, one effect of new kinds of interactions between the sexes. There are consequences here for ideas about reproduction once channelled through body payments. There are also new claims to ownership of resources and rights in persons. Property created by rights of invention has an explicitly 'hybrid' (complex) character, Chapter 7 argues, akin to that which Latour finds endogenous to Papua New Guinea. The issue is explored through reflections on cultural inventiveness and on some of the new candidates for proprietorship of biogenetic material that appeal to intellectual property rights. The chapter criticises certain assumptions about the nature of Melanesian transactions, and touches on the Euro-American view of ownership (possessiveness) as attachment. In Chapter 8, the quandary of a modern Hagen parent is described in terms of a specifically local conundrum: the need to detach children from parents in a context where the old instruments of bridewealth exchange no longer operate with the same effect. At the same time, for the anthropologist, the quandary brings the Hagen parent nearer to rather than further away from her Euro-American counterparts concerned with new formulations of procreative rights.

Issues of form and substance behind many of the new formulations are brought together in relation to one area, signalled by the speculative essay on intellectual property rights which opens Part III. Chapter 9 draws connections between emergent forms of Euro-American property across several domains. Four candidates for potential ownership are identified: the products of collective life (cultural property), of usable knowledge (intellectual property), of the body (through the application of biotechnology) and of professional commitment (academic control). The essay comments on certain kinds of European rhetoric, notably the rush to personify the biotechnological development of human substance as the commercialisation of human beings or persons. There is an international community of commentary here. It was the elevation of a virus to human status that led an American-based non-governmental task force to draw attention to bioprospecting in Papua New Guinea; this lay behind a conference on intellectual property rights. Interpretations are brought to task when the anthropologist is asked to contribute. This is the subject of Chapter 9. Chapter 10 finds another locus for talking about concealment and revelation; this time it is related to questions about the scale of people's activities, and the manner in which values are or are not kept constant. It is an attempt to discuss social change without preempting anything by the freighted vocabulary of change-and-continuity. It thus tries to keep ethographic writing as 'open' to the unpredictable as the social life which stimulates observations on itself.

If the world is shrinking in terms of resources, it is expanding in terms of new candidates for ownership; there are at once new kinds of entities being created and new grounds for property – among other types of ownership – claims. Whether one lives in Papua New Guinea or in Britain, cultural categories are being dissolved and re-formed at a tempo that calls for reflection, and that, I would add, calls for the kind of lateral reflection afforded by ethnographic insight.

In the latter part of the twentieth century anthropologists are as conscious of the appearance and disappearance of social forms as they were at its inception. This is one reason why I offer no apology for the comparative moves here (bracketing together Papua New Guinea and Britain, or, more accurately, the ethnographically conceived Melanesia and Euro-America). If one is ready to contemplate differences between temporal epochs, then it is helpful to be reminded of differences between cultural epochs. At certain junctures in these essays I suggest that ways in which 'Melanesians' objectify social relations could enrich the impoverished conceptual repertoire with which 'Euro-Americans' seem lumbered; however, there are warnings as well as delights here.

Three changes have occurred over the last twenty years, among many others, in the way that Euro-Americans are asked to think about relations between (to use Gell's terms) agents and patients, or to imagine persons and things alike as actants. First is the late twentieth century (re)embrace of technology which at the beginning of this period produced the cyborg literature, images of interdigitated human and mechanical capabilities. At about the same time, the new reproductive and genetic technologies, as they were called, were signalling unprecedented interventions in procreative and generative processes. Second has been the rise of personalised markets, not to speak of personalised money facilitated by communications technologies, and a self-styled culture of enhanced information flow. Finally, firms and corporations, as well as the organisers of new technology initiatives, have begun to pay increasing attention to what has been known all along but has come to be articulated in new ways, namely the fact that technical (and social) knowledge is embedded in persons and in the relations between them. When the capabilities of persons and relations are identified as skills, and the skills are seen as transferable, then they are also commodifiable. The concept of skill works as a kind of human counterpart to the concept of technology.

The commodity seems more visible than ever. Yet the trajectories are complex, and there might be a parallel here to the dual emphasis on corporalisation and conceptual effort noted in relation to reproductive technology. In one direction everything seems to be becoming reified, one thing finding an equivalent in another thing: there seems nothing that cannot be bought or sold. In another direction human effort understood as intellectual as well as material means that there is nothing which does not seem to carry connotations of social identity: there seems nothing that cannot be attributed to someone's authorship. At the very least, forms of knowledge are held to have a social origin, and it is no accident that social constructionism was for two decades a dominant social science paradigm. At the same time, then, as the possibilities of commoditisation reach into areas of human life and creativity that were never open to the market before, so too are commodities becoming personified, in the Euro-American sense, that is. By that I mean that they are identified through their attachment to persons in ways that go beyond simple notions of possession, at the same time as attributes attached to identities may be acquiring a newly transactable (sometimes commercial) value. Cultural property is a good example. Of course many anthropologists (and Chapter 7 briefly takes this up) have argued that the commodity never was the pure product which its standing as an analytical category made it out to be. I do not think that was always a simple case of misdescription. I prefer complex trajectories to blurred genres. They give us marginally more purchase for dealing with the unpredictable.

Lateral thinking might come to grips with the complexity and momentum of these changes; critical thinking could tug at the very concept of 'change', which constantly threatens to spin off its own apparently resource-rich orbit, and pull it back perhaps to the real world of enduring problems and resource-poor populations. Together these point to one kind of response from the social scientist. This can be neither a matter of piling on theoretical antecedents nor a matter of going where no one has been before. I would put it rather that we need to go precisely where we have already been, back to the immediate here and now out of which we have created our present knowledge of the world. That means constructing a mode of enquiry which will enable a return to fields of knowledge and activity in the hindsight of unpredicted outcomes, and which will thus enable recovery of material that investigators were not aware they were collecting. The ethnographic method as it has been developed by social anthropologists, with its insistent demands of immersement, begins to look extremely promising.

ACKNOWLEDGEMENTS

These are gathered at the Conclusion to this chapter (p. 257). I am grateful to Eve Mitleton-Kelly from the Organisational and Complexity Learning Project research project at the London School of Economics for introducing me to the idea of complex evolving systems (the phrase is after Peter Allen), and for her observations in this context.

PART I

EFFECTS

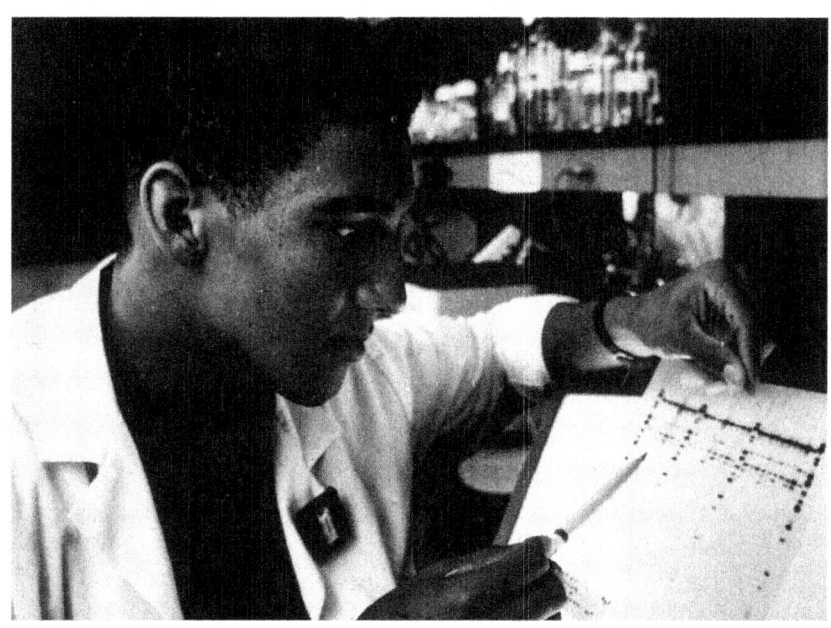

Although the bulk of these chapters have all been written in the last five years, their material spans a period from the 1960s to the 1990s. These figures are taken from illustrations to the second chapter. *Above:* 1960s. A man from Mt Hagen examines a feather plaque which will be worn in a friend's headdress. Each headdress is at once a combination of conventional elements and unique. Photographed by the author. *Below:* 1990s. A scientist from Washington University, Saint Louis, examines DNA fragment patterns. Human DNA is made up of elements which combine for each individual in a unique way. Photograph reproduced by courtesy of Blackwell Scientific Publications Ltd./John Wiley & Sons

Both men are, so to speak, looking at other persons. One theme of this book is 'symmetry' of perspectives – how people see themselves in others. The chapters consistently draw in materials apparently exogenous to their subject matter, whether to illuminate Euro-American discussions of the new reproductive technologies from a Papua New Guinea viewpoint (Chapter 4) or to introduce constructs from Euro-American contests over the ownership of procreative material to illuminate the analysis of bridewealth payments (Chapter 7). The depiction of DNA fragments, then, indicates a particular field of contemporary debate touched on in these chapters: the new reproductive and genetic technologies. Comparison in turn invites questions about comparison across epochs and thus both the 'speed' of time (Chapters 3 and 10) and about 'conceptual time', the epochs from which analytical concepts are derived (Chapters 5 and 7). As for reproduction, the headdress shown here is a sign of male vitality, and Chapters 2 and 3 address the relationship between Melanesian ideas of life force or vitality/capacity and its realisation in things, visited again in a resource-conscious context in Chapters 9 and 10. Intellectual creativity is taken up in Chapters 6, 8, and 9. Finally, the examining pose of the men points to the several junctures at which the book discusses the effect of making things visible/known. Questions are raised about knowledge, information and the effects of communication. Chapter 2 opens with images one might wish to hide; Chapter 4 is concerned with information which, once known, cannot be hidden, while Chapter 10 invites one to think about what is (made to be) half-seen.

CHAPTER 2

Pre-figured Features

'Any body-representation that stands for an individual': this was the rubric for a conference organised some five years ago on *Portraiture and the Problematics of Representation.*[1] It was the subsequent publication (Woodall 1997) which set me a quandary over choice of image – how to illustrate my account. Since the quandary itself illustrates some of the issues I wish to raise, I begin with it.

The man from Mt Hagen in the Highlands of New Guinea whose photograph you see in the frontispiece appears in Strathern and Strathern 1971 (plates 40 and 45) among photographs of several Hagen women and men; the book's subject was adornment. In some cases we had given people copies of the photographs or otherwise reciprocated; with others we had long-term relationships, while in many instances (as in this) the camera belonged to the anonymous interface between spectator and performer. Given that people decorate in order to display, taking pictures had a cultural appropriateness to it; in any case the decoration rather than the person is what is on view. Contributing pictures of people to a volume on portraits, however, made me pause. Not in a position to seek permission from particular individuals, I could not take the liberty of deploying a photograph as a portrait. I have chosen a picture of a man holding up an item of decoration, a feather plaque (*køi wal*), for the camera to take.

On the occasion of the conference I depicted various aspects of self-decoration, but no single picture of a person, or even set of pictures, had to account for everything. Some thirty slides formed a composite portrayal which the accompanying analysis decomposed; my visual sequence was meant to imitate the revelatory force of the way Hagen people present themselves through their decorations. This was impossible in a printed publication. Revelation depends on temporality; open a book, and the illustrations are already laid open. Doing the same thing through an accompanying text, inviting the reader to go back to the pictures with fresh eyes, would be a weak alternative. There is a more serious issue about the weakness of texts. If I reproduce half a dozen slides of dancers from the New Guinea Highlands in their feathers, wigs, and face paint, you will have seen them before, half a hundred depictions of 'warriors' or 'wigmen' posing for the camera – whether for Air Nuigini advertising, on BBC documentaries or in *Time* magazine. They carry the tourist face of Papua New Guinea, and thus raise questions about new colonisations. These questions apply to the anthropologist as much as to anyone, and I could not reproduce such photographs without making them the subject matter.

If photographs of decorated dancers would not do, would group portraits be an answer? Rather than showing individuals full face or close to, I would be able to convey the fact that dancers decorate in order to be seen in their entirety. This would be culturally more appropriate imagery – the facial features or three-quarters bust or close-up so you can see the details of the flaking paint and tired eyes (*pace* Kirk 1981) is not how people intend you see them. A group photograph would conserve the public nature of such occasions. Yet it would suggest to the Euro-American reader that when you look at New Guinea portraits you no longer see the individual but him or her as part of a group. That is not what I wish to convey. A single picture? It could be the subject of multiple interpretations and thus do the work of several photographs, while treating the individual in a respectfully unique way. This would produce another problem altogether: making one person represent everyone else, the stereotype of the informant who doubles as everyman, anonymous and unasked.

In the end I included a single photograph from Hagen, of someone whose name I never learnt but who was seemingly pleased by the camera's interest in what he was doing. He does of course have a name and I call him Ketepa after the bird plumes, but he belonged to a clan group with which I had only passing acquaintance and to whose members I was no doubt another tourist. He is informally decorated with a cassowary plume in his wig and a forehead band of shells; the bamboo tally on his chest tells of the times he has on previous occasions been a donor of wealth. On this occasion in 1967 he was not formally dancing, but was helping one of the dancers, adding to the plaque occipital plumes from the King of Saxony (*køi ketepa*) bird of paradise. The colours are vivid: the long, eggshell-blue plumes complement the shimmering russet of the *raggiana* bird of paradise at the back, while various species of parrot provide deep blue panels to each side in contrast with a bright red centre and at the centre of that a 'pool' of startling blue.

What has this to do with portraits? The man is asking us to look at the plaque. Suggesting how we might (or might not) think of this composition in feathers as a portrait offers a comment on the idea of body-representations as standing for individuals.

INDIVIDUAL FEATURES

Euro-Americans looking at a portrait may well assume they are looking at someone who has a name. Of course the name may not be known but the likeness of the features 'belongs' to the individual just as his or her name does. And although persons can be recognised by their gait or voice, conventionally it is to faces that they put names. It might be disconcerting therefore to think about the Asmat of Irian Jaya who in the past went on hunting expeditions to capture other people's names to give their children, which men accomplished by bringing home the head to which the name formerly belonged (Knauft 1993: 192), or the Marind-Anim who, not necessarily knowing the name, would bestow as a 'head-name' on their children the last utterance of the decapitated victim (1993: 156).

Ethnographers of the Asmat and Marind-Anim suggest that the head-hunters were seeking access to the 'life-force' of other peoples. This was thought of as a potency transferable between persons; what the head contained (this potency) rather than its features was important. Indeed features were of little moment. When heads were kept they were either stripped down to the skull or else remodelled (sometimes with the original skin, but stuffed beyond recognition). If they were then decorated, as they might be with shell valuables and feathers, it was to idealise them as sources of a life-force that now flowed through the living. It would be stretching the imagination, then, to think of these heads as portraits. They obliterated rather than conserved the bodily uniqueness of their original owners. Above all, there seemed to be no interest in the facial features as indicating the individuality of the person. The head might be an individual's head but it was not deployed so as to suggest that it represented the original owner as an individual.

My understanding of the conference rubric was that the individualised Euro-American person is recognisable in the individualised body, with its unique characteristics, especially of the face. These characteristics I take to be 'features'. The notion of portrait draws on this convention insofar as a principal medium is precisely the individual's body features. When other kinds of references are made to bodily character, they may be used as substitutes for body representations. If, however, persons are represented in quite other ways or if features do not refer to a particular person, then presumably we are not dealing with portraits.

The Asmat and Marind-Anim heads might have their origin in individual persons, yet if features once made a person recognisable in life, they ceased to do so when their animation was taken by another. It would be wrong, however, to conclude that these people did not recognise individuals. They certainly distinguished by features, but when they came to represent the individuality of persons they did not use such features to do so.

Individuation lay in the capacities people evinced in their effect on the world. Thus it was in the very act of severing the head that the Marind-Anim man displayed unique access to power, embodied in his ability to bestow a head-name on his children, each child being individuated by name in turn (Knauft 1993: 156-7). For Asmat men, repeated success in head-hunting was a requisite for personal honour, and only someone who had taken several heads could sponsor feasts in his own name (1993: 189). When it came to bestowing the life-force on boys, each Asmat recipient was brought into contact with a specific head. Not only did he take the victim's name, but he also became that particular person's incarnation, and the deceased's relatives might treat him as their kinsman (1993: 191-2). In short, he took the person's individual identity. Individuality was thus evinced by the decapitator or by the recipient of the head. If anyone's individuality was represented, it was that of its new owner.

But is 'representation' what we mean? Representation implies a medium, as features of the body may be deployed as a medium through which Euro-American portraits refer to the individuality of persons. Now in the Asmat case any representation of the individuality of the new owner was simultaneously an enactment. It was the demonstration of a capacity – to sever the head or to absorb its life-force – that was individuating. Individuality was thus an effect, whether of taking action or of being the recipient of someone else's acts. The heads themselves remained as *evidence*: severed by the power of the decapitator and emptied by the recipient who drained their life-force away. They did not stand for the deceased as such. For they did not mediate any relationship with the dead man – the new man appeared to the victim's kin in the stead of the old: a living person not standing for the one killed but standing in for him.

If one were to look for an analogue elsewhere, perhaps it would not be immediately to the twentieth-century concept of a portrait but to another use of the head as evidence, in this case specifically the face. I refer to the *imago* displayed by aristocratic Roman families as described by Dupont (1989). Families of Republican Rome attested their nobility by the right to images of deceased male ancestors. A wax impression was made of the deceased's face that was then (repeatedly, Dupont infers, 1989: 407) used to make wax masks: *imago* designates both the impression in the wax and the features that make the impression. There was nothing representational about the wax masks, Dupont argues; it is 'the trace, not the figuration, of the deceased' (1989: 413). This trace was counted as a material reality or evidence; the wax mask was as much body as the corpse had been.

There was an indigenous Roman distinction between the *imago* as the material presence of the deceased and figurative representations such as those uttered in the form of funerary orations. The *imago* contained an impression of the deceased; words, by contrast, were a medium through which the deceased's exploits became a spectacle. Funeral orations were the oral counterpart of the 'names' written on public signs apparently hung from the chests within which the *imago* of the deceased was contained (Dupont 1989: 409-11). Honorifics were thus attached to the deceased through the medium of words, spoken or written by others, as representations of the person's achievements. Although the oration was personal and the titles civic in import, both had public significance, whereas the wax image was ordinarily kept hidden.

Thinking of the Asmat or Marind-Anim use of heads prompts a further observation. I suggested that there the individuality being celebrated belongs not to the victim but to the decapitator/recipient – the deceased's lifetime achievements are taken away to become a life-force bestowed on another. Perhaps the Roman wax *imago* was the living form of the deceased even as the Asmat boy was the living form of the decapitated victim (the dead form of the deceased was in the tomb even as the spirit of the dead victim was abroad seeking vengeance). Dupont suggests that the *imago* did no more than indicate the singular individuality of particular persons and had no collective import. But if we pay attention to those who handle or possess the image, it would also seem that they receive an individuality of a kind.

Dupont observes that the public identity of the deceased signified at the funerary oration was a limited individualisation, for the virtues praised were gentilic (1989: 411). Now the funeral oration aimed to produce a spectacle – evoking the illustrious past of the family – in the context of praising the newly deceased. The praise had to be in his material presence. To praise his ancestors meant that they too had to be present. The oration was delivered from the rostrum on which the corpse was placed in the presence of the family's *imago*. These images sat in the audience in the form of masks worn by actors dressed according to the highest title of the ancestor in question. This was the moment when, removed from their boxes, the images were in public attendance. What was offered for the admiration of the crowd, however, were the material insignia of power with which they were now accompanied; apparently the images themselves processed anonymously. Now whether or not the spectacle was meant to inspire a sense of glory and virtue in the spectators, a civic act promulgating public values, can it be read as a public claim to individuality?

Such individuality would come not from the wax faces of particular persons, long dead: but it may well have inhered in the very capacity of the living family to make a spectacle in and of their company, to make public the throng of ancestors as a source of glory – if not exactly life-force – for their descendants. Features conserved in wax gave evidence above all of the fact of the impression, and this was the form their own living presence took, uniquely claimed by those mounting the event. Bringing out the ancestors would be an enactment of the very power they had passed on.

We may judge the Roman images, like the decapitated New Guinea heads, to be less than portraits. But they do prompt questions about where we should look for signs of individuality and about the nature of representation. Consider another figure, not the head itself but the feather decoration Hagen men attached to the head, made to be seen, frontally, above the dancer's face, and with (a conceit of mine) a further 'head' of feathers atop the plaque. The Saxony plumes that both border the plaque and make up this 'second head', the spray, are said to be like fresh running water which, when it flows, is a sign of life.

COMPOSITE FIGURES

The feature plaque shown by the man in the photograph is designed to be fastened to the top of a ceremonial wig, usually somewhat larger than the one he is wearing, and without its netted covering so the hair gleams black. It is an extension of a body already enlarged (an effect dancers strive for) by decoration. It is very much to the point that the living head is not severed. Hagen men decorate in order to dance, a strenuous display of energy and endurance in full public view. Men typically arrange themselves in a single line, to be observed primarily from the front for the admiration of perhaps hundreds of spectators. The living bodies support the signs of life that the men claim for themselves. Ketapa has just finished fastening the Saxony spray, and if you follow his eye you will see he is looking at how it is attached, on a flexible cassowary quill. As the dancer moves, so light catches the feathers which then shimmer like flowing water.

If the Asmat head or Roman image imparts life-force or glory to other persons, what spectators see in the Hagen dancer is the one who has attached to himself the life-force or glory of others. The ornaments in which he is decked – birds of paradise feathers, shells, leaves, cassowary quills, face paint – can be thought of as so many bits of *other persons* appended to his person. And their presence is summoned thereby. We shall come back to the significance of this. The feather plaque is a condensed version of the entire process: in what I have fancifully called a second head, you see a man attaching an attachment (the Saxony spray) to an attachment (the plaque that will top the wig). Moreover, of all decorations, no one can wear Saxony plumes without acknowledging (through compensation payments) those from whom he obtained them, in the same way as wearing the plaque at all demands sacrifice to his own ancestors.

Mt Hagen is noted for its fine ceremonial grounds, public places where clans display their strength to an audience. Display occasions are generally political: the dance ceremonialises gifts between allies or enemies in warfare, groups engaged in competitive bouts of prestation and counterprestation. It is the donors who decorate and dance. Gifts, comprising specially mounted pearlshells, livestock and money, are handed over as an aggressive challenge to the recipient to make as good a return later. Dancers carry weapons, usually spears, sometimes steel axes like the one Ketapa has in his belt. There is a pearlshell hanging on the wall of the house at the back, but it is out of sight in this photograph.

At the point of making the gift, men are detaching wealth from themselves and in that act pointing to their own evident capacities to attract the wealth to themselves in the first place. They receive valuables such as pearlshells in the same way as they give them. Valuables, a source of aesthetic pleasure, are themselves decorated for giving away. They come and go between persons: a gift is always destined for and comes from a specific other, and thus travels along relationships. Women, who pass between clans in marriage, encapsulate the possibility of relationship itself, for they make potential exchange roads between their brothers and husbands, as well as creating obligations such as having to acknowledge the importance of maternal kin. On occasion they decorate, but dances are above all men's occasions, and as for the fame they produce, it is, Hagen men and women say, the man's 'name' which goes on top. Gift exchange resembles acts we have encountered elsewhere, in a kind of speeded-up mode: one gives evidence of one's power by showing that it has been taken from others. What gives the speeded-up effect is that this is accomplished not through killing another person or keeping him in a box but through creating a flow, enacted as a flow of valuables/wealth, between living persons. Hagen people are explicit about the fact that one gives to recipients in order to receive in turn, and the wealth, along with hopes for prosperity and fertility, that flows with these gifts constitutes glory for oneself and for one's clan alike. Every gift recapitulates other gifts, evidence of the ability to animate relationships.

A man does not dance by himself: these are group affairs and decorations are never seen in isolation. The plaque was virtually identical in pattern to those being worn by other dancers of the same patrilineal clan (see Strathern and Strathern, 1971, colour plate 6). Indeed this type of ornament is the most standardised of all decorations, worn only with certain assemblages. Men also deliberately synchronise other effects such as the way they paint their faces. Does a group, then, constitute a sort of clan portrait? Is the plaque its emblem?

I ask the question with Townsend-Gault's discussion of institutional portraits since the 1920s in mind. Drawing on the distinction between the 'true portrait' which 'aims to represent the inner individuality of the sitter' and the effigy which 'renders a subject in terms of their role or office, giving them a facade for a face' (Townsend-Gault 1988: 515), she observes how the official portrait situates the subject. The painting (or photograph) is generally hung in the institution to which the person belonged, as the portrait now belongs. 'The institution both represents and reproduces itself through representation of its members' (1988: 512). An official portrait receives power precisely from being *in situ* – for the sitter is being claimed by a specific institution, as a clan or noble family claims its members. Certainly, if an institution is more than the persons who run its boards, the Hagen clan is more than the members who gather to dance: the clan is its history, its territory, its lineage, its settlements, its wealth in cash crops or trucks. An institution also consists in the values of loyalty and solidarity that bind its members, and in evidence of such solidarity. Hagen clan members dance shoulder to shoulder. But the collective impression is achieved through, not at the expense of, 'inner individuality'.

For whether we see a man or a clan is in one sense irrelevant: collective action aggrandises each man's performance but is no different in kind from his own aggrandisement as a single person. You are looking at just one piece of one man's decorations in the photograph, and you are looking also at the *effect* of aggrandisement – plumes attached to plumes. Indeed, like each dancer in the line of men, each item of adornment is the object of care and attention. Does this denote individuality then? Yes, but not because of the singleness of the items – quite the reverse: it is because each item is also a part of an assemblage of items. Let me put this beside another apparent paradox. Recall the head-hunters. I said that features were not being used as a medium through which to represent the individuality of the head, and that it was the head-hunters' acts which were individuating, of the head-hunter. Here (in the short-circuiting that Hageners do to make the living simultaneous givers and receivers of vitality), it is the dancers' own individuality which is being proclaimed. Again, however, it is not proclaimed through the dancers' particular features. Indeed, a dance is only said to be a success if it becomes impossible to recognise the dancers; their decorations must act as a disguise, and are reckoned to have failed if the personal identity of the dancer is perceived too easily. Individuality is proclaimed instead through the decorations themselves.

But how can individuality be proclaimed through the very items which would seem to most institutionalise and standardise these men? The Hagen dancer is situated within the clan, yet the decorations he wears are neither emblems of clanship nor signs of office, and although they indicate certain dance roles they are not otherwise uniforms, costumes or even outfits (Polhemus and Procter 1978). Rather, the dancer's attire is an assemblage, put together there and then from many sources. The crucial analogy is between the clan as an assemblage of men and each man as an assemblage of men (his relations with others).

I photographed Ketepa before the dance began; in the same way as the feather plaque recapitulates the kinds of attachments found in the decorations as a whole, Ketepa's assembling recapitulates the act of gathering ornaments in the first place. He is doing it for the person who will dance (not in the picture), and for an audience (also not in the picture, though you can see the legs of two boys idly looking on). Prefigured in the decorations are the dancer's relationships with other persons. Moreover a man's decorations do not just 'represent' these other persons; they are there through an activation of his relationship with them, as Ketepa's handiwork is evident in the skill with which he has mounted the Saxony spray. It is quite likely that the feathers belonged to Ketepa in the first place. At any rate, decorations literally travel along the road that link people, detached from (the possession of) one person to be attached to another. What is true of the decorations is also true of persons.

Before such an occasion a prospective dancer will have visited, borrowed from and compensated with gifts numerous in-laws, maternal kin and friends here and there in order to get together the decorations he needs. Only some will have already been in his keeping. At the same time, what he obtains from elsewhere is evidence of internal well-being and would not be successfully obtained without that. Inner strength and outer success go together. Now inner strength comes ultimately from the ancestors, and without their blessing a dance will fail and a man's decorations appear dull and drab. Decorations from a previous occasion will be anxiously inspected, as Ketepa may well be doing, for the shine and gloss ancestral favour bestows.

An assemblage of decorations should include both bright and dark elements. Darkness connotes internal solidarity and ancestral protection (as well as outward hostility) while brightness connotes outward connections with others and the ability to take into oneself, to receive and absorb, the fertility of other persons and other clans. The arrangement of feathers on the plaque is not fortuitous: the alternations of light and dark coloration are deliberate, and if the whole effect is topped by the white Saxony spray, it may be flanked by black sicklebill feathers. On this occasion dark feathers are repeated in wands made from the blue (*rudolphi*) bird of paradise worn either side of the plaque; meanwhile they are stuck in the ground near the packaging which kept them clean.

Men's capacity is shown twice over: in detaching wealth from others and in turning it into prosperity for themselves. The decorations are a composite of items, just as the man displaying the wealth he is to give away is a composite of the relationships along which wealth flows. What distinguishes one assemblage from another, one man from another, is that invisible composition. Each constellation is unique. In the same way it is in the relationships that a man gathers to himself that his individuality lies; the accomplishments that bring a person a 'name' come from holding persons together. He attends to his clan brothers, to military allies, to enemies; to his mother's brother and his wife's brothers, and so on. In turn this means that he always acts within a heterogeneous network of relations. In sum, what is prefigured in the assemblages is the dancer's relationships with other persons. As the assemblage is put together there is no 'whole', final product for which the dancer or his helper aims; rather, each act, each individual item, recapitulates the effect of the entirety, each small act of attachment or aggrandisement adding to the overall effect. We may speak of a further analogy, then, between the man and his decorations.

The man is prefigured insofar as the relationships mobilised by the dancer are already there, as ancestors are already there. Simply by virtue of being born, a person is enmeshed in relations with mother's and father's kin, and both are celebrated in wealth exchanges – father's kin in clan support; mother's kin as donors of fertility and recipients of wealth. Such connections are a principal subject of public oration at funerals. When you look at a dancer in feathers and ornaments you may not know which particular persons have lent him this or that or what his maternal kin have helped with; but you do know that he can only stand thus by virtue of the relationships he has with these others, and that he has effectively activated. He is living evidence of this support. We do not know Ketepa's relationship with the dancer who will wear the feather plaque, but only because I was a stranger – not because it was unknowable. In fact I know that there will be a relationship between them that pre-dates the help given in 1967.

The decorations are prefigured in the expectation that a man cannot put together an assemblage by himself. The items are evidence of that activation, the substantial counterparts to other events. Hagen people may think of them as (parts of) other persons the dancer attached to himself. Liabilities follow: he may have to kill a pig to pay for the loans or find other means of compensation, and must in any case observe good feelings towards these people – if he harbours bad feelings the decorations may fail in their effect. And he must have the right inner orientation as far as the ancestors are concerned, or they too will disfavour the event. (They only have to send a shower of rain to make everyone anxious. Do you see the umbrella leaning against the wall behind Ketepa?) In other words, the decorations show a capacity to draw in relationships; they show how they have been animated, and with ancestral help. That much of Ketepa's face is in shadow is apposite: it is round the back of the neck that ancestral ghosts 'sit' when a man dances. Dances are performed under the midday sun. To achieve darkness about the face is truly a sign of ancestral presence.

In what sense is the plaque a portrait? Not a portrait if we mean using a person's body features as medium, for the media are feathers that draw attention away from the dancer's personal features, just as paint is applied to the skin to disguise the face. They are the body. The feathers that come from the bodies of birds make up a kind of bird body (*køi wal* means 'bird-bag/-womb/-container') for the man. The body's enclosure with its bright coloured centre is like the house interior where men keep their valuables, or the maternal confinement of the unborn child, or the inner side of a man's outer skin. Not a portrait if we mean that inner individuality must show in the features, for individuality lies not so much in the appearance as in the act of assembling. Men dance with assemblages almost identical in appearance, but each will have drawn on his own unique constellation of relations to do so. And not a portrait if we insist on representation. Although this is an artefact that points to other events, it is not so much a representation of them as evidence. We witness an outcome: the results or effect of mobilising relations. The feathers, now in the hands of one person and soon to be in those of another, will be attached not to some likeness of the [second] man but to the man's person himself. The plaque will in turn have an effect. It will make the man an example (exemplification) of his own efficacy, and publicise his 'name'. It thus prefigures the presence of the particular dancer whom you cannot otherwise see in the photograph. Whoever puts the plaque on will be making visible the efficacy of the support he has. In making the *køi wal* up for him, Ketepa is looking at one of the effects of his own relationship with the dancer, and in this sense at the dancer himself.

GENETIC PROFILES

I have acted on the supposition that, in the conventions of twentieth-century Westerners (Euro-Americans), portraits attend to people's features in order to represent their individuality. Features in turn have to be rendered in such a way as to denote uniqueness. But the result is that the medium of paint or stone or whatever uses the person's form as a further medium: portraits are in that sense representational. The various treatments of the head presented here raise questions about what is used to denote individuality. I have also raised the question of 'where' individuality might be located, and drawn attention to certain actions. However, the principal effect of the acts is not representation but efficacy. Efficacy is the capacity or ability to bring something about; there can be no substitute – one either does or does not evince it. As in the Roman dogma about evidence having to be part of the real thing, evidence cannot appear as a counterfeit, cannot appear – as portraits do – as 'a representation'. But one may well seek evidence that the efficacy has, as it were, had its effect.

Efficacy is displayed by the head-hunter/by the ancestor's descendants/by the dancer who presents his decorations to the audience. And if it appears in that last instance that the Hagen man owns himself, we would be telling only half the story: the owner of the decorated person is also that composite of persons with whom he has relations. They are prefigured in his very ability to appear to all. It is a man's exchange partners who have elicited the display, his associates (like Ketepa) who have contributed to its composition, and his kin who have given him body. Indeed, the decorations re-make a body that is already there, formed by contributions from maternal and paternal kin, with its white bones, red blood, glistening flesh and dark skin. These are the body features that the body of the decorations makes over again.

Unique and composite, prefigured and relational: a certain kind of visual evidence with which Euro-Americans have become recently familiar might afford an analogy with the feather plaque from Hagen. The second photograph in the frontispiece shows a scientist examining human DNA fragment patterns.[2] (The DNA molecule has been cut at specific sites and then separated by size; when an electric current is run through fragments suspended in a gel, the smaller ones travel further, creating characteristic bands. Band patterning can identify individuals and reveal genetic relationships.)

We do not know to which cluster of characteristics these genetic sequences will eventually relate, any more than we know the name and history of everything we may acknowledge as a portrait. But it is genetic material from someone, not anyone, and, unless it is taken from a foetus, it is from someone who must have a name. (Genetic endowment is like the name most Euro-Americans are given at birth – a unique combination of elements recombined in other persons.) It prefigures that person's features. It is also composite, a sequence created in the combination of sequences, and relational. Like a sort of life-force transmitted from one person to another, DNA sequences are the ancestral traces of connections between the generations, material evidence of the fact that features exist only as the outcome of relationships. That recombinant technology means that DNA sequences can be severed and re-attached also opens up the possibility of extracting life-giving capacity from foreign bodies.

The scientist is looking at a representation produced through the medium of a specific technology. It is a picture of efficacy, a fragment of the 'code' for the appearance of certain features, a representation of the mechanism whose effect will show in that person, and whose effect is always individualising. Indeed it is that individualising quality of genetic makeup which at the same time turns representation into evidence. In the form of 'finger printing', similar depictions may be used as forensic evidence of individual identity. This means that in turn the depiction is itself significantly featured: the patterns of bands appear simultaneously as physical characteristics of the DNA molecules and as physical characteristics of the mechanical or biochemical processes that make them appear. On what grounds one might or might not consider such a depiction a portrait could make us think again about the other material in this account.

A note on exegesis. These four examples suggest different nonrepresentational uses of bodily characteristics (Gow 1988). Comparison has been at the expense of critical appraisal. As far as the Hagen data is concerned, ethnographic amplification can be found in A. Strathern 1971 (ceremonial exchange, the occasions on which formal decorations are worn); M. Strathern 1979 (ideas about inner and outer bodily form); M. Strathern 1991a (singularity and plurality). Writing on their immediate neighbours in the Wahgi, O'Hanlon (1989) also provides a guide to recent literature; his ethnography is a first-rate contemporary account. Many points could have been exemplified by comparison with other materials, e.g. Bateson's 1936 'portrait skull' from the middle Sepik area of Papua New Guinea (Bateson 1958, cf. Bouquet 1988), in commentary on pan-New Guinea preoccupations such as the equation between birds and men (e.g. Gell 1975; Feld 1982; Sillitoe 1988b) or through internal replication (e.g. the way Saxony plumes are repeated visually in the vertical motility of the long ceremonial apron).

Apart from the conceit of the double heads (*køi wal* and Saxony spray as head on head), all statements about the Hagen material come from indigenous exegesis and from analysis of it. It is necessary to add that final phrase, since anthropologists take people's interpretations as part of their data. Symbolic analysis is the subject of much anthropological debate; see, for example, Neich's (1982) semiotic critique of Strathern and Strathern (1971). The present account draws on the prominence of analogy in Melanesian constructions (e.g. Barth 1975; Wagner 1977; M. Strathern 1988), and of the retention (self-scaling) of form that Wagner calls holographic (1986). Instances or exemplars (Goodman 1976; Munn 1986) do not work only as parts of a whole (metonymy) or through relations of substitution (metaphor) but as instantiations that retain the properties of trope across different scales and thus 'appear' as 'large' or as 'small' as any other instances. On liberties with the term 'body' see Leenhardt 1979 (1947); Battaglia 1983.

CHAPTER 3

The Aesthetics of Substance

An image I cannot get rid of is that of a newborn infant having its face pressed to the earth before it has drawn breath. The imperative was once so overriding that even a woman without surviving children might suffocate her baby. I cannot get rid of the image because of the reason. It used to happen (so it was alleged) not because the woman had no wish for a child, nor because the child was malformed or there were too many mouths to feed or the birth was illegitimate, but because of its identity. No: I am wrong in one particular. We are told that the child *was* malformed; its misfortune was to be large. Now everything that one is taught to think about health and infant mortality makes the converse, the desire to have fat babies, unexceptional. So whereas I might find it, at the least, comprehensible if circumstances led to the mercy killing of a puny child, no amount of comprehension will subdue the bonny picture I put together. I cannot 'see' the mother's desperation; it is covered by everything conveyed in the description of the apparently healthy infant. But, no: the fat baby born to the luckless mother was not healthy at all, or at least not for others. Such children were witch-children, identified by a special name. And they presented the evidence in themselves: they were witch-children precisely because they were fat.

DISPOSAL

Rolland Munro (1992) asks how we rid ourselves of unwanted images. For him, this is part of a larger problem about the disposal of meaning. He is speaking of a (Euro-American) world where the production of meaning seems endless, and its excess almost effortless. 'Postmodernity ... is associated with a shift of significance away from conditions of materiality towards a universe of signs ... [S]aturating social relations with shifting cultural signs Baudrillard interprets as "the triumph of a signifying culture" and ... "the end of the social" [quoting Featherstone]'. But that sense of surfeit is there in any interpretive exercise. In a recent critique of the anthropology of aesthetics, James Weiner (1995a),[1] borrows a phrase from the Yolngu (Australian aborignal) artist Naritjin who, when asked to talk about the significance of bark paintings, replied: 'There are too many meanings. Later on, when you know more, you'll know which ones to choose and which ones to discard.' How is that discarding done? The conundrum, choosing what action to bring into play that will not itself add more meanings, has its own twist: the need for dispersal under pressure of excess. For the (desire for) choice has already evoked the 'more' [meanings] which throng at the borders of articulateness. How, then, does one set about disposing of meanings, getting rid of images?

One of Munro's answers is to point to the fact that, mercifully, meanings are often predisposed. We do not live in a riot of unlimited invention – meanings may be already curtailed by convention, and he turns precisely to the social, to the social experience of effecting previous disposals in interactions with others, as an essential conduit that carries them away. But that, so to speak, is an unintended consequence of social life. We may add that there are also situations where disposal is the subject of explicit social work. People offer meanings to others to consume.

Think of those circumstances when attention is drawn to the qualities being conveyed by an image: the point is that anything recognised as an 'image' is recognised as being offered for or as explicitly requiring an act of interpretation. Images are meanings made available, we might say, for consumption. Rhetorical productions – the arts, literature – belong to just such special circumstances, for by them we tell ourselves that this is what we are doing, though the process of acknowledging that images need interpretation is not of course restricted to these media. They bring home the point, however, that the effect of an image depends on the extent to which persons are willing to assimilate it. But does such assimilation diminish or instead increase the quantity of 'meaning'? They are not taken 'away' from the performer or artist or author, indeed may be extended and turned and amplified by the audience. In any case images may have to be reproduced over and again in order to satisfy consumers looking for particular meanings. What is revealed in all this is the author's very ability or capacity to be continuously productive, which would in turn only seem to increase the problems of excess. It would imply that in addition to meanings one might have to think about creativity – that ability or capacity – as itself a subject for disposal.

If this seems too excessive an extension of the meanings to be found in the concepts of production and consumption, let me evoke a set of social circumstances which could almost have been designed to answer the question about assimilation. Here the producers and consumers of images not only may but must come face to face: the persons are made present to one another. And under these social arrangements assimilation can work as a disposal of a kind. There is nothing accidental about it. On the contrary, it seems as though people deliberately put themselves into the position of extracting – draining away – meanings from one another. Two examples are pertinent, and in pursuing them this chapter will both amplify and curtail the account of men's activities given in Chapter 2.

In the late 1960s, not long after the Hagen photograph was taken (page 27),[2] Raymond Kelly was embarking on his extensive study of the Etoro of interior Papua New Guinea. The story of the smothered child comes from his ethnography (Kelly 1993). The reader does not need to know the broader ethnographic background to either Hagen or Etoro in order to appreciate the points that follow, but does need to know that much of the material is historical. The social arangements in question concerned the flow of life-force which Etoro men circulated among themselves and the ceremonial exchanges through which Hagen men circulated wealth. In both cases, men knew they had to seek recipients for their creativity. In the former, it was creativity itself that was circulated and consumed by others; in the latter, men kept the sources of creativity but circulated its products.

Now Munro asks about *unwanted* images. When, as he says, meanings are to some extent predisposed by social convention, as seemingly applies to the fat body of the witch-child, by getting rid of the image then you can at least get rid of a thing to which meaning fastens. The desire is to be rid. But I have wished to put this into a context where the desire to be rid of something may be realised for positive as well as negative reasons. One might wish to dispose of things because it is only by peeling off the products of creativity that fresh, creative acts become possible. If others are construed as wanting these things, then evidence of creativity can be made to rest in the satisfaction of their desire. Both Etoro and Hagen men produced (the products of) creativity in already consumable form, for an audience or recipient, creating images *intended* to be lodged in other people (minds/bodies). And the audience or recipient, however coercive the act (cf. Hirsch 1995a), invariably agreed to consume the product. That is, the image was not ordinarily refused. It could only be refused by breaking off relations between the 'producers' and 'consumers'. We might say that this is exactly the Etoro mother's dilemma.³ She could not discount the evidence of witchcraft before her eyes. She could, however, refuse to be the creature's mother, that is, refuse to activate the relationship.

But beyond agreeing or refusing to consume is the problematic nature of consumption itself. An anthropologist might add that the tragedy of the Etoro witch-child lay in those very practices, the social work, that disposed of meaning in other contexts. For they created the possibility of imagining another type of consumption altogether, consumption that had not disposed of creativity but had instead accumulated it. Etoro put together a horrifying picture of a person not dissipating but hoarding the vitality of others. This is what witches did. And the witch-child reduplicated the identity of its witch-parent(s), at once the outcome of excess and an embodiment of excess. Not itself available to absorption or consumption by others, the image had to be eliminated by different means.

THE QUESTION OF SUBSTANCE

Etoro

Etoro used body size as an image that could be passed between persons. As in places elsewhere in Papua New Guinea (see Biersack 1995), men's universe was predicated on the supposition that the senior generation in effect bestowed their bodies on the junior generation. Younger men absorbed the life-force of older men in this way. The life-force (*hame*) was regarded as in finite supply.

Life-force should not lodge too much in any one body. Rather, it had to flow, and Etoro men kept it in constant circulation in the form of semen donation, meat provision (growth-inducing food) and the distribution of shell valuables (wealth) that were signs of vitality. Men were able to track the enlargement and depletion of this life-force in their relations with others. Over a lifetime, they thus moved from being, in adolescence and early adulthood, recipients of other men's life-force until the moment in their prime when they themselves became donors, and as donors, in middle and later years, continued to bestow it on juniors in turn. Life-force was transmitted to the unborn child through sexual intercourse, to boys through insemination (this is what initiation was about) and to others generally through transactions with shells and meat whose giving was regarded as equivalent to insemination.[4] Hence, in adolescence and early adulthood, men built up repositories of this life-force while, as they moved into the middle years, their own force subsequently became depleted at the expense of the new generation growing up behind them. As their bodies withered through this process, depletion became a source of pride.

As beneficiaries of other men's acts, men who received had also to give. For a man to give there had to be an appropriate recipient: initiates and wives to inseminate, receptacles for the life-force thereby bestowed. The willing recipient was crucial to sustaining this flow and became a donor in turn. Witches, however, men and women alike, snatched rather than received and as a consequence could never get rid of what accumulated inside.

Witches first attacked and then consumed their victims, the size of their bodies becoming a mark of this engorgement. Because their very soul was in a transmuted state, they could never get rid of this predisposition to harm others, until, that is, they were killed themselves (Kelly 1993: 256). The witch-child 'inherited' the same transmuted soul without, it would seem, any diminution to the witch-parents' capacities. Here I might be tempted to note, from the extensive literature that now exists on Papua New Guinea societies, those several places where anthropologists have talked about the moulding of identity through food and the transmission of substance from one generation to the next, of which this might simply seem a perverse exemplification. However, the concept of 'substance' will not quite do.[5]

Etoro conceived of the witch hungering after the victim (Kelly 1993: 263), yet it was not food as such that filled out the flesh, and for all that the witch-child replicated its parents, it was not the transmission of physical tissue in this case that was significant. Etoro did not interpret the growth and form of persons as a direct consequence of the physical ingestion of ordinary food. Now, in dwelling on an image of filled-out flesh, I have deliberately introduced mass, a sense of bulk and weight, the solidity that English-speakers associate with one meaning of substance. Yet we could as well talk here of form as of substance. Although Etoro persons were regarded as composed of hair, flesh, bone and blood derived from their parents (see note 5), and although the witch's body was a manifestation of greed, these effects were – as I would phrase it, comparatively speaking – a presentation or shadow of the primary condition of body.[6] We could call this latter the 'inside'. This primary inside body was invisible, a spirit double the ethnographer called it, and this was the body nourished by its own activities, which grew and decayed, which was cared for by lineage spirits. It was also the body that committed and succumbed to witch attack. Ever present, invisibly foregrounded in Debbora Battaglia's (1994) phrase, it shared with its secondary condition, the corporeal 'outside' body, the capacity to be filled and emptied of life-force (*hame*) (Kelly 1993: 148). The witches' problem was that they filled but could not empty themselves; the state of their soul prevented that.

Witches fed invisibly on their victims; in eating the inside limbs and organs of the primary body they consumed the victim's life-force. The swollen secondary body that Etoro pictured to themselves was an image of this hidden process – not a representation but the *imago*, evidence, a mask pressed on the face of the real thing.[7] The visible 'outside' body, the image, had an aesthetic effect for it communicated this condition to others. But that was all it did. For what was made evident in a witch's body was also true of bodies generally. In Etoro eyes, flesh did not itself have the capacity for growth; food was not nourishment in that sense.[8] It was life-force that caused growth, that filled out a person and was passed on across the generations. Life-force was not otherwise transformed into other things: it simply came to exist in greater or lesser quantity in its capacity to fill and empty a person's (two) bodies. However, and the witches drew attention to it, this life-force could asume a form; as an image it was made material.

By material I mean that it became the subject of people's interactions and thus a quality attached to their relationships. We have seen that in general life-force lodged in the bodies of both donors and recipients. It was made material when it thus passed between persons – as an actualisation of the *act* of transfer or donation. Persons as they appeared to the eye were, in this sense and in themselves, images of transactions. Giving and receiving: that is what the outside body conveyed. The outside body was at once an aesthetic medium for the effect persons had on one another and the enactment of that effect. Relationships, in short, provided the material conditions for life, and in the normal course of events, excess never built up. At the same time, flow was one-way. It was because specific persons in specific relations were there that an Etoro man could move over the span of a lifetime from a condition where he lacked life-force to one where he was visibly grown by it to a position of visible depletion. This was the aesthetic movement: the receiver of the messsage, the consumer of the body, inside and outside alike, was the one who registered its effect. In assimilating the producer's body, he or she also drained it, and thereby enabled its form literally to conform to a cycle of increase and decrease in which it would appear – and ought to appear – at the end of life as 'small' as it did at the beginning.

Hagen

I turn now to a society where enlargement and depletion were imagined as an *alternation* of states, indeed specifically orchestrated through exchanges which depended on wealth given away subsequently returning to an original donor. The flow between men was two-way. Depletion had positive overtones when it referred to wealth already dispatched. But to be thin in body before one was old indicated an inability to attract it back again. However much he gave away in ceremonial exchange, a man's body size was expected to remain in an undiminished state.[9] Here the images of transfer were detached from the capacity for life and presented as though they had a materiality of their own – that is, wealth was seen as mobilising relationships. There was a different tenor to reproduction: disposal occurred without diminution. I would suggest that this was accomplished through a specific invention, the invention of substance. Bodies were transacted between persons, so to speak, not in terms of the flow and ebb of life-force but in terms of the substance of which they were made and parts of which they could always give away.

If it were not for the Etoro, there might be no surprise to the fact that the people of Hagen in the Highlands of Papua New Guinea prized fat babies. But the Etoro ethnography suggests that we need an explanation. We should take note of the form which maternal anxiety took. Anxiety surfaced when labour was prolonged and difficult. Women in labour were often troubled about the kind of evidence of substance they would bring forth; a puny child was a sign of ancestral disfavour for which the mother might suffer or of an incubus who had revealed itself as a spirit changeling. Its lack of substance was the problem. Hagen growth was not due directly to a life-force in the Etoro sense but to what the inside body made consumable (the fertility of the soil was consumed by the mother in the form of food and evinced in her milk) and turned into outside images of itself (a fat child fed off fertile land). The soil made food grow, food gave bulk and strength to parents, mothers nourished children with their milk. These substances were also parts of one substance, 'grease', as visible in the pigs (themselves wealth items) which people reared and exchanged as it was in persons themselves. At the same time, such substance indicated if not 'life-force'[10] then a creative capacity (nutrition, fertility), one best captured perhaps by the English epithet 'procreative'. Elsewhere I have offered a preliminary definition of substance, as procreative body-effort in a completed state, that is, an outcome of people's acts 'held' in the body they have created ('grown'), and which appears as an object available for or demanding of transaction. By contrast with Hagen, Etoro do not embark on transactions which would bring body (creative capacity) to a completed state in this way.

A Hagen child had to show a proper state of nourishment. But maternal anxiety was not only about the state of the child, it was also about the mother's capacity to bring it forth and not retain it within. It had to be detached from her, and posed life-threatening consequences if it could not be. Men showed a similar preoccupation in their efforts to elicit wealth from others. For them, what was at issue was the demonstration of their creativity in relationships.

If for Etoro men we imagine that the object of transfer was a capacity for life, then we might say that Hagen men by contrast used their relations to materialise *the specific capacity for transfer itself*. They used relations to create relations.[11] 'Substance' in the form of fat bodies and plentiful pigs or shells was evidence of this creative move. Men sought to create (sustain and innovate on) relations primarily through the flow of wealth (those pigs and shells). What was thus revealed to be given away, taken outside, was the growing power of a particular capacity – the very ability to give and give again. It followed that every enactment could only exemplify or augment that capacity. For what was given away were images of that capacity in the form of detachable substance: the wealth one produced, not the power to produce it. That power remained intact. Indeed, it was furthered by the social consequences of gift giving; all such gifts stimulated counter-gifts later, so that theoretically speaking the more one gave the more one received. The image now embedded in another would be returned at a future date.

In being brought forth, the created items (food, wealth, children) were thus separated from the fertility that gave birth to them. They could be separated without radical diminution of that capacity. Thus parents bodied forth their vitality in the child, but the vitality, the capacity, the body effort, was not itself bodied forth. Rather, the child gave evidence of *having received* that vitality in its substance, its nourished state. Hagen nutrition, like procreation, like the drawing of wealth to one's house, did its work off-stage. And had to be kept off-stage to work. This introduces a different temporality from, different social conventions for, the disposal of images.

Etoro bodies – inside and outside – fell away and became wasted when their vitality was passed on to and thus consumed by others. In the Hagen case, the disposed-of body became only temporarily 'wasted'; it went into hiding.

There are two bodies here. There was the body of the donor,[12] for which J. Weiner's (1995a) comments on caducity are pertinent.[13] What was discarded was what was left behind – from the recipient's point of view, this was the donor who had released the wealth. In the foregrounding or separation of an outcome (wealth) from its origin (the donor), what dropped off, the discarded image of the donor in his glory, might also be thought of as being momentarily hidden from view.[14] That is, the entities out of which others were brought forth become backgrounded. The cavity of the men's house from which shell valuables came was closed up after the ceremony. It was because the detached element came to stand for the whole process, and thus referred to, encapsulated or exemplified its own origin, that what had once been its origins were now parts located 'elsewhere', and thus concealed. There was also the body of the detached items themselves. Hagen men did not just force others to act as recipients of what they produced; they also disposed of these images by rendering them invisible, for the valuables, once handed over, were hidden away in other men's houses.[15] In the same way, if they were not actually eaten, pigs which had come from the privacy of people's domestic spaces went to those of others. What had been revealed was the very capacity to make things appear in such a mode that they could be detached, and passing them on to others was a means of further concealment. What was kept concealed was growing power, regeneration. Generative capacity was retained (to create more relations) and what was passed on, made material through the relations which elicited them, were the crucial images of detachment which kept up the flow of persons and wealth.

In visualising these flows as flows of substance, men gave themselves a significant purchase. If Etoro men only wanted life-force to lodge in them for a while, and then to pass it on, glorying in the evidence of their own diminishment, they took a lifetime to do it. Hagen men could speed up the process in their circulation of exchange items: they, too, only wanted the wealth to appear at certain times, although in this case what they gave out also came back, an enactment of their own continuing capacity for growth which enabled them to repeat the transactions and thus keep substance flowing.[16] Chapter 10 takes up this argument about speed. In the meantime, note that although giving was a highly creative act for the donor, he could not do it alone. The act required the materialisation of social relations, real time and real people, other persons prepared to act as recipients. That is, the special occasions of ceremonial exchange were predicated on a rhetorical need: there had to be someone who came and demanded the wealth.

VELOCITY

Too many 'meanings': for Naritjin, the Yolngu artist, the problem of the proliferation of meaning appeared to resolve itself through choice. Faced with the task of interpretation, Naritjin explained that it was a 'matter of *refusing* meanings their purchase on our imagination' (J. Weiner 1995c: 5, original emphasis).[17] In one sense, as Weiner implies, this is an absurd quantification. Meanings do not exist in a quantity to be divided up in this way any more, as Munro (1995: 320) points out, than they can travel. Or, any more, the New Guinea Highlands ethnography might provoke a Euro-American to object, than living bodies can shed their substance for others.

Meanings do not travel, Munro says, but inscriptions, that is, the descriptive forms in which things appear, the manner of their expression, do. An image is one such vehicle, and to explore the relationship between meaning and vehicle is to enter a vast theoretical terrain, the discourse of signs. In this terrain, images no more exist in the form of their presentation than meanings do. Indeed, one cannot discriminate sensibly between image and meaning, or sign and symbol for that matter, without reaching for theoretical stabilisation. But let me 'refuse' that handhold for something else which is summoned by the English term 'meaning'. Consider those social situations where people assume that things are being produced for their effect, and thus invite interpretation.

This is the meaning which Gell (1995), following a long line of philosophers of art, wishes to place on the idea of aesthetic impact. That is,

he argues, items become appreciated for their appearance precisely because they become the subject of a disquisition about appearance. Form
is thus visibly and explicitly dependent on a discourse about form, which
itself has to work, as a poetic, with its own impact. Gell's example here
(after Coote 1992)[18] is the beautiful oxen of the Sudan on which people
such as the Dinka lavish aesthetic attention. In this case that attention is
produced through poetry and song. Yet however produced, he adds, we
should be looking for a 'social cult' of attention to appearance. It will simultaneously create and consume, ascribe to and draw out meaning from
form. This is exactly how one might describe the presentation of bodily
increase and decrease of life-force (Etoro) and substance (Hagen). Men
pressed on to others the consumption and thus disposal of what they
were, as a consequence, seen to embody. This body/wealth was intended
to be interpreted as the product of creativity, which thus existed already
in the discourse about it, that is, in the capacity to produce descriptions
for others to consume.

Involving others has its consequences. One obvious problem is that it
subverts the communication of intention, since – as Papua New Guineans tirelessly tell themselves – everyone has their own (intentions).
Moreover, social engagement taken to excess can also pose serious problems for disposability. That is because the number of people who can be
enrolled in an enterprise contribute to the velocity with which things
circulate.

In their staged disposal of what they produced, Hagen men enter-
tained the idea of constant expansion, that they could always extend
their relationships. One of the 'illusions' of wealth (M. Strathem 1988:
206-7), we could also say this extension was an illusion of disposal. Ever
more conduits by which to get rid of it and ever more relationships as
a result. They were constrained of course by having to gather together
the resources and persons to make a show, but then we might also say
that their ability to dispose of wealth was constrained by the wealth they
stimulated to flow towards – not just away from – them. What appears to
have been important, and the subject of aesthetic discourse, was the need
to keep the flow moving. The possibility of increasing the flow of wealth
was in part a matter of velocity, the speed at which items circulated.

Eric Hirsch puts it thus in his discussion of another Papua New
Guinean people (the Fuyuge). Like Hagen ceremonial exchange, at the
centre of their principal and periodic ritual sequence had been an elicitory capacity – above all the capacity to achieve a concentration of effort
– when people otherwise dispersed were brought together.[19] Writing of

the 1980s, he commented on the place that ritual had come to occupy in the Fuyuge world. It was not the case that the periodic performance had nowadays become irrelevant 'but that it must be be performed at a more rapid pace – it need[ed] to be speeded up' (1995c: 67). People were impatient at the time it took to prepare. And they had an alternative to hand: 'cultural forms derived from the metropolitan context ... are seen as a way of achieving the flow and anticipated outcomes of the [ritual] in a quicker manner' (1995c: 68). If Fuyuge discos and guitars became an alternative to old-style dancing, it was because their elicitory capacity could be brought into play at a much quicker pace. The description matches the kinds of uses to which money was being put in Hagen in the 1960s, and even more evidently in the 1990s.[20]

Money has an elicitory capacity of the kind Hageners readily appreciate: it can detach a whole range of things from persons. Money speeds up transactions. I have suggested that Hagen exchange practices realised some of the potential of velocity; in despatching goods that return, one short-circuited so to speak the cycle of growth and decay which Etoro took a lifetime to accomplish, and money enhances this potential. Handing over gifts of money short-circuits more laborious cycles of production and transaction. At the same time money can make accumulation and dispersal visible, and thus becomes 'visible' itself. It was and is the subject of endless discourse, a constant source of amazement that it does both: people wonder at the size of what they can collect together, as when a clan makes a major purchase, and wonder equally at the way it disappears, when they are left as they say with no money on their skins. Today its seemingly ubiquitous presence has become a measure of both the past and the future. Of course Hagen men and women comment by saying there is not enough of it. But in their imaginations, that is, when it is in their wallets, money can do anything and anything can be turned into it. And they complain of this ubiquity: it is, in a sense, in too many places. People buy favours with it, leave home for it, sell their heirlooms for it – and keep it from others. Money has become visible there all the time, a medium whose enabling capacities cannot be hidden. For money that can be stashed away so easily is in another sense hard to hide. It is hard to hide in other persons. And there is a new reason – not the reluctance of the recipient-consumer forced to accept what he is given but the reluctance of the donor-producer unwilling to give it away. Not an image of pure transferability, after all, money at once makes too many things flow and does not itself always flow properly. It becomes only part-detachable. The point is amplified in Chapter 5.

I have introduced money for the conundrum it poses as something at once invested with intrinsic value and excessive in its influence. It is, in contemporary Hagen eyes, in too many places. It exerts pressure precisely just as one might imagine the excessive influence of 'meaning'.[21]

Munro's concern with the disposal of meaning came from his critique of certain theories of consumption. Those who look to meanings in patterns of consumption to interpret the way consumers choose are not really providing an account of how production is restricted. They simply substitute the production of meaning for the production of goods. Production continues to flow. There is no end, he writes, to the consumption theorist's ability to theorise and spin meaning. The Euro-American theorist's ability to proliferate meanings, however, does not in itself require specific theories. Theorists' dominant medium, writing, like money, does it for them. Detachment would seem easy enough – in publication – papers – conferences. But the form of publication also means that meanings are left visible, exposed. One cannot get rid of meanings by hiding them. I am thinking here of the kind of expository or analytical writing of academic papers that lays everything out, that can turn anything with an argument, that yearns for exegesis, and that imagines that the more one can gather in the more comprehensive the interpretation will be. One effect is that everything comes to the surface. So anthropologists devise models (restrictions) to control the need to take into account everything they have laid out. Yet the most elaborately layered account can still end up as excess, accumulation, the repeated evidence of past imaginings.

Expository forms enjoy a kind of limitless and accumulative effect, then; one cannot hide again what has been brought to the surface. Ever greater effort is required to encompass meaning by meaning, only to discover that constructs which appear to be offered freshly for the reader's attention in any case, already, inform the text. That revelatory device in turn points to further deferral, to future revelations. This is creativity of a kind. However, while the revelation that the terms were there all along might work as a momentary discovery, if they cannot be concealed again they cease to work as discoveries at all. Most of the time this hardly matters, yet writers do sometimes want the discoveries to be illuminating and fresh, and thus to make evident the capacity for interpretation. Think of the recent fate of 'culture', a concept that embodies an intellectual capacity to comprehend the world in certain ways. Over the last decade the concept of 'culture' has become a ubiquitous coin – it shoots through all sorts of contexts, able to turn virtually anything into exemplifications of itself. This may be to the irritation of the anthropologist who was once wont to produce 'culture' as a hidden illumination of his or her materials.[22] Although the concept was embracing (anthropological descriptions proceeded against the background of culture), it would be foregrounded only at certain explanatory moments, as an explicit reminder of the nature of the phenomena under study. Such revelations are no longer possible.

Yet if expository practices make it difficult to hide what has been brought to the surface, there is a further long-standing social obstacle to getting rid of meaning. Or rather of being certain that one has got rid of it. Euro-American writers may have to construct their audiences as general rather than specific consumers, and inevitably so when they exist as an anonymous public. So there is no *particular* witness or recipient; what is detached, discarded, disposed of, published, is not axiomatically lodged within a particular other.[23] They cannot rely on effect being evidenced in terms of reciprocity between persons in an ongoing relationship. The materiality of face-to-face interchange is not there. Particular audiences may of course be found in communities of scholars, say, or sports enthusiasts, known to one another so to speak through common interests and a shared discourse. They are prey to a different kind of hazard: failure to contain circulation within the community takes away its 'face-to-face' potential. Gillian Beer (1996: 195) notes that, as has happened in the past, '[A]t present we are again in a moment when scientists are accepting the risks of uncontrolled reception. Writing that had initially sought and required the autonomy of the specialist group is now rapidly and copiously re-interpreted by wider and diversified groups of writers and readers.'

But that is uncontrolled reception from the point of view of the writer. What about uncontrolled reception from the point of view of the reader? Consider Munro's (1995: 320) description of an interchange. It may take a parent-cook longer, he says, to digest the unwonted response of 'not turkey again!', than for the child to finish off the unwanted plate. An image produced by one person is thus lodged in another; the parent's discomfort reassures the child that it has successfully disposed of its disgust about turkey. Yet having 'read' the child's remark, the parent cannot so easily pass the discomfort on and would probably not think it right simply to pass it back. Like parents there to respond to the child's changing moods, readers are targeted for their receptiveness: one of their jobs is to absorb what is written, but without – except in the forum of explicit debate – even the possibility of registering a return. So they have to dispose of things too. But how? Beer (1996: 188) quotes from Don DeLillo's novel *White Noise*: 'We suffer from brain fade', argues one character, 'the flow is constant ... Words, pictures, numbers, facts, graphics, statistics, specks, waves, particles, motes. Only a catastrophe gets our attention.' What of catastrophe, then? What if readers feel themselves at the mercy of texts? Unexpected pictures jump out. A continuing flow of argument seems insufficient to carry the scenes away. Elements of narrative lodge in the memory independently of the river of words or the scaffolding of themes. When images stay in the mind, one cannot get rid of them by an exercise of imagination – that is simply reinforcing. And the reader of books is unable to return them to their creator. I cannot give the image of the fat child back to Kelly.

Ingestion on the part of readers may be involuntary. However, there is a category of writing whose authors speed up the feeding of their unknown audience. Such writing perhaps also helps the reader to discard meanings even as they are consumed. I refer to literary forms which work through figurative rather than expository language, through synthesis rather than analysis, as one finds in much poetry.[24] Condensed, compressed, totalising: it is possible to find literary forms of expression which offer meaning in a mode that can also work to dispose of it. The mode works by forcing the reader or listener to respond to 'images'[25] as though they formed a series or sequence of experiences. Sequencing creates a movement which carries the reader or listener forward, almost as though there were no time to linger on the individual moment.[26] However much reflection is invited, the sequencing makes the succession itself a rapid one. So images hide, in the sense of displace, one another – not quite the movement involved in closing up a ceremonial house in order to open it out again, or decorating and undecorating the body, but with something of the same material effect. A relationship of sorts is set up. For the reader is *meant* to react not just to the writer's words or arguments but specifically to tropic effects. It does not matter if the meanings are shared or not, the reader expects images which will elicit reactions from him or her, expects to be fed and edified, and above all expects to be drawn along, stimulated afresh at each metaphorical turn, a whole gallery of picturings. This is different in turn from the incidental description, the image that appears as an adjunct to an argument, an exposure that repeats its shocking and primal effect every time as the book falls opens at that page.

No: insofar as Kelly's account is expository in intent, it is as vain to wish Kelly to take back the image of the fat witch-child as it is pointless to have wished he had covered it with another.

I thought at this point that I might have disposed of the meanings I wished to attach to different forms of expression. But I have not of course disposed of the meaning of disposal. The term carries too much already. On reading this chapter, Paul Connerton presented me with seven types of disposability (in fact the list grew beyond seven, but they were enough, with examples from the industry created around discarding industrial waste to the shedding of icongraphic knowledge over the generations so that training is required to interpret what had once not needed 'interpretation'). It would be a fascinating task to expand on this, but I shall reduce the possibilities to one outcome. Perhaps the issue comes once again to the difference between what arises inadvertantly and what is made an explicit object of action. Pollution surprises by its untoward nature, an unlooked-for return; yet those involved in the activity of waste disposal know that one cannot dispose of waste, only convert it into something else with its own life – including literary life in DeLillo's *Underworld* (1997). The same is true of interpretation: we never cease to interpret, but when we cease to ignore what we are doing and pay it attention, as do the art historians whom Gell might have had in mind, then we realise that much more is added in recuperating old meanings than was ever lost in the first place. Now these need not be general truths; it is enough that they afford a critical distance on some of the techniques through which people render the world explicit to themselves. There was a moment of explicitness at the beginning of the chapter, in the initial link between the Papua New Guinea example and the author's Euro-American reactions: a (social) practice suddenly sounded all too like my own efforts to cleanse my (descriptive) account of too much resonance. Suppose one went with the grain, then; suppose one wished to put conservation in a positive rather than negative light.

Think, then, of the value that an image has precisely because 'it does not expend itself. It preserves and concentrates its strength and is capable of releasing it even after a long time ... [resembling] the seeds of grain which have lain for centuries in the chambers of the pyramids shut up air-tight and have retained their germinative power to this day.' I quote from Benjamin's (1992: 90) description of the story. He is complaining about the dissipative excesses of information by contrast with the story's enduring power. The value of information hardly survives the moment in which it was new. And that is because of the pains it takes with explanation. Information, he observes, lays claims to prompt verifiability. It must appear 'understandable in itself, present events already shot through with explanation. It thus subverts narrative, whereas 'it is half the art of

storytelling to keep a story free from explanation as one reproduces it'
(1992: 89). In short, a story relates but does not exposit. The connection
of events, he thus adds, is not forced on readers – it is left up to readers
to intepret according to their own understanding.

Here it is explanation which is forced upon the reader, and the story-
teller's effect, like that of the image-maker who deliberately leads a reader along a trail of displacements, offers instead the choice of where to
linger. Here, too, far from exposition keeping everything laid out to view,
it becomes ephemeral, disappearing when the need for it disappears.

The point is that one cannot adjudicate in advance on which forms
will release the values one is seeking to reify. That release is, so to speak,
the work of social life, which is why I have introduced the work that
Etoro and Hagen people do. I have also described a more general consequence of social life. When actors can identify one another, refusing
to be a recipient of meanings can become an expressible act. When they
cannot, different kinds of social conduits may work to greater or lesser effect. The next chapter turns to a situation in which diverse social interests
influence the way meanings are attached to certain forms of knowledge.
Social conventions designed to set up conduits in the general population,
on a mass scale, actually make certain kinds of disposal harder for people,
like kinsfolk, in face-to-face contact with one another.[27] Chapter 4 also
sets up a contrast between two kinds of information, which catches some
but not all of the inflections described in this chapter.[28] In setting these
accounts side by side, I would wish to recapture for exposition some of
the delayed effect of a form which Benjamin sees only in story-telling.

ACKNOWLEDGEMENTS

The topic of the 1996 conference for which an earlier version was prepared (*Cultural Poetics: Materialism and Method,* convened by Peter Middleton and Julian Thomas) stimulated the attempt to enrol materialism
into the argument. I am grateful to Douglas Dalton for his criticism,
and to Gillian Beer and Paul Connerton for several conversations; they
will both see their ideas here as will Rolland Munro who was also most
generous with his comments on the text.

CHAPTER 4

Refusing Information

What is new [in the present epoch] is that people have produced a machine, a discourse, that can absorb any bit of discourse
Paul Rabinow, paraphrased

I wish to capture a particular moment. It is doubtful if it is one with much future. At the same time, current arguments over recent developments in reproductive medicine help make the climate from which that future will come. Here I put in a plea for attending to contemporary complexity.

In almost a throwaway line, Rheinberger (forthcoming) observes that calculation, legislation and instruction have long shaped human society. The history that he writes for molecular biology is to this extent anticipated. In particular, of course, modern state governments are constituted as interventionist, using society as their technical embedding, for what characterises governance but a state of affairs where the tools of manipulation are of the nature and dimension of the procedures with which they interfere? In general, and as a consequence of their own history, human institutions are constantly faced with the effects of their own past interferences. The one I report on here concerns the embedding of scientific knowledge in aspects of Euro-American kinship. My argument also concerns the runaway metaphor of information; regardless of whether or not information models are still apt in other fields, for governmental practices the process of information-gathering appears to absorb anything we wish to know. However, it is not always quite as informative a concept as it might seem.

Recent discussions (e.g. Eekelaar and Šarčević 1993; Robertson 1994) concerning the rights of parents and children have turned to the citizen's relationship with the state and the ethics of intervention, as well as to litigation and the pursuit of claims. In the two decades during which reproductive technologies have become a public phenomenon, both have been arenas for what one can only call cultural exploration. In passing, they endorse the utility of information. The several commissions of enquiry[1] into new reproductive (and genetic) technologies set up since the early 1980s indicate the extent to which governments consider this a field where they should marshal public opinion, while in civil disputes litigants use whatever they can in support of their arguments. Their cultural explorations often push to the limit assumptions about what constitute parent-child relations, in the very act of seeking for limits or establishing reasons for claims.[2]

But there are limits to creativity as well. Some kinds of information come with built-in effects. New reproductive technologies are about procreation and its techno-scientific enablement. They are also about relations of kinship. Now post-Enlightenment Euro-Americans have at the heart of their kinship system a set of core presumptions about knowledge that makes science especially easy to think with: these concern knowledge externally verifiable by information about the natural world.[3] Knowledge about how persons are related to one another is acquired from, among other things, information about biological process. With the new technologies have come new techniques of verifiability. Now such knowledge is integral to the recognition of persons as kin, and has its built-in impact on personal identity. This implication has in turn implications for the public handling of debate through commissions of enquiry and the courts. It seems that these public or semi-public instruments are simply responding to the needs and claims of society or of individuals for more information. Yet the pursuit of information may pose problems for persons as kin.

CREATING KINSHIP

In 1995 I had the opportunity to discuss the story of Louise Brown's birth through *in vitro* fertilisation with Ru Kundil,[4] from Hagen in Papua New Guinea. The story made no sense without the rider that

Europeans thought that one act of insemination was sufficient to create an embryo. Ru's response was instant. Of course, he said, she would not be able to have any children of her own. Because she had been made at just one time, there would have been no possibility for her mother to have nourished her in the womb and endowed her with everything that made a fertile baby girl. In Hagen, it is not only the mother's contribution that is important; development also depends on continued sexual contributions from the father, and must carry on after birth through the food that the child eats, it being significant that the food will have been jointly grown by her mother on land cleared by her father. Insemination is feeding and coitus is work. If he and I were somewhat at cross-purposes in this conversation, I suspect it was because I could not envisage conception as anything but the outcome of a single act and he could not envisage fertility as anything but the outcome of a continuous process over the generations.

So what might we make of some compatriots of mine, from a town not so far from Oldham where Louise's parents lived? Edwards (1993: 59) had been discussing donor insemination with Veronica Thomas [pseudonym].

> Somebody somewhere must be creating this artificial womb. A baby reacts to what you're feeling – if your heartbeat is faster then the baby's heartbeat is faster. It could be fed on just vegetables – how would it react then, through the placenta – not what you fancy like crisps or salads, or Chewitts on the bus, like cravings at different times – vegetables, sweets, alcohol[,] whatever it takes to make a baby. It will have no feelings because no feelings are going through it.[5]

Again the conversation may have been at cross-purposes, since Veronica was imagining what a baby 'reared in a laboratory' might be like. Her question was about the child's emotional development as an individual if it were cut off from contact with maternal idiosyncrasies. Like Ru, then, Veronica is concerned about the kind of influence a parent has on its offspring over time, although he focused on the future capacity of the child and she on its emotional health. I give concern with these practices a name: kinship.

Kinship makes children part of the bodies/persons of their parents. It points to duration, that is, to the effect that the past has on the future. The authors of these two accounts are likely to place very different emphasis on what Veronica would no doubt call 'biology' or 'genetics' and what Ru would call 'investment [through work]', and if we went further the anthropologist would find herself describing two very different kinship systems as far as their consequences for relationships were concerned. But both take the development of the child to be embedded in the activities of its parents. Now by virtue of the very fact that development unfolds over time, there may be a succession of parental figures. One of Ru's female relatives, for instance, has handed a son of hers over to her sister who has no birth children, and through being fed (the object of her 'adoptive' parents' work) this child becomes the sister's child.[6] How far the sister takes over the parental role will be put to the test when the child marries, for that is the point at which the work of rearing a person is acknowledged in bridewealth distributions.[7] Another resident in Veronica's town spoke about her uncle in the following terms (Edwards 1993: 61):

> SM: Well, I mean, we're talking about scientific things now but my uncle was adopted, for instance, and I don't know how much he wondered about his real mother but his adopted mother was always his mother from his point of view. ... [I]t's more to do with relationships than it is to do with birth, I think; and the relationships what you build up. And I had a discussion with me mother some time ago and something to the effect that it wasn't blood necessarily that counted, it was the relationship that you'd built up between you, which I think does count for more. But that can always be disturbed by, as you say, adopted people growing up and trying to find out where they actually come from: which I can imagine will also take place with those who want to find out what laboratory...
>
> MB: They want to know their origins, don't they?
>
> SM: Because they feel somehow they belong somewhere and...
>
> MB: And they want to know which box they slot into. It's funny that, isn't it?

The English-speakers introduce a significant dimension: knowing the conditions of birth can cut or disturb the continuities of relationship. More than that, those continuities can be set aside on the basis of such knowledge; and such knowledge is significant for a sense of identity. This is bound up in the question of what is passed on to the child.

The place that knowledge holds in the way Euro-Americans[8] deal with kinship relations echoes other areas of social life. Making decisions over knowledge – deciding what information is useful, what facts cannot be ignored, how one should act given what one knows – is as fundamental to the kind of exercise which policy-makers undertake through commissions of enquiry as it is part of litigious practice. Knowledge is significantly drawn into definitions of the person when it becomes a means through which persons think about themselves. The quest for facts about the way the world works, and in issues of procreation the role accorded to 'blood' and 'actual' facts, is also part of the Euro-American quest for self-hood: self-knowledge is considered foundational to personal identity, and that includes knowledge about both birth and parentage. However, these are not all on a level. There are situations in which information about biological origins is held to verify relatedness.

Because of its cultural coupling[9] with identity, kinship knowledge is a particular kind of knowledge: the information (and verification) on which it draws is constitutive in its consequences. In mind here is Searle's classic contrast between constitutive and regulative rules as expounded by Martin (Ahern 1982).[10] Now the kind of information gathered together in the Eekelaar and Šarčević volume, for instance, is being gathered in a regulative manner. The intention is to see what will be relevant or persuasive to exploring issues in contemporary parenthood in the knowledge that only *some* information will be useful. Regulative aims impose a duty to be well-informed; from this comes the public value put on freedom of information. At the same time, one can collect all sorts of information that need not be acted upon, a likelihood especially evident in litigation. Nor does the information redefine the activity: whatever the readers find out, the result of the collection will still be an academic work on parenthood. By contrast, kinspersons who find things out about their ancestry acquire identity by that very discovery. Parentage implies relatedness; facts about birth imply parentage.[11] Euro-Americans cannot ignore these connections. The information forms ('constitutes') what they know about themselves. And between parents, a point to which I shall return, this is highlighted in the traditional difference between mother and father. In a way that is not true of mothers, fathers are vulnerable to 'discovering' they are not fathers after all.

As kinspersons, Euro-Americans may well be wary of the information that comes to them. Where the academic or policy-maker or lawyer will gather quantities of data and then screen some of it out in order to establish the basis for knowledge on which to proceed further, the kinsperson can only screen at the initial (first) threshold, that is, the moment at which a decision can be taken as to whether to be exposed to the information in the first place. So people may say they *do not wish to know.* Or they may say they think *others should not know* and they do not wish to tell.

This ought to be a challenge to explorations in the field of reproductive technology. Such reluctance would seem to block the kind of free society that liberal government imagines for us. Of course, kinspersons may be drawn into that imagining; there are many advocates of open knowledge about all kinds of procedures, including adoption, and numerous examples of people who feel better on the grounds of the new identity they have discovered. But we shall not understand the converse, people's reluctance, or their desire to not-know, or anxieties about where information will lead, unless we realise that kinship knowledge has certain built-in effects.

REGULATIVE AND CONSTITUTIVE INFORMATION

Different uses of regulative information

Two schemas serve as exemplars for regulative information; each also throws up questions about constitutive practices.

First, the most notable example of a state equipping itself with information about reproductive medicine must be Canada. The final report submitted by the Canadian Royal Commission on New Reproductive Technologies (Canada, Minister of Government Services 1993) runs to 1,275 pages. It makes its search explicit: the preface claims that over 300 scholars participated in the exercise, across seventy disciplines, involving more than 40,000 Canadians, with a newsletter, research studies, public hearings, symposia and written submissions. Unprecedented as a consultative exercise in this field, its aim was a set of recommendations for the regulation of practices. But before the practices could be regulated, the information had to be.[12]

Government of pregnancy is Weir's (1996) arresting description of liberal principles applied by the state to the field of reproductive medicine. Beyond the fact that knowledge about the population, through census and other social data, is taken for granted as part of the state's care of itself, and beyond the fact that at the end of the twentieth century this has to include cultural data as well, lies its responsibility to enter into dialogue with the population. The Commission clearly saw its duty as seeking out opinion as a potential basis for specifying cultural values and ethical principles. It wished to be seen equipped with information drawn from a wide spectrum of social sources within the population, a 'total society' approach (Massey 1993). Conversely, it was also concerned with its own role as disseminator of information: the scientific data without which people could not be well-informed, the findings from its various surveys, and its unique collection of opinions and attitudes which enabled it to inform Canadians of the views of other Canadians. The Report would seem to endorse the cultural assumption that the more information that can be gathered the better; that the only way to treat a heterogeneous population is to gather a diversity of views; that out of a morass of data, the policy-maker selects what is important or useful in the light of various priorities.[13] When information becomes a taken-for-granted prelude to taking action, some information thereby becomes regulative of other information.

Weir and Habib (1997) draw attention to the Report's vigorous defence of 'evidence-based medicine'[14] in directing public funds towards techniques whose effectiveness has been proven through clinical trials. They comment that making aggregate data a medical arbiter for the suitability for treatment flies in the face of current clinical practice which emphasises variability of treatment forms with respect to the individuality of bodies and disease. Perhaps a similar approach to aggregate data can be seen in the Report's handling of people's attitudes and opinions. Of the thirty-two chapters of the Report, some nine are prefaced by 'Views of Canadians', though such views are by no means confined to these sections. Here is the distillation of all those hearings, consultations and submissions. Each consists of a presentation of a diversity of attitudes, criticism, reservations, in some cases gathered together ('Emerging from this range of views and concerns was a distinct sense that most Canadians see ...' (Canada, Minister of Government 1993: 430)), in other cases the multiplicity of angles being left as a 'spectrum of views' or 'perspectives' (502). One might comment that, as far as its presentation in the Report is concerned, nowhere is this body of information addressed as such or, beyond occasional categorisation, its special nature subjected to analysis. The data is not presented in terms of how it was collected, or how it may have been allocated different jobs in informing the commissioners. Whatever preliminary work went into such processing, it was not thought necessary to be explicit about it. Indeed the catch-all notion of a 'view' reduces everything to a matter of how strongly people hold this or that opinion and how over certain matters there is agreement and over certain others disagreement. That some people might have been thinking about personal experiences or individual triumphs, others what might be best for society, others what kind of advice might be useful or how best to act as an advocate for a particular position or where future research might lead, all seem outside the data rather than part of it. Just by abutting one set of attitudes or values against another, a sense is instead given that everything has been taken into account. The Report as such[15] remains profoundly uninterested in what *kind* of information it is based upon.

In short, the Commission's Report presents a type of cultural analysis which presumes that 'culture' lies somehow in the opinions of a population aggregated into majority and minority perspectives. The analysis provides numerous examples of what Weir (1996) calls the 'constrained conflict' of a liberal rationality; pre-structured for conflict, liberal government must be seen to tussle both with minority views and with criticisms of its own actions. We may add that it thereby conceals the extent to which people might wish to refuse the issues on which they were being required to have views. This last comment sounds a bit tangential. Nonetheless, there were some very different kinds of information being presented to the Commission, to which one suspects the democratising concepts of 'attitudes', 'opinions', and views in conflict, were simply inadequate.

I give one example. Of the 250 organisations which appeared before the Commission, only a small handful represented Aboriginal groups (see Massey 1993: 248; Appendix B to the Report; I follow its capitalisation of Aboriginal). There is some puzzlement in these submissions as to what the Royal Commission wanted to know. The written submission from the Indian and Inuit Nurses' Association of Canada (1990) gives a clue. It urges the Commission to consider in-depth studies of infertility, with the rider that the studies should be specific to the Aboriginal populations. It talks of sterilisation practices, of high rates both of venereal disease and fertility among Aborigines, and of genocide. And that is the point: the consultation exercise appears to have elicited concerns not so much about infertile couples, or the future of society as a whole, as about the reproductive future of a particular people.

Some of the puzzlement seems to have been about the role of the government and, in its seeking information, about the information it was also imparting. That from the Northwest Territories Status of Women Council (1990) talks of the delivery of services and of hospital provision, bringing in issues of basic health, infant mortality and access to obstetrical care. Others talk of reproduction as part of 'community' or the 'circle of life'. The Yukon Indian Women's Association (1990) submission asks what kind of priority assisted conception could possibly be or who set the budget for fertility services, questioning the relevance of the technologies to themselves: 'reproductive technology is not an issue for us, nor is it even on the bottom of the list of our health issues'. The same submission expresses bafflement at having to explain technical procedures to elders. This is not a simple issue of knowledge versus ignorance. It would seem that these peoples are seizing on the information about reproduction in terms of their social identity as governmental subjects ('As First Nations people in the Yukon and the rest of Canada, we are at a critical stage in our quest for recognition of our sovereignty'), even wondering if they have the option not to know ('it is difficult to think of infertility as an issue when our overall well being is lower'). This kind of response does not necessarily mean that these communities do not 'want' new reproductive technologies; it is not a question of an 'attitude' or a 'cultural value' or their views on it. It is a question of what kind of knowledge their response would lead to, and thus what is already constituted in the enquiry.

If an example from Alaska is anything to go by, perhaps one should be looking for the kinds of relationships presupposed by the act of enquiry itself. Bodenhorn's (1994) work on the way Inupiat elders talk about 'reading' (books) makes very clear the fact that knowledge is regarded as something that can only be acquired in the context of a relationship, embedded in interactions between those who know and those who wish to learn; knowledgeable persons are their books, they say. In what relationship, to extrapolate, was the Canadian quest for information about reproductive technology to be embedded? If with the state, what kind of relationship with the state was being enacted *in this exercise* given everything else about that relationship? Perhaps these Aboriginal peoples are asking questions about how fertility bears on government legislation and its delivery of services to them. Perhaps they are saying: we do not know what this consultation means because if we knew it would have to be in terms of what is already built into anything we have to do with the state. If that built-in effect is not the articulating point of a new relationship, what *is* the point?

As it was, these submissions remained something of an anomaly for the Commissioners. Relations with the state might be constitutive of the knowledge Aboriginal Canadians had of themselves, so information given to government agencies implied consequences for governmental presence – with the result, as I have suggested, that what did not touch on state provision could not be heard. Yet what might thus have been constitutive for them appears to have been (not very enlightening) regulative information for the Royal Commission. These were simply views to put beside more views, and in such a minority idiom as to have weak regulative effect.

The second context for regulative information on which I draw is premised not on gathering everything in but on the very opposite: an assumption that there will be dispute and disagreement about what matters, as well as motives for concealing facts and distorting evidence. Here too there are certain built-in effects, embedded in concerns about personal identity. The concerns reach the courts because interests are at stake. Brief details of four cases from newspaper reports[16] illustrate the mobilisation of new procedures of verification. They do not involve new reproductive techniques as such, but belong to the cultural climate within which such techniques are developed. All concern allegations of paternity.

(1) Michigan, US (*New York Times* 7 October 1994). Exhumation of a corpse for DNA genetic testing ('fingerprinting') led to the vindication of a woman's claims about the biological father of her daughter conceived after rape. The daughter has successfully contested his will and will inherit a major share of his estate. His kin talk about the money motives of the two women; the daughter's mother talks about being freed from decades of shame. A story of revenge and just deserts, achieved – after publicity over the case – through change to the law itself, granting inheritance rights to the 'unacknowledged children of rape'. (2) Wales, UK (*Independent* 12 August 1992). A cremation was held up for DNA fingerprinting by a man who had known for years that the deceased was his father, the outcome of an affair with his mother; the revelation of the test confirmed his knowledge. However, the information to which the son had access seems not to have been shared with the husband's kin. Here the revelation had the effect of literally changing relationships. The boy moved onto his father's farm and his father's brother, who said he had not known of the son's existence, had to move out.

In both cases, we see the regulatory effects of information. Proof provided by DNA testing can convert one kind of knowledge into another. The mother's knowledge of the child's paternity turns from secret or suspicion into openly accredited information. With that displacement, the legal entitlement that arises from being a child of an identifiable person comes into play. In both, further proof confirmed what one of the parties always claimed. Gaining external information through the test gave previous information public validity. In the next two cases, the role of new information is much more problematic. Indeed it might have been better for everyone to remain in ignorance.

(3) Edinburgh, UK (*Guardian* 6 October 1990). DNA fingerprinting showed that a man was, in all likelihood, not the genetic father of a girl with whom he had sexual relations over a period of three years. A first conviction had led to a two-year jail sentence for incest, although he was released after one. The new information was brought forward when he was charged a second time, and on disproof of a genetic connection the conviction was quashed. His actions were no longer regarded as incest. This was despite the fact that the man himself had believed at the time that he was having intercourse with his genetic daughter. (4) California, US (*California News* 26 September 1993). On the discovery that his wife had been impregnated by a friend to 'help them out', a man declared that the children he had reared for nine and five years respectively were 'somebody else's': 'Every time I look at them now I see their father's face'. Under the ruling that a claim to non-paternity must be lodged within two years of birth, a Riverside Superior Court judge determined that the man must remain the children's legal father and pay for their support. In retaliation, the father claimed a right not to be a parent. His lawyer was reported as saying: 'It is just the flip side of the fundamental right to parent. You have a fundamental right not to be a parent of somebody else's kids.'

Obviously cases are brought to court precisely because of the need to select between different kinds of information. But aside from this regulatory effect, another kind of effect runs through these examples as well. We are not just dealing with information that can be used to sway a judgement. Each turns on knowledge of birth and parentage altered by the revelation of a previously unacknowledged genetic tie. A man whose identity is revealed by proof of his contribution to conception cannot ignore this information. And not only fathers are involved; a spectrum of persons may have cause to review their relations among one another. The new information has a forward impact on the way relations become reconfigured and thus on how several other parties are going to behave in the future. In sum, three issues are involved. (1) The significance of knowledge for personal identity. (2) The fact that kinship knowledge is about identity in the context of relationships, so that choice between facts is also choice between relationships. (3) The relationships between types of information which means that one piece of information can automatically obliterate another, taking away the status of previous information. There is no choice about it; such effects are built-in. When this happens, information becomes constitutive of kinship knowledge.

Information about kinship can be used to regulative ends – for sifting through the bases of people's different attitudes or in being marshalled to support claims in court. But the material also shows the constitutive nature of procreative facts in the recognition of relationships. This kind of kinship knowledge has particular resonances for Euro-Americans. Another way of putting this would be to say that 'biological' information has immediate (simultaneous) 'social' effect.

Different types of constitutive information

Before commenting further on this element of Euro-American kinship knowledge, I introduce my own regulative strategy (modifying the way some information appears by deploying other information). A brief comparative excursus is in order. This is stimulated by Ru's comments on the Hagen situation where insemination is as much nurture as feeding is, and where feeding after birth continues to create the child's identity. This means that the effects of postnatal nurture remain in the substance and form of the body, and, as a result, a discovery that the prenatal 'biological parents' are other than supposed *cannot take away* the effects of postnatal nurture. Rather, the new information adds other persons whose 'work' went initially into building the child's body, and in no way denies the subsequent work of those who nurtured the child after birth. The new information, we might adduce, simply has a regulative effect. Something similar is also conveyed in the submissions to the Canadian Royal Commission. The Indian and Inuit nurses refer to supernatural forces and to the ante-natal care that a woman had to take in order to please her to-be-born child, while the Yukon Indian Women's Association insist on the significance of people knowing their ancestry, especially the father, because this is of paramount importance in determining marriage rules. These examples are not of course meant to be elided together. To underline their ethnographic distinctiveness, I turn to an Amazonian case with rather special features.

In his account of the Piro-speakers of Amazonian Peru, Gow (1991) specifically analyses the relationship between kinship and knowledge. Children acquire kinship knowledge in the form of what Piro call 'memory', above all memory of their parents. Knowledge is built up as care is built up. The relevant information concerns who has taken care of them.

Kin are said 'always to remember' one other (1991: 164). Remembering is an activity, as English-speakers might say that so-and-so remembered someone in their will, and is most visible in the acts of care that kin bestow on one another, and especially parents on children. This is not to say that Piro deny the significance of procreation, physical connection and shared substance. On the contrary, they may point to cases where a child is raised by someone other than its physiological parents (1991: 158), and this has a regulative effect on other information, such as marriage rules. Physiological connection – and immediate postnatal care when the child is held to lack knowledge – contributes to the child's identity, but as such gives the parents no rights over the child. When Piro distinguish 'adopted' child from 'real' child, says Gow (1991: 159), it is to stress the identity which the child has acquired as an adopted child and the caring which has produced it. The facts of procreation, then, are set beside the fact that it is primarily through food that the identity of the child is created, and in the context of relations with others. The child grows from a state of ignorance to a state of knowledge, and it is through constant acts of feeding that knowledge is implanted, which the child holds as 'memory', and which is expressed in the kin terms it uses (1991: 161). Indeed Piro point to a special kind of 'real food' produced jointly by its parents that 'sets up the relationship of memory when fed to the child' (1991: 193); much food circulates in later life to sustain such memory (1991: 273). In other words, given the role of memory as acknowledging kin through food, only limited knowledge is acquired through information about physiological origins. Procreation does not contribute the kind of information on which the child will later base his or her perception of the kin universe, the relatives towards whom she or he must act. Feeding is the primary process constitutive of that knowledge. We might further say that it is the state of being fed, rather than being informed, which matters.

The methodological point is not that the Piro case is representative or even exemplary; it does not in itself contain any general truths. Rather, information about the Piro serves to rearrange ('regulate') the constellation of factors we might wish to select for consideration, encouraging us to return to the Euro-American material with a different ear. Being informed does matter. It certainly matters to ('constitutes') what I have been calling kinship knowledge.

One Euro-American problem about being a kinsperson is that information about kin is not something which can be selected or rejected *as information*. Information (however incomplete it may seem) has already given the person an identity. The social effect is immediate. Simultaneously, the person learns about relations with others: kinship identity is realised within a field of relationships. Thus knowing something about one's kin is also knowing something about oneself – if one has no option but to deal with the information it is also true that one has no option over the relationships. Any subsequent selection or rejection implies selecting or rejecting those already one's relatives or else revealed not to be relatives at all. Screening out information will have the consequence of appearing to effect a choice between persons. ('Oh, I don't want to know about them.')[17] Whether what one discovers is the basis for deciding never to see someone again, or for cutting off ties or welcoming them into the home, the information is already, so to speak, knowledge, that is, already embedded in the way one acts towards others and perceives the world. In short, in Euro-American thinking, knowledge creates relationships: the relationships come into being when the knowledge does.

There is space for a brief exemplification. We are dealing with bilateral systems of kin reckoning with certain built-in directions given to gender difference. Until recently, difference between male and female parent rested in the two ways in which procreative parenthood was traditionally established, mother through birth and body issue; father, through presumed coitus with mother. These two routes to knowledge supposed two kinds of linkages, a contrast that foreshadowed the difference that common parlance supposes between 'biological' and 'social'.[18] The mother's biological tie to the child is at the root of her social obligations to it; the father's social tie to the mother is at the root of his knowledge of biological connection with the child. In other words, in pre-technology Euro-American systems, motherhood and fatherhood required different kinds of proof to establish the facts of procreation.[19] And fatherhood appeared to require more proof than motherhood.

The question of fatherhood, we may say, traditionally epitomised the role of knowledge in kinship. Fatherhood was a more contentious issue than motherhood. New techniques of information, including the information embodied in new techniques of procreation, enhance or exaggerate these concerns. In the case of fatherhood they are likely to turn on the identity of 'the biological father', while in the case of motherhood it is the diversity of biological considerations which becomes problematic. Indeed, in the way that Euro-Americans talk about kinship, the distinction between the 'moment' of conception and the prolonged nature of foetal development is replicated in the distinction between the instant insemination by the father and the drawn-out contribution of the mother. Taken together, procreative motherhood and fatherhood may be seen as jointly affording a 'biological' basis to parentage as distinct from the nurturance/rearing roles of 'social' parenthood. Either may regulate information about the other (thus social parenting is information about how one assesses biological parentage). However, the idea that the biological tie can be created in a moment, through the conception that is thought to have been completed at a single point in time, also appears to be of another order of fact from the continuing nurture of the child. It belongs to a natural order open to scientific investigation. It has the character of a constitutive finality that cannot be modified, that once known cannot be laid aside. 'Paternity' is presumed in the verifiability of information that exists about that event.

NORMALISING INFORMATION

A group based in Manchester (England) calls itself ODAC: Our Dads Are Canadian. The group, united by its search for fathers, half-brothers and half-sisters, comprises offspring of Canadian servicemen stationed in Britain during the Second World War. 'All we want to do', said one, 'is find out who we are'. This member was interviewed by *The Observer* newspaper (7 January 1996) at a time when she was planning to visit Canada to confront the Prime Minister. She was also writing a campaign letter: 'We, the ... innocent victims, demand what everyone else already has – the right to know who we are.' From one point of view, however, the issue is precisely what she *does* know. What she knows is that she is the daughter of an unidentified serviceman.

One significant relationship is acted out in Euro-American kinship, as the English women told us at the beginning when they talked of the effect of knowing about one's birth. That is *the (regulative) relationship between different areas of information*. The remarks made by Veronica situate personal identity in the context of relations with others that are nurtured over time, including with the biological mother, since Veronica imagined the physical connection as an emotional one as well. Given Euro-American ideas about the inheritance of characteristics ('I see their father's face'), Edwards argues that connections are drawn between different kinds of identities – psychological (personal characteristics), biological (physical origin) and social (the parent positioned in a network of relationships). In the discourses encouraged by the new technologies, these different arenas are separated out again as discrete domains of expertise (cf. Moore 1996: 10). Open government is also about bringing together types of expertise. What becomes normalised in the 'constrained conflict' of those relationships (between domains of information) is the utility or desirability of information itself.

There now exists a large literature and many commentaries[20] on the secrecy with which people may conceal the facts of birth, alongside a general apprehension that as far as the new technologies are concerned Euro-Americans are moving from a situation where concealment was always an option to a position where, in favour of open knowledge, concealment is regarded as deleterious. Society ought to be able to absorb the implications of technology. But while 'society' can absorb any amount of information to regulative effect, information with constitutive effects might make us think again about the partitioning of expertise and the value given to openness.

Perhaps we should not be led by the rhetoric of transparency in government, or *per contra* by detective work needed in litigation, and simply assume that openness is an ethical premise to issues of knowledge raised by reproductive medicine. Or, better, if we do wish to pursue openness then we should know that part of the stimulus comes from certain politics of communication (open information for a free society; truth for the sake of justice),[21] and not from systematic investigation into kinship practices. A moment's reflection tells us that it is precisely because governments have reasons to withhold facts, to be selective about what becomes public, that information is a matter of concern to citizens and investigative journalism is championed as protecting the right to know. In the right to know comes a (regulative) enablement: being able to choose the right course of action. By contrast, I have been arguing that in the case of kinship, as Euro-Americans construe it, there are (constitutive) areas in which there are no choices. The lawyers in the Californian father's case claimed as a right his desire not to continue to be the father. But, as far as the information about the genetic origins of his children was concerned, he could do nothing about what others in his situation might instead have wished, to claim a right not to know.

O'Donovan asks why the blood tie matters (1989: 105). In contrasting the children of donors and the children of adopting parents, she notes the current presumption[22] that absence of information about parental identity is a 'gap' in knowledge. She quotes Tresiliotis's views of adoption: there is a psychological need for personal history material in 'the formation of a positive concept of self'. In his view, such 'information is "a fundamental right" in "the quest for roots, origins and reunions", where adoptees are "seeking to 'complete' themselves"' (O'Donovan

1989: 100-1). But, as she points out, we do not know how many would choose *not* to trace their 'origins'.

This is not simply an English obsession with emotional health (see Morgan and Lee 1991: 162f on English legislation in the context of European practices). Contributions to Eekelaar and Šarčević (1993) couch the alleged need of the child to know in the language of human rights. For instance, Hegnauer (Zurich) suggests that attention on the right of childless couples to have a child needs to be balanced by considering the rights of the child: 'the real or imaginary delight of bringing up a child fills only about a quarter of a lifetime[!], whereas the problems of his genetic origin and psychological identity haunts the child to his end' (Eekelaar and Šarčević 1993: 211). Nielson (Copenhagen) flatly states that a child 'should be entitled to know if it was conceived by donation', and, as a separate though related issue, the identity of the donor. This entitlement should be the basic right of the child, because without it the child 'would be deprived of the possibility of having a true conception of himself' (Eekelaar and Šarčević 1993: 218). And from the US, there is an assumption that when a family discloses the existence of a collaborating donor or surrogate, the 'children will be intensely interested in their missing biologic parent' (Robertson 1994: 124).

Different countries regulate donor disclosure in different ways. However, three kinds of identification are generally recognised – identifying the circumstances of birth, that is, naming the technology; identifying the characteristics of the donor without naming him or her (often called 'non-identifying' disclosure), and identifying (naming) the person of the donor. It is revealing that these do not need to go together. In relation to donor insemination (DI), the Canadian Royal Commission recommended non-identifying disclosure, entailing openness as to the use of DI (creating thereby 'DI families') and secrecy as to the identity of the donor. In this intriguing (Euro-American) view of identity, the manner of birth and the characteristics of the parent still tell the child about itself, even if it is devoid of relationship. Here access to information about the parent is not about creating a relationship with the parent (which would imply the absent parent's willing consent, and therefore the child's right could not be held *against* the parent) but about personal information.[23] By contrast, the named identity of that parent opens up the question of the child's place within a network of other persons. It also opens up the question of continuities: how to deal with the lapsed period, whether the future will lead to continued contact, whether the knowledge is to bring obligations and duties that can now be discharged. One may add, then, that what may be non-identifying information about a donor will be all too 'identifying' as far as the existing parent is concerned. He becomes identified as having no blood tie after all.

Where does O'Donovan's gap come from? It comes from information. This is because, as in the case of ODAC, it is the *information* that a child is born from donation which itself creates the question of origins. Where it is thus constitutive, information cannot be screened for relevance or applicability: one either knows or does not. Hence such information raises questions about the value of not-knowing. Yet ignorance, or even more so the desire to keep facts secret, is rapidly being constructed as a 'deviation' from the normalising desire to know. An overview on donor insemination prepared for the Royal Commission refers to the 'move internationally to be more open about DI practice' (Achilles 1992: 28). However, it cites the Australian bioethics committee[24] who came to the conclusion that the 'social parents' should have the choice whether or not to tell. Robertson (1994: 123) says that 'as a matter of public policy, the question of secrecy or disclosure to the child is best left to the couple to resolve'. The couple of course do not resolve it themselves: they resolve it with the help of the cultural presuppositions which inform their actions. In a cultural milieu where disclosure is valued for its own sake, people may feel under particular pressure to be open. The keepers of secrets as new cultural dissidents!

The English remarks on adoption (above, p. 66) were proffered in the context of a general discussion of secrecy (Edwards 1993: 61; Edwards n.d.). Edwards' interlocutors regarded secrets about parentage as undesirable largely because they are impossible to keep – they have a nasty habit of popping up: 'knowledge will out' – and it is damaging when a secret emerges. At the same time, they thought that revealing genetic origins might send children off to trace their other parents, and it might be best if matters were kept from them – 'if it were not, that is, for the social "do-gooder" ... conceptualised as the expert/professional who thinks it best for the offspring to know "the truth"' (Edwards n.d.). Secrecy may come under attack from professionals concerned with counselling, who themselves can only act on the basis of what information they gather about their clients. They may regard keeping secrets as emotionally deleterious, as Achilles reports, leading to 'adverse interpersonal relationships'. But then they have cases to hand. People who find out about their DI status at a late stage in life may report feeling deceived, and Achilles suggests that part of the problem such people experience comes from their parents' mixed attitudes towards the event: 'if the parents are secretive, the child may feel ashamed, whereas openness about the whole procedure may create a more positive attitude' (1992: 31). O'Donovan (1989) voices much the same hope. I do not, for my part, want to defend secrecy for its own sake. But possibly we should make an attempt to understand parents faced with the difficult 'choice' of either taking on themselves the screening of information from the child or else reconstituting their own relationships to him or her through the difference that the child's knowledge will make to them all. The small point I wish to add is that such choice can only be exercised at a threshold that excludes the child, for it can only take the form of a decision whether or not to tell in the first place.

Achilles quotes an interview with a man who in the cultural idioms of individualism and personality might either make you think he had invented his feelings for himself or else that he was giving vent to a universal human dilemma. He is talking about discovering his DI origins at the age of 37. 'I began to consider myself as a victim of a life-long deception. I cannot understand why it ever had to be secret, why my mother could not have told me at the age of five ... why there are no regulations, why this is supposedly better than adoption, and why I have no rights as a human being to know my own father' (1992: 30). Quite properly she expresses uncertainty about how to interpret anger of this kind. Most of the explanations tend to be in terms of the usually fraught circumstances under which people find out. But an element here could be a displaced disappointment that his parents were somehow not his parents after all. Which might suggest that up to then that is what they had been.

I doubt whether these observations of mine have much future.[25] On the contrary, history looking back to this moment may be amazed that there was ever any debate over concealing parentage – the very idea that Euro-Americans had a problem with telling children about their biomedical origins could come to seem fantastic. That would be a climate in which it will appear quite normal to be open about how children were conceived and by whom conception was facilitated. It could be as normal as today's acknowledgement of the single parenthood and unmarried partnerships which have rendered much of the stigma of illegitimacy obsolete. Only inspection of the historical records of the 1990s might indicate a more complex state of affairs.

The last decade has witnessed a swing in several countries from value put on secrecy in gamete donation to value put on the child's right to know. Looking back, any hesitation about open knowledge may come to seem one of the areas of unfreedom that neo-liberal institutions and interest groups were bound to sweep away. By setting up public debate, then, liberal government has worked to demolish this area of unfreedom (see note 21). One can envisage the new suppositions that will result. The debate on anonymity will be rewritten as a simple matter of concealing the technical facts of parenthood. Scientific knowledge with its premise of independent verifiability will be re-embedded within kinship as molecular knowledge with its promise of rewritten organisms. Euro-American parentage, in short, will lie in those specific facts about procreation and conception, and genetic ancestry, that Euro-American technology can assist.

The future is always too simple. My plea for contemporary complexity is to consider things as they are at present, and thus to remake the present as (always too) complex. I do not mean to recall just the contests and unresolved ambiguities which biomedicine evokes – the present is systemically complex, as Rheinberger reminds us. We do not know which of our current practices will turn out to have been a precondition for the future. This is simply not predictable. We do know that whether those aspects of procreation which technology assists will indeed come to seem all important or else pale into insignificance, is going to depend on other things of which we are not at the moment aware. It could be, for example, that the question of birth origin will become trivial by comparison with ethical issues surrounding other aspects of parentage and parenting. If the very concept of 'biological kinship' becomes absorbed by the concept of technologically-assisted relations,[26] then what we now mark as 'social' will also have become redistributed among diverse ways of thinking about kinspersons. Perhaps people will not want to find out about their personal past. It is extrapolating (aspects of) *present* thinking into the future which renders problematic my thoughts about 'refusing' the technical facts. That is because such facts are how we have come to imagine the facts of life. Isn't this, after all, the information which we imagine we shall be passing on? The answer can only be, for as long as these facts about the techniques and processes of procreation continue to come as information, and for as long as refusing information is conflated with refusing self-knowledge.

The stark portrayal of parenthood by the historian Carolyn Steedman (1986) is apposite. Her own mother, she says, was someone who refused reproduction. She did not want to replicate herself, had not liked herself enough as a child to want children. The social reasons she gave, of which her daughter was constantly reminded, that children were a financial burden or whatever, simply sat to one side of her wished-for refusal to reproduce at all. She did not wish to perpetrate her manner of relating to her world. Since she bore children, her refusal took the form of refusing to mother. Her only recourse was not to behave according to the rules of good mothering. The daughter adds a comment on how few means, social or psychological, women had in the early years of the century to act out such a refusal. At the end of the century, Euro-Americans give information such procreative potential that even to look for the means to refuse it (information) seems pinched and narrow. Pursuing such means would, all the same, enlarge the horizon of possibilities from which the future will come, and thereby enlarge the scope for outcomes at present unpredictable.

ACKNOWLEDGEMENTS

A version of this chapter was first given to an International Sympo-sium on *Governing Medically Assisted Human Reproduction,* University of Toronto, 1996. An abstract is published in the proceedings of the symposium edited by Lorna Weir (Centre of Criminology, University of Toronto, 1997). I thank the organisers for the considerable stimulation. Some will see an unintended irony in my drawing on the Canadian ex-perience to talk about the values of open knowledge, since the conduct of the Commission was heavily criticised on the grounds that the 'research process was cloaked in secrecy' (Eichler 1993: 196). A fuller version was subsequently presented to the *Culture of Biomedicine* conference noted in the Preface.

My thanks to colleagues for permission to cite unpublished papers. I am also grateful to Barbara Bodenhorn for an extensive commentary, to Frances Price for her many insights into the issues and observations on the text, and to Lorna Weir for both sending me materials and offering comments. Melissa Demian added an important clarification. I have also benefited from criticism in various venues including the Lucy Cavendish College Archaeology and Anthropology Society.

PART II

PROPERTIES

CHAPTER 5

New Economic Forms: A Report

Both those who think they exemplify the new and those who think they exemplify the old may, in pursuing that very division, be radical agents of change. If there is a kind of congruence or interdependence here in their efforts, perhaps it is part of what Otàvio Velho has described as the *fait accompli* of globalisation. He puts a concrete image before our eyes: for the anthropologist the experience might be akin to seeing people going Pentecostal all over the world (Velho 1996: 101). The battle between God and the Devil that Neo-Pentecostalism enjoins is a dualism to undo other dualisms. Moreover, while it was a nominally Lutheran pastor from Hagen who took me aside in 1995 with a message he wanted to relay to England, Velho's remark (1996: 116) about Pentecostalism in Brazil spreading across the entire religious field was also echoed in the Hagen area. Public meetings of the long-established Lutheran church, as well as Roman Catholic, can now resemble those of the much more recent Assembly of God,[1] with its promise of charisma and fellowship, and work in the name of similarities. Observing that Papua New Guinea is now one of the most Christian countries of the world, the pastor said I must return to England where he knew there were few believers and bring people back to God.

From that perspective, this is a report from the past. I have not joined the 'new fellowship' of the late 1990s. Rather, this is a report from thirty years before (1964-65): what 1995 seems like from the perspective of descriptions that were valid then. We might still ask what time the analysis is in, a question I return to in Chapter 7. Here I make specific some of the horizons from which I have had the opportunity to ask it.

The Hagen of 1995 certainly recalled the Hagen of 1964-65 ('1965' for brevity and symmetry) in the extent to which people commented on the divergence of old and the new in their lives. That is not new. But now it seems a division to undo other divisions. It is against a kind of generational battle that people enact the new order. Yet what to a Euro-American might seem familiar developments in its wake, a new kind of individual on the one hand and on the other expanded opportunities for consumption, from the viewpoint of 1965 also call for something of an explanation. I suggest we look at the evolution of certain specific relationships. This chapter considers the individual as an emergent product of the state, and consumption as entailing an efflorescence of certain kin-based relations. The following three time horizons reflect fieldwork opportunities.[2]

THREE HORIZONS

Thirty years ago, in the mid-1960s, the processes of pacification which had been interrupted by the Second World War had had their effect throughout the Papua New Guinea Highlands: no fighting, people quietly buried in the Christian manner even though Christian converts were few, local government councils just set up and coffee coming into cultivation as a cash crop. Everyone in Hagen was predicting the end of the *moka* system – ceremonial exchange between clan groups – and the future of business. Indeed some anthropologists (notably Finney 1973) had argued that the style of Highlands bigman 'leadership' was preadapted to entrepreneurial activity. Men wanted tradestores and the government should provide roads. 'Roads' became a metaphor for what people saw as a dividing of the ways; the past and the future were both present, and one could be as it were either a past or a future person,[3] follow the ways of the ancestors or follow the ways of commerce.

Meanwhile, clans in the Northern Melpa area of Hagen were capitalising on the huge influx of shell valuables that had come with the opening-up of the Highlands just before the Second World War. The Australians had needed trade goods; at one point Highlanders were extracting cowrie and other small shells from the tiny expatriate population at an estimated rate of half a million per month (Hughes 1978: 315). These shells moulded the form of bridewealth and other life-related payments;

above all they stimulated clan groups into competitive exchanges, based in the 1960s on the then receding horizon of warfare; the underlying rationale for massive *moka* gifts was homicide compensation.

The staple sweet potato was divided between pigs and people, and pigs accompanied shells in exchange. In men's eyes such transactions eclipsed the productive activity in which men and women both engaged. That division between transaction and production was a stimulus to my much later stressing a gender divide between same-sex and cross-sex relations. The former captured primarily the stance of men in their relations with other men, which led to clan-based, collective activity in a way not true of same-sex relations among women. Cross-sex relations referred to ties between men and women that always had a particularistic cast to them, rendered in terms of conjugality or kinship. What was true between persons was also true within: persons could so to speak align their various elements – aspects of the body, behaviour – into a same-sex state, while their makeup as members of paternal agnatic clans at the same time nourished and protected by maternal kin simultaneously provided a cross-sex template.

Cross-sex relations were more the focus of women's than men's concerns. To men it was a question of securing a home base from which to engage in the world, while women demanded from men recognition of their input. The horticultural division of labour – men clearing gardens and women planting and harvesting them – was the idiom in terms of which this relationship was presented as one of (unequal) reciprocity. Women took such advantage as they could in pressing their particularistic claims in other ways; thus blood spilt in a quarrel would lead to claims for compensation, generally satisfied if the husband paid her male relatives. Women were structurally 'in between' groups of men, their multiple loyalties showing in a constitutional multiplicity of minds. Men on the other hand were alleged to overcome their conflicting emotions and orientations much more easily, and display the 'one mind' that was the predicate for successful action.

Ten years on, in the mid-1970s, the newly emergent state of Papua New Guinea had from the outset to deal with a problem no one had foreseen: what was called 'tribal fighting' in the Highlands. Reasons were many. They included the enlarged electoral boundaries which had destabilised old alliances, and the high coffee prices which had turned men's ambitions from tradestores to trucking and passenger vehicle business, with a toll of road deaths. Workers from outside Hagen provided labour for the large coffee and tea plantations in the process of transferral from expatriate to local ownership, and there was trouble when immigrants got caught up in disputes. (Many Hagen people themselves despised labouring – they could earn so much more locally from their own coffee and market gardening.) Above all, the introduced judiciary system proved inadequate to coping with the political dimensions of homicide, and people took the law into their own hands. Homicide payments took on a different character, huge sums being demanded in cash, paid directly from the killer's to the victim's clan or tribe. Some might turn into reciprocal *moka* exchange – *moka* certainly had not disappeared as predicted – but otherwise the effort that went into raising such payments was like the effort that went into the purchase of a vehicle: however the money circulated, it was not channelled back into the hands of the donors through counter-gifts.[4] Shells meanwhile were leaving the area altogether, devalued in favour of money.

If the influx of shells with the first advent of the Australians had had a democratising effect, as Andrew Strathern argued, producing bigmen with a losing battle on their hands trying to maintain their monopoly by channelling the shells through themselves, then the effect was specifically on relations among men. Cash crops and market gardening had a second democratising effect, and here women were also involved. Since money came in 'small' as well as 'large' amounts, it seemed all right for them to have access to small amounts while men commandeered large ones. As a consequence, women not only emerged with resources of their own (however tiny) but were also seen as visible supporters of their menfolk when men came crying for extra money. Women owned money in the way they never owned shells. At the same time, it was also possible for men to deny women's input into their activities; the pig that had been the prime symbol of joint conjugal effort was if need be obtained through purchase.

I found myself at this time (1970s; see M. Strathern 1981) writing about the rhetoric of consumption. Consumption, expressed above all in women's stated desire that they reared pigs to eat, had before seemed part of the cycle of production and consumption which concerned those particularistic cross-sex relations focused on conjugality and kinship. These were both insulated from and eclipsed by the sphere of transaction. So when I wrote earlier about production and transaction, production subsumed consumption. But now the issue seemed rather men's rhetorical contrast between production and transaction on the one hand and consumption on the other. Production and transaction together helped define the new sphere of commercial enterprise (Pidgin, *bisnis*). As far as the lucrative coffee was concerned, for instance, men and women were both producers of cash. Men's large sums of money ideally went towards collective prestigious purchases or transactions, more businesses or 'money-*moka*'. Whether or not the final payment was for something that would be returned to them, on the analogy of exchange, the very activity of collecting the money involved any number of side transactions. Men also looked to their home base, calling on women's 'small' amounts to supplement their transactions. But women were liable to spend their money on children, on food when they were short, and on clothes, soap (women spending on soap and thus making themselves alluring might be a source of male suspicion), kerosene, school fees, and so forth. This 'consumption' could be rhetorically construed as spending on oneself, and was claimed by men to be typically female. Women complained of men's consumption in turn – what with their beer drinking and sheer capacity to squander large sums of *kina* (dollars) on useless activities by contrast with their own virtuous garnering of hard-won *toea* (cents).

Meanwhile, land was being taken out of the horticultural cycle for coffee growing. There was a kind of pioneering spirit about 'business' under the newly independent state. Some Northern Melpa had returned to settle on land they had once occupied along the banks of the Wahgi river in the Central Melpa region; the control of the malaria introduced when the Highlands were opened up and the draining of the Wahgi swamp (for plantations) had rendered it re-inhabitable. If by the mid-1970s the number of returnees had grown substantial, by the mid-1990s this new settlement area was stretched to population capacity. The effect of drainage had been to bring a lot of peat-rich land into cultivatable use, and it was regarded as supremely fertile. I was told that crops planted here cut the interval between planting and harvesting, in some cases by as much as a third, by contrast with the thinner mountainous soils of Northern Melpa. The popularity of this area was further enhanced by its proximity to Mt Hagen town, declared in 1995 Papua New Guinea's 'third city'. Mt Hagen was a place to buy things – suits and jackets, kerosene stoves, calculators and cassette players, dietary supplements to make one fat, Christian tracts in Pidgin and English, fast foods and air tickets. It was also a place to sell. The marketplace boasted fresh produce – broccoli, mangetout, aubergine – that went far beyond the cabbages and Irish potatoes introduced in the 1950s. Women planned contract-growing in order to take advantage of the bulk buyers who flew produce to Moresby.[5]

In 1995 I watched a chip garden being brought into cultivation. Sharleen worked in a fish and chip shop in the town and her idea was that she would become the sole supplier of potatoes. She hired non-Hagen labour (unemployed immigrants living in the town) for the heavy work of ditching and turning the soil, bringing in women from her husband's place to help plant the plots. Everyone was pleased to see her come, and made it quite an occasion. Before the planting began, she poured (white) chemical fertiliser over the black peat soil. Sharleen had been given the land by her mother's parents, since her mother herself lived in Moresby and had only intermittently cultivated gardens there. This was unusual. Daughters often maintained claims to their father's land but did not pass them on; here, in the absence of the daughter, the daughter's daughter was using her natal land.

Other sisters/daughters had taken up not just usufruct rights but permanent or semi-permanent residence in the new settlements,[6] invariably with the reason that the land was so good and money came easily. It was not possible to establish how widespread a phenomenon this concentration might be, but it was certainly marked in this particular area. Not only daughters but their husbands, and other relatives who could claim a tie through women, joined the settlements. And not only contacts from within Hagen – there was a sizeable population of non-Hageners, from the lone Indonesian to a whole number from the Southern Highlands to men from Enga Province married to Hagen wives or retiring there after government service in the town. In the name of the dominant tribal group (Kawelka) to which the land belonged, residents claimed they were the fastest-growing group in the region.

Four points conclude this narrative. First, people were recovering from a series of deaths for which several clans, with varying degrees of responsibility, were paying in pigs (now worth K500-800, the largest up to K1,000) and money (K20,000-30,000 might be demanded for one homicide). People were fed up with fighting and paying, and flocked instead to charismatic and fellowship worship (some congregations the offshoots of the Pentecostal church), helped by the drinking ban in the province that made the vow not to drink easier to keep, and worried in any case about heaven and earth ending at the millennium. Second, marketing was ubiquitous: there was no public event that did not bring forth rows of vendors spreading out their nylon sacking (old imported wheat flour bags) on which they put not just sugar cane and cucumber for refreshment but cooked food, roasted corn, buns and scones, sweet potatoes. Women earned regular amounts from this, and a man late on his way home could buy a snack in case there was no meal when he got there, while wifeless men could provision themselves in a way that had never been possible. Third, pressure on land around the settlements was severe. Forage areas for pigs were seemingly being reduced by the month, and instead of pigs roaming during the day when they grubbed up all sorts of food, they had to be tied up. This was very labour-intensive, because they needed to be moved around with the sun, and the ropes constantly broke as they tugged to be free. Finally, women's bodies had changed shape. They are not I think stooping in the gardens less, and they continue to hump burdens, but many no longer wear netbags hanging down over the nape of the neck which gave a bowed effect to their composure, or turn their feet and legs inwards in the contained manner they had had. Instead, women march about with uncovered heads and swinging arms, and school leavers sit in any which way. The netbags they do carry are usually bright and decorative; one of the first sights a tourist at Hagen Airport has is of a large section of the perimeter fence covered with rows of vivid bags for sale. To those looking for signs of women's laxity, such decorativeness may arouse as much ire as toilet soap. At the same time, netbags have become a ubiquitous sign of local tradition, whether 'Hagen' or 'Highlands' or even 'Papua New Guinea'.[7] Making such bags, for women but also versions for men, and men's associated netted caps, is perhaps the only exclusively female work I saw. Most people are also fatter.

Perhaps this sounds a familiar story, told countless times. What is its interest?

DIVIDED PERSONS

The discussion starts with something that is also familiar: the observation that money is divisible, all-purpose and a measure of value as well as a medium of exchange. But this happens to be a new observation and at least to the person making it unfamiliar. I am not referring to lecture notes on Malinowski or Firth (see e.g. G. Dalton 1971: 168) but to what Sharleen's mother's brother, Manga, said at the culmination of many conversations about social change.

In the past, Manga observed, people had cowrie shells or pearlshells, and they did not think: if a man came up and asked for a pearlshell one would give it to him, or of it was a question of returning bridewealth at a divorce, then one just collected shells and pigs together and handed them over. There was not any other work for these things.[8] Each item was entire. It was both a single thing and had a single purpose – no one thought about keeping back part of a shell. But money is different. Money has a lot of work to do. One may think of buying food, or finding a bus fare or contributing to a compensation payment. When it comes to giving money to a person, one wants to hold some of it back. 'He has asked for K20, but I will give him K10 because I have another use for the other K10' ... By the same token, money can be divided into small amounts. A man has K100, but then some goes on this and some on that, and the entire amount no longer exists. Too many thoughts, said Manga, accompany its use. The usefulness of money encourages people to hang on to bits of it. And if money can be spent on numerous things then numerous things also have a price. A man looks at a dry casuarina tree and thinks, 'Oh, I can sell that to someone who has no firewood.' A man with a garden in fallow looks at the kunai grass growing there and thinks that someone may want it for thatch. 'In the past we just took the grass – now we have to buy it.'

Too many thoughts accompany its use: money divides the mind. The notion of a divided mind is familiar to Hageners. A person has conflicting thoughts, and action consists in resolving these thoughts into the single one that emerges as motivation. Indeed, this was the context in which I argued (M. Strathern 1988: 282) that the person emerges as an individual agent through the singularity of action. In the same way, a clan appears as a collective individual (Foster 1995a: 10-11 uses this phrase apropos New Ireland Tanga) when it is engaged on one enterprise, acts as a unit. It is the act which, through its temporality, individuates.[9]

Now Manga was glossing things a bit. It was always the case in the past that the clan acted as an individual unit, gathering together as 'one', only by suppressing its heterogeneous constitution in order to do so (and see Hirsch 1995b: 199).[10] Any gift of pigs or shell represented the hard-extracted contributions of persons who invariably had other uses for them. But Manga was using the singular manifestation of the complete shell or pig to say something about money: from this perspective it did *not* have an individuating effect. Money was always too suggestive of alternatives. So in handing only some of it over, one was not resolving conflicting intentions, in the single act, but rather activating the mind's divisions. This last observation on the divided mind had been prompted by reflection on divided persons. I had commented that people seemed to be disputing in court all the time, and Manga said it all came down to money. A wife looks to her husband for money, he said, and the husband looks to the wife, whether for the material provisioning these days called 'service' (*savis*) or for help with enterprises or as 'compensation' (*kompensesen*) for injury.

I take up Manga's analysis on this point of division, or multiplicity, the idea that money *could* be entire *if* it were not divided or fragmented, and his linking to divisions both within persons – their multiple orientations – and between persons – the expectations of parties to a relationship. There is a comparable dualistic cast to the way in which Hagen people phrase many of their reflections about change. Persons are also presented as divided in their minds between following old and new roads.[11]

Social anthropologists have sometimes approached the question of change by dividing culture or society into bits, as though it too could be entire if it were not fragmented. One would have a whole society if it weren't divided up! Of course, cultures and societies are neither completely whole nor completely divided. Nor are persons. Anyone who has lived in a moiety system or who reproduces under a rule of exogamy knows that, for the most significant social division is within the makeup of their own bodies.[12] But the Euro-American drive to think of society as a whole includes identifying conflict 'within', as in the identification of a tension between new and old. With greater or lesser irony, bits of the culture/society will be analysed as traditional and other bits as modern, contemporary, postcolonial, global, or whatever. It will be with irony because anthropologists know that tradition only survives if it is reinvented, and because they know that a valorised and explicit tradition is not the same as the unstated, implicit tradition visible only to the observer because to the bearer of it it is not tradition but life. The person who deliberately or in apathy follows the old ways lives in a world holding out the possibility of that choice. In any case, they know that history is continuous.

However, people in Hagen commonly deploy what Gellner[13] called an episodic rather than evolutionary conception of history. This is not 'change' in the sense of progressive development but the displacement of one kind of sociality by another. The conception holds across several scales.

First, the old world is already eclipsed by the new and people are living in a 'new time'; the new is now divided off from the old by virtue of the very fact that it contains both old and new. Second, these times may coexist, as Hirsch (1995b) has described for Fuyuge. I would understand Hagen people's stress on old versus new as a version of the alternating socialities which in the 1960s underlay the movement between ordinary and ritual time, between domestic and political orientations, between the spheres of production and transaction. Each time or type of social engagement can be seen (anticipated, as Hirsch notes) from the perspective of the other. The perspectival switch between such moments of social life may take the form of reciprocities as in donor/recipient relations, in that the one becomes the other at a future date, or may involve eclipsing identities, as in the transformative move from household production to ceremonial transaction. Third, if persons also afford a perspective on one another, and thus occupy alternating positions, then each person seemingly has within themselves the capacity to act in either an old or a new way. Manga, literate in Pidgin, instigator of many *bisnis* enterprises, with ambitions for future commercial exploitation of land round the settlement, also sets himself up as a traditionalist, conserver of old values and keeper of customary practices. His son Rupert, with tertiary education and full-time employment in Moresby, would have said that he in turn also followed Hagen *kastom* ('custom') in bringing gifts home for his mother and sister, as well as father, when he came on leave. Rupert's Hagen name is Kitim, the one his mother uses for him (see Chapter 7).

Two kinds of men

Work was a local topic of conversation, stimulated by people's activity in turning former pig pasture into garden land. In the old days, I was told, it was possible to get people to help by promising reciprocal work. But these days no one will join unless they are paid. This was especially true of the younger generation, to whom of course it was a means of independence for precisely the reason that older men would then spell out: that in the past young men would come to work because they depended on help later, especially with bridewealth. Young and old acknowledged the contrast between the generations and between dependent and independent persons.

In fact the refrain of self-regard cropped up everywhere. Middle-aged men expressed amazement about the ability of their juniors to ignore the demands of reciprocity. Manga's son, Rupert, seemed notably impervious to his relatives. His mother needed a new house and Rapa, a brother living in the same settlement area, built it for her, expecting that when Rupert returned from Moresby he would acknowledge this act. Rapa was taken aback to find that it simply did not enter into the young man's calculations.[14] The father, wondering why the son gave no thought to investing in relations for the future, paid Rapa for the house himself so that the man would not feel badly towards Rupert. When Rupert did come on leave, the young man largely ignored the garden work going on, neither helping there and then nor paying his father or brothers for labour in lieu. People who spend on themselves or who only want to work to earn money for themselves may be accused of taking resources out of the flow of reciprocities. Reciprocity ordinarily enacts an exchange of perspectives – each person sees him or herself from the point of view of the other. Dependency can thus carry a positive connotation when it refers to mobilising relationships, and people are seen to grow important with the relationships by which they are supported. So why did Manga's complaints fail to affect Rupert, fail to have the purchase they once might have done?

In the past, the person who publicly denied the significance of relationships boxed him or herself into a corner. To be relationless was to be rubbish, the lot of men who had no wives or women who had no natal kin or men who avoided public life. To be rubbish meant having nothing to put on the skin – the wealth that enhanced a person – which is why women were categorically rubbish. The relationless person could respond neither to the collective rhetoric with which bigmen, trying to get their clansmen to forget their own affairs and join together in a group event, inflated the unity of the clan, nor to the multiple rhetoric which worked when people were balancing claims or augmenting clan affairs with extra-clan resource. Is it that today, when anyone can hang themselves around with clothes which indicate money, these ends can be achieved through solitary means? On the one hand, the consumer market allows for the inflation of self-regard; on the other hand, persons can multiply themselves through the range of products available for consumption. If so, we would be in a familiar world indeed, where it is the market that returns a perspective on the consumer.

There is more here than just a new sense of individual goals and personal independence. Recall the present day *loss* of oneness which Manga observed. This was the individuated self seen from the external perspective of another. Gift exchange could objectify that possibility in dividing off donor from recipient; it mobilised collective relations; it also mobilised a wide spectrum of extra-group relations which turned persons in different directions. In all these, gift exchange appeared as an enhancer of relationships, the very carrier of reciprocity. But it was precisely developments in exchange practices over the last thirty or more years which seems to have presaged the self-regard of the consumer.

Two kinds of relations

In a classic article commenting on Hanuabada, a Motu settlement out-side Port Moresby, in the 1970s, Gregory (1980) distinguished two types of gifts: gifts to men and gifts to God. The former reembed gifts in an exchange cycle which keeps the goods in circulation (investment in re-lationships) while the latter take them out of circulation. He is referring in the second sense to the massive donations that Christian clans were giving to churches at that period, donations made with great publicity and conserving the ranking of the clans which is at the basis of Motu gift giving, but with no return to the donors. This has happened in Hagen to some of the compensation payments given for homicide, and increas-ingly so since the 1970s. While in the recent past such payments had often been the start of reciprocal relations between groups, who kept the flow going, a second and alternative road exists these days (1990s) which takes the form of non-returnable payments. These payments evoke a reciprocity of a kind, insofar as they are intended to pacify the recipients in return for life taken and to assuage angry feelings in order to avert re-venge. Economically, however, they function for the recipients as capital which they are free to invest in other relationships, and for the donors as alienable or 'altruistic' gifts do in a commodity economy.[15] Most impor-tantly, from the donors' point of view, their wealth passes out of circula-tion. So the archetypical gifts to men in Hagen (homicide compensa-tion) can nowadays equally well work for the donors like 'gifts to God'.

The contrast between transactions which keep wealth in circulation and those which remove wealth from circulation corresponds to an in-digenous postcolonial practice: the division in compensation payments between 'restitution', the compensation or equivalent that went to the victim, and an extra amount ('shaking hands') to appease feelings (M. Strathern 1972: 25-6). Sometimes the extra was called *baiim lo* ('buy-ing/paying law'), though that phrase, like *kompensesen* ('compensation')[16] itself, could also be used of the whole payment. In the 1990s, an equiva-lent to the payment for breaking the law was said to be money handed over, in the local magistrates' courts, to magistrates in order to repay them for their trouble. Although there might seem a difference between payment to make a person feel good and paying a magistrate, the fact that an extra amount was provided beyond the restoration of equivalence (compensation) seems to be taken as a significant factor.[17] In the same sense, and whether or not it was reciprocal, the gathering and dispersing of the huge wealth needed for homicide compensation created for the donors a relationship of a kind to the state. Compensation – restoring an equivalence – was encouraged as a strategy to prevent further disruptive fighting:[18] national and provincial governments alike came to have an interest in settlements by such means. Without the cessation of reprisals, they could not guarantee safe passage to coffee buyers and vehicles; did not in certain areas admit war injuries to hospital. The state, we may say, wanted to promote a flow of sentiment towards itself, so that people would think of law and order and stop fighting. Perhaps this was foreshadowed in the public feelings expressed towards the kin of homicide victims in the context of a one-way flow of reparations.

Elsewhere, two-way flows have continued. While it would seem, for the people I met in the 1990s, that group *moka* in the Northern Melpa mode was no longer popular or viable, there was talk of a different kind of *moka*, on the Central Melpa pattern, where sets of clansmen combine to give jointly to their respective maternal kin. The flow of sentiment between kin linked in such particularistic relations might seem the very antithesis of generalised feelings towards the nation state. We shall see there are more connections than one might suppose.

Flows of sentiment

If compensation to enemies is to assuage their feelings, make them feel cool, the idioms are said to be borrowed from the personally-felt sentiments between kin linked through the marriages of women. These are the relations particular to kinship obligations, and prestations accompanying life events, especially brideweath and death payments. In the 1960s and 1970s intermarried allies paying for help given during fighting might have used as a rationale the need to make relations with maternal kin good.

Now insofar as these collective exchanges between groups involved men, we can think of them as predicated on same-sex relations, with all the rhetoric of brotherly solidarity that same-sex gender carried for them. Women had a special interest, however, in those exchanges which their husbands made with their own male kin. This was not surprising, perhaps, for on such occasions instead of being divided by the demands of different men – husband, brother – the woman was so to speak brought together ('composed') through their combination in her. Depending on one's perspective, then, one could see such exchanges either as same-sex transactions between men (e.g. male in-laws) or as mobilising cross-sex relations (focusing on the intermediary tie of the woman). When the woman was thought of as intermediary, those relations between men also divided a man off from other males – between loyalties towards his agnates and loyalties towards (say) his wife's brothers.[19] In short, the enactment of cross-sex relations between men (i.e. men in a relationship mediated by a woman) that had a composing effect for the woman, created both the possibility of a division of interests for a man and the possibility of an expanded base for operations that he 'added' on top of his agnatic relations.

These two gender positions show above all in payments to maternal kin. As Wagner (1967) first argued for Daribi, one of the functions of payments to maternal kin in patrilineal kinship regimes such as Hagen is to separate off a person's agnates from others who have claims on him. The maternal kin who look over the growth and bodily development of, and are thus bodily part of, the sister's child, are from time to time compensated by the paternal kin for their contribution. In making these payments, agnates define themselves (making themselves 'one'). As a consequence, a man's feelings are oriented towards these cross-sex kin in the very acts through which he detaches himself as separate from them. Now in Daribi the child is thought of as literally belonging to the maternal kin unless the agnates make this payment; in Hagen it is much more a case of keeping the feelings of maternal kin flowing towards one in a kindly way so that they will continue to bestow blessing and provide nurture.[20] Hageners thereby exploit the expansive possibilities of this relationship: if they feel well-disposed, then maternal kin will be a source of future support. In other words, Hagen men emphasise both same-sex detachment – groups of men compensating each other – and cross-sex attachment, the flow that was instigated by an initial act of nourishment from a woman. Indeed I was very struck in 1995 by constant expressions of anxiety about making sure people felt well-disposed towards others and felt good in themselves. This was no doubt stimulated by Pentecostal preaching. However, when it involved payments to maternal kin, I was told that it expressed what was quintessentially Papua Niugini *kastom*. Hence I have conserved the present tense.

Here is Pamun, father of several children, active on the local school PTA, and claiming personal responsibility for encouraging families from other provinces to settle nearby. We were discussing various categories of kin who had received at a party (*pati*) an aged man had given to anticipate his funeral and enjoy the distribution in his lifetime.

When someone dies, Pamun said (I am paraphrasing), the close maternal kin will bring a pig to the mourners to eat, perhaps K100 too. The money is for buying food during the first mourning period. At the end of this [a week or so] the agnates of the deceased pay back the maternal kin, perhaps K500 or K800, many times the original amount. *Kandere* [from the English 'kindred' but in specific reference to maternal/sororal kin] is an important thing. They say, 'Oh, our sister's son has died, and if he were alive then he would give us pigs and make *moka* with us, but now the man has died, and only men borne by other women are left, and they will look after their own *kandere.*' So the agnates think of the bad feelings that the bereft *kandere* have, and give them gifts. Or else the *kandere* accuse the agnates for letting the man die, and demand compensation. – The point about bad feelings is that such sentiments will invariably have a forward effect, so that maternal kin will continue to have an interest in the body of kin left, even though their own sister's child has died. If payment (compensation) stimulates positive feelings, it can also serve to detach negative feelings so that the agnates will then be left in peace. – Anyway, even in a man's lifetime, he must make payments to these maternal kin. They complain if a person does not buy their body (*baiim skin*) in this way. This is the old law. In Papua New Guinea, Pamun concluded, *kandere* is a big thing. 'If we do not look after them they will not look after us, and we shall get sick and die.'

However, the normative cast of this statement is misleading. There is tremendous latitude over whether or not such payments are made. Indeed there is a crucial second tier of explanation, which Pamun also supplied: one would only send gifts to those maternal kin with whom relations had been kept up. In other words, if these people do not visit (and bring gifts) then no gifts go in return. In the case of the old man who was celebrating his funeral distribution, his own maternal kin had long faded into the background, and the gifts were to the maternal kin of the next generation. Among all the maternal kin who might receive, it is those who 'work' at the relationship who will also 'eat' subsequently.[21]

As a supporting exhortation, Hageners may present looking after one's *kandere* as distinctively Papua New Guinean 'tradition' (*kastom*). It was as a self-proclaimed traditionalist that Manga was planning a large gift to his own maternal kin, to be orchestrated with that made by a fellow member of his subclan to his maternal kin from elsewhere. The combined prestation would make it quite an occasion. He explained the cultural logic.

> These people have fed us, given us the breast, and in return we give them pigs and money. Because they continue to feed us, and as they

fed us when we were little, so we buy our bodies with pay. After all, a man fathers [bears, in Hagen; the same term for women having children] his child, and he looks after him on his [clan] land, but it isn't only the father who is involved; there is also the mother! She too bore the child. And the maternal kin see that the child's agnates are happy, but if they do not think of the mother then their own thoughts become a little angry [*popokl*]. In the same way as the child drank at the mother's breast, then they [the *kandere*] too should eat.

Now Manga's maternal kinsman had elicited an earlier payment with advance solicitory gifts of pigs, and Manga had already reciprocated with a gift which included two cooked pigs, as well as live ones. The cooked pigs, bought for K500-600 each, were handed over with special instructions. They were to be eaten specifically by the young men of his maternal clan who were to put the jawbones in the cemetery; the ghosts of that clan would then look after their sister's son (Manga). Manga's maternal kin are now pressing for a further prestation. He regards the gift as falling within the rubric of *moka* (compensation to the maternal kin with *moka* 'on top'). 'We no longer give *moka* in the way we used to', he added,[22] and surmised that it would be his 'last'.

Manga thus places the gifts squarely within a traditional orbit. He expressed nostalgia for the passing of *moka*, and emphasised what Papua New Guineans think of as *kastom*. If he is doing it on an inflated scale (though small, he stressed to me, by contrast with the kinds of payments Central Melpa used to make) then this belongs to the inflated regard which cross-sex relations in general and maternal relations in particular are today given. I take these two sources of regard as major motors of economic change.

ABSORBING EXCESS

Inflation in a commodity economy, oriented to productive consumption (see Gregory 1982: 31), implies a readjustment in the ratio of goods and money to one another. What would inflation in a gift economy, oriented to consumptive production, be like? Presumably it would entail changes in the rate by which relationships are reproduced. Inflation in a gift economy might thus be defined as an increase in the quantity of items, goods or money, against the capacity of relations to absorb them, that is, reproduce themselves by them. Relations expand to meet the increased circulation of items. They may expand through intensity of interaction, reproduced so to speak at each new moment of objectification or realisation. The result is not necessarily 'more relationships'; rather the underlying premise of reciprocity or obligation in relationships can simply be evoked more frequently and at a higher level of internal demand. So what is subject to increase are the occasions on which relations are activated. As Manga said, the presence of money has introduced many new occasions for husband and wives to test the basis of their support for one another. In lieu of the year-long division of labour, the fortnightly wage or visit to the market creates short-term expectations. Expectations of mutuality are constantly being put to the test.

My argument will be that, by providing a kind of cultural rationale for consumption, the very relations which absorb consumer items to a heightened degree also enable the development of individualistically minded consumers of a quite different cast. In turning to the sense we might make of the new individualism, as well as the new consumerism, I bring to my aid two recent works, Foster on nation-making in Melanesia and, more briefly than does him justice, Carrier on theories of consumption.

The individual

Foster (1995a; 1995b) develops the Dumontian paradigm of the (old) collective individual in order to contrast it with a (new) possessive individual. He links the latter to the emergence of the nation-state with its set of diffuse, abstract qualities to which people aspire, and which can theoretically be owned by anyone. Contemporary advertising targeted at an urban and middle-class Papua Niugini encourages people to think of themselves in terms of personal practices – what they eat, what they listen to on the radio, the comic strips they read – that locate persons within a national culture.

Foster's construct of the collective individual resonates with Hagen men's identification of an individuating orientation with (not against) a collective one: the capacity to be seen to act with 'one mind' or 'one body', as in a transaction. When people of Manga's generation complain instead about the person who gives no thought to others, they summon the old relation-less, autonomous individual who went his or her own way to his or her own social cost. They have only pity for such persons. Some today do indeed fit this category; on many others, however, this pity is quite wasted. And that is precisely because the new individuals are not relation-less either. On the contrary, if one looks again at the possessive individual whom Foster describes, it is clear that the self-orientation of such persons conceals a very real set of relationships. What the individual possesses is a range of generalisable qualities ('I'm like all those people who read the newspaper'; 'the law will protect my right to freedom') that constitute the basis of the relationship which the person has, *qua* individual, to 'the state', 'the nation', 'society' – these abstract entities each offer a slightly different character to their citizens, populace or members. The possessive individual, in this view, thus incorporates a relational capacity, able to draw to him or herself, as Foster argues (1995b: 165), objects waiting to be personalised through his or her acts of consumption. This is the *analogue* of Melanesian relationism, its displacement rather than its antithesis.

There is a close connection in Foster's account between the possessive individual and consumerism. In the materials which he considers (the representation of Papua Niugini in advertisements), the salient relations are those to the market, and the market, he argues, in providing ways of imagining the nation also prepares such persons for relations with the state. The Moresby newspaper-reading population, responding to direct appeals to national culture, and consuming the idea of a national state, perceive themselves as belonging to a society of similar consumer-citizens.[23] This is their world. No wonder older men in Hagen – and mothers and wives – in many cases simply got nowhere with their criticism of those who spent their money on consuming nationally available commodities.[24]

When it comes to supporting *kastom*, however, in the view that diverse local traditions (*kastom*) emerge as a stylistic variation within a cultural repertoire (*kastom*) (Foster 1992: 284), young and old unite in their appreciation of certain kinds of support to others. The new citizens have appropriated the idea of solidarity on the basis of similarity, as in looking after one's *wantok*, those with whom one shares a language, locality or some other identifying origin premised on similarity, along with a high value put on maintaining relations with *kandere* (maternal kin).[25] Where they can see expatriates operating their own *wantok* system, they regard anything to do with *kandere* as quintessentially Papua New Guinean. From a Hagen perspective we may speak of the former (*wantoks*) as assimilated to same-sex relations, the latter (*kandere*) to cross-sex relations. None of the older people would disagree: these cross-sex relations embody *kastom* indeed.

Cross-sex relations

In discussing *kastom* as a cultural category, Foster (1992) contrasts Hagen with the New Ireland Tanga, pointing out how the 1970s Hagen *moka* incorporated commodity relations (*bisnis*) in the same way as it incorporated money. We have seen that in the 1970s both *bisnis* and *moka* were counterposed to consumption. But if then men produced for exchange, and for collective purchases (production, including *bisnis,* was for 'transaction', whether more *bisnis* or *moka*), then in the 1990s much production work is explicitly geared towards 'consumption'. This affects gender rhetoric among other things. Men's appeal to other men (same-sex relations) to invest in transactions used to be backed up by their pointing to the perils of consumption as feminising and debilitating. Nowadays consumption (enjoying goods of all kinds) appears to have a new legitimacy.

Foster refers to pressure generated by 'expansive (social) reproduction' of the Hagen kind: money enables persons to expand their participation in exchange and augment the name of the donor. I return to the point that initially (1930s/1950s) inflation in shells caused an efflorescence of ceremonial exchange, since social access to these wealth items was considerably widened. At the same time, but especially during the second-wave inflation with the increase of money in circulation in the 1960s/1970s, it seemed that some people were behaving as though there were a 'surplus' of it. Bigmen in relation to little men and men as a whole in relation to women held on to their power base by siphoning off money through collective enterprises such as car purchase. This effectively dumped money outside (in the hands of car merchants). Men's same-sex exchange relations afforded expansion of this kind. They could blow up to huge proportions the competition that did not just speed up circulation but allowed men to simultaneously sweep up money, get rid of it and augment the name of the clan in doing so.

Has there been a third-wave inflation? Is this what we are looking at in the 1990s: inflation in the capacity to spend on consumer goods? If so, another set of relations has moved in, so to speak, with an expansive capability that enhances people's capacity to absorb goods of all kinds, and all-purpose goods, not just the expensive cars or compensation payments that require big sums. While much of this purchasing power is dumped outside the local economy (in the hand of foreign traders), it also keeps a local market afloat and thus keeps the capacity circulating (women selling buns). These are domestic relations, but domestic relations of a particular kind.

Now Carrier, with his colleague Heyman (Carrier and Heyman 1997; Carrier 1995), has recently criticised the anthropology of consumption for failing to take social issues into account, his example being the American housing market, where one cannot understand consumption patterns without also understanding status and class constraints, among others. The authors properly place consumption within the frame of social reproduction, in a context where the relevant unit is the household, although they imply that their analysis applies to other consumer regimes too. Their model locates consumption in the efforts of household members to locate themselves in a world they perceive as containing unequal groupings. The bourgeoisification of households in the English industrial revolution, with their demand for dinner services, wallpaper and sitting-room furniture, is well-known. This household, like the individuals who composed it, were as much products as they were creators of practices of productive consumption. Yet while household goods and items associated with what Euro-Americans regard as house-based activities are prominent as consumer goods in Mt Hagen town, it does not at all follow that the household is the social unit of consumption of such goods. It cannot avoid the purchasing of local services that Carrier and Heyman mention, but perhaps Hagen is becoming a consumer society without having to develop the domestic-applianced house. And that is because what is available for expansion is not contained within the aspirations of householders. I refer to domestic relations of another kind: *cross-sex relations* from a man's point of view and – though I do not develop it much here – same-sex relations from *a woman's* point of view.

The consumption of purchasable items has become locked into a set of relationships where the potential for expansion is enormous. These particularistic, domestic relations are thoroughly appropriate vehicles for increased intensity of interaction. Escalation comes not just from the quantity of consumer goods available, but from the *capacity* of these relations to grow and expand in intensity, variety and realisation. This possibility comes in turn from the fact that these relations are about sustaining good feelings – keeping up a flow of sentiment between kin. The obligation to attend to such relations characterises husband-wife, father-daughter and brother-sister cross-sex ties, and to a lesser extent same-sex relations between women, especially mother-daughter and sister-sister. A clan may increase the number of times it mounts a ceremonial exchange occasion, but it will be in terms of months and years; by contrast visits between consanguines and affines, with the expectations of hospitality, may become as regular as Sunday morning church and Sunday afternoon football.

This may be connected to other features of social life in the new settlement area. There has been a perceptible rise in the numbers of non-agnates establishing themselves on Kawelka clan land, often via ties through women, local groups being willing to absorb families wishing to put their 'contract' (*kontrak*) with them in expectation of support, financial and political. Increasing demands on husband and wives each to provision the other provide a ready set of reasons for the increasing turnover of spouses and rise in number of divorces. Relaxed territorial boundaries (a higher degree of interdigitation of garden claims) and relaxed rules of commensality (menstrual seclusion no longer practised) has exaggerated the feeling of being 'crowded' that some returnees felt.[26] In the place of those separations, the spacing and distancing of relationships which residential patterns and various rules of behaviour once offered, perhaps new iterations of relationships are called for. The effect is to intensify relations in terms of the interactions by which they are seen to be 'reproduced'.

However traditional they may also have been, Manga's payments to his maternal kin were also part of this reconfiguration of cross-sex relations. I do not mean to imply that there was a sudden influx of consumer goods into gift exchange, Pepsi and trainers where before there had been pigs and money. In 1995, bridewealth, child payments and other gifts mobilised the same principal items that they had twenty years ago. Consumer goods were not an object of exchange in that sense at all. For all that people need is money (you do not have to transact with consumer items if you can transact with the medium which purchases them). The very divisibility of money makes it 'useful' in this respect. But why should one link money to consumer goods? The link is pertinent in *the context of these relationships*.

Especially to maternal kin, but also between affines (future maternal kin), and non-agnates in general, ties constructed through women – for either men or women – were in the past regarded as potentially nurturing/threatening. While men always stressed how their children grew large on their clan (agnatic) soil, that was but one part of the agnatic clan's contribution to the growing person's health and vitality. *Kandere* (maternal kin), on the other hand, had a particular interest in the child's body, for it was body which they 'fed', through breast milk, through pork and other food, and through gifts; it was body they could harm through dissatisfaction at the way they were treated; and it was body for which the deceased's paternal kin paid at death to turn aside malignant influence. And this body that was the material manifestation, the objectification, of those substantiating relationships serves equally as the new body of the consumer.

On one occasion Ru Kundil[27] drew up the contrast for me. I was talking about vitamins and medicines to help different body functions, and he exclaimed at the attention that Europeans paid to their own bodies. 'We [Hageners] do not look after them,' he said (and I paraphrase), 'We do not give such thought to our bodies.' He offered a comparison with gardens:

> Europeans plant all different kinds of food so they will always have different food [in the shops]. But we [Hageners] don't: we don't aim to fill it up with examples of every kind, just what comes into our heads or what is at hand. What is important is that we allocate strips in the garden to other persons, distribute the garden among people [who would have claims on it]. This is what people hold on to [as their kastom]. They think of their maternal kin and in-laws and shared the food. Even (he observed a shade piously) in the old times of fighting, a refugee group who was not known at all might come pleading for land, and the hosts would allocate them gardens, give them food, and then later the grateful immigrants would give compensation to the hosts in return. Only today people do not think like that, and the skulmen [the educated] keep their money in their pockets and do not share it. They close their ears to requests from even those who share their blood, their mother's brothers.

In Ru's view, if relationships are in good order then the body will flourish as a sign of them. You don't attend (as Europeans do) to the body parts but to the conditions for personal good health, which rest in the relationships that support you. A person must have a good 'background' (bekgraun), i.e. kinsmen. The difference between paternal and maternal kin in this regard is, as Pamun also said, that in the case of maternal kin their nurture/protection has to be elicited. That is, such relations are a specific focus of reproduction. You can take it for granted that growing up on your father's land you will be nourished by it. But you cannot take for granted the continuing interest of maternal kin, and their blessing can only be secured by continuing, active involvement. That is why these relationships have a potential for expansion, and perhaps why Manga went out of his way to pay Rapa (see p. 96-7) when he could have – and in another epoch surely would have – subsumed Rapa's house-building under a dependent's obligations as a resident non-agnate.

There is a general heightened intensity to relationships through women, both with men and among themselves, to which this public acknowledgement of the importance of maternal kin acts as a kind of cultural background. Maternal kin care for you if you care for them, and in Hagen it shows in the body. What this may have also done is help create the consumer body – which in the end does not need relationships between persons to justify it at all.

Money in and of itself does not produce possessive individuals, nor does what I have called the inflation of the capacity to absorb consumer goods arise simply from their self-evident value. Relations between persons have developed in certain specific ways, and this chapter has given prominence to an enlarging field of cross-sex relations. While this creates a kind of ground for possessive individuals and consumer-citizens, it also produces another kind of individual altogether (Sykes pers.comm.).[28]

Let me come back for the last time to Manga's analysis of money, his comments about the way money sticks. A man cannot detach money from himself in the way he could detach a pearl-shell (say) – and it is that process of detachment which makes him an individual, 'one man' separated now from the debts owed to others, embodied in the wealth item that is handed over (cf. Gillison 1991). We may say that money both flows more than pearlshells did (everything has its price) and flows less (people cannot release it as a whole item but find themselves holding on to bits).

As we have seen, it was once the case that the kinds of payments that Hageners made to their maternal kin performed the double function of separating off sets of men from one another (the men who divided themselves through compensation) and of sustaining a flow of sentiment between kin linked by women who could be drawn upon for support. The first was an exercise of detachment – evinced in the whole shell that was handed over entire – and the second an exercise in continuing attachment – one had to go on working at such relations in order to realise their potential for future growth. The first had a momentarily individuating effect, in the discrete definition of men on both sides, the second an aggregating or heterogenising effect, of implicating persons in their composite dealings with one another. But over time that first individuating effect seems to be becoming harder to achieve by virtue of the fact that collective individuals are less rather than more evident in the 1990s; everywhere one sees *composite individuals*.[29] The efflorescence of cross-sex relations of all kinds, to which Manga's payments to his maternal kin contributed their part, has created different social persons. Those *moka*-like payments to maternal kin have become embedded in a different society.

For who are these people? Indeed, as 'a people', have they become a composite individual? The returnees have not divided themselves into territorial units as distinctly as they once did. That does not mean to say that groups do not come together for common purposes, as they do. Rather, a conglomerate of people is held together by heterogeneous ties, cross-sex as well as same-sex, Hagen and non-Hagen, the point being that any persons who count themselves in will do so on the basis of a specific, particularistic relationship that they have cultivated. For this they will have needed money. A new dignity for prosperity (Velho 1996: 112)? It is not irrelevant that the same kind of individual is also being produced by the present enthusiasm for Pentecostal-inspired Christianity: anonymous mass congregations, each member of whom taking Jesus individually into their hearts, binding themselves by personal protocols, may even have the power to rid people's bodies of the Devil. The diversity of some of these gatherings, drawn from numerous tribes, several provinces, men and women alike, all ages, took me aback. I had not seen anything like it before. Every person with a different sin, they are told, and each one of them seeking the same God of life.

POSTSCRIPT 1998

Since this was written two interesting papers have appeared, germane to aspects of the arguments presented here and pointing to shifts in relationships that are at once similar and dissimilar. Of course, social trajectories come from diverse horizons, and may be seemingly in or out of phase with one another, and within as well as between populations. These accounts from elsewhere in Papua New Guinea extend some of the analytical concepts deployed for Hagen.

The first concerns same-sex and cross-sex relations. I refer to Minnegal and Dwyer's (1997, also 1998) detailed data on the tiny population known as Kubo in the Strickland-Bosavi area. Here recent changes in residential arrangements and pig keeping, including the increased numbers of these animals and a new potential for monetisation, has accompanied a shift in their significance for social differentiation. What seems to have been 'lost' is the special bonding between pigs and their (female) carers, and thus the concomitant particularity of each pig along with the social distinctiveness it bestowed on the carer; among themselves women are as it were less differentiated from one another. By contrast, the sexes have become more differentiated from each other in their daily activities; those whose lives were once characterised by close husband-wife interaction experience a new degree of separation. In some respects, all this resonates with the second Hagen horizon described in this chapter. Now that Kubo pigs can be bought and sold with cash, men have independent access to them, while the identity of the animals themselves has, in the perspective of the market, become that of the generic 'pig', a source of money. Minnegal and Dwyer's analysis also dwells interestingly on a second source of differentiation loss and differentiation gain, namely the impact of a new Christian cult (millennial but not Pentecostal, and in addition to the already established Evangelical Church of Papua New Guinea). The cult has encouraged greater segregation of the sexes, with new protocols of modesty for women, while simultaneously homogenising relations within the two categories (of male and female). In short, some of the sources of the particularity that lay behind people's cross-sex conjugal relations, as in the distinctiveness of women's identity with particular pigs, has become displaced both by generic animals and by same-sex gender behaviour.

The second concerns collective and composite individuals. In describing the effect of Charismatic Catholicism on the North Mekeo peoples and their enthusiastic building of a new church, Mosko (1997; cf. 1985) reminds us of his own analysis of the open and closed body. The closed body renders the sorcery of others 'cold', while the open, 'hot' body has the power to enter the body of others. These were also generalised states of alternating sociality in which Mekeo villagers experienced their defence from penetration by others and, on the offensive, exposure to it. Money is 'hot' in this scheme of things. As he says: actions comprehended through exchange 'consist in the partial decomposition of one person – the giver – for the sake of the composition of the other – the receiver. Sociality is not merely give and take of things between persons, but expansion and contraction, give and take of tokens of the persons themselves.' Charismatic Mekeo open themselves to God, a source of hot power which can make cool and harmless the power of sorcerers. 'What distinguishes charismatic ritual agency from that of more conventional Catholics is that they dispossess parts of themselves [in donations of money for the church building] to make room in their bodies [in the very gestures of spreading their arms in devotion and opening the mouth to sing] for God's grace.' In this view persons retain their partibility, though it would seem that rather than having the power to enter others (e.g. through sorcery) they have put themselves into a permanent state of openness in relation to the church.

ACKNOWLEDGEMENTS

I repeat my considerable thanks to those with whom I stayed in Hagen for seven weeks in 1995, and all their neighbours. Some of them are named in the Preface. The visit was facilitated by the National Research Institute, Port Moresby; the British Academy provided a personal research grant. Keith Hart and Caroline Humphrey inspired the initial presentation of this at a seminar in Cambridge. I am grateful to Eric Hirsch for his comments, both on this chapter and across many conversations, and to James Carrier, Adam Reed and Richard Werbner. I record with appreciation being able to refer to Mark Mosko's unpublished paper (1997) in this context, and note the interest of his material from Mekeo.

CHAPTER 6

The New Modernities

As two examples of the formation of identities in the twentieth century, Clifford (1988: 148) cites first Picasso's cubist response to an African mask and then Leach and Kildea's film *Trobriand Cricket*. 'The film takes us into a staged swirl of brightly painted, feathered bodies, balls, and bats. In the midst of all this on a chair sits the umpire ... He is chewing betel nut, which he shares out from a stash held on his lap. It is a bright blue plastic Adidas bag. It is beautiful.' He then adds that perhaps one can see the Adidas bag as 'part of the same kind of inventive process' as the African-looking masks that suddenly appeared in Picasso's pictures. Built on the missionaries' game, something amazing, he says, has been concocted from elements of tradition. It renders ethnography surrealist. The surrealist moment, he argues, is one 'in which the possibility of comparison exists in unmediated tension with sheer incongruity' (1988: 146). Such 'elements of modern ethnography tend to go unacknowledged by a science that sees itself engaged in the reduction of incongruities ... But is not every ethnographer ... a *reinventor* and reshuffler of realities?' (1988: 147, my emphasis).

Comparison and incongruity: Latour (1993: 10-11) would see these enabled by two modernist knowledge practices. On the one hand are practices of separation ('purification') which create distinct but comparable zones, his own prime example being the distinction between human and non-human worlds; on the other hand are practices of mediation ('translation'), which mix types of being, above all 'hybrids of nature and culture'. Such mixes proliferate, unofficially as it were, as a byproduct of making those pure distinctions – indeed he argues that 'the more we forbid ourselves to conceive of hybrids, the more possible their interbreeding becomes' (1993: 12). Latour argues that moderns tolerate both practices provided they too are kept distinct. But '[a]s soon as we direct our attention *simultaneously* to the work of purification *and* the work of hybridization, we stop being wholly modern' (1993: 11, my emphasis). And that is because we – 'we' appears to mean we moderns who are Euro-Americans – would see our relations with others differently.

In this context Latour extolls anthropology as the discipline that tackles everything at once: 'every ethnologist is capable of including within a single monograph ... the distribution of powers among human beings, gods, and nonhumans; the procedures for reaching agreements; the connections between religion and power; ancestors; cosmologies; property rights' (1993: 14). He is referring both to anthropologists' holistic approach to the description of social life and to the mixes offered by their subjects. Anthropology makes explicit, then, practices of modernism ordinarily suppressed in the purificatory and rational ('constitutional') effort to keep descriptions of (say) the natural and social worlds distinct. His point is that hybrids have always been present: there never has been a modernism of only that exclusively rationalist kind. We always were non-modern. And his model for the non-modern includes parts from worlds he deliberately calls premodern, summoning among others peoples from Papua New Guinea. He could, for instance, have cited the Trobriand Islanders.

Now Latour does not wish to take on the premodern world wholesale; he only wants to borrow bits from it. After all, he argues, the explicitness which premoderns give to hybrids (mixing human and non-human elements) has as restrictive a role as does their dogmatic separation in the hands of moderns. Indeed, by making hybrids a focus of cultural practice, premoderns cannot realise the potential for experimentation which moderns allow by officially ignoring them.[1] Premoderns and moderns alike are one-sided in their explicit orientations; Latour hopes moderns can redress the (several) balance(s). So what new roles are anthropologists' accounts of Papua New Guinea required to play in these democratising gestures?, and we might cite the account just given in the previous chapter. Euro-Americans are being invited to become aware of their continuities with others: 'As collectives, we are all brothers' (1993: 114). Premoderns show moderns a part of the picture, how to be explicit about hybrids.

Where Latour is interested in the separation and mix of nature and culture, Clifford performs the same intellectual operation on the separation and mix of cultures. So if scientific anthropology upheld the distinctiveness of cultures, he can also point to the power of the implicit, here the unofficial side of ethnography that was always juxtapositional, surrealist (Clifford 1988: 147), in response to the hybrid character of culture itself. The two arrive at similar declarations of symmetry, both on account of the hybrid forms they detect: Latour's symmetry between modern and premodern societies resonates with the symmetry of mutual inventiveness Clifford finds in the way cultures borrow from one another. How could one possibly have any quarrel with such a progamme?

SEARCHING FOR SYMMETRY

'Inventiveness' has all the resonances of the enabling role into which anthropologists place cultural consciousness. They are delighted when peoples turn to their own ends artefacts and ideas introduced from elsewhere – the endless possibilities for re-configuration (e.g. Wilk 1995) – especially when that elsewhere is the anthropologist's own culture. Culture appears, in Turner's words (1993: 423), 'as the *jouissance* of the late capitalist consumerist subject, playing with the heady opportunities for self-creation that the ever-growing world of commodities appears to provide'. My interest in Latour's account is because he not only tries to introduce a certain symmetry between social formations (modern and premodern), as Clifford does between cultures, but extends that symmetry to the kinds of mix of human and non-human entities which Papua New Guineans have made familiar to the anthropologist. The first kind of symmetry is an evolved form of cultural relativism. The second symmetry opens up a perspective on the substance of Melanesian (my examples come from Papua New Guinea) knowledge.

Latour argues that the separation of culture and society from nature has both given social scientists their distinctive field and corralled them within it. Thus he extolls anthropology only insofar as its mixed accounts include technology, religion, the natural world and social relations; he castigates it for privileging the social. The anthropologist is all too likely to suggest that the one entity that premodern peoples fail to see for themselves is society. Since such people cannot separate knowledge from society, he says (1993: 99), the anthropologist has to point out the social construction. Moreover, on home ground anthropology fails even in such an attempt. He accuses it of focusing on areas of life identifiably 'social' (arcane rituals or remote communities), ignoring natural science among other things. Here too anthropologists should look to the networks, to the mixes of artefact and idea and person which make up life. In Latour's terms, 'networks' become visible as effects of mediation ('translation'), that is, as links between whatever (non-)moderns perceive as different orders of knowledge.[2]

To reveal the hybrid constitution of an artefact appears a democratising move precisely because its configuration of meanings (its network) emerges as the creation (the network) of many actants. An African mask is at once the work of individuals, the presentation of planes and surfaces, and an object under an artist's eye. Human and non-human combine in the painting Picasso creates. Picasso owns the painting but not everything that went into its composition nor indeed the image derived by others from it. He may sell it, in which case it acquires an alienability which becomes owned by another.

This is of a piece with the discovery that cultures were never pure. Clifford goes to great lengths to demonstrate the impurity of cultures. And he links it, especially in the Mashpee Indian land case, to problems of identity when identity is held to depend on unique continuities of form (culture) and substance (people). Looked at one way, the Mashpee were Indian, another way they were not (1988: 289). (Cross-examination of Mashpee as witness to Mashpee identity: "'You don't eat much Indian food, do you?' 'Only sometimes.' 'You use regular doctors, don't you?' 'Yes, and herbs as well'" (1988: 286)). Clifford's political intention is both to celebrate the hybrid as a form in its own right and to insist that through people's inventiveness all cultures are hybrids. So what is a difficulty for the Mashpee Indian is illuminating for the cultural commentator. A hybrid cannot be pinned down, for its characteristics do not reside in any one part but in the way parts work together. It is thus a perfect trope for culture as re-creative combination, in the same way as Latour's 'network' is a trope for the journeying, nomadic extensiveness of any enquiry that pursues connections. One sees linked in one continuous chain (Latour's phrase) entities as incommensurable as the chemistry, global strategy and personalities that go to make up (say) a report on atmospheric pollution. Insofar as a hybrid identity (of the report) is distributed between diverse components, and insofar as no one can claim to have traversed a network identical to anyone else's, the journeying enquirer in turn has licence for cultural creativity him or herself.

I wish to reflect on the way in which anthropological knowledge enters other people's networks, and contributes its bit to hybrids. It needs to retain a critical edge. For the language of hybridity may otherwise lull cultural observers into a false sense of freedom. There seems no end to human inventiveness: if everything is negotiated all we need pay attention to are the negotiations. We can describe the traffic to and fro, or the networks along which things as they travel change their shape and utility, the plastic bag that becomes a container for betel nut, betel itself going on its own travels (cf. Hirsch 1990). However, the symmetries may not be quite what they seem.

There is already a difference in the role Clifford and Latour accord *inventiveness*. Clifford sees culture as a source of creativity; one symmetry between cultures lies in their capacity to absorb and make hybrids out of one another. Latour sees inventiveness of a particularly powerful kind lying only in the suppressed hybrids of modernism:

> ... we do not wish to become premoderns all over again. The nonseparability of natures and societies had the disadvantage of making experimentation on a large scale impossible, since every transformation of nature had to be in harmony with a social transformation ... [W]e seek to keep the moderns' major innovation: the separability of nature that no one has constructed ... and the freedom of manoeuvre of a society that is of our own making. (Latour 1993: 140).

Freedom as well as a superior inventiveness belong to the moderns.

Behind the democratising concepts of impure cultures and hybrid networks lie other asymmetries. They turn on Euro-American assumptions about identity and ownership: where 'we' see ourselves and what 'we' claim for Euro-American culture. These asymmetries should be leading the anthropologist to new questions about old modernist issues, namely about property and proprietorship. But they would not have to endorse the 'purification' side of modernism. They would not be questions about the boundedness of cultures or about keeping separate the components of our naratives – anthropologists know now not to ask these. Rather, they would be questions about the length of networks. On the horizon are a whole new set of claims to proprietorship (new in the same way as becoming conscious of the modernist work of 'translation' is new). They arise *out of* the very perception of hybrids, out of mixes of techniques and persons, out of combinations of the human and non-human, out of the interdigitation of different cultural practices. Not socially innnocent, not without their own likely effects, they presage new projects for modernity.

I am intrigued by the fresh significance Euro-Americans have found in their concept of intellectual property rights. These establish property in the creative process by which new forms come into being. What is newly hybrid about some current patenting procedures is their innovative mix of human and non-human parts. What should make anyone wary are the massive financial interests which give patent holders political power. Let me return to Papua New Guinea in order to consider why this might be of any interest for the way ethnographers think about their materials.

Impure cultures and hybrid networks

Clifford's Adidas bag is a double take. Something amazing, he said, had been concocted from the missionaries' game of cricket, which had in the process been 'rubbished'.[3] The Adidas bag becomes rubbished too. The aesthetics are not symmetrical: Picasso bestows new value on the African mask, elevates it to high culture, but a plastic bag taken out of its classy sports milieu is detritus. One would have to spell out the fact that Trobriand Islanders appreciate shiny surfaces to things – as a preference for tin roofing over thatch was once explained to me – in order to deprive the epithet 'plastic' of its connotations of tawdriness.

There is a further asymmetry. Although Clifford indicates a state of mutual inventiveness between European artist and Pacific islander, *both* examples illustrate the reach of Euro-American culture. African mask and Adidas bag landed up in their strange contexts through the *same* process of travel and diffusion. Euro-American culture seems to have the longer arm, to reach everywhere, so 'we' can simultaneously recognise ourselves both in what we appropriate from others and in what they appropriate from us. We are not only here, we are also there: traces of ourselves on the Pacific island. So invention may appear either in the inventiveness of seeing new uses for goods or in the invention of the goods which others use. Rendering the Adidas bag intrusive or incongruous in a Trobriand setting is Clifford's technique for undermining the concept of cultural purity; yet it is intrusive only insofar as it is overdetermined as Euro-American.

Latour formalises this phenomenon in terms of length of network. There is a crucial difference of scale between modern and premodern societies. 'Comparative anthropology has to measure ... effects of size with precision' (1993: 114). By this he means that 'the relative size of collectives [actors who work together] will be profoundly affected by the enlistment of a particular type of non-humans' (1993: 109). His example is that of a technological invention – Archimedes' pulley, which enabled the king of Syracuse to build a military force with a quite new dimension of power. Now Latour does not take size as self-evident. Large events may have small causes, as large enterprises are sustained by countless small projects – the very size of a totalitarian state is obtained only by a network of statistics, calculations, offices and enquiries. Nonetheless, it is the massiveness of machines, and the power of non-human devices, which in his view divides (non-)moderns from premoderns.[4] As does, he says, 'the invention of longer networks' (1993: 133).

> [Now that moderns are no longer removed from the premoderns, he asks what best might we keep of each?] What are we going to retain from the moderns? ... The moderns' greatness stems from their pro-liferation of hybrids, their lengthening of a certain type of network, their acceleration of the production of traces ... Their daring, their in-novativeness, their tinkering, their youthful excess, the ever-increas-ing scale of action ... are features we want to keep. (1993: 132-3)

In short, the modern *as inventor.*

What qualifies for inclusion in a network? It can only be an agree-ment that things are connected by some continuous enterprise. The tenuousness of such agreements is described by Mol and Law (1994) through the arresting example of blood tests for anaemia that gather together different sets of 'natural facts' on the journey from labs to hospi-tals to clinics to tropical outstations. What makes us think that the betel container is an Adidas bag is *the length of the network* that we presume: artefacts both flow and remain recognisably Euro-American in origin (cf. Thomas 1994: 40). What renders them hybrid are the multiplicity of factors by which the anthropologist would construct cultural iden-tity: a Euro-American artefact 'found' and turned to new use through indigenous cultural inventiveness. Like us, you see, these Melanesians, although their networks are shorter.

Latour's interest in scale implies a certain mathematics. He suggests that one concept worth saving from premoderns is that of there being a multiplication of non-humans, such as we may imagine the overpeopled universe of the Manambu (Harrison 1990), with its thousands of named entities, persons not necessarily human. But do these enumerations indicate a multiplication of beings? One could as well imagine a clan universe divided into numerous manifestations of itself (Mimica 1988). Melanesians, we might argue, live in an already globalised, already scaled-up world (Wagner 1991). Its power is that it can be infinitely divided. This is certainly the logic of bodily generation, whether one is talking of a clan body (say), or a person's. Conversely, bodies are always capable of revealing their composition, their mixed character. Across Melanesia, people divide themselves by kinship, and borrow from one another sources of nurture and fertility, as a clan is formed and nurtured by affines. Such networks are routed through persons, carried by the human and non-human traffic of spouses, land and wealth, longer or shorter as the case may be. Indeed we may measure the length of some networks in the immediate or delayed return of conjugal partners (Damon 1983): the disposition of debts (compensation claims) indicates who inhabits the networks, or portions of them. Perhaps Melanesian networks are not so much 'shorter' as measurable.

Papua New Guinean hybrids

Latour does not give much in the way of examples of premodern hybrids. I must therefore seek them. Can we find objects of knowledge where the mix partakes of both human and non-human elements? What about the way people relate things? Godelier (1986a) offers an example in the 'combined system' of property rights which prevails in societies such as the Siane of the Eastern Highlands of Papua New Guinea.

As Godelier redescribes Salisbury's (1962) original account, Siane rules regarding material and immaterial property comprise two kinds: men exercise inalienable rights over lineage land, sacred flutes and ritual knowledge and personal rights over clothes, pigs and planted trees. Yet if from an economic point of view the system appears mixed, daily practice works much more like a purification strategy separating sacred from profane. Protocols concerning people's claims with respect to these two types of property suggest that Siane have to ensure that these categories of things are kept apart. At the same time what is being kept apart, in the difference between what a Euro-American might call the human (mundane) and non-human (spirit) world, are different aspects of the person. On the one hand, the person is a clan or lineage member, tied to his (and it is his rather than her) ancestors and descendants alike; on the other hand, the person is individuated through his own actions and claims. We might say that out of this composition of distinct elements persons emerge as hybrids of the human and non-human. Conversly, if sacred goods '"belong" *simultaneously* to the dead ancestors, to the living and to descendants yet to be born' (1986a: 79, Godelier's emphasis), these are all so to speak one person (the lineage) with an interest in property – the lineage being divided between, a composite of, the dead, living and those to be born.

Similar divisions are found in the domestic pig,[5] to Euro-Americans a non-human entity also the work of human beings, a piece of technology that has played diverse roles in the evolution of Highlands societies (Lemonnier 1993). Siane pigs are held as alienable personal property by men, although such rights of disposal are qualified by other interests, not least by those of women (e.g. Sexton 1986). We may recognise in this combination separate interests held simultaneously together. Godelier adds an important piece of knowledge apropos Baruya, on the borders of the Eastern Highlands. Men alone transmit their rights in their father's land to their own children, and possess the sacred objects used during initiation to reproduce the strength of male warriors. Women can do none of this. But, he says, women do transmit to their daughters the magical formulae which will enable them to raise pigs, along with pig names (1986b: 81). Creativity is thus distributed between men and women. Certainly, in the attachment that Gimi women, also in the Eastern New Guinea Highlands, show towards their pigs, procreative overtones are evident. 'Gimi women carry shoats like babies inside netbags to their gardens ... When one of [a woman's] pigs is killed and set out for distribution at a feast, she sits weeping beside the pile of charred slabs, swatting away flies, wearing the pig's tail around her neck and chanting its name' (Gillison 1993: 43). As a non-human child, the pig has a divisible identity, for it belongs as much to men as to women, and those slabs of meat may be payments for her own child's 'head' which its father must give her paternal, and its maternal, kin (cf. Gillison 1991: 187). Like a human pig, the child is hybrid equally by gender and by relationship, containing both male and female elements in its makeup, recognised in just such separations of maternal from paternal kin.

In these brief examples, we encounter networks with distinctive features. If these mixes of beings dead and alive, human and porcine, appear to create 'hybrid' persons, it is because persons create relationships by dividing themselves off from other persons, as they may divide Euro-Americans from Melanesians as brothers elder and younger to each other.[6] Relations make a difference between persons. The discrete interests of men and women partition the child or the pig into an entity composed of different entities. Thus Wassman (1994) describes for Yupno how the body's very limbs may be calibrated for different effects – like a Massim axe (Battaglia 1983) – one side of the body acting as a support for the other's procreative energy. These are not quite the hybrids of Latour's discourse.

We would not have expected such hybrids to parallel a division between nature and culture, for that was a modern Euro-American invention. But there is more at stake than the difference between moderns who deal in abstractions such as nature and culture and premoderns who personify everything. Because nature could not be conceived separately, Latour argues, premoderns cannot experiment on the modern scale.[7] Their technologies, their non-human partners, are less powerful. This puts limits on the effects of their inventiveness. So what kind of knowledge lies in those powers of procreation and creativity attributed to men's rituals and to women's intimate attachment to their pigs? It is knowledge about (that inheres in) relationships. For they have one interesting dimension: such powers are expressible in terms of claims between persons and rights to payment in the form of compensation. Persons are in this sense the composite property of others.

The combination of rights to which Godelier referred is repeated over again in other Melanesian formulations. Living persons are known as just such combinations, and combination is a corollary of the fact that rights are divided or partitioned between persons. The composite substance of persons becomes public knowledge (is decomposed) through mortuary ceremonies, for instance, which render discrete other people's interests – they can be disaggregated through (compensatory) exchanges (Mosko 1983). It is the person him or herself, 'owned' by multiple others, who brings these diverse interests and persons together. Each of these others owns a part, if we wish to introduce the language of ownership; none owns the hybrid. What intrigues me in certain Euro-American formulations is precisely the way the only possible object of ownership turns out to be a hybrid.

But one cannot simply re-assert cultural difference, constructing Melanesian practices by contrast with Euro-American ones. It must be shown that such discriminations matter. I ground my wariness by touching briefly on some of the consequences that anthropological models have had, and on attempts to clean them up; such attempts may bring in items of knowledge already at work in other domains and thus far from innocent in their implications. This will lead us back to the same point about ownership, since it deals with that other part of Latour's modern hybrid, viz. culture, from Clifford's perspective of composite cultures.

FINDING MODERNITY

New culturalisms

In his first letter home to his supervisor, Reed writes of the kinds of relations warders and inmates in Bomana gaol, Port Moresby, appear to have – very different from what he had expected. A group of warders expatiated on the point, contrasting Bomana with gaols in 'the West'. They told the anthropology student that the difference was 'cultural'.[8]

The warders were pointing to practices they regarded as Melanesian: the celebrated *wantok* system through which shared language, region or kinship provide a basis for identity and appeals to solidarity. Warders invariably had *wantoks* among the inmates who would ensure their safety. In borrowing the concept of 'culture', people appear to be doing what is done everywhere, fastening on certain 'customs' as diagnostic of their way of life. Indeed in areas of Melanesia, notably Vanuatu, the concept of *kastom* has become an organising trope for the way people present differences between themselves and Euro-Americans (Jolly 1992). If the anthropologist is tempted to read 'culture' into this concept, the reading is also played back to the anthropologist.[9] But whatever else it may refer to, culture/*kastom* is also used to signify difference.

Now Melanesians have their own explicit practices of differentiation. By gender, group affiliation, territorial defence, not to speak of the partitioning of people's relationships between diverse kin, difference is invariably translated into differences between persons. People divide themselves off from one another by their connections, in terms for instance of the land whose food they eat or the ancestors who keep them in health, or in relation to those who talk in their own tongue. What difference would it make for us to imagine such differences as 'cultural'? None at all perhaps, except that cultural identity has become a sign of the new modernities. Resting, first, on a hybrid person/entity long established in Euro-American thought (in which social anthropology has much investment), it, second, places special emphasis on a form of creativity one might call inventiveness.

First, the human and non-human elements which render the Euro-American person hybrid combine radically distinctive elements from the realms of nature and culture. The idea that persons are duplex creatures, carrying around at once themselves and their social roles, evincing in their individual actions the collective culture of which they are a part, has been one of the contributions of social anthropology to modern conceptions of the world. It has been anthropology's strength to identify the cultural component of people's lives, and to point to those differences between persons that are not innate or given but arise from their societies, from the language they speak and the styles of life they lead. Indeed, this particular apprehension of culture is one of anthropology's exports.[10] Where it is exported, there also the authors see themselves – or versions of themselves. Debates about custom in Vanuatu include debates about how far Euro-American anthropologists may recognise 'their' concept of culture in ni-Vanuatu *kastom*.

Promoting the modern idea of culture to explain differences once put down to identities of a racial kind (that is, locked into the bodily inheritance and disposition of people) has always been taken as an act of enlightenment. 'The demons of race and eugenics appeared to have been politically ... exorcized ... in defense of human equality in cultural diversity' (Stolcke 1995: 2). Her reference is to the work of UNESCO after the Second World War which defended cultural identity and distinctiveness in the Boasian tradition. Since then, such ideas, which 'seemed to be a peculiar obsession only of anthropologists, have now come to occupy a central place in the way in which anti-immigration sentiments and policies are being rationalized' (1995: 2). On the surface appears a new symmetry. Cultural identity is something to which everyone can lay claim; but when cultures are given a homeland and become identified with particular territories or countries, then cultural difference may work to exclusionary or asymmetric effect.[11]

Stolcke encapsulates the widespread and novel exaltation of cultural difference in recent years in what she calls cultural fundamentalism.[12] What is at stake is a definition of culture for a Europe uncontaminated by foreignness. Yet the idea of a European culture is not just racism in new guise (and Werbner (1997: 6) notes the irony of that equation for the anthropologist). On the contrary, there is a perceptible shift in the rhetorics of exclusion, as Stolcke calls them. In the language of the anti-immigration Right, emphasis is not so much on the different endowment of the human races as on profound differences in cultural heritage. This modern separation of culture from other forms of identity is joined with them again in the further idea that people are naturally xenophobic.[13] People, it is held, prefer to live among their own kind.

Contemporary cultural fundamentalism is based, then, on two conflated assumptions: that different cultures are incommensurable and that, because humans are inherently ethnocentric, relations between cultures are by 'nature' hostile. (Stolcke 1995: 6)

Stolcke points out that it is the particular combination of appeal to universal abstract principles (everyone seeks identity) and the demands of nationalism (citizenship), coupled with European ideas about human nature (innate dispositions), that leads to the twin concepts of 'cultural heritage' and 'cultural alien'.[14] These two concepts hold in place the modern hybrid as persons (aliens) carrying culture (heritage) on their backs. In this view, culture makes a difference between persons.

Second, invention abounds. In the anthropologist's eyes Europe is inventing a culture for itself, drawing among other things on the anthropological invention of that concept, which has become imbued with the capacity for inventiveness itself. Social anthropologists might nowadays rush to point out the modernist fallacy of reifying cultures as though they were bounded like territories and not the impure, hybrid creature they (anthropologists) know them to be. Yet anthropology did not only invent cultures as discrete entities. Recall Clifford's shadow surrealism: it celebrated diversity between cultures in the further idea that culture lay in the very inventivenesss with which people played off their differences from one another (Boon 1982). But anthropology's 'culture' is now an embarrassment. If one can lay claim to an invention, can one also disown it?[15] Or should one be inventing something afresh?

Turner feels that the specification of the essential properties of culture is no longer an academic matter, for it has become a political one. So what 'essential property' of culture might a latterday anthropologist identify? Turner answers his own question with reference to the Euro-American movement for multiculturalism with its unpredecented claim that 'cultures' (as such) are worthy of equal support and protection from the state. There is in his view now only one ground on which to elevate culture as a 'new category of collective human rights ... a legitimate goal of political struggle for equal representation in the public domain' (Turner 1993: 425). This lies in 'the empowerment of the basic human capacity for self-creation' (1993: 427). Culture *is*, in his words, the active sense of collective self-production; cultures *are* the way that people have made themselves. If culture generates a capacity for culture, its essential property would appear to be inventiveness.

This is not quite as free as it sounds. In seeming to clean up the act, this freshly minted view of culture turns out to be currency already in circulation, an invention borrowed from others. Turner more or less says so himself. New social conjunctures at work in the late capitalist world, he observes, favour the development and political recognition of cultural identities: 'a metacultural network of forces, institutions, values, and policies which fosters and reinforces the proliferation of cultural groups' (1993: 427). A new modernity then? I would add the new proliferation of claims which have as their very rationale the reduction of proliferation[16] through efforts to limit (competing) claims. Late capital has investments in the ownership of, among other things, inventiveness itself.

New proprietors

The English term 'hybrid' came initially from the Latin for a cross between a wild boar and a tame sow. It emerged in the late eighteenth century with the fresh definition of a cross between species. At the same time it was pressed into metaphorical service for anything derived from heterogeneous or incongruous sources. In British parliamentary language, public bills which affect private rights may be referred to as hybrid. However, of all incongruous sources which create the hybrid character of networks, for Latour the conjoining of nature and culture is paradigmatic.

An example drawn upon elsewhere (see Preface) would also be germane here. In 1987 a Californian corporation discovered the hepatitis C virus.[17] Two forms of Euro-American knowledge are involved here. The virus was a discovery, that is, the unearthing of fresh knowledge about the natural world. But the means of detecting the virus involved an invention in the development of a blood test for which the corporation was granted a patent. The idea of licensing is old, and at least since the eighteenth century, again, has been applied to inventions (but see Brush 1993). This test met all the modern criteria for a patent – novel, produced by human intervention and, in the interests of at once protecting and promoting competition, capable of industrial application. The patent has been a commercial success: the British National Health Service will be charged more than £2stg for every hepatitis C test it administers, estimated to be at the rate of 3 million a year.[18]

What was new about this patent application was that the invention included the genetic sequence of the virus; the very identification of the relevant DNA was an integral part of the test. Gene sequences have 'applicability' on the argument that genes themselves are the technology for the medicine of the future. One outspoken critic[19] has observed that there is only one set of DNA sequences to be identified in the human genome, and no claims to identification could be countered by further inventions/discoveries; the patent is protecting the company from competition, not promoting competition. This particular corporation was in effect laying claims to 'ownership' of the virus and its genetic variants.

What makes such patenting even conceivable is the factor of human intervention in the production of a life form. Here is an American commentary on 'immortal' cell lines, that is, cells made reproducible in the laboratory. Similar arguments have been made at the European parliament (see Chapter 8).

> Many human cells have already been granted patents in the US on the basis that *they would not exist but for the intervention of the 'inventor'*, who extracted and manipulated them to reproduce indefinitely. The US patent office has said it does not intend to allow patents on human beings, drawing on slavery amendments to US law that prohibits ownership of human beings. But the office has not made it clear how it intends to distinguish between human cells and human beings. ... Individual scientists, universities and companies may eventually have the power to design the genetic makeup of a fetus. Should they then be able to patent the DNA that allows them to confer certain traits on the child? (*New Scientist*, 12 January 1991; my emphasis)

The anthropologist would observe that what makes these human cells ownable is their hybrid status, and hybrid in Latour's sense. The gene sequence as an identifiable part of DNA is simultaneously cultural and natural. Neither cell nor technique stands alone. The inventor has rights *only in the hybrid*, that is, in the DNA sequence which he or she has isolated. For 'invention' consists in the way in which culture has been *added* to nature.

Now modern institutions always took persons as having components available to the inventiveness of others, most notably labour which could be bought and sold as a commodity. In the same way as the Euro-American person is an already exising hybrid, at once a living biological organism and a bearer of culture and society, its energies may be distributed between the creativity that is the sign of its own human life and the creativity that is appropriatable in the marketplace. In using labour for ends of its own, capital realises a use the original owner cannot realise for him or herself. Similarly, if the kind of knowledge which science gains from the natural world through its own inventiveness is recognised by patent, then this is because new contexts and uses are created that make the original item into something else. Patents are claims to inventions, that is, to embodiments of inventiveness which others technically could but are forbidden to utilise as inventions. Hence the person from whom the modified gene cells come cannot claim 'ownership' of DNA produced in the laboratory.

One objection to corporation pursuit of certain patents in genetic medicine is that any one invention/discovery is only made possible by the whole field of knowledge which defines the scientific community. There are long networks here, and patenting truncates them: forty names to a scientific article and six names to a patent application.[20] It thus matters very much over which stretch of a network rights of ownership can be exercised. Hepatitis C had been under investigation for twelve years before the virus was isolated. The patent counsel for the company that developed the test was reported as saying: 'We don't claim we did all the research, but we did the research that solved the problem' (*The Independent*, 1 December 1994). The long network that was formerly such an aid to knowledge becomes hastily shortened.

There are numerous contexts of creativity in Papua New Guinean societies. The disposition of labour is one; the role of the intellect in invention is another (cf. A. Strathern 1994a). This chapter has touched on bodily creativity in the production of persons for its suggestiveness about network length.

If it is the interdigitation of nature and culture that makes moderns place such high value on inventiveness (culture), they are valuing themselves as nature with culture added. Persons embody the capacity for invention. Inventiveness is only limited by, so to speak, the technological capacity to realise it. The hybrid nature of the Melanesian person works to rather different social effect. Against Latour, we may observe that there is no limit to (Melanesian) people's capacity to invent, innovate and elaborate on what they think up for themselves or borrow from others. With him, we may agree that the length of networks is limiting. But we need to understand the nature of this limit.

Limitation is not so much quantitative, for any Melanesian artefact is infinitely divisible, as qualitative. Networks have a measure to them insofar, that is, as *social relationships* are measurable. Persons are the products of networks – hybrid mixes of debt, land and wealth – which demarcate the kind of claims they make on other persons. So it is less personal inventiveness that is subject to the control of others than the extent or scale of people's claims. This is true whether one thinks of obligations owed to ancestors or debts with affines or the rules which separate intermarrying moieties or the compulsion with which gifts demand gifts in return. Persons are subject to distributive relations that lead to claims based on the capacity to body forth the effects of creativity. (The creator's efforts, including creation through nurture, are realised in the bodies of those whom they create.) The extent of such claims is in principle known in advance through the protocols of compensation payments.

I have introduced the language of ownership for a reason.[21] Late twentieth-century cultural politics makes it impossible to separate issues of identity from claims to the ownership of resources. This is a field with which Melanesian anthropologists have long been familiar. In relation to land rights or below-surface explorations or reef fishing, anthropologists have been sensitive to the implications of ownership. This extends to the ownership of rights in the personages and identities of the names which kin groups claim as theirs or of otherwise clandestine knowledge which constitutes ritual prerogatives. By and large in Melanesia, however, anthropologists have not had to deal with the ownership of persons, in terms say of child labour or forms of servitude that call for parallels with slavery, nor indeed with idioms of ownership as characterise certain African authority systems. On the contrary, debate over the exploitation of labour aside, 'ownership' of rights in persons tends to surface in the context of claims established through bridewealth and other life-related prestations. Creativity is already taken care of in the disposition of a person's acknowledged sources in diverse others. Those other persons both create the hybrid and are guarantee that the hybrid as such cannot be owned. The compensation networks that keep such interests alive, the relations that sustain the durability of such a view, may prove more important than we think. That, by contrast, the US patent office *has to spell out* the fact that human beings cannot be patented is chilling. One might prefer to be in a world where such claims on persons had already been settled, carry obligations even, as the anthropologist may indeed think of the life-related payments that characterise exchange systems in Papua New Guinea. *Wantok* do not just exemplify custom. They exemplify partitioned persons distributed among many and owned by none.

Here we should disaggregate hybrids and networks. Melanesian networks of relations are, so to speak, persons literally laid out to their fullest extent, measured by their numerous relations, each segment also with its own measure; the hybrid person is the figurative, condensed product of such relations, a composite ownable by no single segment of them. Now it is both the strength of the kinds of networks imagined by Latour and their weakness that there is no pre-existing measurement to them. Seemingly limitless, they can be imagined without anyone having to decide who owns what bits or indeed whether one can own parts of the network at all. If his modelling corresponds to the kinds of chains evident in the way Euro-Americans recognise their own artefacts regardless of whose lap holds them, or evident in the creation of the hepatitis C test, then they correspond to chains that are open, like nature, to appropriation. Hybrid products can be claimed at any juncture, so to speak, and it is when hybrids are claimed for ownership that segments of networks are chopped off to support the claim.

No one would these days want to claim ownership of an idea or artefact on grounds of unique identity, yet there is no refuge for the social anthropologist in the idea of hybrids, networks and invented cultures either. These do not, of themselves, indicate a symmetrical, sharing morality. They are not of themselves the resistant, transgressive stands they might seem; not the revitalised assembly or parliament of things Latour so freely imagines. For neither a mixed nature nor an impure character guarantees immunity from appropriation. On the contrary, the new modernities have invented new projects that forestall such imaginings. We can now all too easily imagine monopolies on hybrids, and claims of ownership over segments of network.

CHAPTER 7

Divisions of Interest and Languages of Ownership

Trobrianders speak of the [unseen] person who 'walks behind' a valuable object

Debbora Battaglia (1994)

'Neither property nor people': this was, in Dolgin's (1994: 1277) words, the conclusion of the Tennessee Supreme Court faced with seven cryo-preserved embryos stored in a Knoxville fertility clinic. The two concepts were connected through the nature of the claims that a man and woman, once a couple but now no longer, enjoyed with respect to what they had created. Earlier courts had offered alternative rulings. One proceeded on the grounds that the embryos were *persons*, children to be brought into the world (the woman wished the embryos to be available to her for bringing this about at some future date, possibly through donation to another woman) and whose best interests must be before the court; the other on the grounds that the embryos should be treated as *property* for purposes of deciding who had control in them (the man had argued that any disposition must – as in the case of property allocation – be agreed upon by both parties) (Dolgin 1994: 1276-7). The Supreme Court sided fully with neither. It described the embryos as lacking '[intrinsic] value to either party', yet as having value in their 'potential to become, after implantation, growth and birth, children' (Dolgin 1994: 1277). Accordingly, it focused on the progenitors, balancing their interests in terms of their procreative intentions.[1]

In some situations procreation itself becomes a metaphor for aspects of property relations, as in certain Euro-American conceptualisations of unalienated labour. This can be so for the products of mental or intellectual labour whose market value includes their accreditation to the producer. They carry the producer's name and the relationship between producer and product is one of identification (Schwimmer 1979).[2] Intellectual property rights define this link in such a way that while third parties may enjoy the property, and create more property from it, its future use is also to the benefit of the original producer. Such property is culturally validated as extensions of persons, often in quasi-procreative idiom, as in the appeal to the moral right of creators to their creations or to the paternity of the author. Indeed, the language of kinship was an important source of analogy in early struggles to establish the recognition of authorial copyright (see Coombe 1994). A background question in the Tennessee case was the extent to which the couple's previous procreative intent was to continue into the future.

From a Danish perspective on embryo disposal, Nielson raises two questions. One concerns the disposition of embryos in other than a procreative context; who then has the entitlement? If, for example, someone consents to the embryo being used for research, the entitlement cannot be on grounds of the future parenting or custody of a child. In her view that is the point at which 'it becomes clear that the embryo is treated as property' (Nielson 1993: 219). The other more general question explored by Nielson is the right to become a parent. This the US legal theorist Robertson pursues in terms of procreative liberty – the extent to which interference in people's reproductive choices is warranted. The right to reproduce he sees as a negative right, that is, against interference, rather than a positive right to the resources needed to reproduce (Robertson 1994: 29). The correlative right not to reproduce can be asserted before pregnancy insofar as it is already legally protected by the courts in upholding the liberty to use contraception. However other issues come into play when a couple are in dispute.

Robertson also refers to the problems posed by frozen embryos and introduces the concept of dispositional control: who has the authority to choose among available options for disposition. 'The question of decisional authority is really the question of who "owns" – has a "property" interest in – the embryo' (1994: 104). He then qualifies his terms:

> However, using terms such as 'ownership' or 'property' risks misunderstanding. Ownership does not signify that embryos may be

treated in all respects like other property. Rather, the term merely designates who decides which legally available options will occur.... Although the bundle of property rights attached to one's ownership of an embryo may be more circumscribed than for other things, it is an ownership or property interest nonetheless (1994: 104).

Dispositional authority might rest with an individual in relation to his or her gametes, with a couple jointly, with the physicians who create the embryos and so forth, but the persons who provide the sperm and egg probably have the strongest claims. (Robertson cites a case where a court found that embryos were the property of gamete providers against the claims of an IVF programme that refused to release a frozen embryo to a couple moving out of the area.) Dispositional authority can be exercised in and of itself and thus would not require coming to a decision about other claims to ownership, nor indeed a decision as to whether the entities at issue were 'property' or 'people'. The concept enables a further principle to be brought into play. Robertson recommends that the best way to handle a dispute is to refer back to the dispositional agreement made at the time of creation or cryopreservation of the embryos (1994: 113). In other words, rather than considering afresh the procreative desires of the parties as they have developed in the interim, and perhaps having to balance their interests anew, it could endorse their intentions in this at the time of first determining to procreate – always provided these were made explicit.

The Tennessee Supreme Court upheld the principle of advance agreements for disposition, but in the absence of such an agreement rejected the idea that freezing alone constituted an agreement to later implementation (of these intentions). In the end it weighed up the relative burdens on the two parties, and found in favour of the husband's currently expressed desire not to reproduce.

LANGUAGES OF OWNERSHIP

The case raises some interesting issues about the language of analysis. The dispute between former husband and wife necessarily mobilised different arguments to litigious effect. Interests at stake were expressed through appeals to interpretations evoking different domains of reasoning (property/people). In academic arguments interpretative choice becomes equally explicit: disputes are often *about* the relevance of the domains from which analytical constructs come. One learns in any case to be self-conscious about the choice of analytical vocabulary; it does not emerge from inspection of data unaided. This is a point on which James Carrier (1998) has commented.[3] I endorse his observation that the Melanesian debates about gift exchange are also debates about property relations. Given, however, that the (Maussian) 'gift' was borrowed from Euro-American discourse in the first place, and with political intent, we might consider what parallels we wish to be drawing in the late twentieth century. This is not just an academic matter. I take the view that the way in which people organise their relations to one another as a matter of control not just over things ('property' in the Supreme Court's sense) but over aspects of life and body (that define 'persons') will loom large on the world agenda over the next decade. We can expect an explosion of concern with ownership.

New resources are coming into being all the time, through the invention of objects of knowledge and utility, as well as new contests over existing resources, and in their wake new negotiations over rights, as the Tennessee case shows.[4] The anthropologist might well be interested in the accompanying cultural search – in the exploration of the domains from which reasons are drawn, in the metaphors, analogies or precedents being pressed into service. Here, the claims were over products of the body for which no prior transactional idioms existed, and the mental intentions of the parties in producing them had to help define what they were. The language of intellectual property rights itself shades into other languages, such as those of cultural rights and all the questions of exportability that they raise (e.g. Gudeman 1995), including reformulations of practices of reproduction never indigenously conceived in terms of (property) rights at all. Thus Coombe (1996a: 217) writes of the descendants of Crazy Horse, 'upset to learn of the appropriation of the identity of their revered ancestor as a trademark by a manufacturer of malt liquor' who 'find themselves compelled to claim that they hold his name and likeness as a form of property'.[5] Anthropologists need to know how and why they might use the language of property and ownership themselves.

Pannell provides a very explicit statement on this from Australia. A particular vocabulary of ownership and repatriation which once shaped debates over the restitution of cultural property (as held for instance in museums) was swept aside by the proclamation of the High Court judges in the 1993 Mabo case. Pronouncing on the death of the legal fiction of *terra nullius*, they also pronounced on the 'corresponding common law recognition of native title [as having] implications which extend beyond so-called "land-management" issues' (Pannell 1994: 19). These extend into the possibility of legal protection for other forms of cultural and intellectual property, inviting a new interpretation of repatriation as reappropriation, that is, making something one's own again.[6] Pannell (1994: 33) also offers a persuasive case for considering possessory rights; one might indeed (after Annette Weiner) wish to reinvigorate the concept of possession, though we should be watching what the concept of possession is doing elsewhere. Like any other construct, it needs debate, especially if it is to be appropriated to demonstrate universal human needs for possessions. The point is that Pannell's argument explicitly addresses the displacement of one set of analytical terms by another.

I follow the contributors to Hann (1998) in deploying property relations as a general analytical construct. Its reference to disposable resources embraces both more than and less than its phenomenological or experiential counterpart, owning/ownership. This is as apparent in Robertson's elisions as it is in the proprietorial but not property connotations of owning as belonging (Edwards and Strathern forthcoming). A further qualification is that a property relation may or may not be construed as one of possession, that is, as an extension of or gathering into the self.[7] In contributing to the division of analytical interests in the concept of property, I wish to point to certain situations where we are made aware of relational preconditions. The Tennessee embryos were in dispute precisely as the product of a relationship between former conjugal partners. An abstract understanding of property as a set of relations is thus explored, in this chapter, through concrete instances where relations are presented twice over, as at once the (invisible) conceptual precondition of there being any claims or rights in dispute in the first place and as the (visible) social grounding of the particular dispute at issue. In English one can thus say that all property claims engage relationships; only some are about 'relationships'. One can say the same for ownership: any property claim can be perceived as implying ownership (of rights, interests etc) but only some imply 'ownership' (possession, certain kinds of title, or whatever).

In discussing the management of knowledge, and envisaging new proprietorial forms, Harrison (1995a: 14) names anthropologists' contribution, 'namely their own knowledge of the culturally diverse ways in which knowledge can be "owned"'. I introduce this reference to culture not to detract from social analysis but to sharpen up the conceptual tools on which such analysis relies, not just to elucidate 'meaning' but to understand the categories of action people mobilise in pursuing their interests. It is probably redundant to say that anthropologists' own management of knowledge already inheres in the concepts they choose to use.

Varieties of timelessness

What connotations does Carrier give to the concept of 'ownership'? In his account of the Ponam of Manus Island, Papua New Guinea, where he focuses largely on property embedded in kin and other relationships, Carrier starts with a description of patrilineal *kamal* groups as land-*owning*. I wonder how the account might have looked if he started with the statistical fact that land is held through numerous transactions which link persons to numerous others; among these others is also a group that lays title to it. If this title constitutes 'ownership', it does not imply that enjoyment of the land and its products inevitably follow. So what does title entail? We know from the detailed ethnography (e.g. Carrier and Carrier 1991) that *kamal* are prominent in political life and were in the past important channels for the inheritance of assets. Are continuing claims to land a matter of dispositional right, to borrow Robertson's term? Or should one be thinking along the lines of intellectual property claims asserted by the originators of places? One would then be drawn into comparative analysis with, say, title to ritual performance or rights held in images or designs, as in New Ireland *malanggan* statuary (see Harrison 1992: 234), while recognising that in the Ponam case the assets in question were tangible – not the intangibles of the kind often associated with ritual (Carrier and Carrier 1991: 42). That would make them more like property that can be enjoyed by a third party while at the same time conserving a value for the original 'owner'. Whatever way, one may add, contests of power were likely to be built into the claims. How then can such contests be a qualification of or deviation from them? To oppose 'practice' to 'formal rules', as Carrier (1998) does, is to beg the whole question of what contests of title or usufruct are about, that is, what they bring about for the people involved. In short, Carrier reifies the notion of a rule or principle, finds it in Ponam land titles, links these to a concept of order, not to speak of propriety, and projects the whole idealist bundle onto a 'Maussian model'! Having located power and interest *outside* this model, he then attributes them to other 'forces'. That is, he divides the material up into domains and then shows how one of them does not encompass the whole.

I certainly could not defend the model that he puts forward as Maussian; nonetheless there remains an interesting question to ask about the story of the free trader (Carrier 1998: 99-100). This is about a young man who travelled to Ponam with bundles of sago to sell because he had heard that people were short. He was not intending to trade with kin or partners, and set out the food in a public place, the price clearly displayed, and waited till he had sold it all (but only after having to lower the price). The story is intended to trump any analytical claims that people can only transact in the context of enduring relationships. Should the question not be whether such actions are a resource for thinking about social relationships? What use do Ponam people make of this act? Does it become a paradigm for other solitary ventures? Consider a Hagen woman going off to a birth hut by herself. Birth may take place in isolation; but when the act of birth becomes a metaphorical resource, an image of productivity or creativity for instance, with the social resonances of regeneration those carry, the hut becomes peopled with others. The mother is not alone: ancestral ghosts affect the ease of labour; the child she bears is already in a relationship with her; all kinds of consequences follow for her kin. At the same time, the act is accomplished in solitude because in another sense only she can effect the birth, and seclusion also signals autonomy of personal action. Acts have to be intentional, purposive; without such personal action there would be no relationships. And without knowing how such acts are imaginatively appropriated, economic analysis cannot begin. For all kinds of values can become present. Battaglia (1994) makes the point through a story about a wealth item which played a determining role in a set of urban transactions without ever appearing – it was (however/only) potentially there.[8] One might ask what is present and what is absent in the actions of the Ponam trader. Among the reasons for his treatment (forcing down the price) was the islanders' view that he was no kinsman of theirs, that is, they summoned up 'other' (his own) kinsfolk for him. It is not immediately clear why Carrier concludes, as he does, that the transactions therefore resemble those of an 'urban, capitalist economy'.

This is a question of description: what analysis makes meaningful. It is also a question of what the object of study is. My own interest has been in forms of sociality developed without regard to the European/Enlightenment distinction between individual and society that has driven much anthropological enquiry. So whatever uses that distinction might have for organising social analysis, there were bound to be some things it left unexplained. The question became how to construct an analytical vocabulary that would make evident those elements previous analyses had hidden. Any choice would entail its own concealments in turn, and I have been conscious of the fact that exactly the kind of study in which Carrier is involved (the study of economic forms) is concealed by that strategy. But there was nothing surrogate or covert about the antinomies I used; they were deliberate artifice. Nonetheless they do, as Carrier correctly notes, make assumptions about timelessness.

Carrier and I both deploy concepts of timelessness, though Foster's (1995a) rapprochement renders the observation somewhat out of date. I hold that the knowledge anthropologists have made out of their encounters with Melanesians poses all sorts of questions about the way they (the anthropologists) might wish to think about human relations. The knowledge does not cease to become an object of contemporary interest simply because practices have changed. I would indeed make it timeless in that sense. Carrier's argument is that historical change is crucial, because among other things that shows up the social and conceptual location of previous practices, and this must be part of – not excluded from – the knowledge with which one works. Yet from another perspective his own categories of analysis remain timeless, as in the very constructs of 'property' and 'ownership', and in his notion that there is such a thing as 'the relationship between people and things'. By contrast, my interest is directed to the historical location of analytical constructs, for none of the major constructs we use is without its history. Let me make this last issue explicit.

I remember at the time of first writing through 'the gift' as an analytical metaphor that I did not want to 'go back' to Mauss. In the end I noted one or two places where others had drawn on his work, and the absurdity of no acknowledgement at all to the inventor 'of the gift' in anthropology led to another reference. But while one might say all this comprised a salient background, in the foreground was a recent study, Gregory (1982), and contemporary interests in the then influential field of marxist anthropology. Gregory's composite model drew on Marx, Morgan and Lévi-Strauss, as well as Mauss; I thus drew on Mauss's work principally as it was filtered through Gregory's. Economist as well as anthropologist, Gregory had a grasp of the economic theories of development being applied to Papua New Guinea at the time, and a lively and informed interest in economic change, and I thought that his appraisal of what was wrong with prevailing economic categories demanded attention.

That is why my definition of the 'gift economy'[9] follows Gregory (a shorthand reference 'to systems of production and consumption where consumptive production predominates' (M. Strathern 1988: 145)). The issue was laid out in ongoing critiques of private property: if the idea of property as a thing conceals social relations then what is gift exchange concealing? (It conceals its own conventions of reification.) Hence the debate with Lisette Josephides (cf. Josephides 1985; M. Strathern 1988) was concerned with what gets concealed or mystified and what is made overt. It was she who stimulated me to consider the conversion process by which wealth is transferred from one domain to another. For the ethnographic problem was that, when pigs are taken off by men, women's efforts and the conjugal relation in which production was embedded are *not* disguised. Returns on work are simply made at a later date. In the meanwhile the man gets out of the transaction a power and prestige that the woman never does. The theoretical problem became how to understand that conversion.

That led me into an analysis of gender relations. The man only takes off the woman's pig in one sense! He is also appropriating his own efforts. To understand the power he has to do this, one has to understand that the husband is taking out of a domestic sphere the pig jointly produced from the work of both of them into a sphere which he alone controls. The point is underlined by Sillitoe for Wola society (1988a). Sillitoe argues that pigs are

> not strictly speaking owned by the men who [nonetheless] hold the right to dispose of them. While men transact with them, women are responsible for herding these animals. The division of rights and duties results in neither owning them. They are jointly custodians, both necessary to their possession. While men hold title to animals, they cannot take possession of them and exercise their right of disposal until they have made a payment, customarily in pearlshells, to the woman herding them, for her male relatives. This payment transfers the creatures from the female productive domain to the [male] transactional one. (1988a: 7)

This is a conversion from multiple relations of interest in the thing to singular ones, equally applicable to Hagen, although no payment as such is made to the woman.[10] A specific instance that unfolded there (in Hagen) recently will flesh out these observations. But, first, a further observation about the historicity of analytical constructs is in order. Which historical epoch is going to supply the anthropologist's comparative vocabulary?

I take Carrier's account as raising two important issues for historical understanding. The first is obvious, that all accounts are contemporary.

That is, they can only come out of the present in which they were written; at the same time that present includes diverse pasts and theoretical antecedents that appear to be for the choosing, as one might for example construct an intellectual pedigree. The second is that the anthropologist searching for an analytical vocabulary may be as much drawn to particular cultural domains as to other theorists, going to some field or area of knowledge for potential connections. This 'spatial' effect may be literalised in cross-cultural comparison when a society in one place is described from the vantage point of another elsewhere. But suppose we also thought about historical epochs as domains from which to draw resources for analysis?

This has been made explicit in anthropology from time to time, as in Gluckman's (1965: 86f) critical appraisal of feudalism in interpreting land tenure systems in sub-Saharan Africa, fuelled by his interest in hierarchies of estates as noted by Hann (1998). Europe remained the reference point, but the observer pursued constructs from a former era. One wonders what fresh purchase starting out 'now', at the end of the century, would yield the Euro-American anthropologist interested in describing Melanesian societies. Anyone drawing on the reach of theoretical resources available from a post-industrial economy might find themselves choosing between modernist, postmodernist and realist approaches to 'contemporary' material. Alternatively, in certain respects 'traditional' Melanesian societies belong much more comfortably to some of the visions made possible by socioeconomic developments in Europe since the 1980s than they did to the worlds of the early and mid-twentieth century. Euro-Americans live these days with the idea of dispersed identities, of traffickings in body parts, but above all what perhaps one could call new divisions of interest in familial and conjugal relationships. Some of these are sketched in Chapter 4. Monetary interpretations of kin obligations and new forms of procreative assets hardly turn Euro-Americans into Melanesians. But perhaps they have turned some of the ways in which relationships are contested in late capitalist society into a new resource for apprehending Melanesian social process. Let me advance this supposition through the specific instance already promised.

Dispute

The following sequence of events took place in Mt Hagen in the Western Highlands Province of Papua New Guinea in 1995.[11] Kanapa had two children, a boy and a girl; she was looking forward to the day when the bridewealth was assembled for her son. It is the groom's kin who assemble wealth items, including pigs reared by his father's and brothers' wives. So that would be the occasion on which Kanapa's pigs would be on public display, and people would see what she had raised. However, one particularly large pig that she had intended as the special 'mother's pig' (for the bride's mother) had been taken off a couple of years previously by her husband for a funeral prestation (when a bigman of the clan died), and her anger with him was one cause of a long illness. The husband, Manga, has already been introduced (Chapter 5).

Discharged from hospital in a weak state, for a month or so she did little more than creep outside to sit in the sun. Her husband complained several times that she did not take the medicine he had paid money for, and had brought the sickness on herself. The routing of her anger through ancestral ghosts (who in the past would send sickness to make the victim's suffering visible) had been diverted by charismatic Christian teaching which held that one should not get angry at all. Local Christian leaders came on three or four occasions to exorcise the bad spirits that were fighting with her good spirit, and the senior cowife and other women of the settlement frequently said loud prayers over her. However her sickness persisted, and several relatives became implicated. This included on occasion her long-suffering daughter who had moved in to care for her. They bickered, and some blamed the continuing sickness on the daughter's getting cross with her mother. The daughter was married into a locally wealthy family, but the initiative that gave her husband's brother a good job with a national company had not passed on to her own husband, a youth who contrived to do no work except mind their little boy. He had a small supply of cash coming from his brother, but his father-in-law saw him only as a drain on resources, contributing neither money nor labour. There were complaints about his not using his education. The same could not be said of Kanapa's now adult son, Kitim (see note 11), who was employed in the coastal capital Port Moresby. The father calculated what it had cost him in school fees over the years to put him through secondary education. For the astonishment there was that he rarely sent money home, and when he occasionally did visit he failed to help in the gardens or contribute money to buy in labour, which would have been as acceptable.

Kanapa loved Kitim but was agitated about his bridewealth. He showed no signs of making a match, and parental promptings had fallen on stony ground. The mother was burdened with the thought of his bridewealth going to waste, all the work she had put into rearing pigs, and – with the pride women take in the size of their pigs – her need to show not just that she was but how she was a mother. Relations with her husband were also involved. The prospect of the son's marriage would galvanise the husband into thinking about the pig he had taken from her. In being the principal person to assemble and dispose of the bridewealth, he would have to make good his promise to the wife to replace the large animal he had taken. At one stage he had promised a sum of money in lieu,[12] and her illness was put down by some to the fact that he had never produced this.

There were various small reasons for displeasure with Kitim; we have seen in the earlier chapter that he had left the rebuilding of her house to her brother, and then given presents to this man rather than to herself; this turned into a quarrel between sister and brother. But Kanapa generally accepted the fact that the son lived away, since it was assumed that one day he would come home to claim his inheritance in land. Had the woman been well she would have taken her part in helping to plant new garden land being developed at the time, as well as clearing the scrub, burning off the rubbish and tilling the soil, while the men did the heavy work of cutting the bush and digging ditches. The men included her husband, her co-residential brother and workers, 'cargo boys'. Youngish men, these latter were recruited from the settlement area on an *ad hoc* basis, prepared to work for immediate cash but not, as might have been the expectation in the past, for food or for the credit of having helped their seniors. These particular gardens were destined for the market, and men and women alike had cash yields in mind. Having to spend on cargo boys was a monetary investment for monetary return. This was work Kitim himself might have done but either could not or did not.

As her illness wore on it became a source of general anxiety, and Kanapa's husband decided there had to be a sacrifice. The only way to get the ancestral ghosts to release their hold on her was to give them something in return, and that had to be one of her own pigs.[13] An animal she had reared from a piglet was selected, for her work was evidently in it. Some would take the killing as an offering to God while others would understand the silent invocation of the ancestors. The husband held the sacrificial pig rope and then handed it to his wife's brother, both of them making short speeches about dispatching the sickness. At that stage they had identified two ghosts as responsible, the dead mother of Kanapa and her brother, and the dead mother of her husband. When she did not get immediately better, suspicion fell on the latter alone as having a long-standing grievance against the living and fertile alike. It was she who had prevented Kanapa from bearing more children and had made her sick on numerous occasions in the past. People concluded that the ghost was reminding Kanapa that in fact the husband did care for her; she should be content and not allow herself to get carried away by jealous cowife gossip.

Sickness is thrown away or detached from the afflicted person in the same way as a man gives away a pearlshell/money in exchange, or a woman a child in marriage (whether it is a daughter who leaves her mother's house or a son whose mother-in-law will receive the large bridewealth pigs she has intended for her). Living people used to fear the too close attachment of the dead who would hang about; at the same time such ghosts can also afford protection, if only from themselves. This is the point at which to repeat the fact that Manga, Kanapa's husband, was already planning a public payment of pigs and money to his maternal kin in order to elicit the positive support of his matrilateral ghosts and perhaps (he did not say this) keep them at bay at the same time. Such payments come under the general rubric of payments for the 'body'. The rationale is recompense for the mother's breast (milk) that is regarded as a source of nurture in counterpoint to the nurture derived from paternal food from a person's lineage land. (There is a direct equation between the 'grease' of breast milk, semen and fertile land: A. Strathern 1972; cf. Carrier and Carrier 1991: 218.) Maternal nurture from the lineage of a person's mother, anticipated at the bridewealth that establishes the marriage in the first place, is paid for again once a child is born, especially at the birth of a first child, and subsequently according to people's inclination or conscience, not terminating until mortuary compensation at death. The special bridewealth pig destined for the bride's mother thus acknowledges the social origin of the girl's nurture, and a division of interests between maternal and paternal kin. Thereafter, the girl's paternal kin become assimilated to 'maternal kin' of her children, a relatively smooth transition, and one that 'new' maternal kin are ready to exploit since they can expect a small stream of gifts in recognition of their special status. The social divisions are thus enacted out as connections to be pursued. One man told me that it was always worthwhile investing in daughters, because a married daughter thinks of her own parents all the time (wants to send things to them), whereas a married man must think of his parents-in-law. He had adopted two daughters in prospect of the flow of money that would come to him by this route.

In short, the 'work' that goes into making a child comes from both parents, but only paternal kin reap axiomatic benefit. So the (already separated) maternal kin have to be specifically recompensed for their lost nurture. It should be added that maintaining connections with maternal kin (and thus the division between sets of kin) is itself 'work', the work being manifest in the swelling and rounded body of the baby and the stature of the adult. A person's spiritual welfare is taken care of by the ghosts, or by God. In fact God has rather upset most such payments, including ones given at death; the missions are said to disapprove of such child payments on the grounds that God makes the body, not the mother's kin. The arrangements are also somewhat upset by the capriciousness of modern marriage, women not necessarily having the input into their husband's land and labour that would be the basis for their kin to claim payment.

This is the view Kanapa would have had from the house where she lay sick. Tethered at the end of the courtyard, in the two or three pigs churning up the soil they stood on, tended by her daughter and chased by her husband when they broke loose, she would see some of her years of work, planning and care – a throng of persons, relationships and events. She would see the division of tasks, and her husband's work on the cleared land in which the tubers grew, the hours of tracking down animals when they strayed, the discussions about how they should dispose of them, the promise to replace particular pigs taken off for an exchange partner. The size of the pigs and their fatness were prime testimony to the abundance of the staple starch, sweet potato, that she cultivates and they eat, and to the fertility of the soil in which it grows. They were also testimony to her intellectual application to her tasks, and the purposefulness of her work. Kanapa wanted to hold on to the pigs long enough to be able to get rid of them at her son's marriage, in a gesture that would make evident her motherhood. If she could not expend them this way, then she intended to realise them for herself by selling them! For she also saw the division of interests between herself and her husband.

DIVISIONS OF INTEREST

This took place 'in Hagen' but, to rephrase the question we have already asked, what time is the anthropologist in? From what historical epoch should I be drawing the tools of analysis? In one sense the events are reassuringly co-eval (after Fabian 1983; cf. Dalton 1996: 409-10) with diverse late twentieth-century global Northern European or American cultures. While bridewealth and the mother's pig, and the need to sacrifice, not to speak of prospective payments to maternal kin, were all in existence in Hagen before people ever set eyes on the money that enables them these days to discharge their obligations, I was assured of their contemporary saliency. I was told that looking after kin on the maternal side was the one distinctive 'custom' (*kastom*) of all Papua New Guinea. It was what marked them out in the modern world, the sign of common identity or national community. But interesting as it would be to join the many commentators on the description of contemporary culture as *kastom*, including Carrier's analysis of commodities and markets, I choose another route.

One of the times Euro-Americans may find themselves in has so to speak only just happened for them. But it may have 'happened' long ago in Papua New Guinea. I wonder if some of the considerations voiced by Kanapa – especially those with their roots thoroughly in Hagen's past – might not *anticipate* certain future economic directions in Euro-American quests for ownership. I refer to the economics of new reproductive forms, of rights established through (pro)creativity, bodily and mental.

Some years ago now, Annette Weiner (1980, 1982) called for the anthropology of Melanesia to look not to reciprocity as a model for gift-based or exchange relations but to reproduction. Although her own model has been criticised for serving the old tautologies of structural-functionalism in new guise (Carrier and Carrier 1991: 110-13), its reference point was not simply the replication of social categories but reproduction in the sense of bodily procreation. She dwelt on Melanesian images of the individual life cycle, of birth and decay, and the circulation of exchange items in relation to these, as generative extensions of body processes. Since that was written, *recent* developments in the Euro-American anthropologist's society of origin are beginning to provide a vocabulary of 'reproduction' that could inform contemporary analysis with the same kind of effect that an economically-interpreted inflection of reciprocity once did. In Hagen, the right to the mother's pig is long established – it has historical antecedents that have nothing to do with reproductive technology and Euro-American legislation and litigation. Yet the emergent quasi-legal concepts that accompany these applications of technology invite Euro-Americans to think of property in persons and property in life forms (Franklin 1995). There is analytical mileage here. One example must suffice: the recently invented concept of procreative intent. It renders some of the enduring forms of Hagen social life newly co-eval with some from the anthropologist's world.

Kanapa's final defiance says it all: the dispute between husband and wife was not between keeping and giving but over the contexts in which either of them could dispose of the products of their joint efforts. Carrier is right to emphasise the work that goes into keeping debts alive in people's minds. Yet it is not just transactions that create debts. Maternal nurture also makes persons indebted to their maternal kin. However Kanapa's huband tried to avoid making good what she thought he owed, he could not avoid the long-term consequences of neglect, his own dead mother's ghost being a ready reminder. Bridewealth has a special poignancy for women, as we have seen, for it is the moment at which the mother's part is made manifest. Indeed, the occasion of marriage is the public 'birth' of parents and children alike, and thus the culmination of a procreative process. One might almost speak of Kanapa, in her deep-felt frustration, articulating the right to be a parent. This means that it is not just, as Sillitoe reminds us (1988a: 7), that men need women to produce pigs, but that women need pigs to produce men. That is, they need a medium which will make visible their maternal care, and then of course for their children to get married. What holds true for both groom's and bride's mother is culturally explicit in the case of the bride's mother. Bridewealth goes to girl's kin because they are her originators, those who produced her, and this is the point at which the bride's kin will utter remarks – as the adopting father did – that could well be glossed in terms of procreative intent. Procreative intent is expressed in people's desire for daughters who will bring their parents (bride)wealth.

This is an openly reproductive system geared to producing persons through the production of things. Yet to locate the principal analytical vocabulary in terms of production and consumption would be to privilege one kind of body product, namely labour, over others. Anthropologists are used to debating the general applicability of market models or the capitalist mode of production to their materials. As I indicated in the previous chapter, here is another debate: the extent to which the technology released by post-industrial/late capitalist institutions has given us new economic forms, including new body products, to think with. The latter includes both body parts previously inseparable from human activity or embodiment, but now capable of externalisation, such as the pre-implanted embryo, and products of the intellect previously embedded in their realisation, but now valued in the way that the potential of inventiveness is valued, such as procreative intent.

The large pig that Kanapa had in mind for the bride's mother was one she had reared, we might say, with such intent. That is, she foresaw the day when it would appear at her son's bridewealth. It would appear both as the product of joint work bestowed on it by herself and her husband *and* as the embodiment of her own actions which subsumed her intentions for it. Like the question of the disposition of embryos in an other than procreative context, the husband's taking it off instigated a conflict over the respective interests of the spouses. We might consider, then, the further concepts that Robertson develops, dispositional authority and dispositional agreements. The issue is not that these are necessarily new in American legal thinking but that they are these days being applied to products of the body. Something of a parallel is offered by Sillitoe's (1998a) discussion (and cf. Salisbury 1962) of personal possessions owned by Highlands men and women and the pigs and shell valuables that circulate in exchange. In relation to valuables he notes that the rights at issue are those of disposal, and that this is a right that only one person at a time may hold, though the item in question (the rights in it) may pass serially between persons. One cannot own valuables exclusively (as 'private property'), but may enjoy custody of them for a while. He thus disputes the relevance of inalienability as a concept; people may cease to have rights in particular items while continuing to have rights in relation to the recipient by virtue of the transfer of those items.[14] What is helpful in Sillitoe's contribution is his focus on the right to dispose not as a concomitant of pre-existing or already established property rights but (precisely as suggested in the case of the Tennessee embryos) as a form of property relation itself. Recall Ponam land titles.

One might elaborate: disposability begins to appear as an outcome of social context, an entitlement to be exercised in the appropriate milieu. Like the Tennessee woman who wished the embryos to live so that she could complete her motherhood in however removed a form, Kanapa wanted to complete her motherhood with the disposal of her pigs at her son's marriage. By the same token, the Hagen woman's entitlement to dispose of the mother's pig is dormant until bridewealth mobilises it. The conventions of marriage prestations here provide a kind of tacit dispositional agreement. In the meanwhile, the potential 'mother's pig' is prey to all sorts of other demands. Until it is realised as such, like the unrealised embryo, other claims may come to the fore. In the Hagen case men have an interest in deferring that particular realisation because they have other uses for the valuable items; in the Tennessee case the man who had no other uses for the embryo simply wished to block that realisation, for it would have made him the father he did not wish to be.

Now through their own exchanges Hagen men create a separate domain of entitlements for themselves; they belong to this social domain
by the authority of the dispositional control it enables them to exercise.
We may further note that it defines desire as desire for valuables to dispose of and identities as relations made present through the dispositional acts of others. In short, what keeps men's commitment to their
collective exchanges is the same as the commitment of husbands and
wives to their joint work: a division of interests. For any or either party
to pursue their interests, such a division must be made visible. But what
is being divided by these interests?

Alan Macfarlane's (1998) analysis of the varying divisibility and
indivisibility of resources (things) on the one hand and on the other
of rights (distributed among persons), at different times and places in
Europe, becomes germane at this point. He points to an ancient difference between Roman and feudal law. Roman lawyers saw things as
property and as divisible (land could be divided or partitioned again and
again among heirs), while for feudal lawyers the thing was indivisible
or impartible but property rights in it could be almost infinitely divided
among persons with claim upon it (there might be several distinct titles
to the same piece of land). Under this second regime, the bundle of social
ties between people was divisible in different ways. He thus quotes an
observation that common law, developed from the tenures of medieval
feudalism and by contrast with civil or Roman law, was the more easily
able to treat abstract rights such as copyright and patents as forms of
property. The point is that partibility and impartibility might rest either
with the object of the property claim or with the subjects making the
claim. The Melanesian material prompts a further question. Suppose the
claims were not about things or rights but about *persons* as such?

In the Melanesian case there is on the one hand a division of interests
among persons with respect to other persons, as evinced through bridewealth payments, for instance, where kin of different kinds have claims
on persons. There is on the other hand, and simultaneously, a conception
of a person's identity as inherently divisible. Thus parts of the person may
be imagined as cut off from having future effect: in patrilineal regimes
a woman cannot transmit her clan identity to the child – it is turned
back through bridewealth, through the wealth which compensates the
maternal kin for the substance they have 'lost' through their daughter.
Where wealth flows, bodily substance[15] may also be thought of as flowing, and body composition becomes an image of the person and his or
her relationships with others. As a consequence, there is both internal

and external partition. The partibility of the person (evinced in flows of wealth) is a counterpart to the person as a composite of the relations that compose him or her. It is as though these people were at once dividing the thing (here the person) *and* dividing bundles of rights in relation to the thing (here sets of relations that at once compose and are external to the person). If we translate that back into Euro-American, so to speak, we might say that persons can be divided both as subjects (Euro-American anthropologists have always argued for a theoretical construct that defines persons as social bundles of rights and duties distributed between various relationships) and as objects (that is, as the objects of other people's interests). But to leave it like this would simply recapitulate the distinction between rights *in personam* and rights *in rem* which Radcliffe-Brown (1952) long ago made a cornerstone of analysis. The kinds of novel partitionings of procreative material offered these days through some applications of reproductive medicine demand new ways of imagining divisible persons and of imagining the social consequences such divisions set in train. These may be interpreted, in Euro-American experience, as fragmenting 'the individual' or 'the body', that is, dividing what is not properly divisible. However, fragmentation does not give us much of a comparative tool. A formula which would be equally apposite for Melanesia is that relationships divide and are divided by interests.

This construct does not map in any simple way on to the difference between inclusive and exclusive relations. Rather, inclusivity/exclusivity seems particularly apposite for the analysis of one type of property relation, namely possession, which resonates with the community/individual axis engrained in European thinking. Now, in the 1990s, there seems a renewed anthropological concern with the concept of possession. If this concern is responsive to a late twentieth-century cultural re-embedding of personal desire and identity in indivisible things, perhaps such a move resists exactly these concurrent perceptions of divisions of body and body products. Perhaps it challenges exactly those emergent quasi-legal constructs of dispositional control – such as the ones presented by Robertson – being developed to deal with divergent interests in life forms.

Battaglia (1994) introduces a scholar, Rosalind Petchesky, who has deliberately sought to construct a critical vocabulary drawn from another epoch, and with resistance in mind. Let us return for a moment then to Battaglia's own story of the potential presence. In her critique of Bhaskar's new materialism,[16] she considers how Trobriand Islanders in Port Moresby drew attention to axe blades, a class of valuable called *beku.* These have been analysed (A. Weiner 1976) as significant for the beginnings of new reproductive cycles, affirmed in the words of an urban Trobriander that they 'represent life'. If one wished to use the terms, they are both alienable (bestowed on recipients without creating continuing partnership) and inalienable (a man hopes eventually to walk after his *beku* and follow its path through successive villages in order to buy it back). 'It would seem,' Battaglia adds (1994: 637) 'that possession, while an important issue for users, is not the only ... issue ... Property models are outdistanced by the way people operate the object and by their quest for it along the path of remembered (or fabricated?) "owners".' This is the juncture at which she draws attention to an article by Petchesky (1995) on the conceptualisation of property in relation to the body: the problem is not the language of ownership but the reification of property as possession. Note that the language of ownership is thus rendered 'unproblematic' through a deconstructive division (on Battaglia's part) that produces a counterpart query, as here in the query about reification, possession conceived as a thing; without that kind of division, one may add, there is no analytical position to take.

Petchesky wishes to recover political purpose for the construct of 'self-propriety' or self-ownership specifically in relation to the body as a point of feminist resistance to other, private, exclusive, conceptualisations of ownership. Against those who decry the language of property altogether she wishes to open up the range of conceptual resources from which we might draw our models.[17] Her inspiration is a moment of resistance that she identifies as having taken place some three hundred years ago. This was a moment at which 'self-propriety' summoned a 'concept of property that is inclusive rather than exclusive and a model of the body that is extensive rather than insular' (Petchesky 1995: 400). (Protest was against the enclosing of the commons, property imagined as a shared rather than private resource.) It was inclusive from the connections that were established with the community, evoking a vision of an 'extended or communally embedded body' as a 'normative ground in the process of self-creation and self-engagement' (1995: 400). The embedding of self-creation *in* community (rather than against it) echoes Gudeman's (1996) analysis of what he calls the community economy as a reproductive system. He draws on Latin American ethnography[18] in order to make a point about the embeddedness of innovation in social practice. It is a specifically 'Western' proclivity, and a late one at that, to treat innovation as a product of the intellect and the products of the intellect as separate from other aspects of the person. He thus asks, apropos the foundations of formal economic knowledge in common practice, at what point it would have made sense to treat innovations in practices and knowledge as clearly independent products of the mind. A historical question about the development of modern European institutions again asks us to historicise our analytical vocabulary.[19]

Now Petchesky deliberately searches for a conceptualisation of ownership in relation to the body that will be relevant for contemporary feminist practice. ('[O]wning our bodies depends integrally on having access to the social resources for assuring our bodies' health and wellbeing; self-ownership and proper caretaking go hand in hand with shared ownership of the commons' (Petchesky 1995: 403).) She finds the construct she is looking for in the writings of Leveller tracts, as well as later slave narratives, of the seventeenth century. The concept of self-ownership, or property in one's person, was being promulgated among folk who were collectively opposed to market relations, not defending them. The promulgation, pre-Lockean,[20] summoned a notion of rights in the body that were free from state interference, especially in sexual expression. Early modern radicals were, in her view, taking an oppositional stance against interference by public authorities in sexual and bodily functions, much we might add as Robertson would like to see procreative choices constitutionally protected against restrictive legislation on the grounds that legislation interferes with reproductive liberty.[21] With Locke, Petchesky argues, the radical idea of self-ownership fell away before a new and individualistic interpretation of property in the person founded on rights to one's own labour. There is no 'one' epoch here. It would be interesting indeed to know how these diverse formulations related to the seventeenth-century beginnings of intellectual property rights (copyright) and the emergent idea of authors' proprietory rights in their work.[22]

Here we find in miniature a recapitulation of the European history of inclusive and exclusive notions of ownership ('possession') which suggests a creative re-use of them. The need comes from the pressure of contemporary social change. Against the background of an emergent Euro-American discourse about property in persons and body products, especially in the context of kinship created by transactions, it is not only anthropologists who are thinking anew about what 'ownership' entails. The current language about reproductive rights is also developing in conscious collusion with and contest against commercially driven definitions of body products. It may endorse or defeat other connotations of proprietorship, for instance in Britain those evident in indigenous

(Euro-American) kinship thinking. It may find an echo in the indigenous (Melanesian) comparison of socioeconomic systems, prompted for instance by the Papua New Guinean way in which commerce and *kastom* are played off against each other in radically different trajectories of commoditisation. These all afford analytical choices. In devising their own contemporary lexicon of property relations, social anthropologists need to know the lexicons developing around them.

ACKNOWLEDGEMENTS

I am most grateful to Alan Macfarlane for initial stimulus, and to Debbora Battaglia and Eric Hirsch for further comments. A version of this chapter was read as a paper to the Royal Historical Society's 1996 conference at York University, and to the Sociology and Social Anthropology seminar at Keele University. It received some pretty hefty criticism from which I have benefited. James Carrier has as always given me much food for thought, and I record my warm thanks.

PART III

SUBSTANCES

CHAPTER 8

Potential Property: Intellectual Rights and Property in Persons

This chapter has a simple aim: to gather together certain issues of potential interest to social anthropologists. These concern concepts of ownership.

There is an emerging constellation of (Euro-American) property interests in which potentiality, as the capacity for development as yet unrealised, plays a central role. This field is dominated by a well-established (legal) category, viz. intellectual property rights, but for non-lawyers the legal category as much serves as a vehicle for experimenting with new conceptualisations of ownership as it delimits a recognisable phenomenon. 'Intellectual property rights' (IPR in the singular) will appear not as the organising rubric of this account but as one location in it.

Euro-Americans are used to entities emerging which are initially difficult to categorise. The embryo outside the human body is a case in point; in other cases, such as the identification of medicinal plants, new uses transform future expectations of what already exists. When the application of 'technology' is involved, the creative work of human effort in these transformations becomes visible. Technologies enabling the embryo to live outside the maternal body render it a new object of knowledge (e.g. Franklin 1993) in part because the embryo is seen to have been produced in new ways. But objects of knowledge may also be appropriated in new ways, and human intention for the use of them is another indicator of creativity, of the capacity to anticipate future possibilities. These processes are conflated in the explicit production of novelty (Campbell 1992). Perhaps the recent salience of intellectual property rights as a public issue echoes the speeded-up tempo of the kind of life imagined by the media and constantly brought forward by commerce (Brennan 1993). 'The ultimate success of the firm depends on the potential of [its technological and scientific] creativity and infrastructure in response to market demand' (Gibbons et al. 1994: 47). Potential becomes an asset, and establishing intellectual property is one way of securing control over the potential life of creative ideas with reference to both their production and their future use.

A long-established form of Euro-American anticipation comes from expectations that persons should enjoy the products of their labour, not just now but also as investment in the future. When those products have a future themselves, as a useful invention does, then continuing ownership may bring continuing returns – the proprietorship that is cut off in some commodity transfers has in others a forward future of its own. The following examples of proprietorship, a handful out of many, all look to the future.

The examples do not necessarily add up, and a methodological point must be made at the outset. If I were to point to similar idioms being used in disputes over embryo conservation and cultural property, this starts looking like word play with the terms people happen to choose. The field could as well be a discontinuous terrain, no more than sightings of places that happen to be visible from particular vantage points (Singleton and Michael 1993) – as aspects of university quality assessment exercises might seem visible from EC deliberations on gene patents. At the same time, the anthropologist is practised in making patterns out of recurrent values and repeated images or in identifying the geology underlying surface diversity. One can always argue that culture consists in making analogies, and then let the similarities and repetitions 'speak for themselves'. Or reinstate analytical divisions that have served anthropology in the past and show up the field as already mapped into domains.[1] In any case the problem would seem these days to be taken care of outside the discipline, in work such as D. Harvey's (1990) which links together cultural and economic transformations (only the surface seems discontinuous) or else by the network theorists such as Law (1994) who make narratives out of getting from one location to another (you can still travel, and the journey connects). On the historical continuity of intellectual property rights, there is a burgeoning enquiry[2] into how types of claims Euro-Americans nowadays take for granted were with difficulty created in the seventeenth and eighteenth centuries. However, I follow none of these courses. For there is a small reason for not making greater claims than that of assemblage.

An assemblage is suggestive. It points to a heap of situations where one might watch for developments, to potential places of interest for the anthropologist. The concept of a multi-sited ethnography (Marcus 1993), diverse sites within the one programme of research, captures some of this.[3] Marcus observes that tracing cultural phenomena across different settings may reveal the contingency of what began as initial identity – the tracing both defines and queries the chain of associations.[4] I would hope that this chapter works the other way round. It avoids discursive connections, making a story, in order to avoid both the false negative appearance of stringing surface similarities together and the false positive appearance of having uncovered a new phenomenon. For *what the locations presented here have in common has not necessarily happened yet*. What I believe they have in common is their potential for reconceptualisations of ownership, and specifically for raising the possibility of persons as property. What has not yet happened is the way in which these sites may in future connect up.

That connections – of a causal or interactive kind – will emerge is not in doubt. Coombe (1993) refers to the recurrent associations that eighteenth-century advocates of copyright laws made between the author and his work and the father and his child.[5] I anticipate similar connections in the future. Given that many of the situations I describe are open to conflict, we can expect lawyers, commentators, spokespeople and social theorists to cast around for analogies, parallels, precedents, whether from their own experience or beyond. Exactly the routes that they follow, or what chains of association they set up, will be the subject for future ethnographic enquiry. (Only) the potential is present.

I start with a brief reminder of the power of connecting otherwise distinct domains of ideas: two American situations in which explicit parallels have influenced the outcome of claims. They concern interesting, if idiosyncratic, readings of potentiality. I then assemble four areas of enquiry, which offer candidates for ownership. Here the idiosyncrasy, in touching on a few out of the myriad issues they raise, is mine.

BORROWING CATEGORIES

The paragraph with which Chapter 7 opens is paraphrased here. 'Neither property nor people': this was, in Dolgin's (1994: 1277) words, the conclusion of the Tennessee Supreme Court faced with seven cryopreserved embryos stored in a Knoxville fertility clinic.[6] The two concepts were connected through the nature of the claims that a man and woman, once a couple but now no longer, enjoyed with respect to what they had created. Two preceding courts had ruled, alternatively, on the grounds that the embryos were *persons*, children whom the woman was now wishing to bring into the world and whose best interests must be before the court, and on the grounds that whatever the status of the embryos they should be treated as *property* for purposes of deciding who had 'control' in them (Dolgin 1994: 1276-7). (The man's lawyers had argued for a division of property rights.) The Supreme Court sided fully with neither; the embryos (only) had the potential to become children. As we have already seen, it described the embryos in terms of 'having value in the "potential to become, after implantation, growth and birth, children"' (Dolgin 1994: 1277).

Now potential can be taken either as not yet realised or as about to be, an equivocation that seems to have influenced the final outcome. According to Dolgin, the Supreme Court bypassed the interests of the embryos and focused on those of the progenitors, balancing the interests of each party by considering the parties' 'intentions'. The embryo's potential to become a person was thus embodied twice over – not just in the capacity for the life of the organic being to unfold but in the intentions of progenitors who had wanted a child in the first place (they had not wanted 'an embryo').[7]

If it can be imagined of future persons that they were once controllable like property, then the reverse, property as person, is with not much more imagination recoverable from the concept of unalienated labour. In Euro-American culture this is especially allowable of the products of mental or intellectual labour whose market value *includes* accreditation to the producer. The point has already been made in Chapter 7: they carry the producer's name and the relationship between producer and product is one of identification (after Schwimmer).[8] When intellectual property rights define this link, third parties may enjoy the property, while its future use is also to the benefit of the original producer. Such property is culturally validated as extensions of persons, often in quasi-procreative idiom as in the appeal to the moral right of creators to their creations.[9] But idioms flow in more than one direction.

One of the now famous surrogacy disputes to have been heard in American courts, *Johnson v. Calvert*,[10] dealt with the question of identifying the mother, since state law allowed that there could be only one such person. The majority opinion was that where the claims of genetic consanguinity and giving birth did not coincide in one person, then the woman who had intended to be the mother should be regarded as the natural mother. This opinion was backed by a legal commentator's advice that since the child would not be born but for the efforts of the intended parents, then the intending parents were the first cause or prime movers of the procreative relationship (parenthood established through the anticipation of it). Another commentator had argued that the 'mental concept of the child is a controlling factor in its creation, and the originators of that concept merit full credit as conceivers'.[11] A dissenting opinion seized on this second formula for its familiarity. Justice Kennard, dissenting, pointed out that the originators-of-the-concept rationale is frequently advanced when justifying the law's protection of intellectual property.

Kennard developed the connection at length, quoting a work on the philosophy of intellectual property which stated that an idea belongs to its creator because it is a manifestation of the creator's personality or self. Kennard's interpretation was that in the same way as a song or invention is to be protected as the property of the originator of the concept, so should a child be regarded as belonging to the originator of the concept of a child. But, she asserted, the problem with this argument is that children are not property. Unlike songs or inventions, she went on, rights in children cannot be sold for a consideration or made freely available to the public. No one can have a property right of any kind (intellectual or otherwise) in a child because children are not property in the first place. The implication of the dissenting view is that although an idea might 'create' a child, it does not automatically follow that rights to its realisation can be owned.

Of course the majority view had not argued that children were property either. They had simply talked of the conceivers and prime movers who produced the child. But a parallel was possible.

ASSEMBLAGE

I phrase the four candidates for ownership as products: of collective life (cultural property), of usable knowledge (intellectual property), of the body (over which questions of property are in constant dispute) and of professional commitment.

These are different orders of phenomena. Social anthropologists are particularly likely to have a stake in the first, as it begins to take shape in the literature, especially from the United States. It deals with a recognisable object ('culture') and recognisable claims ('identity') in settings that make new conflicts of interest out of them. The second incorporates types of interest more than two hundred years old (five hundred, according to some) which have suddenly spilled over from largely legal argumentation, and a technical legal literature, into general use. The third touches on a multiplicity of contentious developments. Biotechnology is a source of passion and concern on which numerous interest groups and lobbies offer their perspectives, and there is a huge outpouring of writing, from political protest to ethical evaluation to explanations of science to the layperson. The last reminds academics of their own interests. One question might be as to which of these other fields will provide borrowable parallels and analogies for the products of university departments.

Products of collective life

Greaves introduces the (American) Association for Applied Anthropology's handbook on *Intellectual Property Rights for Indigenous Peoples* by referring to the astonishing growth of the topic over the preceding three years (1994: ix; see Posey 1990). What is interesting about this collection is the lively dispute as to whether IPR is the appropriate vehicle for conserving peoples' rights to the benefits of their own heritage. Greaves argues it can be, provided one recognises that it is being used in a specific way. For instance, at stake are rights not to new knowledge but to old. So this is about the search for the appropriate parallel or analogy. The search is stimulated by the desire to secure possession, in terms that will have international legal purchase, of natural resources and ways of life in the face of encroachment. If IPR suggests a legal instrument that could be used in defence of indigenous rights, this is a creative and determined use of the concept of 'ownership'. 'Among those of us who seek equity for the world's indigenous peoples the thought arises, why couldn't indigenous peoples *own* their cultural knowledge' (Greaves 1994: 4, original emphasis); he adds, 'and then, if they allowed it to be used elsewhere, secure a just share of the money it generates?' Some contributors, such as the Zuni team (Soleri et al. 1994), voice a sceptical view, wondering whether a device of European capitalism is appropriately extended to cure problems capitalism created in the first place.[12] Posey (1994) queries the appropriateness of IPR to empower indigenous people but points to its power in challenging models of property.

It is recognised that IPR is 'housed in' (Greaves 1994: 5) (embodied, contextualised in) Western law.[13] The problems are spelled out. IPR is not the solution, a new legal instrument is, but it is at least a promising avenue. Yet monopolies can be used both with and against original owners, as in the famous example of Mexico's protection of steroids derived from Dioscorea which led to drug companies turning to other sources (Brush 1994: 137; also 1993: 665). One issue raised by Greaves is 'the rapidly developing technology for transforming any initial phenomenon into something else. Whether it is a new medicinal drug, or a novel sound from a musical instrument,[14] increasingly it is the *idea*, not the phenomenon, that is of value' (1994: 13, original italics). The market thus disembeds what is usable, whereas the thrust of the indigenous IPR movement is to re-embed, re-contextualise, indigenous ownership in indigenous traditional culture. Tradition, we may remark, is an embedding concept.

The crux is that intellectual property rights – whether recognised in patents for inventions, trade secrets, copyright, plant variety rights or trade names – cannot ordinarily be applied to general knowledge. Activists for indigenous claims challenge this limitation when they draw a parallel between intellectual and *cultural* property. Thus Soleri et al. suggest (among other possibilities) that private plant breeders' rights could be balanced with a version of 'farmers' rights'. Many countries recognise the special position of the farmer who depends on being able to duplicate seed; if farmers' rights were defined at a *group* level, they could be extended to rights in folk varieties. 'To those supporting farmers' intellectual property rights in their folk varieties ... the communal effort in developing folk varieties as an integrated part of making a living over generations [is] as legitimate as the individual efforts of scientists' (Soleri et al. 1994: 24). Greaves (1995: 4) is explicit: 'in the indigenous context IPR is claimed as a group right. Further, it is understood as a cultural right, an implementation of their inherent right to defend and continue their ancestral culture.' While fully cognisant of difficulties of assigning rights, advocates of IPR for indigenous peoples in resting their case on traditional knowledge rest it on a collective possession.[15] By conserving their cultural base, it is argued, people will have a core around which they will adapt to the future. At the same time, Brush (1993: 663-4) refers to the 'group identity problem' as one of four obstacles to implementing intellectual property rights for indigenous knowledge.[16]

The anthropologist's concept of culture was first and foremost a heuristic, its individualising function in essence a problematising one (it both defined and queried the entity in question). The difficulty of identifying cultural ownership must include the fact that cultures are not discrete bodies; it is 'societies' that set up boundaries. Social communities may claim common cultural identity, and claim rights in corporate images, but it does not of course follow that cultures reproduce as populations do.[17] Recent diaspora for instance, not to speak of global spread, have familiarised anthropologists with the notion of dispersed cultures.

Products of usable knowledge

In academic and especially scientific communities, the dispersal of knowledge is often taken to be crucial to its reproduction. Like windborne seed, success is measured by the number of sites at which it grows. (Patents are deliberately intended to encourage the publication of inventions by preventing others from re-creating them.) The concept of intellectual property rights is dispersed throughout this chapter.

IPR is a form of property protection which, developed as patents, copyright, license and royalties, the state took over from guilds (see Brush's brief history, 1993). Today it has been drawn into a cultural whirlwind that sweeps up the potential of anyone's creation.[18] Indeed, the National Academies Policy Advisory Group (NAPAG) in the UK remarks (in their 1995 document, *Intellectual Property and the Academic Community*) on a tendency for intellectual property to be used as a synonym for discovery or research results, as though there were some overarching legal recognition of originality; however, this is not so. National intellectual property laws are highly selective, and relate to products from which demonstrable material benefit accrues (authorship of literary works that bring in royalties; inventions with marketable application). A particular origin point in a process must be identifiable, and a particular originator (in the case of patents, the first inventor in the US; the first applicant for patent in the EU). The originator can be an individual author, research team or the corporation/institution (employer) which provides funding and facilities, such as a university (NAPAG 1995: 37). In the case of cultural property, one of the tests of a group's claims may be the transmissibility of cultural knowledge over the generations: it is authentic because it can be shown to have been handed on. Intellectual property is claimable precisely because it has not. So dispersal has to be controlled.

The personnel and resources that lead to new objects of knowledge may form social clusters more like networks than groups. This is quite apart from the fact that communities promoting 'collaborative' effort conceal their own lines of exploitation (see Born 1995: Ch. 9). Communalistic metaphors such as 'common' knowledge or 'community' for the context in which ideas breed and circulate conceal another social phenomenon. Where knowledge is dispersable, then ideas travel along networks. Networks can break into competitive segments, so that the lines of lengthy interchanges of information leading to a piece of usable knowledge, such as a commodifiable invention, are truncated when the time comes to apply for a patent (see Chapter 6). If we are living in a 'knowledge-based economy' (Gibbons et al. 1994), then such social/collective formations, and their severance, are crucial to the innovations on which the market depends. We should be thinking not of individual rights as against collective rights, but of different kinds of collectives.

The increasing functionality of dispersed knowledge has been formalised by Gibbons and his co-authors (1994; and see Hill and Turpin 1995). They contrast two modes of knowledge. Mode 1 depends on institutions and disciplines pursuing specialist goals. Mode 2, by contrast, is transdisciplinary, acquired through application and distributed across institutions.[19] Hence they refer to *socially distributed* knowledge. Echoes of the multi-sited ethnography! Accompanying social forms may be transient and shortlived, like research teams made up of constellations of personnel who come and go, although 'the organisation and communication pattern persists as a matrix, from which further groups and networks, dedicated to different problems, will be formed' (Gibbons et al. 1994: 6). No enduring groups, but perhaps a suggestive counterpart to the collective element in cultural property lies in the 'tacit knowledge' that such dispersal assumes. This is the embodied, incorporated skill that people carry around with them, learnt in specific contexts but transferable to other sites. Gibbons et al. put tacit knowledge *in opposition* to the proprietory forms standardised by IPR. Now the (tacit) knowledge that people carry with them is also learnt from others; in fact Hill (1994),[20] who argues along similar lines, observes that social skills are among the most important aspects of tacit knowledge, and this includes skill about how to operate networks. Such a notion of dispersed sociality may speak to the experience of those 'indigenous' people whose cultural knowledge locates them not in a community but in their own person and own relationships.[21]

There is an obvious parallel between the potential of a product to bring in future benefit and the reproducibility of money. Money produces money via its embodiment and discharge in labour/consumption. The prospect of future gain means that one *wants* others to exploit one's property, just as academics want to have their ideas used, to have them re-contextualised, embedded in other minds, as widely as possible. But the dispersal that, flowing outwards, creates more money (reputation) also has to be channelled if returns are to flow back; here money (less true of reputation) may be one of its own criteria for restricting claims to ownership. Where IPR rests on the idea that money-producing products should go on producing money for the originator, it also acknowledges the originator who starts an enterprise off with money. Hence an employer or funding body may be a future beneficiary. Originators as authors who 'invest' energy, labour and ideas in products are aligned with originators as investors who help 'author' projects through their support.

Products of the body

In March 1995 the European parliament[22] brought to an end eight years of debate on protection for biotechnological inventions. The scientific community was hoping for a Council Directive to harmonise the patent laws of member states. Persons or property? – there was, for instance, lack of clarity over existing provisions which excluded from IPR 'biological processes' for the production of plants and animals (e.g. selective breeding) and included 'microbiological' processes or their products (e.g. cell lines). This particularly affected the standing of genetic material, the production of new 'gene constructs' and the genetic modification of organisms. US law allowed patents on all modified organisms to the benefit of those who could industrially exploit them, whereas European laws were equivocal. They have remained so: the draft Directive on the Legal Protection of Biotechnological Inventions fell.

Many issues stood in its way, including the fear that monopoly patents on genetically modified crops would mean that farmers could not reproduce from their own seed but would have to buy fresh seed each year from patent holders.[23] However, that most widely reported was genetic modification of the human 'body'. I put 'body' in quotation marks because a number of substantives could substitute for it. These, with varying emotive force, recast the subject of the debate in wider or narrower terms.

The British newspaper *The Independent* had the heading 'MEPs set to agree patents for *human life*' on the day of the parliamentary debate (1 March 1995: my italics throughout). Its text referred to *human genes and cell lines*. One lobby group (through its broadsheet, *Patent Concern*, n.d.), noting that the patenting of *human genes and cells* was already with us,[24] warned that the principal ethical problem with the directive-to-be was that 'it does not contain a clause prohibiting the patenting of *human beings*'. The European Federation of Biotechnology Task Group on Public Perceptions of Biotechnology produced a briefing paper (1993) entitled simply *Patenting Life*. They reported that some see it as wrong 'to confer on anyone the "ownership" of *living things*'. They also report on the US courts which decided that microorganisms were not excluded from patentability simply because they were alive: the *modified organism* was taken to be not nature's handiwork (and thus mere discovery) but man's (and thus invention). They cite the US Commissioner of Patents' subsequent declaration that patents would be granted for non-naturally occurring non-human multicellular living organisms including *animals*, and for plant and animal *varieties*. The EC Directive would be addressing itself to *biological material*, and cover *living matter* such as viruses, genes and other types of DNA and RNA; as far as human beings were concerned, it would specifically exclude the *human body* and *parts of the human body*.

Concern on this last point was reflected in an amendment to the draft Directive to the effect that, while material would not be excluded simply because it was of human origin, it would be if ascribable to an individual. It should be possible to patent inventions 'including industrially applicable parts obtained in a technical manner from the human body in such a way that they can no longer be ascribed to a particular individual [person]' (quoted in the press report of the debate in the European parliament).

I draw on the summary version of the debate put out in English. Willi Rothley, who had instigated discussion in 1988, addressed the integrity of the whole entity, saying that no patents would be allowed on *parts of the human body* or any *component of the human anatomy* as such, and 'Any talk of patenting *people* was pure demagoguery'. He referred instead to *human body elements* discovered in the course of research.[25] The amendment had been specific: 'in the light of the general principle that the *ownership of human beings* is excluded, the human body or parts of the human body as such, for example, a gene, protein or cell in the natural state in the human body, including germ cells and products resulting directly from conception, must be excluded from patentability', by contrast with the products of scientific and technological expertise that removed them from their identification with a particular individual. The exclusion was regarded by some speakers as a clarifying guarantee of human dignity that would be lost if the legislation fell. However, other speakers used the larger issue to contrary effect. One appealed to the sacredness of *human life*, this sanctity making it impossible to patent any modifications of *genetic identity* (Roberto Mezzaroma); another (Hiltrud Breyer) was quoted as saying that patenting an isolated human gene was in effect handing over *life* to private ownership, while *the human body* was brought in again as an inappropriate object of commercialisation (Roberto Barzanti).

When the human body, with its cells and organs, was invoked in the debate, appeal was being made to the (natural) integrity of individual entities. However large or minute, and whether or not *also* part of another entity, an entire entity is valued for the discreteness of its form. Now in the case of farmer's seeds, returning to (the patented) source each time would presumably have a de-genealogising effect, reproducing the identity of the original plant without change of form. In human reproduction, on the other hand, each generation can be regarded as a new one and each offspring as having an individually recognisable form. There is an interesting half-way house between such replicating and non-replicating modes of reproduction in certain computer software licensing agreements. These protect the company's future ownership rights in programs even though they are modified, perhaps daily, so that the 'form' of the software licence first bought by the customer may be very different from its 'form' years later (Stephenson 1994: 183).[26] (Stephenson offers this as a model for perpetuating indigenous rights in knowledge transformed by subsequent users.) Here, changing form becomes irrelevant to the continuing life of the product.

Products of professional commitment

Ideas may be embodied in products to differing effect. Patenting an invention confers value on inventiveness, the spark of creativity, however it is materialised. It is the ideas that are marketable, chemical formula rather than plant, blueprint rather than substance – hence the parallels with knowledge as a subject for cultural property. However, as we have seen, there are many parallels that can be made for cultural property, including copyright. Copyright confers value on form – on the performance, the phenomenal manifestation, the substance of words or images. It is precisely the materialisation of ideas in particular texts or stretches of data that is property; in UK copyright law, a work is protected but not the ideas behind it. In addition, products may be created in a context where the ideas themselves *remain* so to speak as much 'outside' the product as within it. This thought is promoted by what academics produce.

My example concerns universities in the UK. I do not deal with the commercialisation of inventions already an issue for many university enterprises, nor with plagiarism which pre-empts authorship regardless of whether commercial benefit is infringed. Rather my interest is in the kind of environment in which scholarly work is produced. Universities suggest parallels with 'cultures', where products are brought to fruition in a collective environment of knowledge and ideas. I do not mean 'communal' in the sense which Brush (1993: 656) perhaps means when he compares the 'collective inventions' (involving 'the open exchange of information among a community of producers') of peasant cultivators with the development of the English steel industry in the nineteenth century. I do mean that there is an identifiable social formation (collectivity). But more than one such formation may have an interest in 'collective' inventions, and the institutional environment of the university academic is not necessarily the intellectual environment of the scholar.

This separation has become an operational one in the Research Assessment Exercise (RAE) at present (1996) being conducted by the UK Higher Education Funding Council.[27] The aim is to assess the research output of institutions (universities), through the performance of individual subject groups (departments), primarily by scrutinising the publications of staff members. Funding consequences for institutions are serious. However, the financial gains and losses that come to the collectivity (the institution) may or may not be felt directly by departments, and will probably fall only remotely on academics.[28] At the same time, the collectivity acquires its research capital[29] not from the anonymous output of workers, as in an industrial corporation, but from the fact that each output (publication) is individually ascribed (and must be so ascribed: there are elaborate measures for allocating individuals to institutions) to a named author to whom individual works must (whether in part or whole) be wholly credited. Now these works are only in one sense produced in the environment of the institutions; they are also produced in the environment of a second collectivity. As named individuals academics belong, *in just that capacity in which the RAE is interested* (as authors), to a collectivity of scholars.

The first collectivity, the university, provides resources, is the channel through which salaries are funnelled, keeps academics alive. The productive activity of academics depends on their separately being scholars recognised by their peers. This second collectivity, instituted among themselves, works as a dispersed community network and as one which exercises an informal proprietorship over ideas which circulate in the form of paradigms and methods ascribable to the discipline. Moreover, ideas remain in this environment whether or not they become embodied in particular works in which individual scholars claim copyright, though scholars may add 'new ideas' to which they initially lay individual claim. This is guaranteed by the proprietory nature of the collectivity, as disciplines or (increasingly) topic-based cross-disciplinary fields.[30] The products which are accredited to, even nurtured by,[31] the first collectivity (the university) will in the RAE be assessed according to criteria recognised by the second (disciplines). This second body has virtually no material base of its own, being limited to a publishing network, sustained by scholars' subscriptions, purchases and so forth. Without the first collectivity, individual practitioners could not exist to be animated by the second. We might, then, look upon the ordinary single-discipline department as having a distinct identity as a hybrid of the two, the institution and the discipline. The unit (department) that is individually appraised thus in one sense is a part of the university and in another has integrity as a whole, if hybrid, entity.

As far as anthropology is concerned, I do not have to add that the discipline is animated by further collectivities. Posey (1990: 15) asks some frank questions about the implications of IPR in cultural property for those who make culture their subject matter.

FINAL REMARKS

Coombe (1994: 404)[32] enlarges on the two-hundred-year-old metaphor of an author begetting his book as a father does his child; its notion of creation goes beyond the idea of property as possession or commodity: 'A father's child is his own, not because he owns it or has invested in it, but because this child will carry the father's name and likeness.' This careful exemption of the child from ownership was being made in a world used to slavery. Today we have to take new care with our exemptions. In relation to twentieth-century fertility treatment processes, Cussins (1996) refers to the ontological choreography by which embryos can go from being 'a potential person' when they are part of the treatment process, to 'not being a potential person' as when it has been decided that they can be frozen or discarded, and even back again as when they are defrosted.[33]

That (rights in) persons might be the subject of property ownership is not unthinkable – the connection is simply forbidden. Every warning against conceiving of relations between persons in property terms still airs the idea. This is especially so when Euro-Americans consider the body or genetic design (both signify the person as an individual). If the child that carries its father's features suggests parallels with the immortalising functions of copyright, the potential child suggests to me parallels with the animating function of patents – one already possesses the blueprint.

Note the double candidates for ownership between these two types of IPR: both the realised entity and its animation, by which I mean the 'life' or 'inventiveness' that goes into a product. The double was there in the EC debate over biotechnology. Diverse terms were employed for the objects of knowledge created by potential proprietorship. One set dwelled on the whole entity, on the given integrity of cells, organs, bodies. A second referred to forces of creation – the 'life' that is more than the cell, the 'modification' that alters the functioning of the organ, the 'people' who are not just bodies. This gives us the familiar Euro-American hybrid or duplex: the supposition that at the core of entities in the phenomenal world, human and non-human, one can always discern what is given and what is open to modification, including the anthropologically familiar idea of nature as culturally constructed or individuals as socialised. The significance of the added element that turns 'nature's handiwork' into the inventor's has its antecedents in an ancient cosmology of animation: matter requires form (see the discussion in Oyama 1985: 11-12).[34] Form appears as ideational, a potential, precisely when it is not matter or materialisation. And at least two instruments of IPR would seem to be immortalising this ancient formula. 'Form' is given value both as the unique realisation or materialisation of being (copyright) and as the essence of this being in the creative impetus of information or design (patent). So culture can be rethought as works plus invention, the organisation of activities in schema and classifications constituting knowledge.

Such categories are open to comparative investigation. A starting point could be Harrison's account of ritual prerogatives. Ritual, like a play or musical composition, is a conceptual entity, and intellectual property is usefully thought of as 'the ownership not of things but of classes of things, of their images or typifications' (Harrison 1992: 235; cf. 'classes of ideas', NAPAG 1995: 46). An archetypal performance might be an example – what is owned is the potential of its enactment. Like Harrison, Gunn[35] uses the specific concept of copyright to talk of types of malanggan-sculpture ownership in New Ireland which involve rights, held not by the artist but by the commissioner, over both the sculpture in its final form and the image on which the sculpture is based, and which signifies the owner's relationship with the dead. Elsewhere, body form and image may be the subject of separate but analogous mortuary exchanges at death (de Coppet in Barraud et al. 1994).

The manner in which the components of the Euro-American hybrid are regarded as separable – the body given form or life – has new meaning in contexts where the latter appears to have an autonomous potential. Technology transfer is about needing the knowledge not the artefact, genetic engineering about needing the genes and not countless generations of flies or mice. We can talk of disembodiment when people seek to create the creativity that otherwise operates through the instrument of a whole body. This is of course a formal observation; the germ may be whole in itself, but disembodiable as an extract from a seed from a fruit. Hence the amendment to the EC Directive-that-was-not-to-be: even if those human elements subject to patent take the form of entire body components, they do not necessarily have that (formal) status of entirety. This leads to a final observation on the desire for ownership.

A thread running through this chapter has concerned processes of contextualisation and de-contextualisation involved in the flow of knowledge. *Ownership re-embeds ideas and products in an organism* (whether a corporation, culture or individual author). Ownership gathers things momentarily to a point by locating them in the owner, halting endless dissemination, effecting an identity. We might even say that emergent forms of property signify new possibilities for corporeality or bodily integration in lives that observers constantly tell themselves are dispersed.

I have not tried in this account to systematise the links between these various fields. But I have pointed to short stretches of linkages. Parallels and analogies come to assume significance in particular locations, and it is of interest to see how concepts themselves shift locations. If a division between matter and animating form can be refigured as a difference between outer form and inner design, design can be further refigured as appearance. The following passage, taken from a recent publicity document put out by the British Patent Office (1995: 5), describes a new intellectual property right, in design, which like any other business property may be bought and sold:

> While patents protect the kernel of a new apparatus, product or process, the outward shape or decorative appearance of products of all kinds is protectable by either a registered design ... or by the (unregistered) design right which gives weaker, but automatic protection ... So a new mechanism in a camera will be patentable, but the 'look' of the casing that encloses the mechanism will be protectable by ... the design right.

ACKNOWLEDGEMENT

Conflicting Interests, Divided Loyalties was the subject of the fourth EASA conference in Barcelona 1996 on culture and economy. I acknowledge the stimulus of this topic to the present exercise. [With minor editing with respect to material already presented in the preceding chapter, this account is given as published in 1996. The EC Directive (p. 171) has since been brought forward again, and been adopted.]

CHAPTER 9

What is Intellectual Property After?

What have we done to 'culture' by insisting that all signifying
forms be treated as information?

Rosemary Coombe (1996b)

In seeking momentary anchorage in actor network theory, I am caught
by its formative tussle with the division between technology and society.[1] Surely there is an after-life to its success in overcoming descriptive resistance to dealing with persons, things, artefacts and events all in
the same breath? Perhaps we have learnt to treat these heterogeneous
phenomena even-handedly. Fresh divisions, though, seem constantly in
the making, and there may be after-life enough in reinventing some of
actor network theory (ANT)'s original rationales. It is illuminating to
consider a situation where its lessons appear to have been learned, yet
where analytical symmetry is challenged by new social differentiations.
How even-handed do we always wish to be? A seminar on intellectual
property rights organised in Port Moresby, Papua New Guinea, in the
context of policy discussions over biodiversity protection, is my net. [The
seminar was still in the future when the present account was written; see
Postscript.]

THE PARLIAMENT OF BROTHERS

ANT's anchorage in a division between technology and society has been its own netting within science/technology studies.[2] Its insistence on treating human and non-human entities alike has endorsed the democratic potential of that programme. Humanity should never have been constructed in opposition to extensions of itself, an axiom which Bruno Latour has extended to all kinds of societies and circumstances: a parliament of brothers follows the parliament of things (Latour 1993: 142-3). Yet something akin to a human/non-human divide lingers in certain social formulations, evocative of the pains that officers of the British or Australian colonial service once took *not* to regard peoples under their jurisdiction as different kinds of human beings from themselves. Indeed, having to banish any hint of that divide (having to banish because it was still there) was a kind of minimal threshold for entry into the international community after the Second World War, endorsed in the United Nations declaration of rights for the human family. This gives me half of the present argument. The other half lies in a corollary of sorts: how to apply the insights of ANT to social heterogeneities in the particular absence of a signifying division between persons and things. One would not want the neutralising language and even-handed analysis of actor network theory to lessen the observer's capacity to perceive loaded rhetoric and persons' far from even-handed dealings with one another.

From the perspective of peoples of the Papua New Guinea Highlands, continuities of identity between persons and things may be taken for granted. People imagine one another in terms of the food which sustains them or the wealth by which they can be measured. Now to Euro-American ears that may sound a familiar enough situation; however, as we shall see, it is what these imaginings compel people to do with their 'things' which marks them out. In the meanwhile I make particular note of wealth because their former currency (such as the otherwise inanimate shell valuable) was held to share many attributes with persons, most notably mobility, reproductive power, attractiveness; it was the machinations which people attributed to other people that rendered these things intractable and obdurate. It is discontinuities between persons that are the persistent objects of local analysis. So while Papua New Guinea Highlanders personify the natural world in the same breath as they reify one another, they do not necessarily presume that these are symmetrical processes. Above all, it is to the actions and intentions of persons that all kinds of effects are assigned. One wonders, for example, which ancestor is blocking a business enterprise or whose persuasion it was that got the election campaign to come to this particular place rather than that. As a result, people are divided not so much by what they possess as by what they do with their possessions and attributes with respect to others.[3] They capitalise on the fact that that you cannot tell by looking at a motor vehicle whose it is, or the power it mobilises. That not being able to tell is a subject on which Papua New Guinea Highlanders elaborate endlessly.

Imagine that radical distinctions hold between persons, then, rather than between persons and things;[4] if one includes the spirit world, persons may be both human and non-human. So how are distinctions between persons established? Very simply, people achieve division through relations. They are divided by the positions they occupy in relation to one another: male and female, donor and recipient, a clan of this ancestry and a clan of that. Relationships separate out capabilities for action. A speaker holds an audience by virtue of their acquiescence; between them they create moments of (social) asymmetry.

Where interests are the phenomenal form of relations, interests divide people from one another. Different interests are addressed in ANT through Michel Callon's (1986: 208)[5] interressements, the devices by which actors detach others from elsewhere in order to attach them to themselves, not to speak of counting allies and the points of passage through which they squeeze debate. Indeed ANT analysis implies that people are always negotiating their relationships with others. If I dwell on persons as actants, it is to plead a special case not for human agency (cf. Singleton and Michael 1993: 230-1) but for the diversity of social heterogeneities which people create out of extensions of themselves. Consider Callon's (1992: 80) definition of an actor as an intermediary regarded as having the capacity to put other intermediaries into circulation. His example of Euro-American ideas on intellectual property – a work being attributed to an author or the right to exploit an invention being attributed to the salary paid to an inventor – has in one sense taken care of anything I might want to say about how Papua New Guineans attribute the appearance of the world to personal intervention. But it is important that Callon's formula allows for controversy and the conflict of interest. The symmetries in which ANT is otherwise interested prompt me to exaggerate the social divisions in this account.[6]

The situation I have in mind, or rather one half of it, is of people being forced to swallow a set of conceptual divisions long familiar to

ANT. Papua New Guineans are being inducted into the mysteries of the divide between Technology and Society. How did this come about? It has come about through a democratising impulse to render human beings symmetrical to one another. For global interests in sustaining the division are being drawn in with the best of intentions, specifically to ensure an equitable distribution of resources and thus to make sure that people are not (too much) divided by what they possess. Just as national sovereignty is promulgated on an international stage, or appeals to traditional social forms are made in a context of mass education, instruments which actually promote the distinction between technology and society are being introduced into a situation where the distinction did not exist so as to protect the indigenous order from some of its effects (the effects of that distinction). One intermediary here is the very category Callon used for his example, intellectual property rights (IPR). Already the focus of considerable controversy in the Third World figured through the peasant farmer (e.g. Brush 1993; Greaves 1994), there are some interesting passages ahead to be shaped by the particular way in which many Papua New Guinean societies deal with persons, their attributes and their effects, and the way as a consequence they also deal with things.

Perhaps part of ANT's after-life will be its effectiveness in having us recognise now familiar confrontations such as these. Being able to see how its very own demon (the separation of technology from society) gathers allies to colonise new terrain may tell us why its analysis remains necessary. And how does this separation combine with the concomitant separations of nonhuman from human or things from persons? John Law (1994) has asked about the difficulty, or ease for that matter, with which phenomena persist and have any durability at all, and that goes for the characteristic distinctiveness of these entities. The seminar on intellectual property rights in Port Moresby promises to mobilise all of these. Along this axis I predict two contrasting passage points for its deliberations. They offer two halves to my commentary on actor network theory. The first, set up by this demon, I have touched upon: the difficulty of aligning different interests in heterogeneous resources and thereby devising the appropriate social procedures for technological development. The second is my other half: in the absence of a hegemonic person/thing divide, the very ease with which all kinds of translations from resources into social claims can be made and the fears of proliferation to which this seems to lead.

First passage point: the Biodiversity Convention

Papua New Guinea is a signatory to the 1992 Convention on Biological Diversity (CBD).[7] The convention's objectives include 'developing national strategies or programmes for the conservation and sustainable use of biodiversity' (article 6), in relation to which the principle of *in situ* conservation frames a whole series of recommendations (article 8).[8] Among them is the contracting party's agreement:

> Subject to its national legislation, [to] respect, preserve and maintain knowledge and practices of indigenous and local communities embodying traditional lifestyles relevant for the conservation and sustainable use of biological diversity and [to] promote their wider application with the approval and involvement of the holders of such knowledge, innovations and practices and [to] encourage the equitable sharing of the benefits arising from [their] utilisation. [8j]

The category inclusion of indigenous communities is an outcome, among other things, of a decade of NGO campaigning on behalf of indigenous rights. Alongside this has been vigorous debate over indigenous knowledge and its protection[9] – serious attention being given worldwide to this double issue at the very point when Euro-Americans speak of their societies as 'information societies' and of 'knowledge' as industrial capital (cf. Coombe 1996a; cf. Brush 1998), and when genetic and biological materials come to be treated as informational resources (Parry 1997).

Intellectual property rights have entered the picture in diverse ways. They comprise an existing instrument for securing the international recognition of copyrights and patents. Papua New Guinea (PNG) is also in the process of becoming a signatory to the World Intellectual Property Organisation. The international aim is to break down divisions between peoples – to give as much protection to developing nations as to the technologically advanced by extending not just the benefits of technology but the procedural benefits of technology-protection to all. In any case, PNG needs procedures in place to encourage (overseas) companies who seek protection for product development. There is also the matter of new works of art, music and other exportable 'Papua New Guinean' artefacts.

Then there is the conceptual potential which IPR regimes open up. The notion that creativity could have commercial protection provides new scope for indigenous claims to resources. Here Papua New Guinea is being introduced to legislative efforts already attempted on behalf of indigenous peoples elsewhere; representatives from Peru and the Philippines are invited to the Port Moresby seminar (hereafter 'seminar'). After decades of unsatisfactory debate over land claims comes a new set of formulations: the possibility of being able to attribute 'authorship' to products of the intellect, and thus turn the focus of property rights from the nature of possession to that of creation. Property in cultural knowledge ('cultural property')[10] suddenly seems a construct realisable on a new scale. IPR could allow indigenous communities, then, to give voice to new kinds of claims, for example to ethnobotanical knowledge (Greaves 1994),[11] thereby enabling a beleaguered Third World to assert itself on the international stage. The seminar programme, under the title *Intellectual, Biological and Cultural Property Rights,* includes 'knowledge, information, inventions and techniques', 'genetic information and products', and 'cultural practices and production'.

On the surface, it would appear that ANT's lessons about symmetry between the human and non-human have already been learnt. Intellectual property rights protection promotes human knowledge on a par with other resources. More than that, the Biodiversity Convention explicitly recognises that knowledge may be embedded in people's practices ('communities embodying traditional lifestyles relevant for ... conservation'), and seems prepared to deal with a range of entities of both a social and natural kind. There appears a new readiness to accept all manner of phenomena as relevant to agreements. Yet this hybrid embrace entails, as we might expect, new practices of purification (after Latour 1993). IPR pursues its own differentiations between technology and society.

Differentiation starts with the simple question of profit arising from the utilisation of knowledge. Using knowledge to gain knowledge would not qualify for IPR protection; using knowledge to produce a commodity would. For the problem is how to make knowledge socially effective, how to make it transactable – knowledge must be turned into something else with its own independent value. The process of transformation may be attributed to an author of a work ready for consumption (copyright). However, it may instead be embedded in a tool which becomes part of the capital needed to exploit other resources. Any tool thought of as making knowledge useful acquires the attribute of 'technology'; the term points to the human resources contained within it. The more widely available the technology becomes, the more evident the continuing usefulness of knowledge: possessing the machinery to cut down a forest helps to create the interest in doing so. At the point of invention, then, an after-life is given to the application of knowledge (patent). Patents are regarded as crucial to technology development – for technology both is a product and produces products. And it captures people's imagination. One impetus for the proposed seminar is alleged international interest in local resources; outside commercial enterprise is regarded as being able to mobilise the technological base to exploit them. Thus the seminar rubric refers to 'the plans of an Australian biotech company to research and market products derived from snake and spider venom from species unique to PNG'.

So where does Society come in? Copyright and patents are premised on the specific need to give a secondary social effect to 'works' and 'technologies' which are already in themselves social effects. People first author or invent a device and then lay claims to its anticipated utility. They have to mobilise 'society' in order to lay such claims. In Euro-American convention, society here lies not only in commerce but in the procedures, such as legislation and contract, which also govern access.

This is the point at which society finds more representatives than it thought it had. On its behalf have come trenchant criticism of IPR as a quasi-legislative device, and criticism has been given impetus by the very challenge of the Convention on Biological Diversity. The movement for Traditional Resource Rights is a case in point (Posey 1995; 1996; and see note 9), one of its programmes being dissemination of information between different non-governmental bodies concerned with these issues. The question they ask is whether IPR could really offer appropriate procedures for aligning social interests with new resources. Far from it liberating the rights of indigenous peoples, many see in IPR only the spread of Euro-American forms of property that will legitimate the extractors of resources and make it more not less difficult to promote indigenous claims. However useful the notion of intellectual resource remains, the formulation of property right is extremely contentious. The principal criticism which indigenous spokesmen are reported to be making of IPR is that it confers individual ownership (see the several contributions to Brush and Stabinsky 1996). International NGOs and others point out that IPR is constructed around the figure of the solitary author or corporate invention, and is likely to work against peoples for whom 'knowledge and the determination of resources are collective and inter-generational' (quoted in Posey 1996: 13). Bringing in the state, from this point of view, does not help. For the Biodiversity Convention only adds to potential injustice in affirming state sovereignty at the expense of local resource holders. Against both market and state, alternative appeals are made to indigenous 'communities' and to the collective basis of knowledge.

Here are old differences rendered anew. This fresh polarisation of society is itself an artefact of international interests: persons are divided by the very debate which provides the key points at issue. For the debate is constituted around apparently axiomatic polarities (frequent candidates are commodity transactions versus sharing, individual interests versus collective ones, companies versus communities, nation-states versus first nations). This in turn generates further divisions. If it is agreed that indigenous collective claims are the starting terms of the debate, then the question becomes how to allocate property rights to specific social identities (seniors versus juniors, women versus men, clans versus villages)? Who will be delegated to represent whom? Social difference could proliferate infinitely.

Thus does the hybrid lead to new practices of 'purification'. Entailed in the potential for IPR to extend protection to diverse forms of resources, human and non-human, is the way in which knowledge is made effective through technology. Bringing social procedures from technology-rich states and companies to bear on what are perceived to be technology-poor ones perpetuates divisions between world powers/ multinationals and indigenous peoples/Third World enterprise. Both sides may well attribute to the former an already socialised technological competence (they know how to profit from their knowledge) whereas the latter have to be made to see first that they have technology (as in the way they implement knowledge about tree products, for example), and then to realise that they have to develop social institutions to protect it. The chances are that Papua New Guineans will feel that they must temper their internationalism with a specifically indigenous response – a response to endorse a specific sense of national identity. Certainly the language is there in people's talk of 'the PNG way' (cf. Foster 1995b). Yet the presence of Technology will no doubt remain a point of reference, and Papua New Guineans will in turn no doubt find themselves imagining an 'indigenous' response that summons a 'traditional' (non-technology-driven) Society. For one effect of the international criticisms is to present the Third World as though it were dominated by 'the social' and by community values. Such communities seemingly look towards the past, since it is existing social relations which are being summoned. The social and the ancient are combined in appeals to tradition, and 'indigenous peoples' across the world have responded to IPR for its attack on traditional values.

In short, IPR has become the subject of international debate through enrolling two concepts on which both sides – those who have hopes for it and those who despair of it – agree. One world has knowledge made effective through 'technology'; another world has society made effective through 'community' (cf. Latour 1991).[12] The former is driven by the material necessity to produce new generations of products, for the technologically advanced somehow owe it to the intrinsic nature of things to exploit their potential, while the latter is, whether as a matter of self-dignity or self-interest, pushing claims of social identity.

And who and what will represent the indigenous order which is the basis of the claims that Papua New Guinea exercises on the world stage? We might look for representatives in their own descriptions of themselves. That brings me to the second half of the argument.

Second passage point: compensation

Papua New Guinea already has a representative of its own indigenous order (so to speak) in the concept of 'customary law', formally part of the underlying law of the country (Law Reform Commission 1977).[13] It is there (as the seminar intends) to be enrolled in the translation from international agreements to local realisation. One particular area generally attributed to 'custom', which has much exercised the implementation of recent claims to resources, is to do with the way claims are negotiated – with procedure. I have been pointing to divisions of interest over the suitability of IPR. There are fundamental problems with how one translates community or collective ownership into internationally valid practice. Indeed, these are imagined exactly as problems of translation. What is to be negotiated? Does intellectual property fit local needs? What appropriate mechanisms can be found? I turn now to the opposite problem, and with it to the fear that intellectual property could fit all too well into existing practices of negotiation and translation. Mechanisms do not need to be found! However apparently heterogeneous the mix of resources, claims and social groups, the procedure in question will fit almost any contingency. Heterogeneity in matching technological and social means is not an issue; the issue is the way procedure itself exaggerates heterogeneity of a social kind.[14]

So what is this universal translator? It is known by the Pidgin/English word *kompensesen*/compensation.[15] Compensation translates persons and things into power-holders with a special competence: they both acquire the capacity to effect further translations.

'Compensation' as it is generally understood in Papua New Guinea does everything which an English-speaker might imagine, and much more. It refers both to the payment owed to persons and to the procedures by which they come to negotiate settlement. It can thus cover recompense due to kin for nurture they have bestowed, as in bridewealth, as well as damages, as in reparations to equalise thefts or injuries. It can substitute for a life, in homicide compensation, or for loss of resources. Car fatalities, war reparations, mining royalties: all potentially fall under its rubric, although since it is generally agreed that people frequently make exorbitant demands, compensation is seen as the enemy as well as the friend of peace-making ceremonies and of commercial exploitation alike. (One might ask, after Latour, how 'exorbitant' is exorbitant: and see Chapter 10). Its outcome is – from a Euro-American viewpoint – hybrid, insofar as it consists in an equally easy translation of persons into things and things into persons. And its procedural capability is of the utmost simplicity. Liabilities and claims are defined by the positions parties take in relation to one another over the issues of compensation itself. I return to this.

The concept of compensation has only recently spread across Papua New Guinea from what is taken as its Central Highlands origin (Filer 1997). Not only was it never ubiquitous, different practices characterised different regional areas; comparative analysis of some of the cultural and social differences in the substitutability of items for one another, for example, may be found in Lemonnier (1991). So wherein lies the ability of Highlands-style 'compensation' to travel? What follows is a synthesis from a Highlands and, in its detail, specifically a Hagen perspective. It suggests two crucial features.

First, compensation enrols a rhetoric of body expenditure,[16] covering both physical and mental exertion, based on an image of body process as the giving out and taking in of resources. What is embedded as substance in artefacts and bodies is the energy with which persons have acted (see p. 52). If the fertility of land lies within until it is drawn out in transactions with others, then anything that the land yields – oil, timber, gold – can be taken as evidence of the owner's inner resources. Observing foreign ventures in mining and logging, anticipation of company profit prompts nationals to construe the counter-idea of recompense. There is a logic to current interest in land as an object of investment that commands a price insofar as substance (company profits) extracted from it can be taken as evidence of substance (ancestral fertility) that has gone into it.[17] By this logic, local politicians and businessmen may persuade companies to enter into reciprocal transactions on the grounds that social welfare is at stake. What an economist might call the opportunity cost of lost subsistence production, nationals voice as 'compensation', reimbursements which they can invest for future development. Paying for loss of future benefit can be likened to compensation for bodily injury in warfare or personal payments for nurture. No wonder there is some apprehension among some policy-advisers at what the idea of intellectual property might do in a regime like this: it would add to an already heady mix the concept that knowledge is also an inner resource with a potential price.

Second, and this is the point on which I dwell here, compensation travels by its own means of evaluation. A transaction which transforms human energies into other values, it offers the promise of harnessing any order of material worth to realise them – an insult costs a fortnight's wage, assistance in war is measured by twenty full-grown pigs, mother's milk leads to claims over a piece of land. Indeed I would argue that the potential of compensation as a ready mechanism for summoning a modernised indigenous order lies in the very way in which equivalences are set up between persons and things. There are Highlands regimes where one can these days pay for almost anything, because the fact of transaction in and of itself need not drive a wedge between different phenomena.[18] The most intimate acts between persons may material-ise in transactions and a wide range of material effects may be laid at people's doors. Moreover the applicability of these procedures is much facilitated by money, which offers infinite scope for drawing new goods into existing facilitations and relationships. This means that there need be no procedural problem about sweeping into the arena of compensa-tion practices all manner of intellectual products – creativity, innovation, work carried out with intention – whatever can be rendered in terms of energy spent. That energy may be stored for the future, and not be im-mediately disposable (as in many land tenure practices in Papua New Guinea) or it may be detachable from persons through the very process of substitution (that is, compensation) itself. The point is that there is no predetermined discontinuity between persons and the products of their efforts (cf. Gudeman 1996). One corollary is that almost anything can be attributed to people's work, someone's, somewhere. If not in known human persons, the source may lie in ancestors or spirits or heroes, with a mythology of inventions and interventions to prove the point. In any case, since so many things are the ultimate result of such interventions, there is little that cannot be made to show the imprint of exertion, in-cluding the exertion of thought and intent.

Remark again on the simplicity of the procedure. The compensation process itself defines what is transactable (compensatable). This is no tautology. For compensation entails making relations between persons visible through the flow of payments, and making them afresh. The vehicles for compensation (usually conceived as wealth of a kind) are thus pressed into the service of creating, limiting and expanding social relationships. Relations are infinitely open to redefinition and reiteration; their definitive capacity is that of absorbing new transactional moments. IPR would expand by huge volume the number of items that may fall into the category of objects with which Papua New Guineans can transact, insofar as it would be enlisting persons seen in the light of new resources, and thus new categories of social actors and new grounds on which to create relationships.

Unlike claims people make on one another with reference to territorial area or group membership as some predetermining set of attributes, compensation itself works as a species of social organisation. It can create new social units. For it may be given or received by any order of social entity – an individual or a clan or a district. But that is really the wrong way round. Rather, collectivities differentiate, identify and, in short, *describe themselves by their role in compensation,* a kind of functional heterogeneity. Compensation is part of the wider field of transactions by which social units are defined through exchange.[19] So, for instance, clan or subclan identity may be claimed on the grounds of people's joint action as givers/receivers of bridewealth. If social entities justify themselves through the very act of giving/receiving compensation, collectivities in turn become infinitely divisible, and any order of social grouping can be united or divided through its procedure. Transactions act as a source both of social continuity (actors coming together for one purpose) and of social discontinuity (actors separated either as contributors towards or else as recipients of payments).[20] In short, they bring social units into being and thus offer an indigenous mode of communication through which people describe themselves.

All that remains to be added is that in its present guise compensation has become a new passage point, in Papua New Guineans' relations with one another and with outsiders alike. Kirsch (1997: 142) has argued that 'economic' explanations of conflict between landowners and resource developers allow 'developers to continue business as usual in the face of landowner complaints about environmental impact, which are redefined as [exorbitant] demands for increased compensation'. They equally allow developers to limit liability to material claims and to avoid other questions about responsibility. Compensation is also new from another point of view. While it works as an intermediary to which actors attribute the value of tradition, its 'traditional' status is questionable. Quite apart from the issue of its ubiquity, Filer (also see A. Strathern 1993) refuses to agree with people's wholesale equation of compensation and tradition. He argues that despite its reference to old practices of body compensation, the new phenomenon of resource compensation speaks to a very recent history of relations with developers and with the state. In any case, traditional attributes do not bind people to 'traditional' behaviour. Hence Filer (1997: 175) observes that expatriate developers may package their relationships with local landowners through 'traditional' compensation agreements intended as signposts to their mutual obligations, while indigenous landowners seek their own private means to remove elements of balance from the relationship – demanding favours on the one hand, resorting to coercion on the other.

COMBINATIONS AND DIVISIONS

The interesting conclusion to derive from this Papua New Guinean sketch is not that people run together technology and society, or things and persons, but that without ideological need for either of these divisions their own prevailing divisions (as ANT makes us see it) are elsewhere. People divide people. What that means is both that old social divisions are used to create new ones, and that the work of division (after Hetherington and Munro 1997) itself creates social distinctions. Technology is no more nor less at issue here than aesthetics, the spirit world, food, good health and reproductive power. For Papua New Guineans do not have to demonstrate that difference is inherent either in or between any of these kinds of phenomena. Difference is constantly created in the conduct of social life. It has always been a vague puzzle to economists that Papua New Guinean Highlanders (among others) should spend so much energy on exchanging like for like, shells for shells or pork for pork – or for that matter money for money. The difference between the items which go back and forth between persons, the significance of their materiality, is precisely a matter of social origin and social destination. They have come from or are intended for specific sets of people. Similarly, the reason why some are lucky and some have power, or have good or bad soil, or advanced technology or not, can be attributed to previous relationships. And, in converse, anything is transactable that can be pressed into the service of the differentiation of persons (after Sahlins 1976). Perhaps this makes 'persons' different kinds of actants from those persons of Euro-American property thinking who struggle, Thurber-like, with the intractability and peculiarity of things.

Perhaps, too, something like this arises when IPR is criticised for introducing alien forms of possession into indigenous communities where relations with people are the basis for laying claims. One has a right because one is a cousin or neighbour, and in claiming the right gives substance to being, even sometimes becoming, a cousin or neighbour. Now while we can extend the Papua New Guinean metaphor and speak of Euro-Americans using persons to divide persons, through inheritance for instance, ANT knows that the latter have what is, for them, a far more articulate set of indigenous mediators at their disposal: precisely the properties of 'things'. Kodak cameras, hotel keys: perceived as 'things' with properties of their own these entities require people do something about them.

Take the notorious product derived from the Pacific yew tree, Taxol, as described by Goodman and Walsh (1997; cf. Walsh and Goodman n.d.). After years of largely American development with public funds, this emerged as a drug eventually used in human trials for cancer treatment, some time after which its name became registered as a trademark of the company Bristol Myers Squibb. Over time, from the first assays of the 1960s to a period between 1982 and 1994 when clinical trials began and nearly 3,000 articles on it were published, 'Taxol' acquired several identities. These corresponded to the several sets of people who had discrete expert interests in it. To paraphrase the authors, the substance changed from a property of the yew tree that was otherwise unknown and unidentified to a crimson-coloured liquid, thought of as a bark extract to be used in screens to detect potential anti-cancer activity, to a sample of white crystals, which was the 'pure compound' according to chemists, to a chemical formula subsequently revised in a second chemical formula. These diverse attributes are summoned by diverse (expert) interests, although the attributes or properties to which these interests correspond, notably chemical and biological ones, are regarded as inherent or natural to anything which can be classified as an organic substance.

This is a prime Euro-American example of what Law (1994: 102) means by relational materiality. If people were not divided into different kinds of experts then we would not have an expert description of the substance divided up like that. Moreover, because experts get themselves into permanent positions of competence, as the authority on this or that aspect, they presuppose that there is no substance which could not be divided up thus. Any organic substance can have a biochemical analysis done on it. Whether anyone wishes to will depend on other interests, but properties attributed to the thing will summon forth their own experts, and thus justify the divisions between people. Things come to seem intrinsically heterogeneous this way. So, like the genetic description which bypasses the tedious collecting of medical histories (Wexler 1992: 227), the thing itself will identify what people have to be mobilised. This is what ANT has been telling us all along about (Euro-American) heterogeneity. You do not necessarily want to reopen all the negotiations. You do not reinvent the conventions of commerce with strangers each time you handle money: it is there in the banknote. Of their own accord, things fetishise people's past decisions. It then becomes a matter of surprise or discovery how people rearrange themselves anew around things – the fracas over the private company taking over Taxol is like the difficulty of trying to find the right social constellation, the appropriate protection procedures, for indigenous resources.

In IPR, as it is internationally pursued, a separation between things and persons turns out to be a *necessary* precondition to implementation – at least to the extent that attributes are taken as independently awaiting discovery or utilisation. What is attributed to the thing in question (design, invention, resource) will be used to drive divisions between people (authors or resource holders against the rest of the world). For while an author may claim copyright in a work, *the work itself* must show, in its makeup, that it has been authored (cf. Callon 1986: 80). Patent claims rest on showing what bit of nature, or what part of a previous tool or application, has been modified, by technology or by the new invention. Unlike other forms of property, IPR rests crucially in the evidence given by the artefact itself.

This can be imagined in several ways. Let me turn Macfarlane's observations in Chapter 7 to momentary use, as though the division between the two systems he describes were also internal to one.[21] If IPR rests in the evidence given by the artefact itself, then it disregards other Euro-American possibilities of establishing ownership. People take possession of all manner of things, through purchase, donation, inheritance, and so forth; such property rights (drawing on Macfarlane's formula) use people to divide things. In brief, rights in each entity are split among persons who have claim on it, so it has as many parts as there are persons who have rights, like a sum of money divided between several claimants. By contrast, there is a sense in which IPR uses things to divide people, since the claim is specifically to the embedded nature of (intellectual) activity in the product. For IPR can only apply to things (human arte-facts) already notionally divided into components, with that part indi-cating the commercial potential of knowledge or creativity being seen as among several components of the whole. It is as though the money itself indicated which bit was to buy subsistence items and which bit was for luxury expenditure.

It was suggested that if, in the view of the 'international community', IPR were to be extended to indigenous resource claims, it would re-create at one stroke the division between Technology and Society (rec-ognise your technical potential and take social action), and between First and Third Worlds (show new nations the social procedures to cope with commercial potential; biological rights and cultural rights may need dif-ferent instruments). To this set of views we can now add a division be-tween Things and Persons (the inherent nature of resources as things indicates the appropriateness of the social claim: this is a biological specimen, that a cultural monument). It is likely that the internal social relations of indigenous peoples to one another will matter only insofar as they bear on the passage point of their relationship to international players; that will no doubt be translated into the 'thing' in which both parties are held to have an interest.

Sustaining symmetry

Policy-makers charged with implementing articles of the Convention on Biological Diversity may search, as do those who resist the extension of the concept of intellectual property, for parallels and comparisons in 'local' and 'traditional' arrangements with which to deal with the new international imperatives. Custom is brought forward as a counterpart to common law. Should not the ANT observer join in? Is there any theoretical interest in that traditional anthropological activity of com-parison? How, for example, would one compare networks? Comparison would force the observer to find parallels and equivalences, to treat one's cases symmetrically, within a presumption of difference. Now looking for parallels in the manipulation of persons and things will simply re-inforce a sense of difference. But that is to start, so to speak, with al-ready purified terms. Suppose we took a cue from a conceptual hybrid, compensation, and looked for other parallels in Euro-American practice. One candidate with an equally limitless capacity for translation suggests itself. It translates knowledge into a power-holder of a now familiar kind, a competence which acquires the capacity to effect further translations. I refer to the Euro-American penchant for self-description.

Self-description is an instrument which, like compensation procedure, encourages social entities to proliferate. And like compensation, which defines the unit that can claim it, such description creates units radically distinct from one another. However similar they all look to an outsider, self-description establishes the uniqueness of each through enrolling the radical divide between self and other. We see this, for instance, in the cascading effect of claims to ethnic identities. Observers who attempt descriptions from the outside are sometimes confused by the hybrid composition of ethnic groups, as though their mixed constitution were a bar to collective identity. But all you need are the instruments for *self*-description.[22]

The Papua New Guinea seminar on intellectual, biological and cultural property rights is a hybrid of a kind, at least as far as its social orientations are concerned (being convened by a new NGO organisation in conjunction with a statutory government body). But its own mandate joins these together in its very description of aims and intentions. On the one hand, the executive summary states its concern with 'promoting conservation and sustainable management of natural resources at the grassroots level in Papua New Guinea'. It thus targets organisational levels outside state apparatus. On the other hand, it points to its own capacity to articulate that concern, especially in the context of networking with similar organisations in the Pacific, which will make it a voice in the context of any legislative move the government is likely to make. Here it is not 'self and other' which is a motivating factor in the self-description, but a definition of competence, the description of the particular power or effectiveness it can deliver, what it can enable others to do.

Since the early days of colonisation, the Papua New Guinea administration has depended on independent service organisations, most notably the various churches, to help implement its policies. This particular alliance of enablement is also part of a late twentieth-century global phenomenon.[23] It is a microcosm of the traffic that Willke identifies between interest organisations and the state. In contrast, he writes (1990: 235), 'to the liberal format of influence and pressure politics ... [many] countries are moving towards an officially organized collaboration between the state and large interest organizations in public policy making'. These organisations are resourceful and self-determining, to the extent that the state becomes dependent on them for detailed and specialised information, while having to recognise their decentralising effect. They act as ('corporated') societal sub-systems. Willke argues that the state trades in its competence at policy-making for access to the knowledge and skills at these organisations' disposal; they in turn comply with state policies, while gaining the chance to reproduce themselves in numerous fields of expertise.

Their capacity for reproduction is immense. When Posey assembled the documents for his volume on *Traditional Resource Rights*, he drew on a range of organisations, from the UN to various bodies in the burgeoning field of 'soft law',[24] to local interest groups. But this is not any random collection of social entities: these groups are mutually recognisable, produce similar documents, speak a common language, and thus communicate with one another.[25] They are all experts. What enables them to multiply is, among other things, *the generative language of self-description* in a field constituted by entities communicating their descriptions to one another. Self-description is a form of self-reference. The self-description which Papua New Guinea produces of itself (the 'PNG way' rendered concrete in customary law) is a description made for a field of similar descriptions circulating in the international community. Each evokes particular competences or sources of enablement. This is the parallel to be drawn with the self-constituting nature of compensation procedures.

Willke argues that modern societies have reached a level of organisational complexity which surpasses the intellectual capacity of individual actors. No one asks, he observes (1990: 238), how to link the turmoil of management activity into democratic process – offices of risk assessment, concerted actions, conferences on nuclear plant security, guidelines for experimental work on retroviruses, world trade agreements, and so forth, not to add to his list the CBD. Each writes its own agenda, each develops its own rationales and goals, and the state is at the limits of its powers of guidance. He calls this functional differentiation (after Luhmann).[26] We can also call it social proliferation.

As service bodies informing the state, these quasi-governmental organisations thus contain their own drive to reproduce; they compel social division. What is written, for example, into the UN-led CBD is endorsed in the interest organisations which spring up to inform states how to take care of social heterogeneity. As Posey says, in his executive summary on behalf of the IUCN (the International Union for the Conservation of Nature) (1996: xiii), the intention is to guide the development of *sui generis* systems, that is, locally appropriate mechanisms for protection and conservation, subject only to the requirement that they are seen to be effective. This calls forth, as we have seen in the case of

Papua New Guinea, the efforts at self-reference I have been noting: systems have to communicate their uniqueness to others. Customary law is an apt example because 'customs' are axiomatically unique by virtue of the social identities to which they are attached. Arguing that self-referentiality is necessary for a system to deal with its own complexity, Willke observes that systems thereby control their borders, deciding which among myriad contingent operations fit into their own procedures, thus producing some kind of operational closure. That very closure is a condition of heterogeneity.

I have been borrowing from some of the concepts associated with models of complex systems in order to underline the self-propelling nature of social heterogeneity in international regimes. For while one might say that these proliferating organisations are all the same, they do promote functional differentiation. That is, they have models of themselves as offering distinct and unique competences, capable of combining with one another, but different from one another by virtue of attributing organisational (operational) closure to themselves. Now Willke seems to take it for granted that 'systems' are bound to conserve difference. ANT would query that axiom of difference. For it problematises the attribution of attributes (e.g. Law 1994: 23). One response would be to point out that many artefacts, things and events are harnessed to facilitate each organisation's self-description, but are not in themselves the source of heterogeneity – each imitates others in their mission statements, databases and executive summaries. But in deploying knowledge about itself, each also makes asymmetrical its claims to expertise vis-à-vis these others.[27] In short, the incorporation of self-description into the operational activity of organisations, as at once part of their knowledge about how they work and a currency through which they communicate with others, becomes a precondition for further division. Describing itself is the first move a new organisation takes (this is what makes heterogeneity functional). Heterogeneity may thus be communicated though common media and identical-looking documents, exactly as Highlands compensation payments mobilise similar items of wealth in an endless round of reciprocities: in both cases the substantive focus of these transactions is the social uniqueness of every participating actant.

The success of ANT is to have overcome descriptive resistance to divisions between technology and society, and everything that follows in relation to things and persons. In actor network theory, anything mobilised in the course of action is an actor/actant: they are all potential agents. One could say that a decade of effort among NGOs and others has overcome descriptive resistance to talking in the same breath about governments, multinationals and indigenous peoples. In this language, these bodies all have rights; indeed potentially they all have expertise, their own competences and above all organisational capacity. Yet people may be as divided by what they share as by what they do not. It may be agreed that everyone has knowledge embodied in their practices: the question becomes how (commercially) useful it is. If claiming access to knowledge leads to functional social differentiation, its utility turns out, like any other resource, to be distributed among people in uneven quantities. The moment one suggests that technology – or procedures for technology-protection – could liberate the usefulness of knowledge for particular social units, one reintroduces the distinction between society and technology which sustains the new international programme. ANT's location within science and technology studies is there as a constant reminder.

At several junctures I have referred to emergent social divisions. The principal examples have been the way in which international debate polarises people's standpoints (p. 180) or compensation procedures define the span of grouping party to a transaction (p. 184). Daniel Miller's twofold concept of diversity, developed in relation to practices of consumption, is pertinent. Rather than seeing mass consumption as covering up discrete and separate indigenous traditions, diversity *a priori*, he argues that one should instead pay attention to the 'quite unprecedented diversity created by the differential consumption of what had once been thought to be global and homogenising institutions' (Miller 1995: 3). This is diversity *a posteriori*, diversity created in the course of people participating in apparently common practices. It is this diversity which emerges as an effect of international language and of generic compensation payments alike. We may either welcome this effect or else wish to treat it with some caution. Either way, it points to new social configurations of considerable interest to the social scientist.

Any primitivist prejudice likely to flourish with the rhetoric of intellectual property could simply be entrenching an *a priori* diversity, that is, the sense that the world is already culturally different: 'their' intellectual property is cultural tradition, invented long ago; 'our' intellectual property is a still productive, progressive, irresistible, technological inventiveness. At the same time, the universalising language which contrasts the technology-advantaged and -disadvantaged introduces new divisions. It is perhaps here, and above all in practices of remuneration (the way in which 'compensation' demands are framed and met) that one finds fresh reasons for (a *posteriori*) diversity. Transactions which accompany the exploitation of resources create new social distinctions between persons, new reference points for what people might obtain in return for what they have transferred, handed over, had taken from them or otherwise lost. This might be an idea or a design (in which case inventiveness is recognised as intellectual property), or it might be the enjoyment of the resources as such, including the benefit of exploiting resources for themselves, and the vision of future benefit this brings. The point is that the possibility of recompense has its own social effects.

The Biodiversity Convention's endorsement of redress was to strike a new balance between the technology-poor and the technology-rich. It invited one to imagine what forms of remuneration would be possible for the new range of resources summoned by the utilisation of (for instance) indigenous knowledge (art. 8). It suggested procedures for resource protection. Its partner, Agenda 21, advises governments to adopt policies that 'will protect indigenous intellectual and cultural property and the right to preserve customary and administrative systems and practices' (Ch. 26). Together these have created a field of expectations, to which IPR contributes its own particularly potent idea (property in intellectual products). These are expectations about what is realisable as an asset. The Biodiversity Convention, and associated instruments, has thus put something of a spin on the concept of property in the diverse forms of remuneration it stimulates and thus the diversity of transactional relations we can expect to result.

Miller welcomed *a posteriori* diversity in terms which give it the stature of an ethic. For him the co-production of diversity through consumption is part of a much larger issue, the realisation of how

> very little of what we possess is made by us in the first place ... [T]o be a consumer is to possess consciousness that one is living through objects and images not of one's own making. (1995: 1)

Living through others *could* be made evident through the economic explanations of which Kirsch (see p. 184) is otherwise so properly doubtful. Every transaction that returns some part of one's energy or effort is life looped through another person. Possibly what Miller has said so boldly of consumption will in the future also come to be said of some of the emergent forms of transaction which resource exploitation has brought in its wake.

POSTSCRIPT 1998

The 'predictions' about the two passage points (p. 177) were not borne out at the Port Moresby seminar[28] in 1997 quite as imagined. The two points were already translated into the international language of resource 'protection' on the one hand and of property 'ownership' on the other. The desirability of protection was voiced as self-evident, and assertion of (national/indigenous) ownership was for many participants the obvious corollary. However the specific notion of intellectual property and how one sets about protecting 'knowledge' elicited an inventive response. One of the questions presented for small-group discussion was what types of intellectual property protections Papua New Guinea should implement, if any, and what types of information they should protect. Some of the arguments which were put forward departed interestingly from the framework of property protection as such.

Of course property protection in the sense of conservation (and cf. Brown 1998) is a byproduct of the IPR agenda: IPR is about encouraging the flow of ideas independently from profiting from them (it is the rights to profit which are being protected). (Thus, with patents, if you can protect the author's interests, there is no need to hide the knowledge.) Something along these lines seemed to be contained in people's appeal to tradition, generally pitched as it was.

Seminar participants claimed that the flow of information between groups in Papua New Guinea was a characteristic of local culture, and it followed that it was traditional channels of information exchange that had to be protected. Indeed it was not 'owning' information in the sense of holding on to it that emerged as a salient issue in the discussion, but what kind of mechanisms and regulations might best *promote the exchange* of information. There were three points which Papua New Guinean participants made here (and I quote in part from a summary prepared by Nick Araho).[29] One, culture constantly changes and cannot be preserved as a static entity; you would not want to stop interchange – if there are threats, these threats come from inaccurate information, from practices and beliefs being misunderstood and misinterpreted. Two, as far as biological resources were concerned, protection was necessary in order that future generations and future farmers could benefit; the participants included in that category future researchers, that is those who would produce more information. Finally, reciprocity was not to be construed only in monetary terms but in terms of knowledge flow: what people wanted back from information was information – the results of research or study. By this they seemed to mean not the technology or the skills of research so much as the substance, the detailed content, the facts, which researchers could unearth. And the value of information would be increased, it was concluded, 'because it will have value to local communities and its reciprocal exchange will create the potential for partnership ventures'. Finally, in the words of Araho's summary, it was said that the very definition of property in international treaties and conventions was a Western concept, and 'it was vital to figure out what the characteristics of property are in PNG and to work within our particular cultural framework'.

Michael Brown's (1998) criticism of what he calls the moral alchemy by which multiple interests and diverse questions about fair use and fair expression are converted into narrow disputes over commodities is well-taken. Thus he attacks the way in which property discourse replaces what should be discussion about the moral implications of (say) subjecting people to unwarranted scrutiny or sequestering public domain information, or of the way in which complex ethical issues are submerged in favour of comprehensive claims to ownership. He is absolutely right to point to the excess and absurdities of some of 'the dramatic expansion of the intellectual property of Native people' (1998: 23). However, if we shift into the world of already existing (*a priori*) social inequities, then IPR is also a force to be harnessed. Precisely because it rolls so much up into a bundle, precisely because it has rhetorically inflationary potential, and precisely because it invokes property, it is a political slogan of (international) power. I would go further. It would in fact be a pity if Euro-American objections to commodity transactions obscured the potential of some of the (*a posteriori*) transactional innovations mentioned in this chapter. On the Papua New Guinean side they spring from rather different rhetorics of power, elicitation and the involvement of people in one another's lives which concepts such as property or commodity do not begin to address. The caution is not to mistake either of these potential bases of power for social analysis.

ACKNOWLEDGEMENTS

I owe my introduction to ANT to John Law, whose inspiration is cheerfully recorded. My thanks to Françoise Barbira-Freedman for extensive advice, to Darrell Posey for the stimulus, and, for their comments and help, Cyndi Banks, Claudia Gross, Charis Cussins, James Leach and Vivien Walsh. The role of the National Research Insititute, Papua New Guinea, and of Conservation Melanesia is acknowledged in the Preface; I am very grateful to these bodies for their generous sharing of information.

CHAPTER 10

Puzzles of Scale

It has become something of a commonplace in the social sciences to comment on the illusion that the pace of life has speeded up. When distance is measured by time, getting there faster makes the globe seem smaller, and speed becomes a shorthand for space-time compression. Electronic communication multiplies by several factors the velocity with which messages hurtle around the world, and in seeking out the margins for competition, capitalist production methods increase the rate at which materials get transported, distributed and consumed (Brennan 1993: 150).[1] By whatever scale, people's capacities seems expanded. Yet there is a quite other set of effects to do with this same rising tempo – doing more simply to stay in the game. Life becomes ever more expensive in terms of resources and energy.[2] Food is wrapped and then packed in boxes which are wrapped; it takes universities these days a whole information technology infrastructure to do their business. This is like the homely experience of earning more to spend more (on more things it costs more to produce) – not expansion but inflation. One is not further forward after all.

The ability to live in both modes simultaneously is germane to my theme. One runs faster and keeps still at the same time. In the first mode, people experience increased activity. In the second, variations of scale make no difference to the relationship between activities. Which of these presents itself as in the ascendancy will depend in part on how the measuring is done.

Measuring makes the world available to the imagination in most interesting ways. That is because of the different kinds of relations it exposes. When what is being measured is independent of the means of measurement, we talk of the means of measurement as scales. Space is metered out as distance, so many yards or miles: it is because yards and miles do not change length as he or she goes that the traveller has an independent means of reckoning how far away home is. A quite separate operation is matching – house-prices against food-prices for example. Here, part of the measurement is also what is being measured: one item valued in terms of another yields a ratio. And ratios can be applied whatever the scale of the operation (what is held constant is not the values on the scale but a relation between values).[3] In the case of inflation, the thought that nothing has really shifted might be rather depressing – it negates any sense of increased benefit. Yet we might after all say that it is *only* ratios such as relative cost which give any meaning to scales (the 'real' value of money). Sometimes, as in the relation between earning and spending, a ratio also implies an equation or works as an analogy; while the cost of houses will not in itself indicate the cost of food, the capacity to earn will tell us something about the capacity to spend – they are not the same activities at all, yet information on one also provides information on the other.

So what has this to do with Papua New Guinea? Everything: I am speaking of Papua New Guinea's world. On the one hand, people's horizons have expanded; distant places have become accessible in shortening periods of time, and a whole culture of consumption has increased absolutely the quantity of things people need in order to get by. Whereas it was once possible for an anthropologist to describe the total number of portable items in the material culture, that number is now virtually infinite.[4] On the other hand, although for a while there seemed an expansive moment when new technology enabled food production time to drop, much of the rural population is nowadays concerned with land pressure and much of the urban population with having to spend wages on buying the food which could be grown at home without money. As for the velocity of communications, and all-night radio sessions, houses built ever closer together require increasing assertions of privacy. Like anyone else, people in Papua New Guinea are both running faster and keeping still.

But what, we might ask, are their measurements? I start with a case which might have interested Ernest Jones.

COSMOPOLITAN TROBRIANDERS

Ernest Jones's most famous intervention in social anthropology concerned the people of the Trobriand Islands and the dialogue between their ethnographer, Malinowski, and Freud. These people, who reckon connections of descent matrilineally, through the mother, professed ignorance of the male role in conception. The seventy-year-old debate which ensued is not yet over.[5] Anthropologists have been largely preoccupied with the issue of cultural knowledge, or else with the ethnographic assertion that while the Trobriand father may not be a procreative figure he is a nurturant one. Jones's original comment on Malinowski's thesis is recalled from time to time, but usually in terms of his (Jones's) argument about the child in a matrilineal regime transferring feelings of hostility from father to mother's brother. However, his main point, that paternity is denied and disguised rather than unknown, has recently been given central place by an anthropologist of the Papua New Guinea Highlands who has for a long time been interested in the dovetailing of the work of the unconscious and the work of society. Gillian Gillison (1993: 21) quotes Ernest Jones: 'the father disappears from the scene only to reappear [in a disguised form] ... [as] an ancestral spirit, who in a supernatural manner impregnates the mother' (Jones 1925: 122; cf. Malinowski 1927). As we shall see, there are all sorts of ways in which people from this part of the world deliberately create the effect of making things disappear and reappear.

The space that Trobrianders occupy has expanded since Malinowski's time – these days they live in Australia, in America and, introduced briefly in Chapter 7, in the capital Port Moresby they are among the political elite. National civil servants and company employees have to carve time out of other pursuits in order to attend to demands that once needed no such calculation, above all maintaining food gardens; as well as eating imported rice and steak, they grow familiar root crops, the most prized being the yam. In fact some have gone so far as to mount displays of urban produce, extensions of the harvest competitions people hold at home.[6]

The First Annual Trobriand Yam Festival in 1985 was sponsored by the then head of the National Planning and Budget Office (Battaglia 1995). It was a re-placing of the Trobriand Islands in Port Moresby. Participants built cone-shaped mounds of yams resembling the kinds of constructions made at home, not just in order to evoke the appropriate 'traditional' connotations (and hence the ethnographic present in the elucidation which follows) but to bring the past into the present and thus extend the reach of their effectiveness (1995: 79). And what exactly would the sponsor and his fellow Trobrianders have been imagining?

Such constructions are at once displays of and tests of a gardener's capacity to turn his effort to effect, and are thus meant to impress others.[7] Now this effect requires a temporal distinction between a past period of time and the present moment. Of course, a man does not know until the yams are harvested what his magical and horticultural labours will have produced. But the period when yams increase in size and number in the ground is not simply assumed to be distinct from the moment when they are harvested and displayed, the two moments must be *kept* distinct. What is the significance of this? It is that by virtue of having happened already, the past activity is thus emphatically categorised as off-stage (hidden), and what happens off-stage is growth.[8] So what is the gardener concealing? I am tempted to call it energy or potency but that would do violence to the ethnographic record, which speaks of prowess or strength. Let me use the term *capacity,* and thereby suppose that it is the capacity for growth.[9] What gardeners would be concealing, then, is their capacity to increase the tubers they have planted in the ground; in the past the analogy with the child in the womb would have been explicit in the magical spells accompanying the work. Yams in the garden might be referred to as 'children'.[10] Now those put on display are above all destined for the gardener's matrilineal kinswomen: he grows yam-children for his married sister(s). Other yams help feed his wife's child.

As far as the procreation of human children is concerned, the mother is, as Jones remarked, impregnated by matrilineal spirit.[11] The father's job is rather to nourish the child and form its body. What is interesting is that a man's capacity to grow the food which feeds his wife's child becomes in relation to his sister an explicit capacity to grow the child (the yam). Rather than saying that there is no father, we might say there are two fathers, the one who produces yams to form children and the one who produces children in the form of yams. In this sense, in the guise of a yam gardener, the father reappears twice![12] (This could be so whether we take a Euro-American view that hiding the energy/potency with which yams are produced hides a generative father, or that in Trobriand procreative idiom it hides a nurturant father.)[13]

Yet there are different time scales here. To reproduce a human child takes a whole cycle of life, with former matrilineage members returning to the land of the dead where, off-stage so to speak, they are metamorphosed into new spirit children before returning to human life. The periodicity – the reproductive time in Brennan's phrase – is generation-al.[14] But suppose reproduction could also be measured in the maturing time of plants? This is exactly what happens. The reproductive time of persons becomes speeded up in the reproductive time of yams. There is no need to wait for the next generation to emerge in its entirety: each year a man harvests testimony to the power of his efforts. Compressing time, growing yams where he might grow children, expands his capacity to make his capacity evident. This sense of speed depends of course on Trobrianders keeping in place the equation between the fertility of yams and of persons. And that imaginative possibility finds a cultural mechanism in one very public arena. The equation between yams and persons is constantly re-imagined through the competitive nature of harvest displays. For here the yams are used as a measure of one man against another.[15]

Men confront other men with their displays, whether as gardeners vying as to whose output is the largest or between gardener and recipient of the harvest. If male capacity is the object of measurement, the means of measurement are the yams he harvests as 'children' for his sister. As we shall see in a moment, it is these which are displayed in the cones and then transposed to the store houses of his sister's husband. In growing such plant bodies, a man (or a group of men such as a set of kinsmen or members of a village) produces a mediated version of himself in a form which can be measured along a scale. This involves specific cultural techniques which allow measurements to be compared. The resultant scales make possible that imaginative leap from a gardener's expansive sense of effort to an assessment of the material results of that effort.

In the old days, one way of settling a dispute would be through harvest competition,[16] yams being displayed in special crates. But the regular shows of yams intended for a man's sister and sister's husband, or for the households of chiefs, were also measured. Each prestation was first assembled in the form of a cone near the garden site. (Battaglia notes how today the conical stack has to be composed in one go, a manoeuvre demanding a fine judgement of dimension and in particular of the size of the base.[17] The builder must project the correct dimensions for the base from the number, sizes and shapes of yams, to make a stable and comely form. Its size is recorded, with a length of rope round the circumference of the base.[18]) The stack would then be disassembled and reassembled in the store house of the recipient. In the past the yams were put into special circular measuring baskets before being transferred to the store house in carrying baskets. A tally was kept of the number of measuring baskets a cone had filled, the tally being displayed to the recipient when the stack was reassembled. For each standard measuring basket, a leaflet was torn from a large cycas frond, every tenth leaflet having only its tip taken, so, as Malinowski (1935: 177, also 213) remarked, 'one glance at such a leaf shows how many decimal figures and units have been measured out'. In competitive displays, after recording the individual contributions, men of a village amalgamated their yams. Malinowski observed more than two generations ago that individual stacks of exceptional size could reach nearly 2,000 baskets; the total bulk of one competitive harvest in 1918 approached 20,000 (1935: Appendix (Document II)); this was said to be the dimensions to which people regularly aspired in the past (i.e. pre-1918). An important man who found himself the recipient of many donations might be gathering in baskets in the hundreds if not thousands.

But what do measures such as these indicate? I implied that competition over the scale of people's enterprises depends on keeping constant certain values which themselves are not affected by scale, and indeed must not be. In this second way in which values are brought into relation with other values, equations are set up between them. And what keeps one equation in place can only be other equations.[19]

Take the premise of these competitive displays between men: the equation between capacity and prestige. Whether on the Trobriands or in Moresby, the quantity of yams will only indicate prestige if they first indicate the capacity of the gardener. And a capacity that is only effective when it is hidden has to have an outward cultural sign to indicate its presence. The timing of events is one such sign. Very simply, two temporal moments (concealment and revelation) are kept distinct from one another. The activity being celebrated might be categorised as off-stage, and what happens off-stage might be growth, but once the growing is complete, the yam-children can be seen and indeed *must* be seen (those on the outside of the stack may have their outsides painted).[20] In addition – almost as though it were a comment on the Euro-American problem of ascertaining paternity – there is the question of the identity of the gardener. One has to be certain that the yams come out of the producer's own body and not someone else's.

The Moresby events which unfolded in 1985 are illuminating here. The occasion was problematic for the city dwellers. In setting up the competition, they had wanted to be able to mobilise or realise the equation between capacity and prestige across the distance separating Moresby from the Trobriand Islands; they would achieve renown that would get back to the people at home, despite the harder work they had in Moresby wresting the yams from the much poorer soils there. That change of scale (harder work, poorer soils) both would and would not make a difference; they wanted to enhance the capacity to which they could point while at the same time wanting the evidence of that capacity to bring them, as it always did, prestige. Yet they could not keep certain ancillary equations stable. In the eyes of some at least, both spacing and timing went awry.

Basically, the men were unable to make the cones of yams next to their own gardens, and thus amass the tubers as they emerged from the ground. For fear of theft, they relocated them in residential areas. So instead of exposing the crop to view as it was harvested, they had to hide the yams again, packing them carefully to prevent damage in transit, and transporting the now invisible tubers in cars and pickup trucks across the city. *This* increase in distance became a hazard. Gardeners fell under suspicion for surreptitiously adding tubers from foreign sources, collecting extra as they went, combining their own produce with other people's on the way. As a result, 'displays were growing [in quantity] at a time when growth ought to have ceased' (Battaglia 1995: 85). The distinction between concealment and revelation could not be held stable by the usual temporal and spatial markers and raised questions about whose productivity was being measured anyway. There was criticism not just of individuals but of the event as a whole.

Time has appeared twice in this account. First, note that two sides of an equation are not necessarily in view simultaneously. In the very equation between the capacity to grow things and public prestige, one of the two elements is in either the past or the future and therefore not present. Through insisting on a distinction between the moments of revelation and concealment, men literally tell themselves that the visible points to the invisible. In this sense what is held distinct is also identified: the visible yam mound is equally well-imagined as secret male capacity. Revelation is thus 'the same as' concealment – but each occurs (and must occur) at its own moment. In short, the relationship between displaying and hiding is itself an equation of sorts. It is precisely the difference between two moments of time which points to an identity between the activities; the one is an earlier or later form of the other.[21] What was momentarily concealed is now revealed; and what is now momentarily revealed will be concealed again. One could almost read these as techniques which people have developed for *commenting on* the very activity of pointing to what they also hide.[22]

Second, displacing the generational time of human reproduction with the maturation time of plants[23] has enabled Trobriand men to speed up the rate at which their 'children' (the yams) appear. They were of course doing this before they ever went to Port Moresby or became the cosmopolitans they are today. The elite in Moresby were seizing on the new space as an expansive potential for themselves, for they had increased opportunities for display they did not have at home.[24] The metropolis enabled them to run further so to speak. But they also had to keep still: the crucial equation between capacity and prestige depended on the spatio-temporal sequencing of the plants as things now grown, now harvested. Without those values being properly orchestrated, the exercise would not work.

Now in other areas of life Trobrianders deploy valuables which have no such reproductive time, and whose rate of 'production'[25] comes from a velocity of a different kind. To this kind of speed I now turn. But here I leave the Trobriands, and do so with a reminder from Jones. When Trobriand men grow yams to give away, their urban ethnographer observes, it accomplishes an aesthetic and political supplementation: 'A man is *more* for gardening – experiences more *of* himself and his relational capacity' (Battaglia 1995: 80, emphasis in original). Jones, in conversation with Evans, said, 'That's the aim of analysis, isn't it? The aim of analysis is to make the person more himself; that is to say, to make him the whole of "himself", not only the visible part but ... the hidden part'.[26]

A HAGEN PERSPECTIVE

I

The man from Mt Hagen whose photograph you see on page 219 is transfixed by the pearlshells streaming out of the mouth of a men's house.[27] He is looking at shell valuables laid in line for a compensation payment – recompense for wartime help to allies, and to both allies and enemies recompense for loss of limb or life.[28] One person's loss of limb or life is also loss to the corporate body, the (clan) group to which the person belongs. However, such payments acquire a competitive momentum of their own among men,[29] developing into reciprocal exchanges between groups – in this case patrilineal clans – who vie to out-do one another.[30] The phenomenon bears a final iteration. Donors challenge recipients to make as good a return of wealth. So we have a sense of what he might be imagining on this occasion.

It is not being treated as the kind of major event which would compel the donors to go into full decoration. All the same, he may well be reflecting on the corporate strength evinced in the capacity to draw shells together and disperse them again. He is probably in any case scrutinising their visible quality, their 'skin' (cf. Küchler 1993). Individual shells can be worn directly on the body's skin too; he happens to sport a bamboo tally on his chest which records his own achievements in transactions – every slat indicating an occasion on which he has in the past given away a set of eight (or ten) shells. So he is also bound to see in these shells transactions from the past, and yet again other shells that will come in return, or perhaps return gifts of a different kind in the form of pigs. Both shells and pigs are tokens of wealth.

The Hagen economy, like that of the Trobriands, is based on root crop horticulture. Unlike the Trobriands, however, and unlike many of their Highlands neighbours for that matter, Hagen people do not use food crops in their exchanges. They both slow down and speed up the reproductive time of plants. The staple, sweet potato, is not displayed as it is harvested but it is displayed in the form of the pigs who eat it daily. Pigs take several years to grow, and this introduces a certain rhythm into exchanges based on pig production. But pigs can be exchanged for shells. And for shells you do not, overtly at least, have to wait on any growing time at all; it depends how fast you can receive them. All men need do to encourage others to give is give to them in turn. The circulation of these items acquires its own rationale.

Nonetheless shells contain many references to persons and their bodily growth. The very iconography – a curled-up embryo or fetus, light-coloured, in the red womb – evokes the idea of reproduction. Moreover, the whole gift is also regarded as a kind of replacement person. If group gifts like these are ostensibly for homicide compensation (thus a replacement of a kind for someone killed), smaller gifts may comprise payments given at marriage, birth or at the end of life. Those who assume primary responsibility for the bride or child or deceased compensate those who helped nurture him or her. This is in order to replace the care which resulted in the person's bodily substance with something of substance in return.[31] Whether one gives away the products of creativity, or has them taken, one is due back the substance, the bodily effort ('the body'), that now lodges within another, as we may imagine a child or bride lodged within the corporate body of the father's or husband's clan. In short, compensation fuses exertion of effort with bestowal of substance ('nurture'). Both are seen to come from people's internal capacities.

Here we may see analogies with the Trobriand mounds. If Hagen men measure themselves by their wealth (shells and pigs), that is the same as saying that men measure themselves against one another by their capacities. However, by comparison with Trobriand harvest gifts, Hagen exchange practices both speed up and slow down measurement. Instead of sizing up different piles of wealth on a single occasion, one set of men brings out its wealth in order to donate it; that is, one clan body lodges the results of its effort in the body of another. Recipients take the items away, into their own houses, then produce their counterdisplay, a return-gift, at a future date. They have to return at least the equivalent of what they received in order not to lose face, and the return has to be the results of their own capacity, pigs and shells which they have found from elsewhere (they cannot return the self-same items). While this introduces a delay – the return gift is not immediate – timing now becomes a political matter, and can in turn be speeded up or slowed down at will.

Demonstrations of capacity thus take place at intervals negotiated among men; every man, like every group, has his own exchange partners, so on most occasions each gives to and receives from specific and known others. Alternately, they occupy the positions of being now donor, now recipient, to one another.[32] Donors are in display mode; recipients are not. While each person is thus an alternative version of his counterpart, seen at different temporal moments, each is also at the same time the measure of the other. The more the recipient receives the more he is challenged to give in the future, and that occasion then becomes the retrospective measure of his partner's success. If I give twenty pigs now, you later have to return me twenty pigs, perhaps with an increment, or else you have failed to match my size and in that sense I have failed to find a good match.

We may imagine the man in the photograph imagining the absent kinsman whose loss he has suffered. This is the body laid out. Becker's observation from Fiji (1995: 126) may be apt here: people suffer in the body but the suffering is not privatised. It is not incidental that our spectator is at the same time calculating the number of shells extracted in recompense and assessing whether they equal the quality of the ones his partner received from him earlier.

II

How is equivalence between gifts established over time? Hageners use a set of independent scales while keeping in place an equation that depends not on size but on matching.

First of all, measurement by scale.[33] Measurement is public. Special open-air ceremonial grounds are cleared for the purpose; pig stakes will be laid out and can be counted by anyone. The quantity of people present is also a measure of a kind – the degree of success depends on its scale effect, the more people who come to watch the greater the hosts' evident capacity to draw the world to themselves. Indeed their visibility is explicitly staged; donors act as the hosts, expose themselves under the midday sun, and on major occasions will also dance to show off both their decorations and the number of men they have mustered. Counting follows a numerical system which allows the rapid computation of units and multiples of units. The overall effect is of numerical extent, often presented as a straight line, a scale made visible either in the line of the pig stakes erected down a ceremonial ground or in the ladder-like tally of shell gifts worn on the chest. Any magnitude of gift can be quantified.

Second, measurement by match. The numerical scale would mean nothing if people did not also hold certain equivalences in place. What above all is being compared are the donor's and recipient's respective capacities. In social terms, prominence is measurable by the extent of someone's network, and networks extend with the gifts. The amount of wealth a man attracts becomes an element in his very ability to exchange, and thus his public standing.[34] Indeed, the measurement of one man's capacity is enabled by another. Obviously the measurement cannot be free-standing: every gift is compared specifically with a prior gift, present performance with a past one. Hence the minute scrutiny of items; each individual item must match the quality of the item for which it is a return. The only measure for one shell or pig is another shell or pig – visible wealth points to its now invisible counterpart on a particular previous occasion.

The whole effort of these events, in other words, would mean nothing without the same link between capacity and prestige which we encountered in the Trobriands. That equation has to be held constant in Hagen too. Here the very process of exchange makes reference back to the bodies out of which wealth is drawn.

In order to effect the display, the preceding period of wealth accumulation will be marked by behind-the-scenes activity; only what is kept hidden will grow. Men negotiate secretly in their houses over the planning and staging of events. Houses are normally shut fast, and one cannot ordinarily tell by looking the wealth its residents command. What is thus subsequently made public is the outcome of growth that has occurred in private, and 'display' is the revelatory moment at which that is communicated to others. The individual identity of the creator is in turn guaranteed by what is most hazardous, the success of the collective display. As in Wahgi (O'Hanlon 1989; 1995), outward presentation is a public test of authenticity. Here, the performance as a whole will only be blessed if it matches inner capacity. Only if the wealth has truly come from the insides of these men, and thus emerges with the spiritual blessing of (clan) ancestors, will their decorations have their intended effect – otherwise they simply fail to impress. This is not just a question of whether the items really come from this man's body or that man's, it is an imperative. Wealth *must* come from the inside, the same kind of imperative I suggest by which excavated Trobriand yams must be made visible. How is this imagined?

Part of the cultural apparatus again lies in the iconography.[35] That sets up a whole series of (aesthetic) equations itself. An enclosed space points to an interior, like the interior of a house. In two dimensions this may be imagined as a centre within a surround, or in terms of colour imagined as something 'red' within a border of darker or lighter hue. Thus the men's house which draws people to the ceremonial ground is also the conceptual source of the wealth that will stream from its interior, in the same way as the man's own head is regarded as the fount of his inner, secret prowess. The head itself may become the focus of enlargement, an object of adornment: the man in the photograph has a handkerchief over hair only slightly padded out, but behind him is someone whose height has been increased with the addition of bird of paradise plumes (in a style typical of 'second best' wear for minor public occasions). In full decoration, on major occasions, the head becomes centred as the mid-point of a figure elongated by feather plumage above and swinging apron below. The dancer's own face may have a bright red centre. Or the effect may be repeated within the adornments themselves with their own centrepiece.[36] These are all depictions of the bodily 'insides' whose capacity has grown the wealth made visible on the outside. The activities are also taking place because the men themselves have been grown by the very land on which they stand, and I shall come back to that further evidence of interiority in a moment.

A recipient contemplating the quantity and quality of shells is looking at an extension of himself, that is, at his relations with others. We could say he is looking at himself through the bodies (the embryo-children) of other men, his own earlier capacity gathered up, grown, and returned to him, transformed, by his exchange partners.

III

Whatever else this man is gazing at, he is gazing at inflation. The photograph, and the account I have just given, date from 1964. Thirty years before that, the area had been opened up by outsiders. As described in Chapter 5, an influx of shells into the local economy on a quite massive scale followed Australian pacification in the 1930s. Gold prospectors, civil servants and missionaries flew in veritable planeloads of shells with which they bargained for food and labour.[37] Those most prized in Hagen, goldlip pearlshells, now became available in great number. They were absorbed into men's transactions through a speeding-up of wealth circulation, leading to an increase of competitive displays of wealth between clans.

At this period, the 1960s, people looked back to the days when one shell was equivalent to one pig; it was not long before it would take eight or ten. But rather than bemoaning the relative drop in shell value, they tended to regard themselves as more fortunate than their ancestors; their sense of importance was in no way diminished. Instead, men became more demanding over the quality and quantity of specimens. Hagen appetite seemed infinitely extensible, and for a while their imagining knew no bounds. So there seemed no end to the flow of shells – at least until the 1960s; the photograph comes from a moment in time when shells were being overtaken by a second influx of wealth tokens, money. For the present, however, our man is looking at his desire for wealth as it was returned to him by expatriate Europeans and Australians, the origin and sources of these very items.

The amount of wealth which flooded into the New Guinea Highlands in those early years had major repercussions, and no historical account can ignore the scale of the changes. In the 1950s, the whole Highlands region (half a million people, of whom Hageners comprised some 70,000, although those in the 'contacted' zone would have been a only a fraction of this number at that date) were, according to one estimate, extracting half a million shells a month from the tiny expatriate population. (The figures include all kinds of shell, the majority being small species whose individual values were low.) High-quality shells were especially in demand, and continued to be in demand, because of what was kept constant, the equation between capacity and prestige, and the value put on (visible) wealth as a sign of (invisible) strength. Without the constancy of these equations, we cannot complete the description of the effects of increase. As I have suggested elswhere (see note

38), individual care and attention kept pace, so to speak, with inflation. Nonetheless, with more shells circulating faster between more partners, men's power seemed expanded, for they could bring more partners into their orbit. At the same time, the prominence which that power had in the colonial past given to one or two persons who took the lead in such exchanges was also being gained at costlier price. Keeping in place the ratios between capacity and prestige took more resources. In sum, that meant both finding the extra wealth to do so, thereby increasing the scale of diverse enterprises, and working to keep unchanged the value placed on wealth as a sign of influence. For ambitious men in Hagen, this was evidence of the capacity to dispense resources through public exchange, for that in turn, as we have seen, was a sign of a commensurate ability to elicit or extract resources from others.

Since then inflation has had its final effect; there are no shells in circulation these days. Money has long since moved in to fill the vacuum. We might say that Hageners' own kind of speed has been overtaken by events.

In sum, I have described the apparent speeding-up of reproductive time that occurs when people make plants, as in the case of the Trobriands, and in Hagen plants converted into pigs, the subject of competition.[39] In both societies, although I have only dwelt on the Hagen case, the circulation of shell wealth stimulated further production but insofar as it relied on speed of acquisition and distribution also had the potential to create its own plane of space-time. It is not a new point to argue that men were able to draw new items – and later money – into their scheme of values precisely *because* of the equations they simultaneously held stable. Keeping that imagining in place required the cultural apparatus of measurement by ratio or analogy to which I have referred.

As a consequence, the shells and money which in one sense comprised an autonomous and self-reinforcing sphere of values also retained references to body substance and to reproductive rhythms.[40] Their appearance and deployment evoked their immediate origins in the interior of the person; they equally pointed to the interiority of the land. Shells were always potentially exchangeable for pigs, and pigs in turn embodied food that grew from the same clan lands that fed people. Hagen men might not use food directly in their exchanges, but the act of revelation recalls women's digging tubers out of the ground, or the way men or women unpack food ovens.[41] Moreover, although shells and then money poured into the region from the outside, as far as Hagen people were concerned both were mediated at source by work. These things could be obtained from the incoming Australians and Europeans in return for people's work. Human bodily strength was itself seen as a product of land – it is the land that makes people strong, they say – and people regarded wages as compensating for their efforts. So what does pointing to the land in this way mean?

Now in this patrilineal regime, 'the father' was apparently revealed at every possible juncture.[42] So we might remark on what happens at the birth of his children. This is the moment from which the particular human father must absent himself, on the grounds that the birth process is polluting to males. It is also the point at which land comes into view as a receptacle for the child's umbilical cord, which used to be specially planted in a small enclosure and thus 'inside' the ground. It is in any case paternal land which gives children their birth identity, and as elsewhere in Papua New Guinea human beings are referred to as 'planted people'. Land points to collective (clan) power. It is also regarded as a source of supernatural fertility. The sign of this lies in what the land grows: people, pigs and plants. Tall trees, high crop yields and fat bodies, like an impressive crowd, indicate what is otherwise hidden: male capacity and ancestral support.

Today, in the 1990s, Hageners may regard their settlements as overcrowded, complaining that there are too many houses too visible all at once; yet when relatives from other parts flock to an area of special fertility, they are pleased to have attracted so many to themselves (see Chapter 5). Yet land is also short for the very reason that it is a measure of resources; for thirty years now, through cash cropping and vegetable marketing, land has been a supply of money, and here everyone looks for expansion. Very simply, soil fertility is made visible by the income it earns. Only recently, however, have people begun to purchase fertilisers for their food gardens, pesticides for the cash crops. What is the rationale? The more money spent on land, they argue, the more (money) it should yield.

When they sell food, these items are at once the products of work, and, coming from patrilineal land, evidence of male creativity. When they sell working time, a similar reference is contained in their nurtured bodies. As activities which generate income from the land, these remain to that extent mediated by the body rhythms of persons and the reproductive time of the plants and animals which they eat. However, we have seen how Hagen men speed up the time it takes to profit from their own transactions by exchanging measures of their capacity for other measures, notably the shells, and then money. A further speeding-up was in store, and one that would both mimic their own exchanges and short-circuit this network of associations between persons, land and fertility.

Increasingly, people have become conscious of the possibility of selling land itself, not so much because of what is happening locally as because of what they hear of elswhere in the country. Purchasing land gets directly to source: money for ancestral capacity. What began in the colonial era as occasional purchases for establishing plantations has turned, since Independence (1975), into something rather different. Unlike the plantations in which land was bought up and then planted with the crops (coffee and tea in the Highlands) that generated income, now they learn that there is overseas commercial interest in what the land itself yields – primarily timber and minerals. Not people, or domestic plants or animals, but the trees which grow spontaneously upon it and the ore excavated directly from inside its centre: there is money to be had for the very measures of the land's inner capacities.[43] Papua New Guineans are caught up in other people's speed. For the remainder, I leave Hagen to talk about Papua New Guinea more generally. Only I do not quite leave it: it will reappear.

MEASURES FOR MEASURES

Hundreds of yam baskets, thousands of shells, and these days the millions of kina (the national currency) which the country earns from timber leases and mining and oil royalties: these gross figures all contain finely negotiated individual computations. K5 per hectare basic occupation fee; K15,000 per hectare for unimproved bush; K35,000 per hectare for land under cultivation; K520,000 for loss of 40 hectares of forested land, all as part of a payout of K35 million over half a decade: these are figures quoted for what is called 'land compensation', administered under the Papua New Guinea Mining Act, paid out for land absorbed into the operations of a gold mine (in the Highlands but not Hagen). Local landowners had in 1988 signed a Compensation Agreement.[44]

The concept of 'landowner'[45] is used by people whether they are claiming royalties on minerals or timber extracted from the land or claiming compensation for loss of imagined resources such as enjoyment of future development. They simultaneously evoke tradition ('custom'), appealing to the depths of their ancestral association with particular territories, while also calling themselves 'owners' in an international language which gives them negotiating purchase with overseas companies, a term now part of the new vocabulary of 'resource compensation'. Often the sums seem exorbitant to the developers, who complain that demands are set only by what 'nationals' imagine the developers can pay. The new landowners are accused of scaling up their demands according to the company's perceived wealth. But it is not only the concept of landowner which had emerged. The very concept of compensation has a new resonance. We might say that it has undergone a kind of inflation.

There are new arenas for satisfaction and more reasons for demanding it. As described in Chapter 9, the idea of 'compensation' has expanded in various directions. In those societies where it was used in the past, there is an increasing range of activities to which it now applies. The Pidgin (Neo-Melanesian) term *kompensesen* covers a wider range of payments than former categories did. It tends to be used for any situation where people feel they have lost something to another person, or – even more generally – simply where someone owes them something.[46] In addition, the concept of compensation itself has spread across the country, becoming a kind of generic Papua Niugini 'custom', and is now deployed by people who before had no equivalent. Indeed, it has been argued that there is little evidence that compensation was ever as ubiquitous as it is to people's current advantage to make out; Papua New Guineans themselves have pointed to its origin in the Highlands.[47] Hagen is one of the archetype origin areas, and that is how it comes back into this account.

Why should 'compensation' have grown so successfully – so successfully in fact that it has become a major actant in issues confronting development efforts and political stability alike? In the context of the present chapter, it is germane to repeat my earlier question: what are people's measurements? What imaginative work do measurements do?

It was not inappropriate from that point of view either to have dwelt on the Hagen case. Its counting systems enabled men to keep precise tallies of the quantities of wealth that passed through their hands. We have also seen that they lodged these computations with others. One means of keeping track of the numbers of pigs on which claims could be exercised was to give them away to an exchange partner who then safeguarded the debt, so to speak; he kept the account. Similarly those tallies worn on the chest represented debts lodged with others, as though what were taken from one body could be put into another for safe keeping. Hence my axiom: men became the measures of one another. But the cultural apparatus, the technology of measurement, had its own outcome. Enhancing size and number became – and this is a comparative, not an historical, observation – an aim, and became competitive. It also led to a double analogy, first between what was given away (in gift exchange) and what was taken from one (in homicide, theft, marriage and so forth), and, second, *between what someone else has obtained and what therefore one must have had.*[48] These worked as equations of a kind.

The manner in which Hagen men – and certain other Highlanders – imagined the male body giving evidence of its inner creativity has taken off with extraordinary effect. In many of Papua New Guinea's numerous societies the human body is held to reveal in its activities inner resources of some kind. To speculate on what it was that the Hagen-like techniques added, note that on the one hand they brought together the competitive scaling-up of measurement devices and, on the other, a potent demonstration that extracting wealth from others matches what has been extracted from oneself. The Trobriand gardener puts magic and work into the soil from which the produce comes. The Hagen negotiator puts his wealth into his exchange partner, and the 'produce' comes back in the form in which it was inserted. People thus measure what is taken out by what was put in; their own power to extract wealth is measured by the power of those who had extracted it from them in the first place.

Measures for measures. If what a donor gives is a measure of what he has taken, this prepares the way for the idea that *what commands a price indicates a resource.* I have suggested that Hagen-and Highlands-inspired ideas of recompense translate new and unprecedented possibilities into the widespread idiom of body vitality, growth and depletion. And that what applies to the capacity of persons also applies to the fertility of land. Substance, profit extracted from the ground, can be taken as a sign of the substance, fertility, that has gone into it (see above p. 182). Witnessing the inroads of foreign commercial ventures, of which the most visible are mining and logging, it is precisely the thought of company profit that prompts people to construe the counter-idea of recompense.[49] In short, if fertility is a hidden quantity until it is revealed, it follows that anything that the land yields – oil, timber, gold – can be taken as evidence of inner resources. No wonder people do not pitch their price according to some preconceived value of the land but scale up their demands according to the developers' ability to pay.

Whatever commands a price, then, also triggers calculation of compensation. This model conveys its imperative with the most direct iconography: body expenditure is imagined as a perpetual taking-in and giving-out of resources which, equally perpetually, requires periodic replenishment. The model has the potential to cover almost any negotiation because the fundamental idea of recompense for bodily exertion can be so widely applied. Indeed, all that now has to be kept constant is the relationship between body exertion and body loss.

Any account of social life would have to ask of this model what are values, what is rhetoric and what is opportunistic. In the context of the arguments of this chapter, however, there is a different kind of observation to make. Regardless of how they are deployed, these techniques of measurement enable people to move simultaneously in two planes, with two modes of orientation to the world, along two trajectories, now making scale relevant to the measurement of things and now making it not. For that model of bodily activity is able to cross scales, that is, to be replicated in all kinds of contexts. It offers a ratio of values which can be quantified at any level of loss or recompense. Perhaps, indeed, this insensitivity to scale was the doorway to letting in its opposite, extreme sensitivity to scale expressed in reckonings of the immense profit of others that could be computed into one's own compensatable losses.

There is a postscript to the speeding-up here. If previous historical moments have been anything to go by, we may, as Filer (1997) implies, expect 'resource compensation' to take off on a trajectory of its own. The rhetoric allows one to seize on land as though it were body – to talk about land compensation as though it were like bridewealth or homicide payments. Yet literally being prepared to accept money directly for the land bypasses the reproductive time of a horticultural regime (the reproductive time of plants, and by extension of shells, and of money as it was originally earned). We should not be surprised if not all the old equations continue to hold. Direct payments perhaps render obsolete some of the former temporal and spatial markers. It is under this pressure that there is a new sense of something else coming to the surface: questions about future generations of children, human children. On many occasions Papua New Guineans talk openly these days about the consequences of present decisions over land exploitation for the future of their children.[50] It is as though in people's spoken thoughts other kinds of reproductive time have reappeared as generational time

The anthropological puzzle is how to make scale both matter and not matter in accounts of social life. The question is how to render as concurrent the relationship between the effects of scale change on the one hand and on the other the capacity of social and cultural systems to retain their features. For the puzzle is not so to speak of life as it is lived, any more than anyone has any problem in describing themselves as running fast and standing still at the same time. We are used to human beings acting in divergent modes. The puzzle is a puzzle for the ethnographic imagination. It lies in the rendering of the data, how to *describe* in non-contradictory ways. The particular description I have in mind concerns being true to just the kinds of societies I have been illustrating from Papua New Guinea.

I have wanted to bring to attention material that I find fascinating without making 'social change' its focus, and in particular without falling into the chasm between tradition and modernity. It does not help to label parts of Hagen as 'traditional' and parts as 'modern', even if people there do. That would put bits of Hagen society on a scale, a continuum of the kind which Ernest Jones might have imagined from more primitive to less primitive, with everyone working their way towards being just like Euro-Americans. Nor does it help to make equations all the time between this bit of Hagen and this bit of English culture (say), as though they were in some kind of ratio, so that they come to seem either entirely different from or exactly the same as one another, a comparative hare which Malinowski started. (It would be perfectly possible to produce a hundred photographs without a feather or shell in them. Yet to measure these people by an outward appearance of Euro-American-ness would be to embark on another discourse of power altogether; they might be surprised, in any case, if analysis focused on outward appearance rather than the hidden capacities it indicates.) Hence I have instead tried to make a puzzle out of comparison, out of measurement, itself.

One effect of Hagen display was the spectators' realisation that they were only seeing a part of it.[51] When you look at the man, you do not see the complete picture in himself; he is completed by everything – and all the persons and powers – he has kept concealed. The interest for the ethnographer is in the social techniques which these people deploy to point to just that realisation.

ACKNOWLEDGEMENTS

This is the expanded text of the 1997 Ernest Jones lecture (the title was 'Scale, culture and the imagination: an anthropological puzzle from Papua New Guinea'), with some editorial adjustments, and I do thank the British Psycho-Analytical Society for their invitation. My account presents several arguments made familiar, and in places controversial, by a substantial Melanesian anthropology not specifically acknowledged here. Quite separately, I was spurred by Nicola Abel Hirsch's unpublished paper 'Creating minds: some aspects of the digestion and generation of ideas'. The power of Teresa Brennan's ideas is evident in the text. Help and advice has come from diverse sources: Paul Connerton, Karl Figlio, Gillian Gillison, Sarah Greaves, Henrietta Moore, Christina Toren and Elizabeth Wright.

Photographs taken by the author, Dei Council area, Mt Hagen, in 1964 and 1967. They are the subject of Chapter 10.

The Ethnographic Effect II

This is the juncture at which to return to some of the observations offered at the beginning of Chapter 1, and to the ethnographic moment which has dominated this book. I have been bemused at my own constant return to the Hagen gesture of ceremonial exchange. The risks to the credibility of the writer are evident. In the canonical form of *moka,* these particular kinds of performances are fading fast, so that recall runs the risk of nostalgia; there is also the problem of perpetuating exotic body images, while their apparently all-male context challenges feminist credentials. Above all, this moment reinforces a kind of economism, one which I have even exaggerated in the heuristic fiction of the 'gift economy' (1988, and see Chapter 5). Indeed the economistic cast is susceptible to the same criticism which Kirsch makes not just of resource developers (Chapter 9) but of much writing on Papua New Guinean dealings with resource developers – focusing on compensation trivialises other highly important dimensions. I both recognise the force of that criticism and want to suggest that looking more closely, not less, at the implications of the exchange which has captivated my writing about Mt Hagen yields a perspective on a range of other issues as well. These are not in the past and include among other things gender relations.[1] At the same time, I also want to indicate how that particular ethnographic moment conceals its own, 'invisible', blind spot.

Kirsch's (1997) criticism is well taken. He describes how the widespread stereotype of Papua New Guineans as greedy landowners, out for what they can get, is familiarised at home as well – jokes about the unscrupulous who would sell anything for money are relished by Papua New Guinean audiences. And anthropologists can query who is really being greedy[2] while still taking economic motivations for granted. Of the Yonggom people who live along the Ok Tedi and Fly rivers, Kirsch has something else to say. The pressing issue for them is not what they can get in return for the use of their land, including its river system, but its degradation and pollution.

This is (if I may hazard) one of Kirsch's ethnographic moments, and for him the question it implicates is that of moral responsibility. Who is liable? Yonggom can pretty accurately point to the effects of this open-cut copper and gold mine: the tailings it has emptied into the Ok Tedi river has created a 40km corridor of deforested land, buried sago (the staple) swamps under sandbanks, killed fish and made people wonder where the turtles and crocodiles have gone; they know that the sediment which covers once productive alluvial soil is waste washed down from the mine. The closest idiom they have for pointing the finger of accusation is sorcery, and it is this which seems to give Kirsch his moment of insight into moral responsibility. One man said that people now 'live in fear' of hazardous chemicals, 'live in fear' being what they used to shout after a sorcery killing (1997: 146). The mine is seen to have powers, with all kinds of visible effects, like the powers of a sorcerer; importantly, the framework of sorcery means that the register of those effects is what happens *to people,* and the people are identifiable. (A Euro-American might say that the register is 'the environment' or 'society'.) So, Kirsch observes, while they are not identical processes, all kinds of events that in the past would have been attributed to sorcery are now attributed to the mine. Someone poisoned by a catfish, hurt by a falling tree, drowned when a canoe was upturned – the mine has been blamed for all these misfortunes. If pushed, people will point to the environment in which these events occurred – the river water which contains chemical, the mudbanks which make it difficult to get out of the way of obstacles, the speed with which the now shallow river flows. He writes (1997: 149): 'claims against the Ok Tedi mine pair its destructive environmental impact with specific cases of misfortune. They represent moral assertions about how the mine has affected their lives, and they seek to hold the mine accountable'.

Kirsch emphatically states that through the idiom of sorcery Yonggom 'reject the view that the mine's liability is limited to material terms.

Instead they recast discourse about the mine as a moral issue' (1997: 150). It is an issue which involves agents and patients (see above Chapter 1 p. 15), that is, it divides persons by the social positions they occupy with respect to the land, with its bad-tasting fish, toxic colour and canoe accidents. In short, the relationship (between misfortune and the causes of it) is simultaneously rendered an object of attention in personal terms (a relationship between social actors) while being reified through the appearance of the land itself. Alterations to the environment brought about by the mining – and some Yonggom hold that the total environment has changed, from departed animals to poisonous rain and harmful sun – make manifest the form of a world which contains both villagers and a mine company and its workers. Is it not precisely because these effects are visible aspects of what is perceived as a social relationship (between these people and the mine (owners)) that one can write of an issue of 'moral' responsibility at all?

The land always lay between persons. It once gave people their biographies, imagined in spatial terms as events linked to particular named places (Kirsch 1996). People thus saw their lives as a set of movements across land that was also landscape (Hirsch and O'Hanlon 1995). However, for the Yonggom, it seems that time has since become a new axis, and lives are measured against a chronology of when missionaries came, the mine opened, the river changed. This echoes the kind of apocalyptic difference which people elsewhere in Papua New Guinea see in the 'new time' which has come upon them (Chapter 5).

Themselves some way away from the Ok Tedi mine, the Duna described by Stürzenhofecker (1994) have nonetheless seen prospecting helicopters overhead and have had tracks made by surveyors cut through their own forests. Here is an anticipation of benefits. Apocalypse is her term. For Duna are confident that change will come, and that it will be total. When one man talked of their lake being dried up and of mountains levelled to find gold, his vision resonated with other, sometimes eager, prospects, such as the fantasy of rural enterprise development to sell water to Port Moresby. The future will come out of the ground.[3] Duna know about drilling operations elsewhere, and '[t]he activities of companies who drill into "the ground" for wealth can be seen as a new form of contest between them and the agencies within "the ground". These spirit agencies do not yield their secrets easily.' She continues: 'Observed surface transformations of "the ground" constitute a concern mostly for men who try to deduce meaning by "reading" the surface or the skin of "the ground" ... just as the skin of people is seen as an indicator of sickness' (1994: 39-40). Men comment for example on new kinds of grasses that are invading the area. The surface of the ground thus takes a form through the grasses, plants and fruits that grow upon it; the ground was formerly evidence of the state of relations between persons and spirits.

The spirits of this sacred landscape did not themselves live beneath it but made their own tracks over it, and required sacrifice from time to time to keep the ground fertile (1994: 36). Certain spirits were also seen as a source of pigs and shell wealth. Indeed Stürzenhofecker argues that the land that was de-sacralised by missionary teaching has become re-sacralised by Duna witness of mineral exploration and their own hopes of new wealth coming out of the ground at places associated with former spirit activity. Technology will make the ground yield what ritual did in the past. 'The negative change in the surface of "the ground" exhibited by altered patterns of plant life is counterbalanced by the positive changes seen to be achieved by exploring the depth of "the ground" and bringing its wealth to the surface' (1994: 42). The sacrifice required by Duna spirits sustained the division between themselves and men.[4] There was, we might say, a two-way flow of effects. However, when one side snatches (see Chapter 3), the outcome may be lethal. Stürzenhofecker describes the opening of a mine in a neighbouring province (at Porgera, briefly mentioned in Chapter 10; see note 44) and the reddening of local rivers which resulted; reminiscent of Kirsch's account of Yonggom, she writes that deaths which had been attributed to the agency of witches were now attributed to the Porgera mine.

The two landscapes imagined here, Yonggom and Duna, register the impact of persons on one another.[5] The Yonggom are now caught up in a cycle of malevolence whereas the Duna, at the time of Stürzenho-fecker's writing, were anticipating a still productive future. They drew on techniques of inspection, looking at the surface of the land, as a man inspects a feather headdress for the qualities to which it points (Chapter 2), in order to 'see' the relations it indicates. Duna were drawn thus into relationships with spirit persons (and cf. Biersack 1982): the state of the land showed the impact of persons, spirit and human, upon themselves.

It is of course with the appearance of 'wealth' items in Duna, that the way in which anthropologists write these accounts starts looking to Euro-American eyes economistic. Yet in Yonggom too I suspect we are, and as I have suggested in other instances in these essays, only a step away from ceremonial exchange of the Hagen kind. The apocalyptic view which both Yonggom and Duna have of a totally transformed world is a cosmic version, I would argue, of the transformation of social positions into which exchange partners put one another, even though the potential for the reversibility of these positions is different. Perhaps we can liken the changing appearance of the land's surface to the shells and pigs which Hagen men say is on men's skin. One does not see (or hear) the travelling, the landscape traversed, except for a moment when pigs are driven squealing along the paths between settlements or shells disappear over the horizon slung between two pairs of shoulders. The Hagen landscape is not so much gathered into the wealth items as shifted by them: their passage makes the places they are going to/coming from change position.

Not all that is economics need be economistic. Here one becomes conscious again of the effect of writing (analysis) insofar as it creates a context within which phenomena take on particular properties. I would remind the reader that the ethnographic moment is, as I have described it, a matter of analysis as well as observation, involving writer as well as fieldworker. Without wanting to labour the point too much, or repeat what has been already abundantly repeated, and oddly as parts now resonate, I return to an earlier attempt (1992) to put ceremonial exchange into a context that might take some of the economistic out of economics. It was written in response to an invitation to consider the 'science of writing'.[6]

WRITING SOCIETIES, WRITING PERSONS[7]

'Since the iconographers are already committed to "reading" images as texts, and social histories of art to treating them as cultural artefacts, the really innovative task is to look at these images critically' (Starn 1989: 206). The images are fifteenth-century frescoes in the castle of the Gonzaga lords at Mantua. Reading the paintings would simply reduce 'brilliantly assertive and demanding pictures [to] passive illustrations of prescribed themes' (1989: 209). Rather than determine what the pictures represent, Starn is interested in how they represent – the kinds of demands that position the viewer in relation to them.

Renaissance theories of perspective would map the paintings as co-ordinates of the viewer's capacity to see, and what the fifteenth-century viewer thereby sees is princely power. Thus classical motifs on the ceiling disguise the privileges of wealth and power as the rewards of study and learning. For knowing the events and figures to which they allude makes the viewer – and Starn is thinking now of the prince – aware of his own knowledge. 'Because he must move around the room to take in the ceiling, the prince becomes an active participant and instrument of the design, and what he sees in it – those emblematic figures calling to mind any amounts of lore and learning from ancient myth and history – invites further participation' (1989: 231). The seeing person, in short, is painted in. This is literally exemplified in three figures whose eyes look down from the ceiling: 'the beckoning function *requires* the response it pretends only to solicit, for by positing a contingent response, the painter acknowledges the need for a beholder' (1989: 211, original emphasis). Indeed, the viewer's presence completes the room, in that without him (or her) the perspective has no effect. The person *qua* viewer is also completed, being presented with (made present by) the extent of his or her visual extensions. Yet the one thing Starn's interpretation (through writing) cannot do is bring about that effect. Instead, he comments on the inconclusiveness of his own endeavour, on the lack of completion, for 'many loose ends and missing links remain to be considered ... much more needs to be said': 'I can hardly pretend to have given a full account' (1989: 232).

Did this twentieth-century critic intend to elicit a sense of completeness, then? He half-says so in that his treatment of certain modes of interpretation was 'meant to clear the way for a full ... range of responses to the formal demands of art' (1989: 232). But these demands are rendered quite differently from those required by the fifteenth-century painter. The painter specifies that the eye of the beholder will meet that (painted) on the ceiling of the room in the castle. Starn evokes responses that could be lodged in anyone anywhere. One wonders what a full range would be – as many as possible perhaps – in which case fullness is subverted by the limitless. The number of possible views is infinite. Indeed, when interpretation is imagined as *taking a view*, then incompleteness is made manifest by the interpretive exercise itself. I wish to take this particular view of infinity as an origin point for the following supposition.

One way to access the idea of writing as a human science is through the role that interpretation plays in responses to both what and how persons make and act (cf. Smith 1988: 44). Now a particular limiting condition governs the kind of response for which a social scientist would settle. For social scientists know that interpretations are always of a world already occupied by 'societies'. A society, like a culture, is so to speak both already written and forever remaining to be so. It is a context that is evidently a text. And interpretation rewrites. We might say this is true everywhere; but, as an anthropologist, I would want to add the possibility that perspective – including the techniques by which persons take a view on other persons – will make a difference. I briefly introduce a contrast between infinite and finite worlds. If (human/social) science presupposes a particular kind of infinity, this in turn is presupposed by a society of a particular kind, namely one thought to be constituted in the consciousness of persons as at once collective and plural.

Displacement

Derrida is clearly the origin of a decisive conceptualisation of 'writing' but, as he points out, is not (cannot be) the origin of writing. Perhaps Derrida's metaphor works, then, insofar as it supplements other Euro-American conceptualisations concerning the extent of human enterprise. Thus, when extended enterprise is understood as society in its largest sense, society appears to contribute to a metaphysics of presence. It seems to speak. Indeed, I would suggest that for twentieth-century moderns, society has had a presence similar to that of the person as individual subject. Certainly, interpretive social science (cf. Rabinow and Sullivan 1987) has been concerned with the dialectic presumed between them.

Anthropologists professionally invest in the presence of society when they see social organisation as the origin not just of its own structure and relationships but of ways of acting and modes of consciousness. Yet the author of social organisation is known only through its productions. Thus, in their effort to describe social reality, anthropologists must resort to 'writing' it so it can be read as a text, rather in the manner that the islanders of Sabarl (Battaglia 1990: 6-7) like to read their immediate surroundings as reminders of past social action. Given that the difference between societies is presupposed in their analysis, moreover, anthropologists both work with what is already there and, in moving from case to case, discover that each simultaneously adds to and displaces knowledge about previous cases. Cross-societal comparison carries 'supplementation' to a decisive extreme. So here is a difference.

The people of Sabarl tell stories, an activity which at once fixes events and opens them up to contest; but it is on the bodies of persons that manifest traces are left. We may say they thereby write persons.

A person's body is 'a map of the basic relationships and processes of Sabarl life' (Battaglia 1990: 53). Now in marking this or that relationship (as through body decor), people thereby cover others. Nurture from paternal kin, for instance, at once presupposes and displaces ('masks') that from maternal kin. In short, persons are completed by, supplemented by, and thus become relative to, other persons.

But to write society, as anthropologists do, is another matter altogether. Persons are involved, yet what completes them seems to be society itself, whether through 'socialisation' or through the analytical strategy of putting people's acts and artefacts into their 'social context'. When they are supplemented by society, persons are being supplemented by an entity of a different order of abstraction, with its own properties, its own presence. These include the necessity that persons represent society to themselves, which generates an incompleteness of a particular kind: a demand for interpretation. The Euro-American vision of society further presumes a plurality of persons; insofar as their interpretations are held relative to one another, so too may interpretations of societies seemingly supplement and relativise one another.

Commentators on 'Derrida' invite us to imagine a difference between the closure or finiteness of meaning assumed in the metaphysics of presence and the deferred closure deconstructive critique forever reveals. However, the paradox of partial closure suggests that instead of a difference between the finite and infinite, we could as well imagine these as two kinds of infinity. The logocentrist possibility that things have finite characteristics engenders the idea that the world is full of a number of (individuated) things. The result is an arithmetic of sorts: things are countable/countless insofar as one can always start counting even if there are too many to finish. This becomes an alternative infinity to the grammatological understanding of recurring equations: a constant substitution of functions such that terms simultaneously express and displace previous terms. That process is theoretically never-ending. The person as subject confronts a pluralist universe of subjects; the person as text inhabits an anonymous one that is itself a continuous text.

Society, in the twentieth-century Euro-American sense, is, as I have suggested, already evidence for such conceptualizations of infinity. First, society is held to contain diversity within it – to be made up of countable/countless different subjects, each with their own view – whether those subjects are institutions, groups, categories or individual persons. Second, it is regarded as a set of techniques by which individuals communicate through relationships, structures, norms, and so forth. In that society can seem the origin both of social organization and of ideas about it, instead of looking to the origin of ideas in specific persons, we may see those persons as society's several mouthpieces. Each individual subject makes do with what is 'already there' in the cultural repertoire, and insofar as the person's own subjective intervention is displaced thereby, it looks as though the person is merely inscribed, already written into a text. Hence the effect is to imagine the person as having to be completed by society. What is added also works as a displacement. One presence (the individual subject) is displaced by another (society) that in itself evokes both the illimitability of interpretation and the inevitability of the already written.

The interpreting subject appears, then, always positioned to act from a point of view, to take a perspective on events that is never exactly reciprocated by another. At the same time, society is at once regarded as made up of innumerable points of view and as furnishing the individual subject with a technology of communication. The subject thus receives certain interpretations, not just from others but from society at large, which reveals his or her own 'extent' – for the perspective from society is one that no single subject can equal.

Now it does not, in such a world view, matter whether interpreting decision presumes fixed meanings or demonstrates the strategies of deferral, insofar as from either point of view the *act* of interpretation 'adds' to previous ones. At the very least, the interpreting subject is supposed to be enhanced by his/her fresh understandings, even as society is enriched by the collective activity of active minds. This presumption of enrichment invites ideas about the fullness of comprehension. The double meaning of supplementation (surplus and displacement) is constantly reduced thereby by the possibility of quantification, by questions – as in Starn's case – about how many and how much. Even if one loses as much as is gained, creates absences through making present, the measure of response remains the individual subject's journey of interpretation; and that enterprise is regarded as perpetually added to, extended, by its own exercise. The journey has no limit, for society tells the individual he or she will never equal all the possibilities it (society) embraces.

Perspective

At first blush, it might look as though the individual subject and society at large each provide a perspective on the other. But there is no mutuality or reciprocity in their regard. They are not analogous abstractions: neither has the dimensions or proportions of the other, and moderns regard them as different orders of phenomena.

We might contrast this with the recursive perspective to which Starn refers, where the dimensions of the subject are returned to him (or her). The Renaissance schema imposes, he observes (1989: 220), 'a strict visual discipline in return for the image of a finite world mastered by the beholder and proportioned to the beholder's eye'. As I understand it, the viewer, who is completed by seeing the dimensions of his or her vision, is being completed by a structure that also personifies princely power. But while that power depends on being acknowledged by the other, a non-princely viewer can never embody it. I wish to turn to a different kind of recursive perspective that rests directly on a mutuality of embodiment, and which therefore animates rather specific modes of interpretation. It is found in those societies of Melanesia, such as Sabarl, where interaction has the paradigmatic form of 'gift exchange'. By this, I mean that 'the other' is always another person. Persons are separated from one another by their relationships: mother from son, donor from recipient, and so forth. Those relationships are at once the cause and outcome of their acting, so that each act requires taking a perspective on another person. In exchanging gifts with one another, persons exchange perspectives, not just as knowledge of their relative positions but as parts of the other that each incorporates.

The concept of 'writing' avoids the assumption that a text is authenticated by its origin in a speaker; the issue becomes the effectiveness of the text. A speaker, by contrast, is the archetype of an intentional agent, a subject assumed to be the origin of meaning. If it is the Euro-American metaphysics of presence which by convention thus attributes consciousness to the speaking subject, it is an equally Euro-American deconstructive practice that would prefer to see even speakers absent from their words. This conjunction gives interest to the Melanesian view. Here, by convention, persons are significantly present, but as the objects of interpretation. Here, presence ceases to be a guarantee of authenticity. Far from a person being regarded as the cause of their own acting or speaking, and the meanings put on them, the cause lies with those who – present or absent – have elicited that person's response.

The same convention requires that the objects of interpretation – human or not – become understood as other persons; indeed, the very act of interpretation presupposes the personhood of what is being interpreted. A Melanesian response to a configuration of plants or to the pitch of a landscape is likely to refer to the intentions of others – whether of spirits, enemies or kin. What one thus encounters in making interpretations are always counter-interpretations: to think that a chief is holding back the rains from the gardens, or that the ancestral potency of the land is being revealed in an abundant crop, become simultaneously one's interpretation of the meaning of certain events and evidence that one is also the object of chiefly, or ancestral, attention. Evidence comes in the form of one's own effects on other persons.

These Melanesian suppositions have a mathematical dimension. Interpretation and counter-interpretation produce the plurality not of addition but of division – do not so much add to the world as divide it up. It would thus be a mistake to see such moves as replaying the Euro-American dialectic of 'self and 'other'; what are being distributed between persons are their relationships. Above all, knowledge of the world is not rewritten as the subjects' self-knowledge (cf. Weedon 1987: 84). Rather, knowledge of oneself is distributed among all those who interact with one. They, too, are the keepers of it.

This gives rise to an illimitability of a certain kind: knowledge is always relative to what a person knows of others and they of him or her, and can only be gauged from how people act. One must constantly scrutinize people's acts, therefore, for each action generates new possibilities and uncertainties, to be tested by counteraction. One's own actions in turn yield one's interpretations of those others. An act is thus a critical moment,[8] instantiating a decision about the cause of events, at once displacing previous acts and demonstrating one's critical effectiveness (what one causes others to do). Yet the world is never incomplete: every act is also a finality, for it will also reveal how one relates to others, and one is never unrelated.

Melanesian initiation sequences are characteristically based on knowledge being established at one juncture in order to be taken away and replaced (thus displaced) by new knowledge at another. They make explicit a general state of affairs. The point of establishing an interpretation at each juncture is in order to act; the action 'is' the interpretation, and through it persons analyse others and reveal themselves by finding their efforts embodied in others. If the outcome (effect) of their acts lies with other persons, so too do the causes, and thus the origin of their being in the world. I would emphasise a consequence of interest in the present context. Different 'points of view' cannot add to what is already there when what is already there is embodied in other persons. The donor of a gift does not discover the recipient; the recipient is notionally present as the cause of the debt that compelled the gift.

Giving gifts provides a simple Melanesian model for the exchange of perspectives. But there are other devices by which one person's dimensions are measured by another person. I adduce an example that also shows how people can control the activity of interpretation, exemplifying not just a world already made but a world already complete.

Number

What might interpretation look like in a society that does not regard the world as affording illimitable extensions of perspectives? The Iqwaye of Papua New Guinea, for instance (Mimica 1988), imagine a universe infinitely divided, producing a multiplicity of differentials, but what is divided is always 'one'.[9] Difference is generative: this is a reproductive model in which every two generates another one. At the same time difference is contained: the idea of an ultimate unifying entity is given a name, Omalyce, an androgynous being who is the single origin of all differentiation. Indeed, Omalyce embodies all number.

Iqwaye enumeration is literally based on the body, twenty (digits) being summated as one (one person). It allows abstract permutations up to a number far higher, Mimica observes, than is ordinarily called for in the pragmatics of counting. He suggests that the generative possibility of the system derives from the entire universe being seen as the opening up of the primordial body into its recombinatorial parts. The doubling and division of entities are thus aspects of a single ontological process. Four hundred is not 'more' than one: it is one in the form of a body of as many persons (twenty) as one's digits (twenty). As a result, each person is both an instance of Omalyce and hence of the whole, and a dividual product of Omalyce's capacity for differentiation; both a homologue of the totality and a re-embodiment of its partibility and divisibility. Each person shows the effect of Omalyce's generative power. Wagner (1991: 168) underlines Mimica's further observation that however sophisticated the statistical measure, one could never count the whole Iqwaye population, for it consists of all those ever born and to be born, and any number short of the total (one) would be incomplete.

Another Papua New Guinea society has worked out such suppositions to a fine degree: everyone who has been or who will be is already named. I draw from Harrison's (1990) account of the Manambu living at Avatip, neighbours of Bateson's Iatmul. Avatip people suppose that there is a finite set of personal names in the world. In fact, these personal names encompass all manifestations of the universe – including what Euro-Americans would call natural objects, features of the landscape, astronomical configurations – for in their invisible aspects these, too, are 'in reality men and women' (1990: 56). The entire world is divided or distributed betwen groups who claim a totemic relationship to refractions of it. Groups are thereby distinguished in their ownership of names, including secret versions for things also named by others. It is the version (the 'person') they lay claim to, not the thing (1990: 52). This is also the case with human beings: all subclans produce children, but each jealously guards the unique names only they can give them. Yet the extent of a group's ownership is constantly open to interpretation.

A subclan owns between one and two thousand personal names, a perceived totality of all its parts, human and otherwise, past, future and present, and the entire community perhaps mobilises some 32,000 names.[10] However, names have to be actively claimed. It is possible for a subclan to take an unoccupied name from another group, as it is possible for subclans to steal secret names. Only through public debate can a group demonstrate that they have kept their secrecy intact. This is no small matter, because with each secret goes the magical power invested in one's ancestor, and the origin of one's identity, as well as in many cases ritual prerogatives.

Rivalry between related Avatip subclans is periodically played out by men in what we might call contests of interpretation. Contestants compose themselves into two sides. A man from one side walks up to the vine rope that divides the two and whispers a secret name into the ear of his opponent, who acknowledges or denies its correctness, a response taken under oath. The name is not one that belongs to the speaker; the aim is to show that he knows the secret names of the *other* side. If a subclan does reveal that it knows the other's names, then it shows it already holds an encompassing order of knowledge, and has appropriated what the other claims are its origins.

The identity of each subclan thus rests in its names, and its identity is also its power. Since the number of names is held to be finite, brought into the world at its beginning, the body of names that a subclan possesses for its members divides a totality composed of the names possessed by all subclans. The universe of names marks the fact that everything already exists. In the same way, all the yams that could ever be grown exist in the ritual powers it takes to release them from mythic time (Harrison 1990: 63). Things are not being added to such a world: rather, groups compete among themselves for the power of possession. 'Supplementation' works, so to speak, by extraction, the displacement of possession. It is the extent of their power that groups thereby measure and test – and, since they do this constantly, they forever introduce uncertainty into their dealings with one another. Thus, men never know that their names have not been stolen until a debate proves the case, in the same way as they keep guard of their stock of members' names only by reacting the moment they hear of an encroachment. Every claim is thus validated only by the refutation of counter-claims: it requires an opponent to challenge one's knowledge in order to know that the names are still one's own.

'The social world of Avatip is divided in such a way that the idea that groups require each other comes close to being a kind of necessary truth. ... What is assumed to be prior to all actual social groups is a closed system of archetypal categories forming a kind of organic totality' (1990: 65). What is constantly adjusted, therefore, is the relative claims of persons towards one another. Since competitive groups are assisted by their allies, who hold secrets on their behalf, the whole work of debate activates the interdependence of all groups who must collaborate 'to maintain the total world order' (1990: 3). And since names are objective properties of the world, neither created by human beings nor dependent on them (1990: 72-3), there is no debate as to whether their attendant power exists but simply as to which group embodies it.

A subclan acquires prerogatives by taking them from elsewhere; what is specific about this Melanesian version of limited-good thinking is how attrition and addition are measured. Attrition and addition equal one another insofar as they are embodied in the relative claims of coeval groups (persons). An Avatip debate is literally a duel, an arena for finding another by which to size oneself, the dimension of one man given by another man. Measure or extent exists in the knowledge of another party, and can be known only through the knowledge that the other reveals.

Harrison likens control over knowledge to the values of wealth objects that circulate in the exchange institutions of other Melanesian societies. Indeed, the debating stance echoes the mutual embodiment of an exchange relationship: each party puts itself in the place of the other by trying to imagine what its secret names are. But the mutuality is short-lived, for to have imagined accurately is to have 'stolen' the name. If the contest of names is an interpretive activity, the objects of interpretation are other persons. And since, through its names, a subclan embodies the powers of its originating ancestors, the effect is a redistribution and re-embodiment of powers. Indeed, interpretation implies having an effect – it is the decisive enactment of what is now seen to have already happened.

In the distribution or division of power between groups, where every gain is another's loss, we see also the division of interpretive work. Each group is required to engage with the other's attempts to establish what the state of affairs is. The work of interpretation is – not shared but – shared out between them.[11]

Writing

Elsewhere (M. Strathern 1991a: 198) I have suggested that the Melanesian counterpart to Western 'social analysis' is the manner in which persons decompose themselves by revealing the relations (persons) which they embody. In the Avatip debates, the object of the debate is not to create new perceptual distinctions – not to interpret what is known but to discover who knows it. Power cannot be measured until it is tested, and then it is known by its effects. For all the divisibility of the world into a multiplicity of names, then, knowledge of names always returns to power as the 'one' outcome (cf. Gillison 1987). Yet all that a subclan/person can demonstrate at any moment is that power is also relative. If one subclan loses a name, it is because another has gained it, even as one person is thus displaced by another person. As a consequence, persons are no guarantee of 'presence'. That is, even if a particular man is there, what is *under debate* is whether or not that man is an originator. He may or may not know the relevant names – and what has to be made present is the power of knowing. The originator is not conceived as an individual subject in the Euro-American sense. A speaker is a mouthpiece – not for society but for persons in another aspect; he speaks for the subclan, and thus for an enlarged version of himself.

If persons do not guarantee presence, presence is no guarantee of authenticity. In this sense the debates are not 'speech'. Names are authenticated not by the originators of them but in the partition of knowledge between claimant and rival, so that it is the active intervention of other persons that delimits what a subject knows. The rival's utterance of one's own name is at once theft and repossession, a claim to an origin that has come from elsewhere. Are the debates 'writing' then?

Battaglia (e.g. 1990: 194) comments on the way Sabarl mortuary ceremonial works to perform persons; that is, a person's relations and capacities are acted out, distributed in the knowledge of those around him or her, in order to allow the generation of new relations and capacities. She calls the ceremonial (activity) writing, to capture both the decisive critical moment at which the deceased is presented in summarising form, and the displacement effect of so marking him or her as now absent. That effect is an object of explicit activity, its enactment sending out, she says, new stories like new shoots of growth. Now whereas Sabarl mortuary rites work to render the deceased absent, Avatip debates work (we might say) to make the living present, that is, to ensure persons embody power.[12] As Harrison notes, by virtue of the fact that power must always be efficacious, constant demonstration must be given that power is with the powerful. What is arrested or blocked is further manipulation or interpretation of the moment itself, insofar as absence in the first case and presence in the second are momentarily written. The outcome is to create a newly usable identity (Battaglia 1990: 194).

We might take these Melanesian forms of interpretation as analogous to the concerns of a social science, yet neither 'society' (the authorless text) nor the individual (the speaking subject) is presupposed. Persons interpret the acts of already existing social entities already related to themselves through their counter-interpretations. It is that division of interests which creates a finite world. For Euro-American moderns who live in a proliferating one, such possibilities appear simply to add to the infinite number of social worlds their own interpretations might address. But our interpretations also encompass the description of both! We think we can imagine both finite and infinite worlds. For 'ourselves', then, it has to be our own world that is finite, in the specific concepts, perspectives – and mathematics – it furnishes us with.

PERSPECTIVES AND BLIND SPOTS

Starn's failure to find completion in his own writerly enterprise is a reminder that the anthropologist is not alone in such realisations, even though there may be precipitating reasons particular to the ethnographic enterprise. At the beginning of Chapter 1, I mentioned that Haddon and Co. imagined they were making records from an incomplete culture. Part of the sense of incompleteness comes from the vision of holism that I have suggested is such an engine to uncovering the unpredictable. (We can never describe the whole of society!) Part comes from the juxtaposition of fieldwork/writing, observation/analysis. However, the sense of incompleteness which such juxtapositions generates also has a general source in Euro-American knowledge practices.

A merographic commentary

This is the incompleteness of shifting perspectives, and Euro-American anthropologists put it at the heart of analytical writing whenever they evoke the comparative method (Parkin 1987). A comparison of entities means that each entity reveals others, each in turn thus affording a perspective which may always be rendered incomplete by those others. It implies a limitless possible number: Hagen, Yonggom, Avatip... It implies taking specific parts of one work and using them in an identifiably different context, although always with the proviso of return (return to their ethnographic source). Descriptions from one society thus lodge in another, as though the substance of particular ethnographic cases were flowing between the texts. But this last allusion to a kind of exchange is fanciful. What we are talking about is the organisation of writing. And however mutually or reciprocally the comparisons are set up, and however equalising the attempt to be even-handed, the effect of moving between analytical locations produces what I have elsewhere dubbed the merographic connection.

The term points to certain practices of knowledge which presume a limitless number of perspectives. Each new angle or perspective eclipses the last; anything may be a part of something else, minimally part of a description in the act of describing it. In this view, nothing is in fact ever simply part of a whole because another view, another perspective or domain, may re-describe it as 'part of something else' (M. Strathern 1992: 73). We might imagine two persons each inhabiting the other's visual field. The merographic connection thus works through turning aside from one vantage point to see things from 'a whole' new perspective. To know Avatip through knowing about Hagen: if what one has to know is the point of view from which author writes, the most important thing is to know precisely 'the point of view from which' his or her perspective is laid out. Each perspective in including another viewpoint as a part of itself must exclude the other *as a perspective.*

In Euro-American eyes, reification and personification would provide two just such radically different perspectives on the way in which people attach things to themselves and themselves to one another. They give us the familiar problem with commodification, when objects seem valued over subjects and persons subordinate to things. There is to hand an articulate working through of this Euro-American problematic which rests exactly on the idea that each perspective is a radical and an individual moment.

Radin's (1996) recent grappling with the topic of commodification first separates out two perspectives and then finds a kind of solution in the notion of (her phrase) 'incomplete commodification'. For this lawyer, and self-styled philosophical pragmatist, the notion is an epistemological answer to questions of value in an arena of moral debate in American, and European, society also touched on in these essays. The arena is created by an increasing technological capacity to detach and transfer body parts, along with arrangements including surrogacy effected through reproductive medicine, all of which have recontexualised age-old practices such as prostitution and 'baby-selling'. The controversies are over what is or is not appropriately detached from the body or the person, commodified, and ultimately on the market for sale. The problem with commodification in this sphere is that it does indeed seem to turn subjects into objects, and Euro-American views of persons as subjective agents cannot hold with that. But Radin wishes to avoid the impasse between either overvaluing or else undervaluing commodification – between according it too much power (seeing its sinister hand everywhere)[13] and according it not enough (in trying to remove whole realms of life from it).[14] The impasse, as she analyses it and with which one can only agree, is to be laid partly at the door of crude notions of personhood and community (individual and society) which do not appreciate that market relations are relations not just between persons and thing but between persons as such. She suggests that if we conceive of the person as related to others, and community as founded on human interdependence, then '[i]ncomplete commodification as an expression of a nonmarket order coexistent with a market order can be related to this shift in conceptualization of the ideals of personhood and community' (1996: 113). In this view, commercialism does not have to be crass, and one can imagine commodification as a matter of degree.[15]

What Radin wants to say is that aspects of transactions involving persons and what they detach from themselves may carry non-commodity values, while one should not be so afraid of commerce as not to recognise the appropriateness of commodity values in other aspects. Thus she defines (Euro-American) practices of compensation for injury as a form of redress, which may take a monetary form but do not imply a commensurable *quid pro quo*, that is, the injury is not totally measured by money. 'Commodified and noncommodified conceptions are well crystalized, and they coexist' (1996: 189).[16]

My purpose in introducing Radin's formulations at this stage is to clarify the description of merographic connections. She herself could not state it more clearly: commodified and non-commodified concepts[17] form distinct, in the double sense of at once separate and crystal clear, orders of interpretation of experience. Nonetheless they coexist. The two perspectives can be connected, indeed comprise a pair. Thus one may think of commodified and non-commodified conceptions, in Radin's language, like market and non-market economies, joined together as opposites or complementarities. At the same time, this joining does not yield a reciprocal or mutually defining relation. On the contrary, while the values can be aligned as positive and negative aspects of each other, each conception simultaneously draws on its own universe of connotations, applications and meanings. Each is connected to a unique, in the sense of self-referential, range of phenomena which gives it its own character: the one differs from the other insofar as it is also part of a quite different context for action. In short, what defines commodification is not what defines its opposite.[18] This means that each provides a perspective on the other, and one may describe processes from either view (as spelt out in note 16). In Radin's formula, commodity and non-commodity values are in 'contest'. Her epithet is, merographically speaking, absolutely right. The outcome of this coexistence is not so much a contradictory or dyadic or bivalent process of commodification as an 'incomplete' one.

This is more than a single example – I believe it is a quite characteristic Euro-Americanism. To repeat an earlier question, then, what might interpretation look like in a society that does *not*, as here, imagine perspectives as self-referential, 'unique' contexts for action and hence with the potential to coexist with, and overlap with, limitless numbers of 'unique' others? I do not believe that the answer can be accomplished in the kind of writing that Radin must write, or that this book is written in. But the writing which cannot exemplify the phenomenon may nonetheless point to it. One must simply be prepared for the unpredictable, including different distributions of what people take as finite and what they take as infinite about their circumstances.

Perspectivism

Suppose perspectives were finite, but not in the Renaissance manner. Suppose, instead of a Renaissance imagination which at times tried to make the whole world the singular object of the viewer's vision, having a perspective were regarded as a capacity belonging to animate life. What the viewer would 'see' would be other life forms. What would be finite here? Could it be the manner in which one's perspective was returned to one? That is, closure would lie in the fact that one simultaneously had one's own perspective and received the perspective of another. Or rather, the point at which the viewer was conscious that he or she had a perspective on things would be the point at which he or she would meet (so to speak) the reciprocal perspectives of other life forms. Each would thus include the other's perspective *as a perspective*. This is exactly what Eduardo Viveiros de Castro (1996; 1998) has described from various anthropological accounts of Amazonian 'perspectivism'.

He writes of a complex ontology of multiple worlds, where experience is in one sense radically divided, in another sense constantly doubled or self-shadowed (1992). These are the Amazonian worlds, of Araweté and others, based on an assumption of continuity between all animate beings; people share with animals the same kinds of soul and thus the same identities and indeed mental constructs. What differentiates them are their bodies. It is bodies which see and which determine what is seen. From out of their human body, human beings can only 'see' animals as non-human; but when the animals' point of view is imagined, these creatures do not see human beings as human beings – to them people appear as animals, and the animals appear to one another as people. Now the body in turn is created by sight. Those who have the view (take a perspective) appear human, as persons, to one another. Being able to see defines an agent: people know they are people because the rest of the animate world appears as non-human. But it (being able to see) says nothing about the identity of other creatures, only about how they appear to the viewer. What determines the form, that is, determines what can be seen, is spiritual state. There are certain moments when people can see the animals in the same way as they see themselves (they see the animals as people), namely when they have access to other worlds through shamanistic trance. Spirits comprise a further axis here, along with other non-human entities. How human being see things, then, is how every other creature perceives, and all animate beings are like human beings in that sense (share the same kind of soul). Certain significant animals most exemplify these principles.

As Viveiros de Castro (1996) put it, seeing is a question of percept not concept. What you see is not what you know. You can only 'see' the manifest form or body that is available to sight because it is with body that you see in the first place. Under special circumstances you can acquire other kinds of sight (that is, other bodies) and 'see' all kinds of entities in different form. Such Amazonian alternations of vision confirm a consequence of these operations, namely that any one perspective is, so to speak, completed or made finite by its reciprocal. If, on the one hand, a human being seeing an animal sees a human being seeing an animal, then, on the other hand, the human knows that he or she has the form of an animal in the other's eyes.

Since being able to see is a condition of humanity, animals and spirits may be said to include former human beings, but not the other way round. Animals are ex-humans, not humans ex-animals (he quotes among others Descola 1986: 120). To repeat the lineaments of this complex ontology: being human consists in the vantage point of seeing and seeing gives the world a particular form. When persons lose their bodies, as in death, they cease to appear as human beings to others (can no longer see and be seen in the same world). In short, the body is an agent of perception. So although animals/spirits perceive just as living people do – they all have similar kinds of souls – without the same kind of body they perceive different things. When tapirs become people they see in the same way but the bodies they see are not the bodies that people see: they see tapir versions of human beings. And that in turn is because this is not simply a matter of knowledge, of switching perspectives in the sense of putting yourself mentally in another's shoes: it is because vision brings about different worlds or orders of being. Hence there is a divide between worlds, 'known' by the travelling that is necessary – it takes shamans to cross it. Shamans activate different bodies.

This is not relativism. The evocation of ontology is quite deliberate here. For what lies behind this description is Viveiros de Castro's concern with the primitive ontological base on which, by contrast, much anthropological exegesis rests. It is epistemology which has become a source of endless complexity, and social anthropology is not the only discipline that has at times turned an intellectual Euro-American obsession with how we come to know and describe things into the issue of how we represent them. After all, what we conceive as an object of study must be mediated by what we make of our knowledge of the world! I also use the term 'world' deliberately: this epistemology constructs a 'whole' world as its object. For life appears divided into the (real) world on the one hand and on the other into how human beings know and represent that world. Indeed, in the late twentieth century of Euro-American academia, a 'perspectival' view has become almost a *sine qua non* for the idea that we all hold different ways of knowing the world and different viewpoints from which to see it. The consequence, Viveiros de Castro would say, is that all the interesting questions seem to be about about how we (subjects) know the world (object) – a simple-minded ontology upholding a fantastic epistemological edifice.[19]

But what do such Euro-Americans have to say about the way in which persons have a view on one another? There may be a mutuality of regard between persons, who each know that the other has a perspective on him or herself, yet only under certain conditions will this work as a finite relationship. Rather, it is likely to take the form of a merographic connection. The other's perspective is encompassed within one's own. For the other's perspective exists for oneself, in this Euro-American view, *as a piece of knowledge.* That is, one is consciously aware that what is true of oneself (having a perspective on events) must equally be true of the other person. This yields the familiar reflexive position of seeing oneself through others, and its anthropological companion, concern about the representation of others. In this order of things, simply 'knowing' about other perspectives may also be regarded as a respectable end in itself.

Amazonian perspectivism, by contrast, makes knowledge a means rather than an end. Viveiros de Castro (1996) puts it forcefully: a point of view does not create the object, as in Euro-American ontology; the point of view creates the subject. A perspective in the Amazonian sense cannot therefore be a representation (of an object). And the world you see cannot be effected through a change of mental orientation – or by an alternative social construction – only by body condition. Attention to body condition pervades people's being in the world. Kinship, for instance, as we encountered it briefly in Chapter 4, becomes a process of the active assimilation of relationships through the absorption of substance and memory; persons constitute one another's bodies as human bodies through interaction.

This does, I believe, give us a useful re-entry into the Melanesian material. It gives us a further vocabulary for the significance of form. If we take Amazonian vision as a kind of traffic between animate beings, the evidence of the traffic lies in the forms of those beings (a human being seeing another human being as an animal). One sees, so to speak, the effect of the relationship. In Melanesia, the appearance of the land, the state of people's bodies, the resources they have at their disposal, are all signs of traffic. The traffic may be conceptualised as between human beings and spirits, as in the case of Avatip or Duna, or in Hagen when people there still think of ancestral ghosts, and variously between humans and animals; however (I suggest) humanity, and thus a division between humans and others,[20] is not the principal ontological axis. I do not think that the difference between 'spirit' or 'animal' and 'human' has been the archetype for perspectival traffic in the Amazonian sense. Rather, it is persons who offer perspectives on one another. By this I mean that the significant lines are internal, between human beings as distinctive social entities, that is, between types or kinds[21] distinguished by their relationships with one another. This is why gender, as a means of reification, giving a form to persons, has figured so prominently in Melanesian anthropology. Descola (1996) makes exactly this comparative point. The ontological axis is the possibility of division between (social) 'persons'.

Such a division is not just a matter of knowing, but of being. This is why gender difference is not trivial. At least as I have described it for the past in Mt Hagen, the crucial difference was between same-sex and cross-sex relations. Someone in one position acts towards another in a counterpart position, and each comes to define the other. One is same-sex to one's same-sex sibling (say), cross-sex to one's cross-sex sibling. These are fundamentally different modes of relating. Similarly, in lineal systems, the differentiation of kin into maternal and paternal, or agnatic and cognatic, kinds points to a fundamental state of being for the person so connected; being a son is not the same as being a sister's son. These are not relative points of view – there are ontological consequences to being a son to these people and a sister's son to those, or to being a consanguine by contrast with an affine. These are at once bodily conditions and social orientations, and Melanesian relations with spirits should be seen as composing a similar configuration. Any of these connections may work as a dyad: the view that a Trobriand child has of her matrilineal kin(s-folk) is returned by them to her as their matrilineal kin(swoman). Perspectives are paired, as perspectives, although there may be many pairs.

It is subjects, in my vocabulary 'persons', who hold perspectives in one another. What creates a finite perspective? Perspectives linked by what passes between them? Coming from Hagen, I have already used an exchange-derived term, 'traffic', and written in general of 'flow', where others might think of seeing or for that matter might think of particles of light. But it is the evidence that is visible. What transpires between persons becomes reified, graspable, 'on their skins', whether it is the skin of the land or the body or the clan with its universe of names. Ceremonial exchange begins looking like a literal version of such traffic. It crystallises flow between persons, makes it into an aesthetic object by making it the subject of exchange between partners who are, most evidently, partners for the purposes of exchange. Visions are not operators, and you do not need shamans. But – and here I borrow from Stephen Hugh-Jones (1994; 1996) – there is a counterpart to the travels of the shaman: the travelling of wealth. The 'Amazonian' shaman makes the traffic of vision visible. In 'Melanesian' exchange transactions, it is holding the gift that creates the viewpoint.

Relations between donor and recipient are predicated on the fact that at any single moment one is either in one position or the other in relation to one's counterpart (a donor to a recipient). If one may occupy either position, this is a situation which gift exchange freezes as a condition of exchange itself: to be a donor is to be or to have been a recipient. The anticipation of this reversal is ever present. This is not a matter of vision, as in the Amazonian case, but of the kind of effect which people have on one another. Through exchanging perspectives, for example, people exchange the capacity for each side to augment itself. In Hagen, this was evinced through a characteristic obsession or anxiety on men's part. What was always problematic was how sufficiently the gift will have been augmented – the amount of power it evinces. This was seen through the size of the prestation and how it compared with previous ones. Quite unproblematic, by contrast, was identity. In any specific interchange, there was never any doubt who was donor and who was recipient; that was indicated in the kinds of gifts they held. Gifts in the hand could almost be like Amazonian eyes.[22] If, from one point of view, a donor handing gifts to a recipient turns the recipient into a future donor, then, from another point of view, the donor knows himself as the recipient due to be handed gifts in return.

Wealth items are transformative:[23] they create two kinds of persons (donors, recipients) by the direction of their flow. As for women in patrilineal systems of the Hagen kind, what is crucial for them is that the direction in which they (the women) move should also create different kind of persons (a woman's own paternal kin become maternal kin to her children), and for that they require that men's energies be diverted into kin-based prestations. They lock male agents into a network of debts and credits, so that men become defined by the way they face one another as transactors in kin relationships (cf. Van Baal 1975). In any event, the flow of wealth between men forces both men and women to take a perspective on one another in a heightened and articulate way – an exteriorised form of the 'flow of relationships' (Wagner 1977) which forces reciprocal perspectives on everyone. Each person sees him or herself from the viewpoint of the other. Here we may return to Kelly's account of the Etoro in Chapter 3 (and see note 5). When he writes (1993: 163) that a male initiate, now visibly linked to his father and agnates by shared bone and hair and to his mother's kin by blood, flesh and skin, 'embodies, in his completed physical and spiritual constitution, all the relational components that constitute the social system', he also shows how the social system re-works these linkages as relationships of exchange. Over two generations the mother's kin turn from being recipients of the initiate's shell valuables to sending valuables back (in bridewealth, according to the marriage rules). The person who is *embodied* in two different ways, by (relation with) father's kin and mother's kin, becomes the rationale for two sets of persons (the two sides) to interact in a fashion which makes each momentarily occupy the position of the other.

Now the Melanesian idea that persons exchange viewpoints or perspectives with one another prompts comparison with the Euro-American reflexivity of selfhood that binds a notion of identity to what can be seen: I know who I am because you can see who I am. In this formula one person's gaze is reflect in another's; a person's soul is in their eyes, and to see is to know. It is precisely knowledge (including self-knowledge) that the Euro-American interaction brings, and 'reflexivity' is a state of knowing.

However the Melanesian exchange of perspectives in which I am interested entails an exchange of 'effects'. Perspectives may be overtly paired, and the positions may be reversible, but a person's gaze is not returned as such; the man does not see himself but himself, transformed, in another body. In brief, like a mother giving food to a child, the donor gives to a person different from himself (a donor handing a gift to another donor as a recipient). And what 'person' is this? It has to be the person engaged in exchange, and thus it is the exchangeability of people's capacities that is at issue. This exchangeability is manifest in the person's body, and gift exchange is one moment at which this truism is made public. In Hagen, as we have seen, gift exchange between men takes the form of an exchange of substance: wealth flowing between donor and recipient indicates the detachability of the donor's assets which go to swell the size of the recipient's body in turn. The enlarged body is made visible through decoration, even as, when the donor's gift has been consumed (momentarily) by another, the depleted body is made visible through its absence. Thus, too, a pregnant mother and her child affect one another, for both grow together, as later the child and his or her clan grow one another (the clan body that is literally enlarged by its own members also nourishes them with food off its land). In short, bodies have effects on bodies, and being 'effective', as opposed to being 'reflexive', is a state of being. It is a circumscribed, relational state. These effects are not mediated by a need to have prior knowlege of the world; they are the outcome of interactions.

Blind spot

The question of knowledge weaves in and out of this account. So, too, the practices of revelation and concealment spin a particular kind of spell. When I began thinking about why I was so dazzled, in fact, I assumed it was because of what made visible, that I had been drawn to the display. On reflection I realise that there is much more to it: that it is the hiding again that exerts an equally powerful effect. One can hide ideas in one's descriptions, after all, so not all of them may be evident at any one time. This leads me to my blind spot. Obviously I have to approach the blind spot sideways, so let me return to Harrison.

The issue is again the language of description, which we know will involve the various Euro-American devices of juxtaposition, of summoning a particular context, of perspective merographically conceived, which all contribute to the axis of comparison that the writer creates. Now Harrison compared Avatip control over knowledge to transactions in wealth objects such as those which circulate in the Trobriands. The specific control over knowledge that affects Avatip people is the manifestation of persons in their names; but he also talks more generally of the creation and circulation of ideas and of incorporeal property such as designs, spells and all kinds of ritual imagery and procedure. The comparison with wealth items[24] is well-taken. For I suggest that this 'knowledge' is not like the kind of knowledge with which the writer-anthropologist is principally concerned.[25] I underline the issue with an account from New Ireland. Foster gives a story about Tanga exchange transactions which depicts them as 'specific instances of revelatory display through which agents constitute and communicate knowledge'; in the story, shells in moving from one hiding place to another move between persons. The knowledge people thus communicate to others is, to complete his sentence, 'about themselves' (1995a: 208). Circulation, he goes on to say, takes the dialectical form of appearance and disappearance. He then adds that '[v]isual apprehension or witnessing ... often entails a proprietory relationship between the viewer and the object viewed, such that the viewer achieves a degree of mastery over the object observed' (1995a: 209). Visual perception is the only reliable source of knowledge, and seeing, in his analysis, constitutes not only knowledge but control, that is, demonstrating an effect.[26] We may conclude that, as in Avatip, the object of knowledge, like the object of an effect, is not some notion of a world at large, but, and more finitely, other persons. The world at large – if they were to imagine the land, the settlements, the weather like that – simply gives off signs as to the effectiveness of this traffic. If knowledge is in the first place about the persons between whom it is imparted, this, it seems to me, is a highly significant qualification on comparing its circulation to a Euro-American epistemology.

Elsewhere in Papua New Guinea are people whose reputation seems built on an almost deliberate recalcitrance to Euro-American knowledge practices, or, more accurately put, where Euro-American anthropologists have had spectacular problems with coming up with adequate descriptions (Crook in press). But has the apparently evident and describable practice of ceremonial exchange, staple anthropological fare since Mauss's *Essay on the Gift*, also been a block to (anthropological) knowledge? Or, again more accurately put, why should I – and I am not of course alone – have made it a source of knowledge? Was it because as a Euro-American I have been trained to equate knowledge with seeing, when what is seen is *the world at large?* I do not see a person but a person in a cultural context, not a figure but a figure in landscape, not just shells being whisked away but a glimpse into a social system, not a gift but economics. The revelatory part of these practices (gift exchange) seemed so obviously to be about making evident social facts and political-economic processes. Their significance had to be in what they revealed to the anthropologist about culture, society and economy.[27] And it seemed so obvious to think of people's relationships as similar exemplifications of a social world. That all remains true and worthwhile to work with. But those (Euro-American) insights into social process obscure certain properties of the relationships themselves.

I re-read the passages in *The Gender of the Gift* (M. Strathern 1988: 180-2) which deal directly with reification, and am struck by a question that troubled me at the time but that I did not allow to appear as a question: what was the underlying motive for making relations visible? I had

247

no account (description) of the apparent need I imputed to these Melanesians to make relations *visible*. It did not have to be asked because the desire to know seemed self-sufficient, the counterpart to the anthropologists' analysis, as the end of the book suggests (1988: 309). It was a blind spot. For it seemed a kind of self-evident fact of social and cultural life that people make themselves explicit to themselves in various ways for which visibility itself is a powerful metaphor. This was the dazzle: they are anthropologists too! The dazzle of technical symmetry, that is, a symmetry in artistry and technique. It had the same grip as the notions of convention and norms had gripped earlier anthropologists in their perception of social order as a matter of rules. However, I suspect now that this (the idea that people must make themselves explicit to themselves) probably came from the kind of productionist view of culture and society which, among others, Viveiros de Castro (1998) has roundly criticised. It implied that people were having to produce and create themselves as participants in some kind of social project. There is another version to be retrieved from those same few pages. All we need do is drop the Euro-American link between visibility and knowledge of the world.

There is no doubt that people in Hagen, as elsewhere in the Papua New Guinea Highlands, strive to make themselves effective in relation to one another. And while I have focused on Hagen men's affairs here, they can of course only be completed by women. Women are in any case effective in the sense of having their presence acknowledged in the claims they can put on husbands and brothers; they wish to have an effective presence between kin. What I now think is mistaken is the axiomatic assumption that visibility is somehow for the sake of knowledge, and that knowledge addresses, and thus gathers information about, the larger world in which one lives.[28] Instead, I would offer a different Melanesian emphasis. What you see is what there is (presents itself) to be seen; what you do not see is what is not to be seen. In Hagen women are mostly not to 'be seen' in the way men are. The reciprocal, with its compelling negative (Munn 1986), is only conceivable because of the finite perspective it thereby implicates; it would be nonsense to speak thus from within an open-ended, infinite world.

This means, however, that a Melanesian view keeps *relations* in view. What you see is not a representation of the world; it is evidence of your point of being in it.[29] What you see is there to be seen because the observer is in the appropriate social condition to register the effect.[30] And the cause of the effect is ultimately another person. Perhaps witnessing them both at once – the visible person and the person who made 'him' visible – would be a Melanesian version of the anthropologist's ethnographic moment: two trajectories (two distinct persons) brought together. A gift, a pearlshell, would do it.

Now, let me choose, from among a growing number of such criticisms,[31] Douglas Dalton's complaint about the anthropological obsession with relations. His reasons are exactly those of finding the right description, and he argues that anthropologists who emphasise relationality simply re-describe their own intellectual project. In one sense, this has to be right (cf. J. Weiner 1993). At the same time, he would point to what, in the case he describes (Rawa in Madang Province), summons the unpresentable absence or missing origins that supply human ends (D. Dalton 1996: 394). He says that what Rawa see, sublimely, in shells is anger, pain, absence (1996: 409). They summon, in his view, the inadequacy or incommensurability that arises between the loss of a person (say) and the compensation offered in their stead. I would be a little sceptical, however, of the transcendental incompleteness and its problem of adequate 'representation' as he attributes it to them. Rather, the removal of persons summons what Merlan and Rumsey (1991: 235) call 'compensation-for-disequilibrium' – a person who moves from one domain to another becomes lost as a recipient or carrier of relationships. Is it not through anger, shame and absence that we may also understand people's effect on one another? For a body or a mind to be in a position of eliciting an effect from another, to evince power or capability, it must manifest itself in a particular concrete way. Foster (1995a: 269, note 20) compares the Tangan who perversely hoards wealth with witches from elsewhere; the retention of wealth 'ultimately denies him the only culturally recognized means for attaching the qualities of those objects to his person, namely, display' (at the point of giving it away). Reciprocity, Foster adds, is willingness to become an instrument of another person's self-definition. One simply has to make or create oneself in a form that can be consumed by others.

I repeat the point that an exchange of perspectives is not to be confused with the European gaze. A mutual gaze in the contemporary Euro-American mode is two perspectives each from an individual standpoint on to the world.[32] In my model of Melanesia,[33] for which I have imagined a visual theory of sorts, any one perspective elicits another. There would not be a visible world to see if the world were not making itself visible towards the viewer. But of course 'the world' is not a perceived object here – persons are. Rendering oneself visible, just as the holder of wealth does, offers a sight which is then reduplicated when at the moment of handing it over men, and sometimes women, on the donors' side decorate themselves. They create a form as it is intended to appear from the perspective of the viewer (recipient). That form is put before the viewer, and thus forced on an audience, (the coercive metaphor is appropriate) for the audience to confront. This in turn offers one reason why self-decoration is such an apposite starting point for the anthropologist's exposition, why perhaps it has also been through the self-decoration of dancers which accompanies ceremonial exchange that this ethnographer at least has been so teased. Decorated dancers do not in this sense see themselves. It is not their job: it is the work of the viewer to see the dancers.[34] The dance decorations mean nothing without the viewer's, the participant observer's, absorption of the effect which the dancer's person makes.

There is a type of knowledge here which consists in 'seeing' relations.[35] Provided we can take this to mean both concept and percept, the aphorism could do as well for twentieth-century Euro-American as for twentieth-century Melanesian. But the Melanesian constructs I have been dealing with in this book do not end up with relations – they start with relations. In fact one could say that relations are what make people 'see' anything at all.

JOINT ACKNOWLEDGEMENTS

I repeat my acknowledgements here to Ru Kundil. I single him out as a scholar; as someone who assisted me in Mt Hagen, the one name must stand for very many men and women. I have not always made separate reference to the fact but the works of Janet Carsten, Donna Haraway, Eric Hirsch, Daniel Miller, Frances Price and Nicholas Thomas, as well as Maurice Bloch, have contributed to remarks in both parts of this Chapter. Colleagues at Cambridge have been at once a great support and a great stimulus.

Eduardo Viveiros de Castro was Simón Bolivar Professor at the University of Cambridge during 1997-8, and the inspiration of his magnificent set of lectures to the Department of Social Anthropology is evident. My gratitude also for several conversations. Special thanks are due to Almut Schneider for extending my sense of contemporary Highlands realities.

Notes

1 THE ETHNOGRAPHIC EFFECT I

1 This is not in itself a simple movement between 'levels'; the two elements are homologous. Compare Riles' (in press b) analysis of a certain type of (NGO-inspired) document, where the language of the document gradually seals over the concrete negotiations which produce each phrase until all the bracketed (debated) material is gone. She writes: 'the fixed and self-contained form of analysis of international negotiation deprives the academic observer and reader of the familiar ethnographic journey through transformations of meaning from concrete apprehensions of facts to abstract analysis'. An unfamiliar rendering, as I find myself attempting here, might bring an aspect of academic anthropology closer to the aesthetics she describes than one might have thought. For Riles' elegant phrase 'a figure seen twice' encapsulates the ethnographic moment. Either observation or analysis, either immersement or movement, may seem to occupy the entire field of attention. What makes the ethnographic moment is the way in which these activities are apprehended as occupying the same (conceptual) space.

2 I have benefited here from the research of both Jude Philp on the Torres Strait and Sandra Rouse on Haddon; and see Herle and Rouse 1998.

3 And Alfred Gell has driven the point home with far more force (and elegance) than can be found in the original [see Conclusion to this chapter, n. 33]. I note that similar points could also be made with reference to language, verbal exegesis and rhetoric.

4   In *The Gender of the Gift* (M. Strathern 1988), where a fuller account can be found; it also provides the rationale for the cast I have given to the definitions in the preceding paragraph. I had not meant to revisit this material so directly, and in particular would have preferred to lay to rest the language of 'persons' and 'things' ('the reification of social relations' was the original subtitle of this book). However, the way in which diverse technologies and inventions have entered the Euro-American imagination over recent years means that they may require address all over again. See for example the central essay in Frow 1997.

5   There need be no literal 'handing over', or at any rate no hand gesture that is witnessed; indeed in my mind's eye are valuables and wealth items collected or lined up in the expectation of being given away, the body gesture of things momentarily detached from one person and destined to be attached to another (see the photographs on page 219).

6   Elsewhere (e.g. M. Strathern 1988: 272-3) I have found it analytically useful to divide 'persons' into 'persons' thought of as objects in the regard of others and as 'agents' who take action. Each creates a perspective from which the other can be seen, and each is of course a figure seen from the one or other perspective. The person is revealed in relationships; the agent in actions. As Gell says of agents and patients, a person is a potential agent, and vice versa.

7   Warm thanks to Simeran Gell and Nicholas Thomas for letting me see the manuscript of this book. My comments here are offered by way of tribute to an incomparable, and incomparably engaging, mind.

8   Miller (1987: part 1), whose anthropological introduction to the Hegelian-derived concept of 'objectification' is most germane here, elucidates the origins of such evaluations and just what is lost to critical analysis in taking them at face value.

9   I use 'dazzle' with Gell's (1992: 46, 51) connotations: objects dazzle as displays of artistry or technical virtuosity, the attitude of the spectator being conditioned by his or her sense of the magical or technological agency behind it.

2   PRE-FIGURED FEATURES

1   *Portraiture and the Problematics of Representation,* an interdisciplinary conference held at Manchester University in 1993, convened by Marcia Pointon and Joanna Woodall.

2 I am grateful to Frances Price for this photograph and to Gail Vines for its description; it is reproduced by kind permission of Blackwell Scientific Publication ltd.

3 THE AESTHETICS OF SUBSTANCE

1 Several of the papers in this collection are germane to my present theme. James Weiner in fact borrows this phrase from Howard Morphy's doctoral dissertation; Naritjin was explaining matters to Howard.

2 In 1967, during a short follow-up visit to an initial fieldwork period in 1964-5. Kelly's data dates from 1968-9.

3 Witch-children were born to witches when they copulated with a witch-like intent, so a witch might have a non-witch child. Conversely, it did not follow that a witch-child implicated its 'natural' parents, since the explanation could be that the mother was raped unknowingly by a witch. But only witches would allow a witch-child to remain alive. As we have seen, the witch-child is identified by its size. (See Kelly 1993: 540, 555.)

4 Cf. the periodic increase and decrease of the bodies of Mekeo men and women (Mosko 1983). In Mekeo, a thin dry body is valued by men as being closed to sorcery attack.

5 In considering terms such as 'substance', 'material', 'form' and so forth, I have been very aware that it matters from which epoch of Euro-American culture and its medieval or classical antecedents one draws one's definitions. It would be tempting to recover a theological definition of substance (spirit essence) that allowed one to talk of material and immaterial form of it. Indeed, something like a theory of transubstantiation fits some of this data. It will also be clear that I give a very abbreviated account of everything that is transactable between Etoro persons. (Kelly himself refers to substances, as in the following account: 'The initiate ... is linked to his father and agnates by a shared bone and hair substance, and to his mother's brother by shared blood, flesh and skin. However, insofar as this has been largely overshadowed by game supplied by men ... this substance connection is now overlaid by and largely replaced by an exchange relationship' (1993: 163.) In the contribution to a Wenner-Gren symposium organised by S. Franklin and S. McKinnon on *New Directions in Kinship Study*, 1998, Carsten lays out a

range of contemporary meanings attached to the term 'substance', and some important qualifications. I should add that my present formula does little more than raise some ethnographic questions.

6　I depart from Kelly's description here in using the terms *primary* and *secondary*. Kelly refers to the spirit body as an immaterial counterpart to the physical body. This primary body is under the special care of lineage spirits. The reader may like to consider Harrison's (1995b) account of the lowland (Sepik) New Guinea people at Avatip where mortal men act out the identities and hostilities of ancestral spirits. Men are the incidental human form in which enduring spirit-beings (associated with particular clans) appear; their personal names come from the clan's stock of spirit names, and in these names – suitably transformed through magic – men go to war *as* the spirits who fight invisibly through them.

7　I recall the *imago* displayed by aristocratic Roman families (Dupont 1989) to which I alluded in Chapter 2.

8　Meat contributes to the life-force but other food simply satisfies hunger. It is not 'nutritive'.

9　A diminution of body energy and size was expected to occur gradually over a lifetime for men, and for women to be accelerated with the bearing of children; but this is not a focus of the extensive kinds of claims to virtue which Etoro men make. Periodic enlargement and diminution were, however, the subject of 'external' adornment and removal of ornamentation. These were aesthetic acts in Gell's (1995) sense: see below.

10　If one were to describe the Hagen soul and ideas about spirit essence and shadow doubles, one could find details very similar to Etoro – but they simply do not occupy the same object position in people's dealings with one another. In this context we may also note Kelly's description of the lack of dependency relations between Etoro child and mother (without dependency there is no nurture), and of the Etoro vision of child as predator.

11　Anthropologists have puzzled over the tautology of gift exchange where relations appear to be activated only in order to create more relations. Note that I restrict this account to ceremonial exchange engagements (*moka*), and do not for instance consider homicide or bridewealth payments. Here shells and other wealth substitute for persons who are thus in a sense rendered visibly absent and in that rendering thereby disposed of (Battaglia 1990). As for the Rawa of Madang Province described by D. Dalton (1996: 399), the Hagen logic of bridewealth entails a kind of death (bridewealth is likened to homicide compensation) for the bride and life (continuing wealth) for her kin, as well as a kind of life for the bride (her children) and death for her kin (their loss); cf. M. Strathern 1987.

12 The body once enlarged by decoration and ornamentation is concealed behind the everyday 'work' body where limp clothes and scanty attire diminish its appearance.

13 J. Weiner 1995a: 4 et seq, after Juillerat (1992) who uses the term to describe an organ – such as a placenta – which drops off once its function is performed.

14 From this point of view Losche throws out a challenge to the 'interpretation' of Abelam (Sepik) figures – houses or masks or paintings – for it is not, she says, interpretation which is communicable but a capacity she calls function. (Asking Abelam what a design means is like asking an Australian what a refrigerator means.) She points to the characteristic shape of these figures which 'might be translated as a container whose inside is invisible but from within which objects seem to be intrinsically produced ... Each aspect, the inside and the outside, the hidden and the revealed, must necessarily be co-present [each immanent in the other]' (Losche 1995: 54). Womb, netbag and bark painting are known by the same term: forms able to give forth.

15 This is also true of the process of body decoration (men's bodies alternate not between fat and thin but between decorated and undecorated state). The effort of collecting together ornaments and applying paint or oil speaks to a material process that is put in reverse when the feathers, shells and leaves are discomposed and hidden away again, whether in the recesses of the dancer's house or back into the hands of the persons from whom they were borrowed.

16 D. Dalton (pers. comm.) correctly criticises the economistic tenor of this rendering, that is, the covert assumption that men strive towards a kind of maximisation. The sense of 'striving' carries too many overtones of rewarded energy. A similar criticism has been made more generally by Eduardo Viveiros de Castro (also pers. comm.) of the concept of 'creativity' which smacks of a productionist ethic. The force of these criticisms in turn relies on assuming that economism and productionism are meant to convey positive values. This creates a nice impasse in the circumstances: how to rid these terms of unwanted resonance, as one might for instance – and

I have tried in the past – rid sociality of its resonance of sociability, relationality of amity and the gift of altruism. In the meanwhile I am sure that the criticism of my current renderings is well-placed, and draw it to the reader's attention. (There is more to the problems of usage than terminological inflection: Dalton's criticism would imply accommodating the Hagen material to the Etoro on the grounds of them both speaking to the impossibility of representation, to the link between fertility and death, and so forth [cf. Dalton 1996].)

17 J. Weiner's own approach to the anthropology of art deals with the concealment and restriction of meaning, following Heidegger's critique of Western productionist bias (J. Weiner 1995b: 35). Heidegger (and Derrida) offers a starting point for Munro's critique.

18 Note that at one point Gell (1995: 25) advances his argument thus: 'Let us agree, for argument's sake, that I have disposed of the idea that...'

19 Once centrality had been achieved, Hirsch writes, the ritual was over; it had served its purpose of making an immanent potential visible. The power of cultivation that is present in the landscape of gardens and pig pasture was made visible, and given coercive force, in the pigs brought together and displayed for consumption in the ritual plaza.

20 Obtained in the mid-1960s from cash crops, especially coffee which was introduced into the Hagen area in the late 1950s, as well as from plantation labouring and other employment. The effect reported here is particularly visible from the 1990s; see Chapter 5.

21 I am further grateful to Paul Connerton for this formulation, prompted by Harold Bloom's writings thirty years ago on the anxiety of influence (see Renza 1990). From pressure of 'meaning', of the knowledge of other poetic writing on poets, to excess of information: excess is inflated in the 1980s by the all-enabling influence of information technology which, in the 1990s, is creating a kind of crisis – at least in academic production. First, the velocity effect of locating or referencing work with respect to others (piling on antecedents) is mocked by the mechanical ability to download generations of writing at will. Second, the value put on authorship seemingly enhanced through legal protection is mocked when frantic concerns with copyright clog the flow of creativity, converting an elicitory power into a product.

22 It no longer works as a heuristic, as it did to powerful effect in the days when it was a term that one could so to speak hide again. It is lost by loss of the capacity to hide it.

23 Cf. M. Strathern 1991b. I mean that, beyond the days of patrons, there is no social category of recipient apart from the general one of reader (however 'generalised' or 'specialised' the reader may be). Writers may of course produce with individuals in mind, but they are rarely in a position to demand evidence of consumption from other persons.

24 Of course these forms can be – and often are – mixed. One of the rare volumes on anthropological poetics (Brady 1991) takes anthropologists' occasional flights into poetry as exercises that rise to various challenges to the imagination – what it is to be human, to know the subject (as in subjective), to counterpose literary to scientific modes of narration, to convey otherwise ineffable experience, not to speak of the hope of conducting yet ever edifying conversations. None of these is my concern here. However, I follow a lead from Preston (1991: 76): if basic materialist assumptions in science rest on the idea of knowledge attained through the measurement of direct sensory experience, then one issue is the means of measurement. If scientific instruments as themselves objects thereby mimic the objects they measure, then Melanesian persons mimic the measurement of one (person) by another (person). See Chapter 10. The witch is measured (known, sensed) through the witch-child.

25 That is, images are presented as 'images'. This is a (Euro-American) cultural statement; I mean it in the way one might refer to personality. One can both speak of everyone having a personality – and equally well of persons having or not having 'personality'! All expressions evoke images, but we also articulate certain specific modes of expression as 'evoking images'. (Preston [1991: 76] refers to *collecting* 'a range of images' from various populations from South Asia, Native America and so forth.)

26 I allude here to the power of symbolic obviation (e.g. Wagner 1986).

27 I am grateful to Monica Konrad for observations on this point.

28 In merographic manner (see pp. 234-35), contrasts already introduced in this present chapter work off this further contrast in ways that multiply without quite replicating one another (the diverse contrasts cannot be added up).

4   REFUSING INFORMATION

1   All but one of the seven member states of the then European Community had by 1991 set up enquiries into aspects of the new reproductive and genetic technologies (STOA [Scientific and Technological Options Assessment], *Bioethics in Europe* 1992), and the EC had also commissioned its own (*The Glover Report* 1989).

2   One reason why anthropologists have been drawn to such material. Critics point out the special nature of both kinds of material, given the interests at stake. See note 16.

3   I follow Cheater's (1995: 120) divergent use of the terms *information* (which takes an object, i.e. someone must be informed, so that information implies communication) and *knowledge* (a sensory or mental construct referring to an individual person's perceptive state). I do not however sustain any distinction between information as a readable sign and as what is read as meaningful. Note that 'science' (that is, scientific techniques of description and verification) remains external to kinship (that is, the management of relations) in this model; it simply offers enhanced 'readings' of the natural world. Elsewhere in reproductive medicine new relations are being 'written' through technological intervention.

4   I take this occasion to thank Ru personally for his innumerable kindnesses and willingness to share his insights. A self-account, originally written by Ru in Pidgin English and translated by A. Strathern, is published by the Institute of Papua New Guinea Studies under the title *Ru: a Biography of a Western Highlander* (1993).

5   Edwards continues: 'It is variation that makes persons. In these remarks, Veronica is concerned with the developing tie between a mother and child. The placenta mediates the relationship and the placenta comprises shared substance. Variation and spontaneity in the mother's diet is thought to have an effect ... on the child's development, as do emotions ... which emanate from the mother.'

6   The role of feeding in creating kin has long received attention in the anthropological literature. For a recent appraisal, see Carsten 1991; 1995.

7   Items are exchanged between bride's and groom's side, with a balance going to the former. The 'pain of childbirth' is acknowledged in the mother's share, but payments only follow where connections have been sustained. Bridewealth claims are further explored in Chapter 7.

8   The 'American' here derives from North America, the 'European' from Northern Europe; I refer to a discourse not a people, although sometimes I personify the discourse, as on this occasion (speakers of Euro-American as 'Euro-Americans'). It has global spread, is locally patchy.

9   Compare the 'structural coupling' between a specific (Euro-American) kinship system and family law noted by Weir and Habib 1997.

10 Constitutive rules define an activity such as a game of tennis; without them the activity does not exist (not to play according to the rules of the game is not to be playing the game). Regulative rules, on the other hand, govern behaviour but do not define it (tennis matches should be conducted in a certain manner, but failure to do so does not mean the players are not playing tennis).

11 Constitutive elements include rules for treating kin (cf. Schneider's [1968: 29] Euro-American contrast between relationship as natural substance and as code for conduct); Barbara Bodenhorn (pers. comm.) draws my attention to the issue of trust as a component of relations between close kin. Indeed, the following argument might take a different turn if it took trust as constitutive of parent-child relations. Trust is built among other things on knowledge (that children are told the true facts; nothing is concealed between close kin).

12 I say this in an analytical sense. Unfortunately it also turned out to be the case to a political extent no one had foreseen. The reader who wishes to assess the evidence for the claims about these numbers should consult Basen et al. 1993.

13 E.g. in the deliberations on the British Human Fertilisation and Embryology Act of 1990, the 14-day rule re embryos was based on information which could be acted upon (discussed in Franklin 1993).

14 Evidence-based medicine is defined as 'medical practice and management of the health care system based on knowledge gained from appropriate evaluation of treatments and their results' (Canada, Minister of Government Services, 1993: 70).

15 I have not examined the background research papers.

16 With triple caveats, as to (i) the status of newspaper reporting, (ii) the status of utterances and decisions in the context of contested claims in court and (iii) the influence of reported US defences of individual liberties on how people from other countries think about such matters (see Wolfram 1989). Young (forthcoming) compares attitudes and assumptions between Canada and the US.

17 On choice in English kinship also see M. Strathern 1992; for North American (US) see e.g. Hayden 1995; Ragoné 1996; Robertson 1994; Weston 1991.

18 That difference is at the heart of European kinship systems of the English kind, the two kinds of parents also pointing up status and contract as two rationales for enduring obligations over time (cf. Dolgin 1990a; 1990b).

19 As many have pointed out, with the new reproductive technologies, new modes of paternity become the model for thinking about maternity (cf. Eichler 1996; Strathern 1996b).

20 Here one would refer, among other things, to work on concealment in adoption (e.g. Modell 1986); discussions of anonymity in gamete donation (in Britain e.g. Haimes 1992), and the information paper on international legal issues prepared for the Royal Commission (Cook 1991). This last details various substantive rights, explicit, implicit or contested in Canadian law. The 'right to marry and found a family' is followed first by the 'right to private and family life' and then by the 'right to information and education'. It quotes article 19.2 of the International Covenant on Civil and Political Rights, noting that any decision to discourage practices such as surrogate motherhood or private resort to IVF must be justified. That access to information should be perceived as a 'right', however, suggests that information as such is a good, and those circumstances in which it is withheld or has deleterious effects have to be specified. Beside the 'right to private and family life', however, one may wonder at what point information becomes interference with reproductive privacy. Ambivalence between openness and intrusion is examined by Eichler (1996) in her analysis of the kind of family imagined by the Royal Commission.

I take heart from an unpublished paper by the lawyer Caroline Forder which argues that universal and unrestricted disclosure fails to achieve any kind of balance between rights which may be in conflict (e.g. the right to be informed and – in her view – the right to not know one's origins). (Forder 1998: permission to cite gratefully acknowledged.)

21 I include here Weir's (1996: 285-6) Foucauldian state that governs in accordance with freedom: 'Freedom is part of the rationality of liberalism, but the practices of freedom [must be] elaborated polymorphically in dialogue/tension/struggle with claims of unfreedom. Along with its capacity for autocritique and renewal, liberal government works against areas of unfreedom in its own practices as well

as outside. It is no accident that, in a cultural climate of governmental accountability, the concealing of all kinds of information may be identified as restrictive.

22 As opposed to earlier presumptions where unforeseen knowledge of genetic heredity was thought to interfere in the lives of adopting families and the family had to be 'protected' from such knowledge.

23 This form of kinship knowledge appears unrelational. Apropos some of the literature on semen donors, Morgan and Lee (1991: 163) report that in a limited survey conducted in London, a third of the donors were opposed to having their identity revealed, while two-thirds were in favour or reserved their opinion; the finding is likely to be long outdated. An interesting comparison is provided by Ragone's (1996: 361) study of American surrogate arrangements. Once the child was born, fewer than 50 per cent of the couples whom she interviewed chose to have the paternity test that was routinely offered to them.

24 The Australian National Consultative Bioethics Committee, given statutory standing in 1988 but then subsequently disbanded. (On individual states, see Waller 1997.)

25 I draw here from Ronald Frankenberg's several apt comments on an earlier version of this chapter. My thanks also to Monica Konrad in this context.

26 I have pointed generally to the role of assistance in the way that culture absorbs nature (M. Strathem 1992: 1767-7; on society and nature see 150), a version of the collapse of the distinction between them promoted vigorously by new reproductive rhetoric (which promotes the distinction and its collapse simultaneously).

5   NEW ECONOMIC FORMS: A REPORT

1 Under whose aegis Pentecostalism first spread; see A. Strathern (1993: 169-74) for a brief early history.

2 Initial fieldwork in the now Western Highlands Province was carried out in 1964-5, in the company of Andrew Strathern. We lived off and on in Papua New Guinea for the next decade, my last field visit to Hagen being in 1976. The opportunity for more than a brief subsequent visit did not come again until 1995.

3 My gloss, after the title of McSwain 1977. See also Errington and Gewertz 1996.

4   At the same time (A. Strathern 1993: 213): In the 1970s the switch to money in *moka* led to a re-creation of exchange', especially between former military allies.

5   But the surfeit of food in the market discouraged some; there was always more than could be sold, so often they made only K10-12. In the coffee season, a man setting off on a journey twenty years before might have humped a small bag of coffee beans with him to sell on the way; men from the new settlement wanting KI0-12 or so could always take a bunch of bananas to Hagen market.

6   Homesteads were built in much greater proximity than had formerly been the case, giving the impression of housing dotted regularly over a wide area; people referred to a named cluster in Pidgin English (Neo-Melanesian) as *viles* (villages).

7   In his study of Bomana jail (Port Moresby), Adam Reed (pers. comm.) found that newly jailed women were put to work making such bags, being taught how to do so if they came from areas where there was no such tradition.

8   A man's point of view of exchange; it was one they also tried to extend to pigs, which embroiled them in disputes with women.

9   As I have defined these terms, socially the person is a relation, by gender androgynous and by origin the product of other persons' actions. The person appears as an individual as the outcome of a process of (internal or external) unification, and thus as one sex or the other. Clumsy as these renderings are, common English terms need to be problematised, if only to raise a question against the kinds of issues of detachment which Manga himself raises. Otherwise we would simply have to treat as ironic the fact that in liberal economies money serves to detach persons from one another by registering the subjective individuation of (market) choice. My thanks to Keith Hart for conversation on this point, and see Callon (forthcoming).

10   The point is of course that at the moment of handing over, the pearlshell *does* incorporate the 'one-ness' that had been achieved in the act, i.e. heterogeneity is suppressed. J. Weiner's exposition (1995b: 27) on the uniqueness of the pearlshell for Foi contains that possibility. I remain here with my original formulations about attachment and detachment, while taking his point also for Hagen that these are unreconstructed metaphors for 'the projection of a form that completed acts of productive consumption take in Foi social life'.

11 As in the BBC1 film *A Death to Pay For* by Charlie Nairn, broad-cast on 11 November 1995. The young man Nykint describes how his mind is divided between thinking about what he can steal and thinking about going to church. The division is represented as something he can so to speak do nothing about, even though his actions will take him off on one or other course.

12 This returns the anthropologist to an old point (cf. Josephides 1982): the role of the outside observer in making practices explicit is obviously different according to what is already explicit. When divisions are only implicit, then conflict can be uncovered as concealed by social practices. When division and conflict is explicit, then we may look for the implicit connections such a division sustains. The former has a commonsense appeal to Euro-Americans who like to uncover the 'reality' of conflict from beneath a glossy surface of harmony; the latter produces the rather stiff functionalist arguments familiar, for instance, from Radcliffe-Brown's work on joking and avoidance relationships. (See Foster 1992: 287 on the self-conscious representation of exchange practice in the Pacific.)

13 In E. Gellner (1994) *Thought and Change,* Chicago: Chicago University Press, cited in a Papua New Guinea context by McDowell (1985).

14 A relative had visited Rupert in Moresby, and Rapa sent a message with her, but the amount Rupert sent back was derisory. A 1970s account of the view from Moresby is given in M. Strathern 1975.

15 See Gregory (1980: 630) on the Hanuabadans who told him that these payments were 'gifts' (in the Euro-American sense of alienable gift) and it was wrong that they should benefit. I emphasise the status of the gift here, in its Euro-American 'commodity' sense, in order to make a contrast with the Melanesian gift. The former is characteristically 'altruistic', and the notion of altruism has dogged (mis)understandings of the latter. In the original text I had included a reference to sacrifice and to Biersack's (1995) theorisation of indigenous exchange as sacrifice (see Chapter 3). Hers is a fascinating argument, but I reserve judgement on the appropriateness of the analogy.

16 I use the orthography of the *Wantok* newspaper. For further on compensation, see Chapters 9 and 10.

17 'Shaking hands' was thus in a sense the precursor of payments to the state.

18 See A. Strathern 1994b: 62 on organs of the state being treated as super-clans.

19 No inevitable contradiction here: a man might expand his agnates' resources by drawing in his affines. I refer to a division between social orientations.

20 Receiving nurture is necessary but can also be hazardous – this is not just a benign interaction.

21 Someone who discovers that the people he thought were his maternal kin were not blood kin (through adoption, say) will still send them gifts if they have been nurturing of him.

22 The Central Melpa people had always orchestrated *moka* along these lines, several members of a subclan/clan together combining to give to their respective maternal kin on the same occasion.

23 Carrier and Heyman (1997) refer to status groups in terms of imagined and idealised patterns of consumption.

24 When Rupert returned to Moresby, he was kitted out in 'Hagen clothes' (clothes bought in Mt Hagen, since he had arrived in 'Moresby clothes') – including contributions from three men of his own age cohort, married or about to be married to various sisters of his. Manga deliberately kept out of it; this was the younger generation's affair.

25 A sentiment which would in theory, from the viewpoint of conjugal households, support matrilineal as well as patrilineal regimes.

26 And was a reason for some staying back in the Northern Melpa area, despite it being harder to earn cash there.

27 A continuation of the conversation noted in Chapter 4 (I give his own name; the other names in this chapter are pseudonyms, and some personal details have been disguised.) It was no doubt a statement idiosyncratically expressed; Merlan and Rumsey (1991: 232) describe the intense fascination with which a neighbouring people, in the Nebilyer valley, regard what men and women eat.

28 I have since seen Karen Sykes' (1997) examination of entrepreneurial projects in New Ireland which takes as its starting point concepts of personhood that render the way in which 'persons' desire 'things' opaque to the logic of possessive individualism. The magic of trade casts wide the net of interests in particular items and sustains an intensified consumerism (through increasing the numbers of partners involved). People desire connection to the (business) enterprise. Items such as trucks become 'a composite of social relations'. I am grateful for permission to cite this unpublished paper.

29 Given earlier usages (M. Strathern 1988), this is a deliberate terminological solecism, bringing together two distinct analytical categories, the composite person, singular but divided, and the collective,
undivided, individual. I might add that the model of the composite
person lies behind Foster's (1995a: 9-10) inspired development of
the notion of the collective *individual.*

6 THE NEW MODERNITIES

1 Anyone who wishes to locate within a wider intellectual/cultural
history the very particular versions of 'hybridity' discussed here
should consult Werbner and Modood (1997). I note that social anthropologists always had their counterpart purifications, not only in
themselves subscribing to nature and culture as ontologically distinct zones, whatever other peoples thought, but in effect treating
as distinct zones societies and cultures in relation to one another.
Assumptions about the naturalness of cultural distinctions, about
internal congruity and external difference, upheld the scientific side
of anthropology to which Clifford refers (see below).
2 This 'network' is not to be confused with that of standard sociological usage. See Law's discussion of networks in actor network theory,
which he characterises as a 'vision of many semiotic systems, many
orderings, jostling together to generate the social' (1994: 18).
3 From a Trobriander's comment in the film.
4 From the moderns, as he lists them (Labour 1993: 135), one would
want to retain the separation of free society from objective nature,
while from the premoderns the non-separability of signs and things,
and from the postmoderns denaturalisation. But also to be saved
from the moderns are 'long networks', 'scale' and 'experimentation', while it is 'limits on scale' that are to be discarded from the
premoderns.
5 There is no such single entity as 'the domestic pig'; the role pigs play
in the circulation of values varies enormously. Law's emendation
of Latour's 'immutable mobiles', materials easily carried that retain
their shape, is pertinent. Mobility and durability, Law argues, are
themselves relational effects. A material 'is durable or otherwise as a
function of its location in the networks of the social' (1994: 102).
6 After Burridge 1960; my thanks to Melissa Demian for reminding
me of this division. Andrew Strathern's (1994b) recent comments

on how local groups may treat a multinational company or even 'the government' as a 'rival clan' could be understood the same way.

7   But scale, and limits, are also *defined* by the field of effect. Lemonnier (1993) demonstrates how different regimes of production and exchange in Papua New Guinea mobilise the domestic pig to different ends. Its apparently pivotal role in some societies is taken in others by human beings (women) or by life-substituting substances (salt); conversely the animal may take on the characteristics of persons or of inanimate materials. As a consequence the pig works as a pulley or lever on human relations with quite unpredictable results. There seems no single relationship between animal husbandry, horticulture and politico-economic system; with neither particular social values nor particular technological developments determinant, people's experimentations result in 'some unexpected technical choices' (1993: 146). We may ask how 'large' the fields of effects are here.

8   I am grateful to Adam Reed, then undertaking a study of discipline and punishment with the cooperation of the Corrective Institutions Service (his PhD dissertation is called *Anticipating individuals: Contemporary sociality in Papua New Guinea in the practice of imprisonment,* Cambridge University, 1997) for letting me quote from his letter (24 October 1994). See Sahlins 1993: 3-4.

9   Lissant Bolton (*Dancing in mats: Extending 'kastom' to women in Vanuatu,* PhD thesis for Manchester University, 1994) has articulated several reservations about the equation.

10 E.g. M. Strathern 1995b. Turner (1993) argues the opposite thesis. He suggests that anthropology's definitions of culture have been left behind in the new movement of multiculturalism. This has as its aims a democratisation of cultural difference – challenging cultural hegemony 'by calling for equal recognition of the cultural expressions of nonhegemonic groups' (1993: 412).

11 Turner distinguishes between critical multiculturalism, which seeks (within education) to use cultural diversity as a basis for relativising both minority and majority assumptions, and difference multiculturalism where culture 'reduces to a tag for ethnic identity and a license for political and intellectual separatism' (1993: 414). He identifies the latter with neoconservatism. But helpful as introducing such distinctions is, they also overlook 'translation'; different meanings bleed into one another. 'Critical' and 'différence' stands will only hold apart momentarily, as his own citation of

a similar, constantly collapsible, distinction in feminist politics makes clear.

12 Compare Josephides' (1992: 159) critique of 'cultural functionalism' on the part of anthropologists.

13 Cultural fundamentalism builds its case on traits supposedly shared as a universal by all people everywhere (cultural identity, xenophobia), which either leads to the demand that immigrants assimilate culturally to the world around them or else works as an ideology of collective exclusion.

14 Thatcher (the then Prime Minister of Britain) stated in 1978 that 'people are really rather afraid that this country might be swamped by people of a different culture' (quoted by Fitzpatrick 1987). Stolcke notes differences between the British and French versions, among others.

15 Latour would disown segments of modernity in selecting from premodern, modern and postmodern regimes his hopeful amalgam for a non-modern world. Inventions are easiest to disown when they fall into the hands of aliens – when the creative act of appropriation implies they (the aliens) have 'their own' uses for it (see Thomas 1991).

16 Latour voiced a need to slow down and regulate modernity's proliferation of hybrids (1993: 12), but through bringing them into his new democracy, not through controlling them through new forms of possession!

17 From *The Independent*, 1 Dec 1994. The observations which follow rest on a couple of reports and a broadcast. For a British statement of some of the complexities of the concept of ownership in relation to human materials, see Nuffield Council 1995.

18 The occasion of the newspaper report was a High Court ruling in November 1994 that the corporation could exercise a legal monopoly on the testing kits. Current tests cost about 50p each.

19 The geneticist Martin Bobrow speaking on BBC Radio 4 (3 December 1994).

20 Apropos breast cancer (case cited on BBC Radio 4).

21 Quite apart from the fact that the naturalness of possession is being newly championed in interpretations of Melanesian ethnography; Battaglia's critique of this includes some pertinent comments on ownership (1994: 640). For an important elucidation of the way persons' sources in others must be acknowledged, see Errington and Gewertz 1987.

7 DIVISIONS OF INTEREST AND LANGUAGES OF OWNERSHIP

1   The Supreme Court considered the parties' intentions in terms of their current interests in wanting or not wanting to procreate, whereas the trial court which had granted custody of the embryos to the woman, on the grounds that they were (already) children, focused on the pre-conception intent of the couple 'to produce a human being to be known as their child' (quoted by Dolgin 1994: 1278).

2   Schwimmer discusses the variables of alienation and identification, use value and exchange value, in a four-way matrix. The world of literature, music and art is a Euro-American example of identification involved in the creation of exchange values; the Melanesian counterpart he cites is contributing labour ('cargo work') to starting up businesses.

3   This chapter was originally conceived as a rejoinder to Carrier, and appeared in the same volume as his (see Hann 1998). (Some small amendments and additions have been made to this version.)

4   The rights concerned neither contraception nor pregnancy but an entity only recently come into existence, a pre-implanted, extra-corporeal embryo. A quite separate source of renegotiation lies in conditions of deliberate social innovation that explicitly take property relations to be the core of social justice. One example is Verdery's account (1998) of the redefinition of property rights under changing political and bureaucratic regimes in eastern Europe.

5   Coombe points here to the recent legal discovery in the US that litigious strategies related to trademarks are likely to be more successful than appeals to the violation of sacred emblems; 'claiming that the nominations of Cherokee [et al] ... are already the marks of nations and were held as properties by the governing bodies of national peoples' is a powerful proprietory idiom given that assertions of theft, as she observes, seem to have greater rhetorical value in American politics than assertions of harm (1996a: 218). One should add however that the range of things regarded as 'stealable' is also likely to be a variable (Harrison [1990] describes how the Manambu of Papua New Guinea steal from one another's stock of names; elsewhere special practices or emblems may not be released to others without due compensation, and so forth).

6   She argues that this interpretation resonates with anthropological positions, such as those of Nancy Munn, which take sacred and

other objects alongside land as phenomenal (consubstantial) manifestations and transformations of one another.

7 These overlapping denotations are typically 'merographic', that is, each appears at once to summon a whole order of phenomena and to be but part of other orders of phenomena.

8 The two cases are not entirely parallel. In the latter, the axe had a powerful effect by being withheld and thus as something which might have appeared; in deriving, as Battaglia says, its saliency from concealment, it created an effect other than its appearance would have had. In the former, ancestral ghosts always remain concealed, and there is no potential appearance at issue, while the social presences of kin have a certain constancy whether or not they are there in person. I simply draw the cases together as a further comment on analytical decisions – what the anthropologist chooses to make present *in the account or description* of the event.

9 'Economy' in quotation marks since it was a route to trying to solve general problems in the interpretation of Melanesian 'society', not an investigation into economic life as generally understood. Such interpretation remains necessary. Foster (e.g. 1995a: 19) can argue that the different types of social reproduction in Melanesia 'have differently conditioned the process of commodization' precisely because of that general interpretative work carried out by many ethnographers of the region.

10 In Hagen women expect pork, but at some deferred date – they look to the future. In the area of which Sillitoe speaks, women also participated in bridewealth prestations (cf. Lederman 1986).

11 Based on events told and witnessed then, some details are disguised. Kanapa ('sweetcorn') is not the woman's name, though she may be called this by some people. (Kanapa is a common food-name, that is, a name bestowed on someone with whom one has shared the item in question.) Rupert, who appeared in Chapter 5 under a Christian name, is here given a Melpa pseudonym.

12 Money would have enabled her to purchase a substitute pig, mindful of the work bestowed on the one reared earlier, and thus standing visibly for her achievements.

13 A man's pigs are given to his wife to tend, so that 'his own' pigs are also 'her own'. In this case it was important that it was a pig into which the sick woman had put her own effort – only this would sway the ghosts.

14 This is the context in which I argued (1988: 1651) that Highlands people do not have alienable items at their disposal; inalienable *property* only makes sense in a context where other things are alienable.

15 In many instances; but see Chapter 3. If we take Kelly's own usage of the term 'substance' in *Etoro*, the observations in Chapter 3 note 5 can be completed as follows: 'The initiate now embodies, in his completed physical and spiritual state, *all the relational components that constitute the social system*. He is linked to his father and agnates by shared bone and hair ... [Now] the initiate has given to his mother's brother shell valuables [semen] and received tree oil [blood, maternal semen]. In the next generation, the mother's brother's son will inseminate the initiate's son and marry the latter's sister ... shell valuables will then flow in the opposite direction in bridewealth' (Kelly 1993: 163, my emphasis). Whether or not we use the term 'substance', body components appear both inside and outside the person, whereas in much Euro-American thinking substances make up a singular, indivisible 'body' equated with the (individual) person. Euro-American notions of divisibility of identity and so forth, such as psychoanalysis deals with, then become a qualification on or critique of such suppositions.

16 Her argument about presence and absence is made in the context of a widely renewed anthropological interest in the material properties of objects which require, as she points out, presence for effect, a critique she extends to Bhaskar's 'critical realism'.

17 She thus offers a critique of the narrow conceptual framework adopted in prevalent feminist objections to commercial traffic in bodies and body parts. To attack 'ownership' only in its bourgeois, privatised, individualistic sense, she argues, is already to cede the ground of meaning.

18 He draws, too, on a tradition of thinking of social life in terms of 'communal' behaviour and 'communities', constructs with their own history as Petchesky hints.

19 In order to find appropriate analogies for his argument about the ownership of ritual knowledge in Papua New Guinea, Harrison (1992) considers intellectual property (and religions as the property of groups) in a range of historical contexts, including the Protestant Reformation in Europe, Germany under the Third Reich and ancient Rome. In acknowledging the interest of Harrison's work here, I should note that he adopts a *non*-reproductive model of intellectual property in his view of such property as the ownership of

classes of things (image, typification [design]). He argues for similar continuities of forms as does Gudeman, namely, that in Melanesia ritual action and beliefs are experienced in the same way as objects, objects being understood not as what people 'own' but as what they 'are'.

20 Locke, she suggests, appropriates the radical language of the Levellers but channels it to different ends. 'It would not have occurred to the authors of the Leveller women's petition [presented to Cromwell in 1651] to see a dichotomy between individual claims to integrity and ownership in one's "person" (body) and communal claims to justice and free use of the commons. ... Only at the end of the seventeenth century ... did "privacy" become a synonym for "freedom" and "goods" take precedence over "lives, limbs, liberties"' (Petchesky 1995: 393).

21 But, as noted above, this is not an argument for claims on commons provision.

22 The state conditioned its recognition of authors with 'a system of press regulation intended to hold authors and printers accountable for publications deemed libelous, seditious, or blasphemous', while authors' proprietory rights to works as commodities with an exchange value did not exist (Coombe 1994: 402, after Rose).

8 POTENTIAL PROPERTY: INTELLECTUAL RIGHTS AND PROPERTY IN PERSONS

1 An obvious one rests on making it explicit that property is a set of relations, property in persons thus being rights in respect of them: the anthropological distinction between rights *in rem* (in relation to a third party) and rights *in personam* (duties laid on the person). This would pre-empt the very potential described in this chapter, how Euro-Americans *do* entertain the possibility of 'owning persons'.

2 Coombe's 1993 review of three recent books lists several others. I am grateful to Richard Werbner for drawing my attention to Rosemary Coombe's work.

3 Franklin (1995) uses the same concept, drawing on Donna Haraway's image of a (cultural) hyperstack that ignores dimension or distance — any order of phenomena may be in the pile.

4 A revival, Marcus suggests, of an earlier form of constructivism in which the artist appears as engineer, making 'useful objects'. Chains

may be formed from following the people, or following the commodity, or metaphor or plot or biography and so forth.

5   Coombe discusses Rose's and Woodmansee's work on the efforts it took to establish authors as individuals responsible for the production of a unique and original work, rather than being regarded as vehicles for received truth or divine inspiration, a displaced theology according to Woodmansee (Coombe 1993: 413). (M. Strathern 1995a explores certain twentieth-century analogies between conceptual and social relations, and between ideas and children.)

6   In a BBC1 documentary ('Heart of the matter', 25 June 1995), the same phrase was used of frozen embryos facing extinction at the five-year limit under which they are 'kept' in Britain. Shortly after the Tennessee embryos (referred to as fertilised ova or pre-embryos) were frozen, the couple divorced; the dispute turned on the wish of the woman to donate the embryos to another couple, a move to which her former husband objected. His wish prevailed.

7   The Supreme Court considered the parties' intentions in terms of their current interests in wanting or not wanting to procreate, whereas the trial court which had granted custody of the embryos to the woman, on the grounds that they were (already) children, focused on the pre-conception intent of the couple 'to produce a human being to be known as their child' (quoted by Dolgin 1994: 1278). Presumably that court decided that the first if not the second part of this intention influenced the woman's wishes to donate.

8   Schwimmer (1979) discusses alienation and identification, use value and exchange value, in a four-way matrix. As noted in Chapter 7, footnote 2, literature, music and art are Euro-American examples of identification involved in the creation of exchange values; a Melanesian counterpart is contributing labour ('cargo work') to starting up businesses. An original account of how one might imagine intellectual property in a 'gift economy' is given by Harrison (1992).

9   Including enterprise morality, the 'instinct for justice that seeks to reward a creative thinker for the results of mental activity' (NAPAG 1995: 2).

10 I am grateful to Derek Morgan for sending me a draft transcript of the California Supreme Court hearing 1993 (and see Morgan 1994).

11 I have drawn on this elsewhere (M. Strathern 1995a). I quote without further acknowledgement from the draft transcript; an analysis may be found in Dolgin 1994: 1281-95.

12 Communities 'are finally acknowledged as rightful owners of "the environment' only to the extent that they agree to treat it (and themselves) as capital' (Escobar 1994: 220). A similar point has long been rehearsed in tribal lands conflicts in North America, Australia and elsewhere (land must be subject to tenure and tribes to cultural identification).

13 Brush (1993: 654) observes that IPR rests on the precept that state power is necessary to create monopoly rights over these goods. Some of the scope of UN (counter)activity is given in Suagee 1994; Posey 1994.

14 He makes an explicit association: chemists in laboratories seek out parallel compounds with fewer side effects to substitute for the original material; so, too, musical sounds need no longer rely on instruments but on electronic synthesis.

15 They may also be drawing an implicit parallel between culture and public discourse. If we follow Coombe's (1993: 414) discussion of IPR as enabling the commodification of symbols, imagery, text and thus creating 'limited monopolies over representational forms', it would seem made for characterisations of culture as the public discourse of representations. See for instance P. Harvey's (1997) elucidation of a transcultural context, nation-states exhibiting themselves at Expo 92 in Seville, in which the very idea of cultural *context* is commodified. Presumably any item attributable to a specific cultural origin could be a candidate for cultural property; but general knowledge will not do for establishing intellectual property – that requires precise specification (Brush 1993: 663). Conversely, Brush takes all inventions as collective in the sense of drawing on ideas that are common property.

16 For comparative comment on indigenous constructions of the collective individual (the collective individualised as a distinct entity) see Foster on New Ireland lineages (1990; 1995a: 216-17) and Handler on Québécois ideas of the nation (1998: 40f.). The latter embraces a moralistic concept of common cultural identity; the former is an amoral, transcendent, gathering of power.

17 The question is prompted by Carlos Alberto Alfonso's analysis of 'non-reproducing' communities in the Terra Fria region of Portugal (pers. comm.). His scepticism about reproduction as an explanatory concept, in this context at least, promises an interesting comment on those ideas of property that are suffused with metaphors of paternity and generative potency.

18 In the words of the British Patent Office (1995: 3), 'they give legal recognition to the ownership of new ideas or brand names ... [creating] for the innovator a system by which he can benefit from his ingenuity'.

19 Mode 2 knowledge production is marked by an increase in the number of potential sites where knowledge can be created, including multinational companies, hi-tech firms, government research institutions; by these sites being linked in heterogeneous ways, electronically, socially, organisationally, and by the simultaneous specialisation and recombination of subfields (Gibbons et al. 1994: 6).

20 I am grateful for permission to cite this, one among several papers on research cultures and new forms of knowledge organisation from the Centre for Research Policy, Wollongong, Australia.

21 I refer both to peoples who have 'communities' only in an orientalist sense, and to those who this century have been dislocated and dishoused from their homes.

22 A brief history is found in Nuffield Council on Bioethics 1995: 85. I owe thanks to both Maryon McDonald and Suzanne Hoelgaard for documents and guidance. My comments do not begin to consider the obvious language differences on the part of members, on which McDonald has worked.

23 This abbreviates a complex situation that would depend on member states' enactment of various forms of 'farmer's privilege'. Brush (1993: 654) details the difference in US law between 'utility patents' applied to plants and 'plant variety protection', the latter allowing farmers to duplicate seed without paying the royalties due under utility patents if the new plant retains the protected characteristic.

24 Alluding to a famous American case, it referred to the patient 'who did not have an automatic right of ownership over tissues deriving from his body'.

25 The Nuffield Council on Bioethics' report on human tissue (1995) gives an excellent overview of what is at present ownable with respect to human tissue, by those who take it and those from whom it is taken, and discusses the English common law presumption that there can be no property in the human body.

26 NAPAG (1995: 25) criticises the EC Directive on Copyright in Computer Programs for not addressing the question: 'when Program II is in some sense derived from Program I, what is to count as sufficient borrowing' to infringe copyright in I?

27 I draw here on several of Penny Harvey's observations (pers. comm.).

28 Basically in terms of continuing employment, that is, the extent to which the employing institution remains viable or the extent to which their individual contribution might make them candidates for redundancy. The RAE assesses routine productivity but is not about routine rewards (individual salaries).

29 Bourdieu (1998) contrasts the domains of academic and intellectual activity within which university members accumulate different kinds of capital. I emphasise their separateness rather than the way they also merge.

30 It is fashionable to deride disciplines and their 'boundaries' in favour of cross-disciplinary enterprises. My own view is that disciplines provide positions from which to critique other forms of institutionalisation, and their proprietory nature is an important instrument here. At the least we should investigate the politics of interdisciplinarity at a time when other potential claims to scholars' work are in the air. NAPAG refers to government interest in increasing the productivity of research, and to the fact that in the 1992 RAE exercise people were asked for tallies of patents and copyrights (1995: 35); they warn against these as measures of research ability. The suggestion of cross-disciplinary 'themes' as the focus of research funding mooted in 1995 by the UK Economic and Social Research Council puts the initiative for determining research priorities into a public (read, government) domain that makes for greater control over scholarly activity.

31 Through (for instance) defence of 'academic freedom'. NAPAG recommendations include the following: 'University academics should retain ownership in their writings, so that they may publish them when and where they wish, without control by their institution.' (Academics are of course hired for and required to pursue their scholarship.)

32 Summarising Rose 1993.

33 Cussins' phrasing, from an earlier draft of this paper, quoted with permission.

34 Oyama opens her account (1985: 1) by observing it matters little to the structure (of the hybrid/duplex) 'whether it is God, a vitalistic force or the gene as Nature's agent that is the source of the design of living things'.

35 In an unpublished conference paper ('An indigenous system of copyright from the Tabar Islands', European Society for Oceanists, 1994), which I cite with thanks.

9 WHAT IS INTELLECTUAL PROPERTY AFTER?

1 The conference for which this was written was called *Actor Network Theory and After*. For those looking for an introduction to ANT, I would recommend Latour 1993 and Law 1994 and their guide into the literature (e.g. Callon 1991). In the same way as it is not necessary for the reader to have a background in Melanesian anthropology in order to appreciate most of the Papua New Guinean material, it is not necessary to spell out the lineaments of this theory for present purposes. I hope therefore that the reader will forgive some unexplained allusions. The original note here, for instance, read: Like scallops, one wants to be caught in the right nets. I am not sure that Callon's (1986) Breton scallops would behave like Inuit ones (if there were any). Inuit scallops would yield themselves to fishermen directly (cf. Bodenhom 1995: 187).

2 I am struck by the axiomatic location of Actor Network Theory (ANT) within studies of science and technology. (Callon [1986: 197] begins with the hope that the 'sociology of translation' offers an analytical framework for the study of 'the role played by science and technology in structuring power relationships'.) I must thank Vivien Walsh for furnishing me with several relevant papers.

3 Needless to say I have specifics in mind: specifically Highlanders from central Papua New Guinea, and transactions predicated on 'gift exchange'. In my paradigmatic case (from Hagen in the Highlands of PNG), men deliberately put themselves into asymmetrical relationships as donors and recipients within an exchange relationship.

4 On the kindedness of human beings see Astuti 1995.

5 'To interest other actors is to build devices which can be placed between them and all other entities who want to define their identities otherwise' (Callon 1986: 208, and forthc.). This cutting disassociates actors from their previous associations.

6 ANT's appeal to symmetry requires the enrolment of the social observer him or herself as another neutral party. However here, not neutral at all, I am definitely exaggerating various analytical positions, and especially in relation to the Papua New Guinean material give something of a caricature, in order to press home my own points. Haraway (1997) is the contemporary classic on problems of scholarly neutrality (modest witnesses).

7   The Convention on Biological Diversity was an important component of the UN Conference on Environment and Development (the 'Earth Summit'), Rio 1992. It also contained other agreements, such as the Rio Declaration and 'Agenda 21', an action plan aimed at the local integration of environmental concerns across a range of activities.

8   The text is printed in Posey 1996.

9   I am grateful to Terence Hay-Edie for several documents here. Instrumental in dissemination has been the Oxford-based Programme for Traditional Resource Rights: see Posey 1995; 1996; Posey and Dutfield 1996. Posey (1986: chart 1) summarises UNCED and other UN-based agreements on the rights of indigenous, traditional and local communities. The Appendices of Posey and Dutfield include texts of the following agreements and draft agreements: Declaration of Principles of the World Council of Indigenous Peoples; UN Draft Declaration on the Rights of Indigenous Peoples (1993); Kari-Oca Declaration and the Indigenous Peoples' Earth Charter (1992); Charter of the Indigenous-Tribal Peoples of the Tropical Forests (1992); the Mataatua Declaration on Cultural and Intellectual Property Rights of Indigenous Peoples (1993); Recommendations from the Voices of Earth Congress (1993); UNDP Consultation on the Protection and Conservation of Indigenous Knowledge (1995); UNDP Consultation on Indigenous Peoples' Knowledge and Intellectual Property Rights (1995). (1993 was the UN International Year for the World's Indigenous Peoples.)

10 The newly independent state of Papua New Guinea promulgated a Cultural Property Act in 1976. This referred to 'National Cultural Property' and was intended to prevent the export of property of 'particular importance to the heritage of the country', including objects 'connected with the traditional cultural life' of people (Preliminary). Its target was principally items of art and artefacts which had value in international markets. My thanks to Mark Busse of the National Museum for his help with information here.

11 See Nabhan et al. (1996: 190-1) who observe that it would be possible for tribal rights to a folk variety of plant to be asserted through the US Plant Variety Protection Act already in place, although no 'tribe' has to date deployed this mechanism. It should be noted that Papua New Guineans are able to equate *national* with *indigenous* rights (vis-à-vis the international community) in ways unheard of

in either North or South America; the concept of tribe is only used in very specific locations, e.g. 'tribal warfare'.

12 There are attempts to put these on an equalising basis. Thus Article 40 of the Charter of the Indigenous-Tribal Peoples of the Tropical Forests ('Programmes related to biodiversity must respect the collective rights of our peoples to cultural and intellectual property') is followed by Article 44: 'Since we highly value our traditional technologies and believe that our biotechnologies can make important contributions to humanity, including "developed" countries, we demand guaranteed right to our intellectual property and control over the development and manipulation of this knowledge.' However, as Françoise Barbira-Freedman adds (pers. comm.), one reason why actors cannot be on the same level of agency lies in the history of commoditisation which long preceded the IPR debate and has already created a particular kind of 'added value' to products not matched in non-commodity conceptions of products and work.

13 Procedural rather than substantive uniformity has been noted as a feature of Papua New Guinean customary law.

14 For a trenchant critique, which should be compulsory reading for anthropologists interested in these issues, see Coombe 1996b.

15 By 'universal' I mean that under certain circumstances it can translate anything into wealth, not that it is a universal feature of Papua New Guinea societies. I am simplifying a case which could be argued in its specifics from the Mt Hagen area, although it is not unrecognisable elsewhere in the country. However, it is not necessarily accepted everywhere either (see Chapter 10), and in any case 'traditional' barriers to the substitutability of certain classes of items for one another have long been the subject of anthropological interest (e.g. Godelier 1986b). I would add that while, from the viewpoint of the new generic standing of compensation practices, the synthesis which follows is not out of place, it (the synthesis) does not of course pretend to be a historical accounting of the way in which these ideas have developed (see e.g. the contributions to Toft 1997).

16 Filer (1997) disputes the connection here. He is at pains to distinguish the recent politico-economic history of resource compensation from the field of body compensation.

17 By no means the only kind of equation; see for example Leach 1998 on ideas of place.

18 With the caveat of note 15; different *kinds* of transactions ('spheres of exchange') may under certain conditions do just this, through setting up restrictions on circulation.

19 The classic statement is Wagner 1967. Groups come into being through the role they take up in relation to the exchange of wealth or persons, and exist as givers or receivers of specific types of items. There is interplay between what is already attributed (the outcome of past interactions and performances) and what is created during new interactions or performances.

20 With fluid 'collectives' goes fluid rhetoric. '[For] when we try to investigate or conceptualise the substance of their mutual conduct, we may find that we are no longer dealing with any actual pattern of relationships between real individuals in concrete social settings, but only with snatches of rhetoric which, like the abstract opposition of "landowners" to "developers", are applied to "development discourse" in a certain type of public forum' (Filer 1997: 174).

21 I borrow from an analytical conundrum observed elsewhere (e.g. M. Strathern 1991a). A reminder of Macfarlane's formula: Roman law emphasised the divisibility of material things among persons (people divide things [into different shares]), while feudal and English common law emphasised the divisibility of persons in the multiple 'bundles of rights' held in entities themselves indivisible (things divide people [into different right-holders]). We might say that scientific classification (as a project that divides by inspection, that is, by virtual or intellectual partition as in componential analysis, without having to divide the entity) transposes 'bundles of attributes' onto the things.

22 The reproductive power of combination and recombination which produces 'cultural hybridity' (Werbner 1997) does not do away with fundamentalisms in identity when identity summons a division between self and other (cf. Yuval-Davis 1997).

23 NGOs have become a phenomenon of interest in themselves; for an account of NGOs in the context of relief work see Benthall 1993.

24 Posey and Dutfield (1996: 120) draw attention to the development of soft law: 'strictly speaking it is not law at all. In practice, soft law refers to a great variety of instruments: declarations of principles, codes of practice, recommendations, guidelines, standards, charters, resolutions, etc. Although all these kind of documents lack legal status (are not legally binding), there is a strong expectation that their provisions will be respected and followed by the international

community.' They add that the evolution of 'customary international law' can be accelerated by the inclusion of customary principles in soft law agreements and non-governmental declarations. These become hardened through use and worldwide acceptance.

25 Both in terms of their participation in the culturally recognisable activity of document production and in terms of relations between specific sets of organisations among whom the documents produced by one may be crafted so as to encompass the documents of others (Riles in press a, b). Françoise Barbira-Freedman (pers. comm.) notes the virtual nature of claims and counter-claims (as between land-owners and developers) which may be inherently incapable of locking into the social constellations called for by IPR practice. Finally, Jasanoff (1997) points to the role of technological expertise through which NGOs establish credibility, and the 'epistemic networks' they create. Thanks to Charis Cussins for this reference.

26 Luhmann (e.g. 1990: 100) describes the systemics of society as a 'network of communication'; within that system Euro-American societies have a huge investment in communicative sub-systems whose function is to describe (communicate information about) society.

27 Willke's point is that there is no common (or transcendental) basis for exchange across systems: any exchange involves intervention into the otherwise autonomous organisations of other bodies. This is most acute for the state: 'the traditionally basic guidance function of the state is severely limited because any type of societal guidance predominantly means self-guidance of resourceful organized actors (1990: 248, italics omitted).

28 Convened by Meg Taylor and Caroll Poyep, and organised by Leslie Harroun, Natural Resources Attorney. The proceedings are to be edited by Marke Busse and published by the National Centre for Development Studies, Australian National University, Canberra.

29 Of the Papua New Guinea National Museum and Art Gallery, Port Moresby.

10 PUZZLES OF SCALE

1 Of particular interest is Teresa Brennan's analysis of speed which I follow in a number of places. She argues that the speed of production is foundational to perceptions of the speed of 'living'. She also offers an important and specific argument about speed as the

displacement of time by space which I do not pursue here except in a most tangential sense. (Brennan writes of those practices of consumption in which 'the artificial space-time of speed (space for short) takes the place of ... generational time. For to the extent that capital's continued profit must be based more and more on the speed of acquisition, it must centralize control and accumulation more, command more distance' (1993: 147). Caught up in this process is the fact that capital binds 'living energy' in forms which cannot reproduce themselves. And 'as more and more natural substances assume this form [become non-regenerative], and as more and more substances are bound in fixed capital [including technology], they require more and more supplies of external energy to enable them to keep on producing' (1993: 148, 145).)

2 A criticism made long ago of conventional notions of progress and poverty still applies: increasingly sophisticated technology has a struggle to keep up with the ever increasing productive task created by ecological pressure (Wilkinson 1973).

3 A ratio is one type of 'scale'; however, for ease of exposition I give the terms separate connotations here.

4 Much more like in fact the tens of thousands of personal names for individual elements in the world over whose recall – in some parts of Papua New Guinea (Harrison 1990) – men once competed with one another. The reference to the anthropologist is to Sillitoe (1988c) and his complete inventory of some 150 portable Wola artefacts.

5 The literature which has flowed from this amounts to a minor industry in its own right. Glass 1996 gives a good recent overview.

6 The Moresby event was to include non-Trobrianders as well, and to be evidence of national, not just Trobriand, cultural vitality. Battaglia notes that one effect of this expansion was that Trobrianders became newly distanced on themselves and their yam self-objects (1995: 90).

7 Size and quantity are significant dimensions. 'Yams ... as much grow their subjects [the gardener] as the other way round. Gardeners trade on their ability to embody supplementation, incorporating others in exchanges that expand their own political parameters' (Battaglia 1995: 80). Note that the generalised account which follows is drawn from diverse writings on the Trobriands produced at diverse times. Other temporalities evinced through yam gardening are the subject of Claudia Gross's thesis, *Following Traces, Creating*

Remains: Relatedness and Temporality in Upper Awara, Papua New Guinea, Manchester University, 1998.

8   Generally true across Papua New Guinea; one classic source is Biersack 1982.

9   Malinowski (1935: 160): 'The harvest thus rewards the industry of the gardener and gladdens his heart with the perennial discovery of his living treasure underground. "The belly of my garden" ... – as Bagido'u in his spells calls the soil he has charmed – has at last brought forth its fruits and the fruits of man's labour.' I do not touch on the cross-sex allusion here and elsewhere (e.g. the metaphor of the belly pointing to the procreative capacity of women).

10 There are many, and contested, accounts of Trobriand practices, the notable references being Malinowski 1935; A. Weiner 1976. A specific focus on yams as children is developed by Brindley 1984, and see A. Weiner 1979; Glass (1996: 73) cites some of the Trobriand evidence.

11 The sign of sexual procreation. The orchestration of gardening is under the tutelage of a matrilineage magician, and matrilineal spirits are invoked in gardening rites. The size of yield from a garden is held to depend on this activity and on the gardener's own individual magic. I do not go into the significance of the land the gardens made on it.

12 See Gillison's (1993: 22) extrapolation from Highlands data that what Trobrianders were ignoring in the denial of male conception 'was not the biological contribution of the male but the symbolic presence of the father'.

13 Glass (1996: 55) cites Jones's oedipal contention that pressure was taken off the hated father-figure and displaced on to the authoritarian mother's brother, summarising some of the counter-arguments which in his view invalidate this proposition about authority and conflict (e.g. the child is in its early years under the father's authority). The issue is far more too complex than these few remarks allow. I am not, for instance, in a position to take a view on whether we are dealing with the suppression or repression of desire. My concern is with the comparisons (and measurements) which become culturally available through the act of concealment.

14 On the idea that one person grows at the expense of another see Chapter 3 and the reference to Etoro (Kelly 1993) demonstrations of capacity in production and exchange: as men grow old, their life-force flows into others, younger bodies growing large as the older

bodies shrink, so that the diminishing vitality of seniors is given a measure in the increasing vitality of juniors. Compare (1) Becker's (1995) account of the way Fijians care for one another's bodies, through feeding acts which bring prestige to the food-giver, an orientation she contrasts with those that produce eating disorders focused on 'the self'; (2) Foster's (1990) description of 'force-feeding' in Tanga and the coercive nature of the gift; and (3) the place of coercion in such acts of relationality more generally, esp. Hirsch 1995a.

15 Another version of this would be to say, one man's relationships against those of another. Thus filling up the yam houses of a chief indicates the extent of his social relationships. A. Weiner writes: 'Yams are the symbol *par excellence* of the reproductiveness of social relations' (1979: 333). I should note that I have drastically truncated the sociology of yam prestations here; see A. Weiner's original ethnography (1976).

16 Not the only reason for competitive harvests, and these days often commuted into competition for prizes in the context of a communal enterprise.

17 Being able to complete the building in one go is a mark of aesthetic power also demonstrated in the inspirational carving of canoe prows.

18 The size of the base is measured by the same piece of string or rope used for all the stacks in a village; small flags are attached to mark the different circumferences. As Battaglia (1995: 84) learned from the men in Moresby, when the string itself is laid out this places the dimensions of the yields relative to one another along a single line. This measurement is further rendered in terms of arm-lengths. (Urban Trobrianders compared the expected arm-lengths of their Moresby stacks with those regularly produced at home.)

19 Relations between equations are analogical; when they are replicated across different scales analogies appear (fractally) as 'self-similar' or 'self-scaling' (cf. Wagner 1977, 1991; Mosko 1995 applies these latter concepts to the Trobriand idea of paternal nurture).

20 I would mention Gell's (1993: 24-31) psychoanalytically-inspired note on outward marks understood as the re-attachment of the enveloping womb to the body surface (of person or object). In the Trobriands, painted skin overtly signals the visible form which the father has put on the fetus through his feeding of it.

21 Also that of certain alternations of gender states (M. Strathern 1988).

22 In the context of drawing parallels between the practice of anthropology and psychoanalysis, Henrietta Moore (1995b) has recently problematised the explicitness of this kind of 'cultural aesthetic'. She writes that it is as if the primary processes of identification which psychoanalytic theory seems to suggest are pre-linguistic and pre-cultural have become open forms of cultural exegesis. This is an important and interesting issue. Others (notably Gillison 1993, and see her succinct statement at 1987: 172) would no doubt disagree with the way in which Moore develops it in relation to the imaginary and the symbolic: 'The imaginary connections between self and other which are usually inaccessible to the individual are acted out through the exchange of material items and the revelation of sequences of images in ritual. These connections are worked over in discourse, acted on in marriage and recreated through gift exchange.' (I am most grateful for permission to cite Moore's unpublished lecture.)

23 See note 1 apropos Brennan's argument. She contrasts the generational time of 'natural reproduction' with the artificial time of short-term profit ('speed') (e.g. 1993: 147). I would add that there are different modalities of generational time in the Trobrianders, there being both a 'long cycle' of persons and a 'short cycle' of plants (yam production). I present the latter as a speeded-up version of the former; this is a comparative not an historical observation, but see Damon (1983) on long and short cycles.

24 The sponsor of the festival came from a clan that at home could not lay the kinds of claims to garden magic which would have given him success. This was a matter of social status.

25 That is, appearance for the purposes of display. I refer to shell valuables of the *kula* type, for which the Trobriands, along with other islands in the Massim area, are also famous. *Kula* has some features in common with the circulation to which I now turn, although Trobrianders expand space (the circulation of a man's name or reputation) rather than time (number of valuables as a function of velocity). For a stunning account of extensions of space-time elsewhere in the Massim, see Munn 1986.

26 Evans (1964: 127). I am most grateful to Elizabeth Wright for bringing this to my notice. Note that I have deleted from this quotation Jones's amplification of the hidden part as the repressed part, and as the part in conflict, because I do not wish to be interpreted as offering a view on the mechanism of repression. (Jones described

the disappearance and reappearance of the role of the father as a matter of repression.)

27 An illustration I have drawn upon on other occasions, e.g. M. Strathern 1993. My apologies to the subject of the photograph; I have not given his name, nor been more specific about the occasion because I wish to use the image in expositional ways that would do injustice to the event as it occurred in historical time/space and to his particular interests in it.

28 Andrew Strathern (the classic account being 1971) is the authority on such compensation payments. In relation to the material which appears below, I should add that he has voiced considerable scepticism about the 'authenticity' of many contemporary compensation claims (e.g. A. Strathern 1993).

29 I would draw attention to the gender here.

30 As on the Trobriands, whether between clan members vying among themselves as to whose output is largest or between a donor and the recipient of his wealth from another clan.

31 These gifts also have a capacity to expand under their own rationale, and turn into (more or less) reciprocal exchanges. The direction of initial 'compensation' is established in the opening moves.

32 What Kelly (1993: 146, my italics) says of life-cycle processes in Etoro could also be said of Hagen exchange: 'The life-cycle processes of conception, growth, maturation, senescence, and death are attributed to the acquisition, augmentation, depletion, and loss of life force in these transactions [such as sexual intercourse]. In each instance, *a recipient's growth entails a donor's depletion,* such that one individual flourishes while another declines.'

33 In the sense in which I am using the term, to refer to standardised computable or quantifiable dimensions.

34 And whole clans measure themselves, competitively, by the size of the reparations they can muster and the resources these indicate. Epstein's (1979) pioneering psycho-analytically inspired work on shell money in Tolai should be mentioned here.

35 Munn's work on Walbiri (Australian) iconography is most suggestive; for substantive parallels in the correlative positions of 'coming in'-'going out' see e.g. Munn 1973: 197 ff.

36 See the photograph of the feathered plaque being inspected on page 27.

37 The goldlip pearlshell, as seen here, figured in bridewealth and mortuary payments, as well as homicide compensation. These were

contexts in which pigs were also transacted. The pearlshell was one of the few valuable which the expatriates could use from the outset to 'purchase' meat (pig). Cowrie and other smaller types of shell were accepted for vegetable food and labour. The influx of shells continued in the early years of pacification and (re)development after the Second World War, when the Highlands were reopened to outsiders.

38 Calculated by Ian Hughes (1978). Some of the same material appears in 'Environments within' (see Preface) but the phenomenon of scale is subject there to rather different treatment.

39 There is an increase of production and the values remain 'substantial' by comparison with the plane of 'artificial' spacetime. The distinction between substantial and artificial time is Brennan's. ('If labour, as energy generated by nourishing matter [substance], in turn assists the growth of nourishing matter, then consumption is directly related to ... the reproduction of the conditions of consumption.' But under capitalism, consumption bears no such relation to production (1993: 138).) Chapter 3 touches on conduits of disposal.

40 Creating at once a potentially self-referential scale and an imperative equation with substance. This dual characteristic is not to be confused with the commodity duo, exchange value/use value.

41 These are 'earth ovens' dug into the ground and lined with banana leaves, the food being cooked by pre-heated stones; taking out the food when it is ready involves lifting it out of the opened-up hole. When a woman in an enclosed garden is engaged in domestic production, this is a secluded domain of affairs kept from the public eye, in the same way as shells are hidden in the men's house for private deployment after a display.

42 On the concealing of the mother (and thus by implication the mother's father), see Gillison 1993: 22.

43 Stürzenhofecker (1994) describes how Duna Highlanders try to 'read' the surface 'skin' of the landscape for clues about their own well-being; on 'reading', see O'Hanlon 1995.

44 As well as a Relocation Agreement. These were parts of the Porgera Special Mining lease, said to have been on a considerably larger scale than other leases. The national *Mining Act* (1992) lays out categories of compensation to landholders, as discussed by Burton (1997). (My account here is derived from both Bonnell 1997 and Burton 1997.)

45 On the contentious use of the term 'landowner' see Filer 1997. I rely heavily on Filer's article for my argument at this juncture, and on an earlier unpublished version he kindly sent me; however I note

Kirsch's (1997) caveat about the focus which social scientists have to date put on social explanations for people's reactions as opposed to the significance of the environmental disasters which they (people in the area) have witnessed. What follows is based on the same synthesis as is offered in Chapter 9.

46 For a comparative view, see Banks 1997.

47 From Filer, who himself points to two historical pushes from the colonial state; one was the payment of war damages compensation after the Second World War in many coastal areas, while the second was official backing given to Highlands war compensation payments to encourage peace-making between previously warring tribal groups.

48 A Melanesianist would hear echoes here with millenarian thinking, from across Papua New Guinea, and with the stories of the primal theft which accompany the present disposition of sexual attributes between men and women.

49 I deliberately put it this way round: evidence of what others have attracted to themselves (profit) seems to trigger the counterclaim. Filer notes how the idea of customary 'landowners' has also generated the idea that the salient social grouping must everywhere be the 'clan'.

50 I have since read Kirsch's (1996) description of Yonggom views on present times which he ends in a similar way.

51 This mode of perception is explored extensively in Tony Crook's dissertation (1998), *Growing Knowledge: Exploring Knowledge Practices in Bolivip, Papua New Guinea,* Cambridge University.

CHAPTER 1 CONCLUDED: THE ETHNOGRAPHIC EFFECT II

1 I do not want to comment here on the problems of promoting 'exotic body imagery' (cf. Kirsch 1996), except to add that it is precisely because self-decoration is misunderstood as clothing or ornament that the usual kind of remedy (to provide pictures of people in global/'Western' clothes instead) is a misleading one. So what might be Euro-American analogues to images created through feathers and ornamental shells? The images created through some of the contemporary construction materials with which imaginative architects design public buildings?

2   Christopher Gregory (pers. comm.). For a more general discussion see Errington and Gewertz 1994.

3   Although a principal referent of 'the ground' is land, Stürzenhofecker (1994: 43) uses the term specifically to indicate a cosmic folding in of what is both below and above its surface.

4   Stürzenhofecker draws analogies with earlier ritual preoccupations, and says that these concerns are primarily men's. Men had much more active visions of 'development' than women.

5   Here I must acknowledge the work of James Leach (*The Creative Land: Kinship and Landscape in Madang Province, Papua New Guinea*, PhD thesis, Manchester University, 1997).

6   This was the rubric: 'A science of writing – *grammatology* – shows signs of liberation all over the world ... however ... such a science of writing runs the risk of never being established as such and with that name. Of never being able to define the unity of its project or its object ... [nor] its discourse on method. ... The idea of science and the idea of writing – therefore also of the science of writing – is meaningful for us only in terms of an origin and within a world to which a certain concept of the sign ... and a certain concept of the relationships between speech and writing, have *already* been assigned *(Of Grammatology*, p. 4)'. The text (pp. 225-236) is reproduced in its original form, with a couple of references omitted.

7   The paper owes much to Debbora Battaglia's 1990 monograph, *On the Bones of the Serpent;* I am also very grateful for conversations with Iris Jean-Klein, then at Manchester University, from which I have borrowed extensively, for her comments here and for James Weiner's encouragement.

8   The reference follows Smith's (1988: 45) commentary on the Derridean 'critical decision' that stipulates limits on the theoretically endless process of interpretation.

9   Mimica discusses mathematical conceptualisations of infinity that are beyond the scope of this paper. What I refer to as the sense of infinity given by the Euro-American view of society, as made up of a plurality of persons, would correspond to the pre-nineteenth-century assumption that the infinite was present 'as a more or less tacit horizon of numbers' (1988: 107). This is the potential as opposed to the actual and absolute infinite, which exists as a totality, given all at once. In Mimica's own argument, the Iqwaye 'one' that is present as a finite whole *also* provides Iqwaye with their intimation of infinity

in this latter sense. For the one (digit) presents the possibility of grasping all at once a sense of everything in the cosmos.

10 Mauss's classic essay on the person made famous the case of Pueblo Zuni naming which delimits the number of possible power positions (roles) that clan members can take. Every clan is conceived as being made up of a certain number of characters, so that each person acts out 'the prefigured totality of the life of the clan' (1985: 5).

11 A kind of imploded dialogue – it is not a dialogue that leads to polyphony or multivocality. However, that does not mean one could not apply a dialogical analysis; Werbner (1991) reminds me of the point. Within the general 'sharing out' of Avatip names, I should add that, as a special case, allied (intermarrying) subclans 'share' one another's knowledge, whereas competitive (agnatic) ones emphatically do not (Harrison 1990: 58).

12 Evident in neighbouring Chambri (see Errington and Gewertz 1987) through the repayment of what they call people's 'ontological debts' for life.

13 She cites, for example, Marxist humanist critiques of the commodity which see terror in reification, and a division of the world into subjects and objects as the pernicious outcome of commodification itself (Radin 1996: 81-3).

14 'Prohibition theory' stresses the wrongness of commodification because of its alienation and degradation of the person, while other theories stress the importance of maintaining areas of noncommodified life for the health of society (Radin 1996: 96).

15 Like 'individualism', M. Strathern 1992: 73.

16 To expand her paragraph here: 'There is a core commodified conception, in which payment for injury is like buying a commodity, and a less commodified conception, in which harms are "costs" to be measured against the costs of avoiding them. There is also a core noncommodified conception, in which payment provides redress but not restitution or rectification, and a less central noncommodified conception, in which payment makes up for certain social disadvantages' (Radin 1996: 189).

17 Reification and personification in the same way, for Euro-Americans.

18 And the arguments in her book take off from a commodity perspective each time: there is no examination of what a counterpart domain of non-commodified conceptions might look like, only incidental references to personhood, relationships, democracy, and so forth.

19 As he argues, Euro-Americans hold that human beings are alike in their needs and wants, differentiated only by customs, technologies, societies and cultures. Hence the truism: what distinguishes human beings from the rest of nature, and distinguishes human beings one from another, are their mental constructs. Radin (1996: 82) cites Georg Lukács' formulation that 'commodification entails epistemological foundationalism and metaphysical realism'.

20 This is a rather misleading way of putting Amazonian perspectivism. All animate beings are human in their own eyes; the division is a consequence of having one kind of body rather than another. (Human beings are divided off from or detached from one another by the condition of their bodies.)

21 Again, I use 'kinds' with Astuti's usage (esp. 1995: 154-5) in view. The Austronesian Vezo of Madagascar exaggerate a division (there is a Vezo verb for 'divide') between living and dead to the point that living Vezo regard the dead not as Vezo at all, because their bodies cannot take on the signs of living Vezo-ness. Moreover, quite unlike themselves, the dead are beings divided into different descent groups and thus composed of different 'kinds'. For the living, the evidence for this condition is the separate tombs into which Vezo have put, and thus indeed divided, the dead.

22 As I understand Viveiros de Castro, for the Araweté, eyes are part of a generalised body capacity for sight; in the same way gifts are part of a generalised capacity for extending oneself. The Melanesian gift does not have to be conceptualised as wealth. For the Etoro to whom I shortly allude, shells go to the mother's brother in return for (a 'gift' of) tree toil, reciprocated in the next generation by shells in return for (a 'gift' of) insemination.

23 I follow Viveiros de Castro (1998) in using 'transformation' not in the sense of one entity productively turning into or growing out of another (cf. the observation of Riles in note 1 to Chapter 1), but as making manifest an already present alternative state of being. This is closer, in fact, to Riles' concept of a 'figure seen twice', except that the relationship is one of analogy (same [type of] person in different locations/bodies) rather than homology (different entities in the same place). Analogy presupposes that persons are similar and that what differentiates them are the positions (bodies, places) from which they act (Wagner 1977). Exchange changes-over those positions. In Viveiros de Castro's 'Amazonian' model, production is subsumed under exchange, which becomes the archetype of human

effort, and origins appear as borrowings, transfers, a dislocation from another body. His model translates into 'Melanesian' insofar as we may understand that anything produced, as from the earth, say, owes its social origin elsewhere, that is, in another person; this is an axis of the compensation logic encountered in Chapters 9 and 10. However, Gillison (1993) would argue for wariness – imagining that there is no directionality to such borrowings can also be the work of fantasy.

24 Which he redefines as 'information goods' with a semiotic role, signifying 'social, especially political, relationships' (Harrison 1992: 237). He states (emphasis removed): 'ritual action and belief are in fact experienced in the same way as are objects in Melanesian economies, namely, as a dimension of the self.'

25 In fact Harrison likens control over ritual knowledge to intellectual *property* (see Chapter 8) – not to intellectual disciplines or academic discourses or encylopaedias of the world.

26 And he adds: 'The same practical dynamic of concealing and revealing thus underpins both elaborate mortuary feasts [cf. ceremonial exchange] and ordinary requests for a leaf of tobacco...' (Foster 1995a: 210). I should note the effectiveness of his own argument which stresses the coercive nature of giving and receiving. Not only are recipients 'force-fed', that is, forced into receiving, but the story he recites renders an exchange transaction 'as the aggressive attempt of one agent to publicize the hidden valuables of another', a story which uses sexual exposure to drive home the point (1995a: 208). O'Hanlon's (1995) analysis is germane here.

27 In short, on making social systems visible; on the Foucauldian antecedents here, see Cooper 1997. To 'practices' or 'persons' carved out of an encompassing society, compare the Euro-American notions that 'place' is carved out of a generalised space (Casey 1996) or 'intervals' and 'events' out of some infinite expanse of time (Greenhouse 1996).

28 Although I did not register ('see') it at the time, Monica Konrad had made this very point to me in a set of perceptive comments not fully taken on board there on an earlier version of Chapter 4.

29 I refer again to Viveiros de Castro's perspectivist aphorism (above, p. 252): whereas the social constructionist motto is that 'the point of view creates the object', in the perspective formula 'the point of view creates the subject'. As he notes, object and subject are not concepts of the same order; I would add that whereas the first formula creates

a world capable of being known, the second instead summons subjects already like the knower. We see here the importance of his insistence that (ontological) perspectivism is not (epistemological) relativism.

30 Hence all the emphasis on 'learning to see' which initiates in many Melanesian societies are taught (after Forge 1970), and on putting persons into a condition to be able to see, that is, to activate relations in an appropriate manner.

31 Of which Gillian Gillison's (1993) is the most profound.

32 Like the two parents of the Euro-American child: individualism doubled.

33 See Gell's very apposite exposition (forthcoming), 'Stratherno-grams: or, the semiotics of mixed metaphors', in *The Art of Anthropology: Essays and Diagrams by Alfred Gell* edited by Eric Hirsch and Simeran Gell, London: Athlone Press (LSE Monographs).

34 Where in Papua New Guinea sculptures, paintings, masks or other artefacts are revealed to viewers, it is often under highly selected and restricted circumstances (including restrictions imposed by previous knowledge) that mimic the same situation: the artefact cannot see itself.

35 I was going to write this chapter without footnotes, but as Hoskin (1995; 1996) notes, the subtextual footnote is part of the technical apparatus of the self-examining individual. As he puts it, the origins of this kind of self-examination lie with the 'split self' of medieval Europe: the self enjoyed a two-sided unity that both acted and examined (its knowledge of) that action. It was the visibility of knowledge through precursors of such apparatus that in turn laid the grounds for Renaissance perspectivism and the subjectifying power of 'the gaze'. There is of course a huge and fascinating literature outside social anthropology, to which Hoskin's observations contribute, on changing conventions of vision, ocular(centr)-ism and the invention of the subject as spectator; a starting point for pursuing these issues might be the essayists in Brennan and Jay 1996. Hoskin reiterates the observation that here (in Europe) the visual 'field' has for long been an epistemological field. It has also been a relational field of a particular kind; the kinds of coordinates it introduces appear extrinsic to the individuals they dispose about it.

Bibliography

Ahern [Martin], E. M. (1982) 'Rules in oracles and games', *Man* (n.s.), 17: 302-12.

Astuti, R. (1995) *People of the Sea: Identity and Descent among the Vezo of Madagascar,* Cambridge: Cambridge University Press.

Banks, C. (1997) 'Shame, compensation and the ancestors: responses to injury in Hanuabada and Bena'. In *Compensation and Resource Development,* ed. S. Toft, Port University: Papua New Guinea Law Reform Commission, Monograph 6/Canberra: Australian National University, National Centre for Development Studies, policy paper 24.

Barraud, C., D. de Coppet, A. Iteanu and R. Jamous (1994) *Of Relations and the Dead: Four Societies Viewed from the Angle of Their Exchanges* (trans. S. Suffern), Oxford: Berg.

Barth, F. (1975) *Ritual and Knowledge among the Baktaman of New Guinea,* New Haven, CT: Yale University Press.

Basen, G., M. Eichler and A. Lippmann (eds) (1993) *Misconceptions: the Social Construction of Choice and the New Reproductive and Genetic Technologies* (2 volumes), Quebec: Voyageur Publishing.

Bateson, G. (1958 [1936]) *Naven: a Survey of the Problems Suggested by a Composite Picture of the Culture of a New Guinea Tribe Drawn From Three Points of View,* Stanford, CA: Stanford University Press.

Battaglia, D. (1983) 'Projecting personhood in Melanesia: the dialectics of artefact symbolism on Sabarl Island', *Man* (n.s.), 18: 289-304.

Battaglia, D. (1990) *On the Bones of the Serpent: Person, Memory and Mortality among Sabarl Islanders of Papua New Guinea,* Chicago: University of Chicago Press.

Battaglia, D. (1994) 'Retaining reality: some practical problems with objects as property', *Man*, 29: 631-44.

Battaglia, D. (1995) 'On practical nostalgia: self-prospecting among urban Trobrianders', in *Rhetorics of Self-Making*, ed. D. Battaglia, Berkeley: University of California Press.

Becker, A. (1995) *Body, Self and Society: the View from Fiji*, Philadelphia: University of Pennsylvania Press.

Beer, G. (1996) *Open Fields: Science in Cultural Encounter*, Oxford: Clarendon Press.

Benjamin, W. (1992 [1968]) *Illuminations* (ed. H. Arendt, trans. H. Zohn), London: Fontana Press.

Benthall, J. (1993) *Disasters, Relief and the Media*, London: I.B. Tauris & Co.

Biersack, A. (1982) 'Ginger gardens for the ginger woman: rites and passages in a Melanesian society', *Man*, 17: 239-58.

Biersack, A. (1995) 'Heterosexual meanings: society, the body, and the economy among Ipilis', in *Papuan Borderlands: Huli, Duna, and Ipili Perspectives on the Papua New Guinea Highlands*, ed. A. Biersack, Ann Arbor, MI: University of Michigan Press.

Bodenhorn, B. (1994) 'People who are like our books: reading and teaching on the North Slope of Alaska', paper read at 1994 Inuit Studies conference, Iqaluit.

Bodenhorn, B. (1995) 'Gendered spaces, public places: public and private revisited on the North Slope of Alaska', in *Landscape: Politics and Perspectives*, ed. B. Bender, Oxford: Berg.

Bonnell, S. (1997) 'The impact of compensation and relocation on marriages in Porgera', in *Compensation and Resource Development*, ed. S. Toft, Port Moresby: Papua New Guinea Law Reform Commission, Monograph 6/ Canberra: Australian National University, National Centre for Development Studies, policy paper 24.

Boon, J. (1982) *Other Tribes, Other Scribes: Symbolic Anthropology in the Comparative Study of Cultures, Histories, Religions and Texts*, Cambridge: Cambridge University Press.

Born, G. (1995) *Rationalizing Culture: IRCAM, Boulez, and the Institutionalization of the Musical Avant-Garde*. Berkeley and Los Angeles: University of California Press.

Bouquet, M. (1988) Contribution to catalogue *Melanesian Artefacts: Postmodernist Reflections* (text by M. Bouquet and F. Branco), Lisbon: IICT, Museum of Ethnology.

Bourdieu, P. (1988) *Homo Academicus* (trans. P. Collier), Oxford: Polity Press.

Brady, I. (ed.) (1991) *Anthropological Poetics,* Savage, MD: Rowman and Littlefield.

Brennan, T. (1993) *History after Lacan,* London: Routledge.

Brennan, Teresa and Martin Jay (1996) *Vision in Context: Historical and Contemporary Perspectives on Sight,* New York: Routledge.

Brindley, M. (1984) *The Symbolic Role of Women in Trobriand Gardening,* Pretoria: University of South Africa.

Brown, Michael (1998) 'Can culture be copyrighted?', *Cultural Anthropology,* 39 : 193-222.

Brush, S. B. (1993) 'Indigenous knowledge of biological resources and intellectual property rights: the role of anthropology', *American Anthropologist,* 95: 653-86.

Brush, S. B. (1994) 'A non-market approach to protecting biological resources', in *Intellectual Property Rights for Indigenous Peoples: a Source Book,* ed. T. Greaves, Oklahoma City, OK: Society for Applied Anthropology.

Brush, S. B. (1998) 'Bioprospecting in the public domain', paper presented at Colloquium on Environments and Development Debates, Center for Latin American Studies, University of Chicago, 1998.

Brush, S. B. and D. Stabinsky (1996) *Valuing Local Knowledge: Indigenous Peoples and Intellectual Property Rights,* Washington, DC: Island Press.

Burridge, K. (1960) *Mambu: a Melanesian Millennium,* London: Methuen.

Burton, J. (1997) 'The principles of compensation in the mining industry', in *Compensation and Resource Development,* ed. S. Toft, Port Moresby: Papua New Guinea Law Reform Commission, Monograph 6/Canberra: Australian National University National Centre for Development Studies, policy paper 24.

Callon, M. (1986) 'Some elements of a sociology of translation: domestication of the scallops and the fishermen of St Brieuc Bay', in *Power, Action and Belief: a New Sociology of Knowledge,* ed. J. Law, Sociological Review Monograph 32, London: Routledge.

Callon, M. (1991) 'Techno-economic networks and irrerversibility', in *A Sociology of Monsters: Essays on Power, Technology and Domination,* ed. J. Law, Sociological Review Monograph 38, London: Routledge.

Callon, M. (1992) 'The dynamics of techno-economic networks', in *Technological Change and Company Strategies: Economic and Sociological Perspectives,* eds R. Coombs, P. Saviotti and V. Walsh, London: Academic Press.

Callon, M. (forthcoming) 'Actor-network theory: the market test', in *Actor-Network Theory and After*, eds J. Law and J. Hassard, Sociological Review Monograph, London: Routledge.

Campbell, C. (1992) 'The desire for the new: its nature and social location as presented in theories of fashion and modern consumerism', in *Consuming Technologies: Media and Information in Domestic Spaces*, eds R. Silverstone and E. Hirsch, London: Routledge.

Canada, Minister of Government Services (1993) *Proceed With Care: Final Report of the Royal Commission on New Reproductive Technologies*, Ottawa (2 volumes).

Carrier, A. and J. Carrier (1991) *Structure and Process in a Melanesian Society: Ponam's Progress in the Twentieth Century*, Chur, Switzerland: Harwood Academic Publishers.

Carrier, J. (1995) *Gifts and Commodities: Exchange and Western Capitalism since 1700*, London: Routledge.

Carrier, J. (1998) 'Property and social relations in Melanesian anthropology', in *Property Relations: Sharing, Exclusion, Legitimacy*, ed. C. Hann, Cambridge: Cambridge University Press.

Carrier, J. and J. McC. Heyman (1997) 'Consumption and political economy', *J. Royal Anthropological Institute*, (N.S.) 3:355-73.

Carsten, J. (1991) 'Children in between: fostering and the process of kinship on Pulau Langkawi, Malaysia', *Man* (n.s.), 26: 425-43.

Carsten, J. (1995) 'The substance of kinship and the heat of the hearth: feeding, personhood, and relatedness among Malays in Pulau Langkawi', *American Ethnologist*, 22: 223-41.

Casey, Edward S. (1996) 'How to get from space to place in a fairly short stretch of time: phenomenological prolegomena.' In *Senses of Place*, eds S. Feld and K. Basso, Santa Fe: School of American Research Press.

Cheater, A. (1995) 'Globalisation and the new technologies of knowing: anthropological calculus or chaos?', in *Shifting Contexts: Transformation in Anthropological Knowledge*, ed. M. Strathern, ASA Decennial series, London: Routledge.

Clifford, J. (1988) *The Predicament of Culture: Twentieth-Century Ethnography, Literature, and Art*, Cambridge, MA: Harvard University Press.

Coombe, R. J. (1993) 'Tactics of appropriation and the politics of recognition in late modern democracies', *Political Theory*, 21: 411-33.

Coombe, R. J. (1994) 'Challenging paternity: histories of copyright' [review article], *Yale Journal of Law and the Humanities*, 6: 397-422.

Coombe, R. J. (1996a) 'Embodied trademarks: mimesis and alterity on American commercial frontiers', *Cultural Anthropology*, 11: 202-24.

Coombe, R. J. (1996b) 'Left out on the information highway', *Oregon Law Review*, 75: 237-47.

Cooper, R. (1997) 'The visibility of social systems', in *Ideas of Difference: Social Spaces over the Labour of Division*, eds K. Hetherington and R. Munro, Oxford: Blackwell.

Coote, J. (1992) 'Marvels of everyday vision: the anthropology of aesthetics and the cattle-keeping Nilotes', in *Anthropology, Art and Aesthetics*, eds J. Coote and A. Shelton, Oxford: Clarendon.

Crook, T. (in press) 'Growing knowledge in Bolivip, Papua New Guinea, *Cambridge Anthropology*.

Cussins, C. (1996) 'Ontological choreography: agency through objectification in infertility clinics', *Social Studies of Science*, 26: 575-610.

Dalton, D. M. (1996) 'The aesthetic of the sublime: an interpretation of Rawa shell valuable symbolism', *American Ethnologist*, 23: 393-415.

Dalton, G. (1971) *Economic Anthropology and Development: Essays on Tribal and Peasant Economies*, New York: Basic Books.

Damon, F. (1983) 'Muyuw kinship and metamorphosis of gender labour', *Man*, 18: 305-26.

DeLillo, D. (1997) *Underworld*. London: Picador, Macmillan Publishers.

Descola, P. (1986) *La Nature Domestique: Symbolisme et Praxis dans l'Écologie des Achuar*, Paris: Maison des Sciences de l'Homme.

Descola, P. (1996) 'The genres of gender: local morals and global paradigms in the comparison of Amazonian and Melanesia', paper given at Wenner-Gren Symposium on *Amazonia and Melanesia: Gender and Anthropological Comparison*, 1996.

Dolgin, J. L. (1990a) 'Status and contract in feminist legal theory of the family: a reply to Bartlett', *Women's Rights Law Reporter*, 12: 103-13.

Dolgin, J. L. (1990b) 'Status and contract in surrogate motherhood: an illumination of the surrogacy debate', *Buffalo Law Review*, 38: 515-50.

Dolgin, J. (1994) 'The "intent" of reproduction: reproductive technology and the parent-child bond', *University of Connecticut Law Review*, 26: 1261-1314.

Dupont, F. (1989) 'The Emperor-God's other body', in *Fragments for an History of the Human Body* (Part III), ed. M. Feher, New York: Zone Books.

Edwards, J. (1993) 'Explicit connections: ethnographic enquiry in north-west England', in *Technologies of Procreation: Kinship in the Age of Assisted Conception*, J. Edwards et. al., Manchester: Manchester University Press.

Edwards, J. (n.d.) 'Donor insemination and "public opinion"' (University of Keele, unpub. paper).

Edwards J. and M. Strathern (forthcoming) 'Including our own', in *Cultures of Relatedness*, ed. J. Carsten, Cambridge: Cambridge University Press.

Eekelaar, J. and P. Sarcevic (1993) *Parenthood in Modern Society: Legal and Social Issues for the Twenty-First Century* [International Society of Family Law], Dordrecht: Martinus Nijhoff Publishers.

Eichler, M. (1993) 'Frankenstein meets Kafka: the Royal Commission on New Reproductive Technologies', in *Misconceptions: The Social Construction of Choice and the New Reproductive and Genetic Technologies* (2 volumes), eds G. Basen, M. Eichler, and A. Lippmann, Quebec: Voyageur Publishing.

Eichler, M. (1996) 'The construction of technologically-mediated families: Looking at the Royal Commission Report from a family perspective', in *Families: Changing Trends in Canada*, 3rd edn, ed. M. Baker, Toronto: McGraw-Hill.

Epstein, A. L. (1979) 'Tambu: the shell money of the Tolai', in *Fantasy and Symbol: Essays in Anthropological Interpretation*, ed. R. H. Hook, London: Academic Press.

Errington, F. and D. Gewertz (1987) *Cultural Alternatives and a Feminist Anthropology: an Analysis of Culturally Constructed Gender Interests in Papua New Guinea*, Cambridge: Cambridge University Press.

Errington, F. and D. Gewertz (1994) 'From darkness to light in the George Brown Jubilee: the invention of nontradition and the inscription of a national history in West New Britain', *American Ethnologist*, 21 : 104-122.

Errington, F. and D. Gewertz (1996) 'The individuation of tradition in a Papua New Guinean modernity', *American Anthropologist*, 98: 114-26.

Escobar, A. (1994) '"Welcome to Cyberia": notes on the anthropology of cyberculture', *Current Anthropology*, 35: 211-31.

European Federation of Biotechnology Task Group on Public Perceptions of Biotechnology (1993) *Patenting Life*, briefing paper 1, London.

European Parliament (1995) *The Week*, 1 March (in English).

Evans, R. (1964) *Conversations with Carl Jung and Reactions from Ernest Jones*, Van Nostrand Insight series, New York: American Book Company.

Fabian, J. (1983) *Time and the Other; How Anthropology Makes its Object*, New York: Columbia University Press.

Fardon, R. (1995) 'Introduction: counterworks', in *Counterworks: Managing the Diversity of Modern Knowledge*, ed. R. Fardon, ASA Decennial Conference series, London: Routledge.

Feld, S. (1982) *Sound and Sentiment: Birds, Weeping, Poetics, and Song in Kaluli Expression*, Philadelphia: University of Pennsylvania Press.

Filer, C. (1997) 'Compensation, rent and power in Papua New Guinea', in *Compensation and Resource Development*, ed. S. Toft, Port Moresby: Papua New Guinea Law Reform Commission, Monograph 6/Canberra: Australian National University, National Centre for Development Studies, policy paper 24.

Finney, B. (1973) *Big Men and Business*, Canberra: ANU Press.

Fitzpatrick, P. (1987) 'Racism and the innocence of law', in *Critical Legal Studies*, eds P. Fitzpatrick and A. Hunt, Oxford: Blackwell.

Forder, C. (1998) 'Is there a human right to assisted reproduction?', paper presented to conference in a series on *Reproductive Choice and Control of Fertility*, convened by M. Brazier, University of Manchester, 1998.

Forge, A. (1970) 'Learning to see', in *Socialisation*, ed. P. Mayer. London: Tavistock.

Foster, R. J. (1990) 'Nurture and force-feeding: mortuary feasting and the construction of collective individuals in a New Ireland society', *American Ethnologist*, 17: 431-48.

Foster, R. J. (1992) 'Commoditization and the emergence of *kastam* as a cultural category: a New Ireland comparative case', *Oceania*, 62: 284-94.

Foster, R. J. (1995a) *Social Reproduction and History in Melanesia: Mortuary Ritual, Gift Exchange and Custom in the Tanga Islands*, Cambridge: Cambridge University Press.

Foster, R. J. (1995b) 'Print advertisements and nation-making in metropolitan Papua New Guinea', in *Nation-Making: Emergent Identities in Postcolonial Melanesia*, ed. R. J. Foster, Ann Arbor: University of Michigan Press.

Foster, R. J. (ed.) (1995c) *Nation-Making: Emergent Identities in Postcolonial Melanesia*, Ann Arbor: University of Michigan Press.

Franklin, S. (1993) 'Making representations: the parliamentary debate on the Human Fertilisation and Embryology Act', in *Technologies of Procreation: Kinship in the Age of Assisted Reproduction*, eds J. Edwards et al., Manchester: Manchester University Press.

Franklin, S. (1995) 'Science as culture, cultures of science', *Annual Review of Anthropology,* 24: 163-84.

Frow, J. (1997) *Time and Commodity Culture: Essays in Cultural Theory and Postmodernity,* Oxford: Clarendon Press.

Gell, A. (1975) *Metamorphosis of the Cassowaries: Umeda Society, Language and Ritual,* London: The Athlone Press.

Gell, A. (1992) 'The technology of enchantment and the enchanrtment of technology', in *Anthropology, Art and Aesthetics,* eds J. Coote and A. Shelton, Oxford: Clarendon.

Gell, A. (1993) *Wrapping in Images: Tatooing in Polynesia,* Oxford: Clarendon.

Gell, A. (1995) 'On Coote's "Marvels of everyday vision"', *Social Analysis* (spec, issue ed. J Weiner, *Too Many Meanings),* 38: 18-31.

Gell, A. F. (1998) *Art and Agency: Towards a New Anthropological Theory.* Oxford: Clarendon.

Gibbons, M., Limoges, C., Nowotny, H. Schwartzman, S., Scott, P. and Trow, M. (1994) *The New Production of Knowledge: The Dynamics of Science and Research in Contemporary Societies,* London: Sage.

Gillison, G. (1987) 'Incest and the atom of kinship: the role of the mother's brother in a New Guinea Highlands society', *Ethos,* 15: 166-202.

Gillison, G. (1991) 'The flute myth and the law of equivalence: origins of a principle of exchange', in *Big Men and Great Men: Personifications of Power in Melanesia,* eds M. Godelier and M. Strathern, Cambridge: Cambridge University Press.

Gillison, G. (1993) *Between Culture and Fantasy: A New Guinea Highlands Mythology,* Chicago: University of Chicago Press.

Glass, P. (1996) 'Oedipal or Tudavan? The Trobriand nuclear complex revisited', *Canberra Anthropology,* 19: 52-104.

Gluckman, M. (1965) *The Ideas in Barotse Jurisprudence,* New Haven: Yale University Press.

Godelier, M. (1986a) 'Territory and property in some pre-capitalist societies' [1st pub. 1978], in M. Godelier, *The Mental and the Material: Thought, Economy and Society* (trans. M. Thom), London: Verso.

Godelier, M. (1986b [1982]) *The Making of Great Men* (trans. R. Swyer), Cambridge: Cambridge University Press.

Goodman, J. and V. Walsh (1997) 'Attaching to things: property and the making of an anti-cancer drug', paper presented to *ANT and After* workshop, convenor J. Law, University of Keele, 1997.

Goodman, N. (1976) *Languages of Art,* Indianapolis, IN: Hackett Pub. Co.

Gow, P. (1988) 'Visual compulsion: design and image in western Amazonian cultures', *Estudios,* 2: 19-32.

Gow, P. (1991) *Of Mixed Blood: Kinship and History in Peruvian Amazonia.* Oxford: Clarendon.

Greaves, T. C. (ed.) (1994) *Intellectual Property Rights for Indigenous Peoples: a Sourcebook.* Oklahoma City, OK: Society for Applied Anthropology.

Greaves, T. C. (1995) 'Cultural rights and ethnography', *Bulletin of the General Anthropology Division* (American Anthropological Association), 1 (2): 1-6.

Greenhouse, Carol J. (1996) *A Moment's Notice: Time Politics Across Cultures,* Ithaca, NY: Cornell University Press.

Gregory, C. A. (1980) 'Gifts to men and gifts to god: gift exchange and capital accumulation in contemporary Papua New Guinea', *Man,* 15: 626-52.

Gregory, C. A. (1982) *Gifts and Commodities,* London: Academic Press.

Gudeman, S. (1996) 'Sketches, qualms and other thoughts on intellectual property rights', in *Valuing Local Knowledge: Indigenous Peoples and Intellectual Property Rights,* eds S. Brush and D. Stabinsky, Washington, DC: Island Press.

Haimes, E. (1992) 'Gamete donation and the social management of genetic origin', in *Changing Human Reproduction: Social Science Perspectives,* ed. M. Stacey, London: Sage.

Handler, R. (1988) *Nationalism and the Politics of Culture in Quebec,* Madison, WI: University of Wisconsin Press.

Hann, C. (ed.) (1998) *Property Relations: Sharing, Exclusion, Legitimacy,* Cambridge: Cambridge University Press.

Haraway, D. (1997) *Modest witness@Second Millennium. Female – Man© meets OncoMouse™: Feminism & Technoscience,* New York: Routledge.

Harrison, S. (1990) *Stealing People's Names: History and Politics in a Sepik River Cosmology,* Cambridge: Cambridge University Press.

Harrison, S. (1992) 'Ritual as intellectual property', *Man,* 27: 225-44.

Harrison, S. (1995a) 'Anthropological perspectives on the management of knowledge', *Anthropology Today,* 11(5): 10-14.

Harrison, S. (1995b) 'Transformations of identity in Sepik warfare', in *Shifting Contexts: Transformations in Anthropological Knowledge,* ed. M. Strathern, London: Routledge.

Hart, K. (1986) 'Heads or tails. Two sides of a coin', *Man,* 21: 637-56.

Harvey, D. (1990) *The Condition of Postmodernity: An Enquiry into the Origin of Cultural Change,* Oxford: Blackwell.

Harvey, P. (1997) *Hybrids of Modernity: Anthropology, the Nation State and the Universal Exhibition,* London: Routledge.

Hayden, C. P. (1995) 'Gender, genetics, and generation: reformulating biology in lesbian kinship', *Cultural Anthropology,* 10: 41-63.

Herle, A. and S. Rouse (eds) (1998) *Cambridge and the Torres Strait Centenary Essays on the 1898 Anthropological Expedition,* Cambridge: Cambridge University Press.

Hetherington, K. and R. Munro (eds) (1997) *Ideas of Difference: Social Spaces and the Labour of Division,* Oxford: Basil Blackwell.

Hill, S. (1994) 'The new globalism: implications for ASEAN technological policies', address to ASEAN – Republic of Korea *Workshop on Cooperation and Establishment of Science and Technology Policy in ASEAN Nations,* Yeovil, 1994.

Hill, S. and T. Turpin (1995) 'The new localism', in *Shifting Contexts: Transformations in Anthropological Knowledge,* ed. M. Strathern, London: Routledge.

Hirsch, E. (1990) 'From bones to betelnuts: processes of ritual transformation and the development of a "national culture" in Papua New Guinea', *Man,* 25: 18-34.

Hirsch, E. (1995a) 'The coercive strategies of aesthetics: reflections on wealth, ritual and landscape in Melanesia', *Social Analysis* (spec. issue ed. J. Weiner, *Too Many Meanings),* 38: 61-70.

Hirsch, E. (1995b) 'Local persons, metropolitan names: contending forms of simultaneity among the Fuyuge, Papua New Guinea', in *Nation Making: Emergent Identities in Postcolonial Melanesia,* ed. R. J. Foster, Ann Arbor, MI: University of Michigan Press.

Hirsch, E. (1995c) 'The "holding together" of ritual: ancestrality and achievement in the Papuan Highlands', in *Society and Cosmos: Their Interrelation or their Coalescence in Melanesia,* eds D. de Coppet and A. Iteanu, Oxford: Berg.

Hirsch, E. and M. O'Hanlon (eds) (1995) *The Anthropology of Landscape: Perspectives on Place and Space,* Oxford: Clarendon.

Hoskin, Keith (1995) 'The viewing self and the world we view: beyond the perspectival illusion', *Organization,* 2: 141-62.

Hoskin, Keith (1996) 'The "awful idea of accountability": inscribing people into the measurement of objects', in *Accountability: Power, Ethos and the Technologies of Managing*, eds R. Munro and J. Mouristsen, London: International Thomson Business Press.

Hughes, I. (1978) 'Good money and bad: inflation and evaluation in the colonial process', in *Trade and Exchange in Oceania and Australia*, eds J. Specht and J. P. White., spec. issue *Mankind* 11.

Hugh-Jones. S. (1994) 'Shamans, prophets, priests and pastors', in *Shamanism, History and the State*, eds N. Thomas and C. Humphrey, Ann Arbor, MI: University of Michigan Press.

Hugh-Jones, S. (1996) 'The gender of some Amazonian gifts: an experiment with an experiment', Wenner-Gren symposium on *Amazonia and Melanesia: Gender and Comparison*, convened by Don Tuzin and Tom Gregor, 1996.

IAITTF (International Alliance of Indigenous-Tribal Peoples of the Tropical Forests) (1995) *The Biodiversity Convention – the Concerns of Indigenous Peoples*, London (draft).

Jasanoff, S. (1997) 'NGOs and the environment: from knowledge to action', *Third World Quarterly*, 18: 579-94.

Jolly, M. (1992) 'Custom and the way of the land: past and present in Vanuatu and Fiji', *Oceania*, 62: 330-54.

Jones, E. (1925) 'Mother-right and the sexual ignorance of savages', *International Journal of Psycho-Analysis*, 6: 109-30.

Josephides, L. (1982) 'Suppressed and overt antagonism: a study in aspects of power and reciprocity among the Northern Melpa', *Research in Melanesia*, occ. paper, Port Moresby: University of Papua New Guinea.

Josephides, L. (1985) *The Production of Inequality: Gender and Exchange among the Kewa*, London: Tavistock.

Josephides, L. (1992) 'Metaphors, metathemes, and the construction of sociality: a critique of the new Melanesian ethnography', *Man*, 26: 145-61.

Juillerat, B. (1992) '"The mother's brother in the breast": incest and its prohibition in the Yafar Yangis', in *Shooting the Sun: Ritual and Meaning in West Sepik*, ed. B. Juillerat, Washington, DC: Smithsonian Institution Press.

Kelly, R. (1993) *Constructing Inequality: The Fabrication of a Hierarchy of Virtue Among the Etoro*, Ann Arbor, MI: University of Michigan Press.

Kirk, M. (1981) *Man as Art: New Guinea*, New York: Viking Press.

Kirsch, S. (1996) 'Return to Ok Tedi', *Meanjin*, 55: 657-66.

Kirsch, S. (1997) 'Indigenous response to environmental impact along the Ok Tedi', in *Compensation and Resource Development*, ed. S. Toft, Port Moresby: Papua New Guinea Law Reform Commission, Monograph 6/ Canberra: Australian National University National Centre for Development Studies, policy paper 24.

Knauft, B. M. (1993) *South Coast New Guinea Cultures: History, Comparison, Dialectic*, Cambridge: Cambridge University Press.

Küchler, S. (1993) 'Landscape as memory: the mapping of process and its representation in a Melanesian society', in *Landscape: Politics and Perspectives*, ed. B. Bender, Oxford: Berg.

Latour, B. (1991) 'Society is technology made durable', in *A Sociology of Monsters: Essays on Power, Technology and Domination*, ed. J. Law, London: Routledge.

Latour, B. (1993) *We Have Never Been Modern* (trans. C. Porter), London: Harvester Wheatsheaf.

Law, J. (1994) *Organizing Modernity*, Oxford: Blackwell.

Law, J. and A. Mol (n.d.) *On Hidden Heterogeneities: The Design of an Aircraft*, MS, Keele & Maastricht, 1994.

Law Reform Commission (Papua New Guinea), (1977) *The Role of Customary Law in the Legal System*, Port Moresby: LRC, Report 7.

Leach, J. (1998) 'Where does creativity reside: imagining places on the Rai coast of Papua New Guinea', *Cambridge Anthropology*, 20: 16-21.

Lederman, R. (1986) *What Gifts Engender: Social Relations and Politics in Mendi, Highlands Papua New Guinea*, New York: Cambridge University Press.

Leenhardt, M. (1979 [1947]) *Do Kamo. Person and Myth in the Melanesian World* (trans. B. M. Gulati), Chicago: University of Chicago Press.

Lemonnier, P. (1991) 'From great men to big men: peace, substitution and competition in the Highlands of New Guinea', in *Big Men and Great Men: Personifications of Power in Melanesia*, eds M. Godelier and M. Strathern, Cambridge: Cambridge University Press.

Lemonnier, P. (1993) 'Pigs as ordinary wealth: technical logic, exchange and leadership in New Guinea', in *Technological Choices: Transformation in Material Cultures since the Neolithic*, ed. P. Lemonnier, London: Routledge.

Losche, D. (1995) 'The Sepik gaze: iconographic interpretation of Abelam form', *Social Analysis* (spec. issue ed. J. Weiner, *Too Many Meanings*), 38: 47-60.

Luhmann, N. (1990) *Essays on Self-Reference.* New York: Columbia University Press.

Macfarlane, A. (1998) 'The mystery of property', in *Property Relations: Sharing, Exclusion, Legitimacy,* ed. C. Hann, Cambridge: Cambridge University Press.

Malinowski, B. (1927) *Sex and Repression in Savage Society,* London: Routledge & Kegan Paul.

Malinowski, B. (1935) *Coral Gardens and Their Magic: A Study of the Methods of Tilling the Soil and Agricultural Rites in the Trobriand Islands,* New York: American Book Company.

Marcus, G. (1993) 'Ethnography in/of the world system: the emergence of multi-sited ethnography', *Annual Review of Anthropology,* 23.

Massey, C. (1993) 'The public hearings of the Royal Commission on New Reproductive Technologies', in *Misconceptions: The Social Construction of Choice and the New Reproductive and Genetic Technologies* (2 volumes), eds G. Basen, M. Eichler and A. Lippmann, Quebec: Voyageur Publishing.

Mauss, M. (1985 [1938]) 'A category of the human mind: the notion of person; the notion of self (trans. W. D. Halls), in *The Category of the Person,* eds M. Carrithers, S. Collins and S. Lukes, Cambridge: Cambridge University Press.

McDowell, N. (1985) 'Past and future: the nature of episodic time in Bun', in *History and Ethnohistory in Papua New Guinea, Oceania,* eds D. Gewertz and E. Schieffelin, Monograph 28.

McSwain, R. (1977) *The Past and Future People: Tradition and Change on a New Guinea Island,* Melbourne: Oxford University Press.

Merlan, F. and A. Rumsey (1991) *Ku Waru. Language and segmentary politics in the Western Nebilyer Valey, Papua New Guinea.* Cambridge: Cambridge University Press.

Miller, D. (1987) *Material Culture and Mass Consumption,* Oxford: Basil Blackwell.

Miller, D. (1995) 'Introduction: Anthropology, modernity and consumption', in *Worlds Apart: Modernity Through the Prism of the Local,* ed. D. Miller, ASA Decennial Conference series, London: Routledge.

Mimica, J. (1988) *Intimations of Infinity: The Cultural Meanings of the Iqwaye Counting System and Number,* Oxford: Berg.

Minnegal, M. and P. Dwyer (1997) 'Women, pigs, god and evolution: social and economic change among Kubo people of Papua New Guinea', *Oceania,* 68: 47-60.

Minnegal, M. and P. Dwyer (1998) 'Working for company: ethos and environment among Kubo of Papua New Guinea', *Journal of Royal Anthropological Institute* (new series), 4: 23-42.

Modell, J. (1986) 'In search: the purported biological basis of parenthood', *American Ethnologist*, 13: 646-61.

Modjeska, N. (1982) 'Production and inequality: perspectives from central New Guinea', in *Inequality in New Guinea Highlands Societies*, ed. A. Strathern, Cambridge: Cambridge University Press.

Mol, A. and J. Law, (1994) 'Regions, networks and fluids: anaemia and social topology', *Social Studies of Science*, 24: 641-71.

Moore, H. (ed.) (1995a) *The Future of Anthropological Knowledge*, ASA Decennial volume, London: Routledge.

Moore, H. (1995b) 'Sex, symbolism and psychoanalysis', The Phyllis Kaberry Lecture, University of Oxford, 1995.

Morgan, D. and R. G. Lee, (1991) *Human Fertilisation and Embryology Act 1990: Abortion and Embryo Research, the New Law*, London: Blackstone Press Ltd.

Morgan, D. (1994) 'A surrogacy issue: who is the other mother?', *Int. Journal of Law and Family*, 8: 386-112.

Mosko, M. (1983) 'Conception, de-conception and social structure in Bush Mekeo culture', in *Concepts of Conception*, ed. D. Jorgensen, spec. issue *Mankind* 14.

Mosko, M. (1985) *Quadripartite Structures: Categories, Relations and Homologies in Bush Mekeo Culture*, Cambridge: Cambridge University Press.

Mosko, M. (1997) 'Charismatic persons, charismatic practices: politico-ritual agency in contemporary Mekeo', paper first presented to session on *Charismatic and Pentecostal Christianity in Oceania*, convenor J. Robbins, ASAO meetings, San Diego, 1997.

Munn, N. D. (1973) 'The spatial presentation of cosmic order in Walbiri iconography', in *Primitive Art and Society*, ed. A. Forge, New York: Wenner-Gren Publications.

Munn, N. D. (1986) *The Fame of Gawa: A Symbolic Study of Value Transformation in a Massim (Papua New Guinea) Society*, Cambridge: Cambridge University Press..

Munro, R. (1995) 'The disposal of the meal', in *Food Choice*, ed. D. Marshall, London: Blackie Academic and Professional.

Munro, R. (1992) 'Disposal of the body: upending postmodernism', proceedings of the Standing Conference on Organizational Symbolism, University of Lancaster, 1992.

Nabhan, G. P. and A. Joaquin Jr., N. Laney and K. Dahl (1996) 'Showing the benefit of plant resources and indigenous scientific knowledge', in *Valuing Local Knowledge: Indigenous Peoples and Intellectual Property Rights* eds S. B. Brush and D. Stabinsky, Washington, DC: Island Press.

National Academies Policy Advisory Group (1995) *Intellectual Property and the Academic Community,* London: NAPAG c/o The Royal Society.

Neich, R. (1982) 'Semiological analysis of self-decoration in Mt. Hagen, New Guinea', in *The Logic of Culture,* ed. I. Rossi, New York: Bergin Publications.

Nielson, L. (1993) 'The right to a child versus the rights of a child', in *Parenthood in Modern Society: Legal and Social Issues for the Twenty-First Century,* eds J. Eekelaar and P. Sarcevic, Dordrecht: Martinus Nijhoff Publishers.

Nuffield Council on Bioethics (1995) *Human Tissue: Ethical and Legal Issues,* London: Nuffield Foundation.

O'Donovan, K. (1989) '"What shall we tell the children?" Reflections on children's perspectives and the reproductive revolution', in *Birthrights: Law and Ethics at the Beginnings of Life,* eds R. Lee and D. Morgan, London: Routledge.

O'Donovan, K. (1994) 'Love's law: moral reasoning in the family', in *Constituting Families: A Study in Governance,* eds D. Morgan and G. Douglas, Stuttgart:Steiner.

O'Hanlon, M. (1989) *Reading the Skin: Adornment, Display and Society Among the Wahgi,* London: British Museum Publications.

O'Hanlon, M. (1995) 'Modernity and the "graphicalization" of meaning: New Guinea Highland shield design in historical perspective', *J. Roy. Anthropological Institute,* (N.S.), 1: 469-93.

Oyama, S. (1985) *The Ontogeny of Information: Developmental Systems and Evolution,* Cambridge: Cambridge University Press.

Pannell, S. (1994) 'Mabo and museums: "The indigenous (re)appropriation of indigenous things"', *Oceania,* 65: 18-39.

Parkin, D. (1987) 'Comparison as the search for continuity', in *Comparative Anthropology,* ed. L. Holy, Oxford: Basil Blackwell.

Parry, B. (1997) 'Whose booty is it anyway?', *New Scientist,* 21 June 1997: 50.

Patent Concern (n.d.) *Patenting of Plants and Animals*, London: The Genetics Forum.

Patent Office (1995) *What is Intellectual Property?*, Newport: Department of Trade and Industry.

Petchesky, R. P. (1995) 'The body as property: a feminist revision', in *Conceiving the New World Order: The Global Politics of Reproduction*, eds F. D. Ginsburg and R. Rapp, Berkeley: University of California Press.

Polhemus, T. and L. Procter (1978) *Fashion and Anti-Fashion: An Anthropology of Clothing and Adornment*. London: Thames and Hudson.

Posey, D. A. (1990) 'Intellectual property rights and just compensation for indigenous knowledge', *Anthropology Today*, 6 (4): 13-16.

Posey, D. A. (1994) 'International agreements and intellectual property right protection for indigenous peoples', in *Intellectual Property Rights for Indigenous Peoples: A Sourcebook*, ed. T. C. Greaves, Oklahoma City, OK: Society for Applied Anthropology.

Posey, D. A. (1995) 'Indigenous peoples and traditional resource rights, Conference Proceedings', Oxford: Green College Centre for Environmental Policy & Understanding.

Posey, D. A. (1996) *Traditional Resource Rights: International Instruments for Protection and Compensation for Indigenous Peoples and Local Communities*, Gland, Switzerland, and Cambridge: IUCN (International Union for the Conservation of Nature).

Posey, D. A. and G. Dutfield (1996) *Beyond Intellectual Property: Toward Traditional Resource Rights for Indigenous Peoples and Local Communities*, Ottawa: International Development Research Centre.

Preston, J. J. (1991) 'The trickster unmasked: anthropology and the imagination', in *Anthropological Poetics*, ed. I. Brady, Savage, MD: Rowman and Littlefield.

Price, F. V. (1990) 'The management of uncertainty in obstetric practice: Ultrasonography, *in vitro* fertilisation and embryo transfer', in *The New Reproductive Technologies*, eds M. McNeil, London: Macmillan.

Rabinow, P. and W. M. Sullivan (1987 [1979]) *Interpretive Social Science: A Second Look*, Berkeley and Los Angeles: University of California Press.

Radcliffe-Brown, A. R. (1952) 'Patrilineal and matrilineal succession' [1935], in *Structure and Function in Primitive Society*, by A. R. Radcliffe-Brown, London: Cohen and West.

Radin, M. J. (1996) *Contested Commodities: The Trouble with Trade in Sex, Children, Body Parts, and Other Things,* Cambridge, MA: Harvard University Press.

Ragone, H. (1996) 'Chasing the blood tie: surrogate mothers, adoptive mothers and fathers', *American Ethnologist,* 23: 352-65.

Renza, L. A. (1990) 'Influence', in *Critical Terms for Literary Study,* eds F. Lentricchia and T. McLaughlin, Chicago: University of Chicago Press.

Rheinberger, H.-J. (forthcoming) 'Beyond nature and culture: a note on medicine in the age of molecular biology,' in *Living and Working with the New Medical Technologies: Intersections of Inquiry,* eds. M. Lock, A. Young and A. Cambrosio. Cambridge: Cambridge University Press.

Riles, A. (in press a) *The Actions of Fact: The Aesthetics of Global Institutional Knowledge,* Ann Arbor: University of Michigan Press.

Riles, A. (in press b.) 'Infinity within the brackets', *American Ethnologist.*

Robertson, J. A. (1994) *Children of Choice. Freedom and the New Reproductive Technologies,* Princeton, NJ: Princeton University Press.

Rose, M. (1993) *Authors and Owners: The Conventional Copyright,* Cambridge, MA: Harvard University Press.

Sahlins, M. (1976) *Culture and Practical Reason,* Chicago: University of Chicago Press.

Sahlins, M. (1993) 'Goodbye to tristes tropes: ethnography in the context of modern world history', *Journal of Modern History,* 65: 1-25.

Salisbury, R. (1962) *From Stone to Steel: Economic Consequences of a Technological Change in New Guinea,* Melbourne: Melbourne University Press.

Schneider, D. (1968) *American Kinship: A Cultural Account,* Englewood Cliffs, NJ: Prentice-Hall.

Schwimmer, E. (1979) 'The self and the product: concepts of work in comparative perspective', in *Social Anthropology of Work,* ed. S. Wallman, London: Academic Press.

Sexton, L. 1986. *Mothers of Money, Daughters of Coffee,* Ann Arbor: University of Michigan Press.

Sillitoe, P. (1988a) 'Property ownership in the New Guinea Highlands', *Research in Melanesia for 1986,* 10: 1-11.

Sillitoe, P. (1988b) 'From head-dresses to head-messages: the art of self decoration in the Highlands of Papua New Guinea', *Man,* 23: 298-318.

Sillitoe, P. (1988c) *Made in Nugini: Technology in the Highlands of Papua New Guinea*, London: British Museum Publications and University of Durham Publications Board.

Singleton, V. and M. Michael, (1993) 'Actor-networks and ambivalence: general practitioners in the UK cervical screening programme', *Social Studies of Science*, 23: 227-64.

Smith, P. (1988) *Discerning the Subject*, Minneapolis, MN: University of Minnesota Press.

Soleri, D. and D. Cleveland, with D. Eriacho, F. Bowannie Jr., A. Laahty and Zuni Community Members (1994) 'Gifts from the creator: intellectual property rights and folk crop varieties', in *Intellectual Property Rights for Indigenous Peoples: A Sourcebook*, ed. T. C. Greaves, Oklahoma City, OK: Society for Applied Anthropology.

Starn, R. (1989) 'Seeing culture in a room for a Renaissance prince', in *The New Cultural History*, ed. L. Hunt, Berkeley and Los Angeles: University of California Press.

Steedman, C. (1986) *Landscape for a Good Woman*, London: Virago.

Stephenson, D. J. (1994) 'A legal paradigm for protecting traditional knowledge', in *Intellectual Property Rights for Indigenous Peoples: A Sourcebook*, ed. T. C. Greaves, Oklahoma City, OK: Society for Applied Anthropology.

Stolcke, V. (1995) 'Talking culture: new boundaries, new rhetorics of exclusion in Europe', *Current Anthropology*, 36: 1-24.

Strathern, A. J. (1971) *The Rope of Moka: Big Men and Ceremonial Exchange in Mount Hagen*, Cambridge: Cambridge University Press.

Strathern, A. J. (1972) *One Father, One Blood*, Canberra: ANU Press.

Strathern, A. J. (1993) *Voices of Conflict*, Pittsburgh, PA: University of Pittsburgh: Ethnology Monographs 14.

Strathern, A. J. (1994a) 'Keeping the body in mind', *Social Anthropology*, 2: 43-53.

Strathern, A. J. (1994b) 'Crime and compensation: two disputed themes in Papua New Guinea's recent history', *PoLAR [Political and Legal Anthropology Review]*, 17: 55-65.

Strathern, A. J. and M. Strathern (1971) *Self-Decoration in Mount Hagen*, London: Duckworth.

Strathern, M. (1972) *Official and Unofficial Courts: Legal Assumptions and Expectations in a Highlands Community*. Canberra: New Guinea Research Bulletin No. 47.

Strathern, M. (1975) *No Money on Our Skins: Hagen Migrants in Port Moresby.* Canberra: New Guinea Research Bulletin No. 61.

Strathern, M. (1979) 'The self in self-decoration', *Oceania,* 49, 241-57.

Strathern, M. (1981) 'Self-interest and the social good: some implications of Hagen gender imagery', in *Sexual Meanings: The Cultural Construction of Gender and Sexuality,* eds S. Ortner and H. Whitehead, Cambridge: Cambridge University Press.

Strathern, M. (1987) 'Producing difference: connections and disconnections in two New Guinea Highlands kinship systems', in *Gender and Kinship: Essays Toward a Unified Analysis,* eds J. Collier and S. Yanagisako, Stanford, CA: Stanford University Press.

Strathern, M. (1988) *The Gender of the Gift: Problems with Women and Problems with Society in Melanesia,* Berkeley and Los Angeles: University of California Press.

Strathern, M. (1991a) 'One man and many men', in *Big Men and Great Men: Personifications of Power in Melanesia,* eds M. Godelier and M. Strathern, Cambridge: Cambridge University Press.

Strathern, M. (1991b) 'Partners and consumers: making relations visible', *New Literary History,* 22: 581-601.

Strathern, M. (1992) *After Nature: English Kinship in the Late Twentieth Century,* Cambridge: Cambridge University Press.

Strathern, M. (1993) 'One-legged gender', *Visual Anthropology Review,* 9: 42-51.

Strathern, M. (1995a) *The Relation: Issues in Complexity and Scale,* Cambridge: Prickly Pear Pamphlet No. 6.

Strathern, M. (1995b) 'The nice thing about culture is that everyone has it', in *Shifting Contexts: Transformations in Anthropological Knowledge,* ed. M. Strathern, ASA Decennial Conference Series, London: Routledge.

Strathern, M. (1996a) 'Gender: division or comparison', in *Practising Feminism,* eds N. Charles and F. Hughes-Freeland, London: Routledge.

Strathern, M. (1996b) 'Enabling identity? Biology, choice and the new reproductive technologies', in *Questions of Cultural Identity,* eds S. Hall and P. du Gay, London: Sage.

Stürzenhofecker, G. (1994) 'Visions of a landscape: Duna premeditations on ecological change', *Canberra Anthropology,* 17: 27-47.

Suagee, D. B. (1994) 'Human rights and cultural heritage: developments in the United Nations working group on indigenous populations', in

Intellectual Property Rights for Indigenous Peoples: A Sourcebook, ed. T. C. Greaves, Oklahoma City, OK: Society for Applied Anthropology.

Sykes, K. (1997) 'Possessive individualism and the snatcher: displacements of desire in small business development in Central New Ireland', paper delivered at American Anthropological Association meetings, 1997.

Thomas, N. (1991) *Entangled Objects: Exchange, Material Culture and Colonialism in the Pacific,* Cambridge, MA: Harvard University Press.

Thomas, N. (1994) *Colonialism's Culture: Anthropology, Travel and Government,* Princeton, NJ: Princeton University Press.

Toft, S. (ed.) (1997) *Compensation and Resource Development* Port Moresby: Papua New Guinea, Law Reform Commission, Monograph 6/Canberra, Australian National University, National Centre for Development Studies, policy paper 24.

Townsend-Gault, C. (1988) 'Symbolic facades: official portraits in British institutions since 1920', *Art History,* 11: 511-26.

Turner, T. (1993) 'Anthropology and multiculturalism: what is anthropology that multiculturalists should be mindful of it?', *Cultural Anthropology,* 8: 411-29.

Van Baal, J. (1975) *Reciprocity and the Position of Women,* Amsterdam: Van Gorcum.

Velho, O. (1996) 'Globalization: object, perspective, horizon', in *Cultural Pluralism, Identity, and Globalization,* ed. L. E. Soares, Paris: UNESCO.

Verdery, K. (1998) 'Nationalism, internationalism, and property in the postcold war era', in *Property Relations: Sharing, Exclusion, Legitimacy,* ed. C. Hann, Cambridge: Cambridge University Press.

Viveiros de Castro, E. (1992) *From the Enemy's Point of View: Humanity and Divinity in an Amazonian Society* (trans. C. V. Howard), Chicago: University of Chicago Press.

Viveiros de Castro, E. (1996) 'Cosmological deixis and Amerindian perspectivism: a view from Amazonia', English version from *Mana,* 2: 115-44. [Translation by P. Gow and E. Ewart, *J. Royal Anthropological Institute* (N.S.) 4: 469-88, 1998.]

Viveiros de Castro, E. (1998) 'Cosmological perspectivism in Amazonia and elsewhere', lectures given to the Department of Social Anthropology, University of Cambridge, 1998.

Wagner, R. (1967) *The Curse of Souw,* Chicago: University of Chicago Press.

Wagner, R. (1977) 'Analogic kinship: a Daribi example', *American Ethnologist,* 4: 623-42.

Wagner, R. (1986) *Symbols that Stand for Themselves,* Chicago: University of Chicago Press.

Wagner, R. (1991) 'The fractal person', in *Big Men and Great Men: Personifications of Power in Melanesia,* eds M. Godelier and M. Strathern, Cambridge: Cambridge University Press.

Waller, L. (1997) 'Australian legislation on infertility treatments', in *Governing Medically Assisted Human Reproduction,* ed. L. Weir, Toronto: University of Toronto Center of Criminology.

Walsh, V. and J. Goodman (n.d.) 'Cancer chemotherapy, biodiversity, public and private property: the case of the anticancer drug Taxol', Manchester School of Management, UMIST, unpub. paper, 1997.

Wassmann, J. (1994) 'The Yupno as post-Newtonian scientists: the question of what is "natural" in spatial description', *Man,* 29: 645-66.

Weedon, C. (1987) *Feminist Practice and Poststructuralist Theory,* Oxford: Basil Blackwell.

Weiner, A. (1976) *Women of Value, Men of Renown: New Perspectives in Trobriand Exchange,* Austin, TX: University of Texas Press.

Weiner, A. (1979) 'Trobriand kinship from another view: the reproductive power of men and women', *Man,* 14: 328-48.

Weiner, A. (1980) 'Reproduction: a replacement for reciprocity', *American Ethnologist,* 7: 71-85.

Weiner, A. (1982) 'Sexuality among the anthropologists: reproduction among the informants', in *Social Analysis* (special issue, *Social Antagonism, Gender and Social Change in Papua New Guinea,* eds F. J. P. Poole and G. Herdt), 12: 52-65.

Weiner, J. F. (1993) 'Anthropology contra Heidegger II: the limit of relationship', *Critique of Anthropology,* 13: 285- 301.

Weiner, J. F. (1995a) *The Lost Drum: The Myth of Sexuality in Papua New Guinea and Beyond,* Madison, WI: University of Wisconsin Press.

Weiner, J. F. (1995b) 'Technology and *techne* in Trobriand and Yolngu art', *Social Analysis* (special issue ed. J. Weiner, *Too Many Meanings),* 38: 32-46.

Weiner, J. F. (ed.) (1995c) *Too Many Meanings,* special issue, *Social Analysis,* 38.

Weir, L. (1996) 'Recent developments in the government of pregnancy', *Economy and Society,* 25: 372-92.

Weir, L. and J. Habib, (1997) 'A critical feminist analysis of the final report of the Royal Commission on New Reproductive Technologies', *Studies in Political Economy* 52 : 137-54.

Werbner, P. (1997) 'Introduction: the dialectics of cultural hybridity', in *Debating Cultural Hybridity: Multi-Cultural Identities and the Politics of Anti-Racism,* P. Werbner and T. Modood, London: Zed Books.

Werbner, P. and T. Modood (eds) (1997) *Debating Cultural Hybridity: Multi-Cultural Identities and the Politics of AntiRacism,* London: Zed Books.

Werbner, R. P. (1991) 'Contending narrators: personal discourse and the social biography of a family in western Zimbabwe', paper given to Center for African Studies, Illinois, 1991.

Weston, K. (1991) *Families We Choose: Lesbian, Gays, Kinship,* New York: Columbia University Press.

Wexler, N. (1992) 'Clairvoyance and caution: repercussions from the human genome project', in *The Code of Codes: Scientific and Social Issues in the Human Genome Project,* eds D. J. Kevles and L. Hood, Cambridge, MA: Harvard University Press.

Wilk, R. (1995) 'Learning to be local in Belize: global systems of common difference', in *Worlds Apart: Modernity Through the Prism of the Local,* ed. D. Miller, ASA Decennial Conference Series, London: Routledge.

Wilkinson, R. (1973) *Poverty and Progress: An Ecological Model of Economic Development,* London: Methuen.

Willke, H. (1990) 'Political intervention: operational preconditions for generalised political exchange', in *Governance and Generalized Exchange,* ed. B. Marin, Frankfurt: Boulder Co.

Wolfram, S. (1989) 'Surrogacy in the United Kingdom', in *New Approaches to Human Reproduction: Social and Ethical Dimensions,* eds L. M. Whiteford and M. L. Poland, London: Westview Press.

Woodall, J. (ed.) (1997) *Portraiture: Facing the Subject,* Manchester: Manchester University Press.

Young, A. (forthcoming) 'New reproductive technologies and reproductive rights: whose are they anyway?', *Canadian Human Rights Bulletin.*

Yuval-Davis, N. (1997) 'Ethnicity, gender relations and multiculturalism', in *Debating Cultural Hybridity: Multi-Cultural Identities and the Politics of Anti-Racism,* eds P. Werbner and T. Modood, London: Zed Books.

DOCUMENTS FROM THE CANADIAN ROYAL COMMISSION ON NEW REPRODUCTIVE TECHNOLOGIES

Submissions

Indian and Inuit Nurses' Association of Canada (1990) *Brief to the Royal Commission on New Reproductive Technologies,* Ottawa: National Archives of Canada uncatalogued documents of the Royal Commission on New Reproductive Technologies.

N.W.T. [Northwest Territories] Status of Women Council (1990) *Brief to the Royal Commission on New Reproductive Technologies,* Ottawa: National Archives of Canada uncatalogued documents of the Royal Commission on New Reproductive Technologies.

Yukon Indian Women's Association (1990) *Brief to the Royal Commission on New Reproductive Technologies,* Ottawa: National Archives of Canada uncatalogued documents of the Royal Commission on New Reproductive Technologies.

Reports

Achilles, R. (February 1992) *Donor Insemination: An Overview,* report prepared for the Royal Commission on New Reproductive Technologies, Ottawa.

Cook, R. J. (December 1991) *New Reproductive Technologies: International Legal Issues and Instruments,* report prepared for the Royal Commission on New Reproductive Technologies, Ottawa.

Index